Yellow Roses

Yellow Roses

His Promise Forever Unbroken

Farah Grace

YELLOW ROSES
HIS PROMISE FOREVER UNBROKEN

iUniverse books may be ordered through booksellers or by contacting:

iUniverse
1663 Liberty Drive
Bloomington, IN 47403
www.iuniverse.com
1-800-Authors (1-800-288-4677)

Because of the dynamic nature of the Internet, any web addresses or links contained in this book may have changed since publication and may no longer be valid. The views expressed in this work are solely those of the author and do not necessarily reflect the views of the publisher, and the publisher hereby disclaims any responsibility for them.

Any people depicted in stock imagery provided by Thinkstock are models, and such images are being used for illustrative purposes only.
Certain stock imagery © Thinkstock.

ISBN: 978-1-5320-3356-8 (sc)
ISBN: 978-1-5320-3357-5 (e)

Library of Congress Control Number: 2017914481

Print information available on the last page.

iUniverse rev. date: 11/03/2017

Dedication

For Ajax: your love is true; so pure and devoted that it lives on, forever. Your continual guidance and protection strengthen me to face all of life's challenges.

Acknowledgements

To my special friend, Omar, whose wisdom, patience and understanding taught me the true meaning of unconditional love. Your ability, to show me that to forgive, gives me freedom, enabling me to reach insights, resolve my driving fear, and to finally achieve a main life's goal. With Omar in my life, my story could fully unfold and be told to the world.

To my dear friend, William who has always been there for me. His gentle ways taught me that no matter what happens in life, it's best for me to practice kindness and choose words wisely. In every situation, he is there for me, eager to help.

To my gifted friend and doctor who's talented skills turned a malignancy around, making me whole again. He restored something more precious than jewels or gold: my dignity.

To all the special people who have entered my life and enriched it in so many ways. You have given my story meaning by helping me understand that we can enrich ourselves only to the extent that we enrich others.

To Ajax, most of all. He not only inspired my book; he was also it's very reason for being.

He still sends me beautiful yellow roses and his presence warmly surrounds me.

-- Farah Grace

Chapter One

My story begins on a Florida kind of Saturday night: sticky-humid, smothering, and sub-tropical. Plump drops poured from darkness above, splashing down in a dance of wavering, watery sheets that would suddenly give way to steamy stillness.

Leah, from the drivers' seat, said to me, "I can't believe how many cars are here on a night like this."

"No kidding, me too," I replied, noting puddles under, between, on and around the cars. "Typical Florida weather. One minute it rains and the next minute, it's clear skies again. The only constant is humidity above ninety percent. Not a good hair day. But I'm glad we decided to come, anyway."

After all my efforts before the mirror, I knew, as I stepped out of the car, my long blond hair would hang straight down the middle of my back. In a couple minutes, the downpour ceased and we seized our chance to dash.

The dance hall had been there many years, developing a reputation as a local "meat market." Not my kind of thing. Even as a teenager, I hated walking past someone, noting them size me up, consider their chances, and undress me with their eyes, with a sly grin.

About eight years before, a woman whose insurance office was next to my business argued, "Since your husband of twenty-some years has passed, you need to get out and start living again."

Going out that evening, I realized early on that I was not ready to "start living again." That night, we went out at the suggestion of a good friend who also enjoys dancing. The exterior of the club hadn't changed a bit, even after decades. It still was decorated with cliché Florida landscaping with tropical shrubs and palm trees. Even the typical pink flamingos stood by. One would never guess the space would be as huge as it was inside.

Dusk had fallen already as we paced a crooked path across the parking lot. The lights did not help us know where the deep water was. They reflected from wet pavement, concealing potholes in our path to the door. We had to watch where we stepped to avoid sopping wet feet. Laughing together, we took our time. We jumped over the smaller puddles. Tiptoed through shallow ones. Walked around the lakes.

I was happy that night, pleased that I could get out and enjoy life a little -- something I had not been able to do in a very long time.

"Well Desiree," Leah asked, "are you ready to go in and dance?"

"I sure am," I said, laughing. "And how about you?"

Leah was such a good friend. She always anchored me when I needed grounding. We had met a few years prior at my gym. I began working out to relieve frustrations of my husband's death and dealing with his unfinished business. I had to stop exercising for a year during some surgeries but I got back to it soon afterward.

Leah had lost almost a hundred excess pounds. She needed to tone up. She went to the gym at the same time I did. She worked with a trainer. When our workouts were finished, we would chat. We became friends.

"I'll just watch tonight," she said, giggling. "This is my kind of music. I enjoy music I understand."

I giggled as I stepped over puddles, wondering just how much my little grandson would enjoy running through them instead of around them. As we walked into the cavernous space, my eyes darted across the huge hall. It was so large that there were two bars.

The size of the crowd inside surprised us both. The music was loud and that felt wonderful. The floor was packed. People were dancing to music from the sixties and seventies. I moved rhythmically to the beat of the music as I worked my way into the crowd.

I love to dance. This is going to be fun tonight, I thought.

As I began the seemingly impossible task of finding a good seat, I saw a man standing all alone, across the huge dance floor.

Oh my God! Is he ever handsome, I thought.

I crossed the dance hall going straight to him like the opposite pole of his magnetic force. My eyes never left him. As I got closer, I realized just how handsome he really was. He looked at me and smiled as our eyes locked together. I felt like a school girl, with butterflies in my stomach, not a woman who had experience in life. As I got closer to him, I thought my eyes were deceiving me. He looked at me and smiled. I sheepishly smiled back. I felt foolish as I approached him. I couldn't take my eyes off him. I found it hard to speak.

"Is it always this crowded on rock 'n' roll night?" I asked.

"Yah, it started two hours ago but I just got here too," he said, fixing his eyes on mine. He spoke with an exotic-sounding accent.

Wow, his accent is attractive, I thought.

Just a week earlier, I had told my youngest daughter I would soon meet a man with an accent. I said that would be so sexy when he talked to me. I imagined Antonio Banderas looking into my eyes and saying, "I love you," in his Spanish accent.

She laughed at me and said, "Go, Mom!"

I knew that kind of man was somewhere in my future, but I did not know where or when or what accent he might have. As for how he would look, I had no idea. I would have settled for only the accent.

"I'm with my girlfriend, Leah," I said. "I need to find somewhere for us to sit."

"I do not think so," he said. Then he took a sip of his drink. "You will find somewhere to sit."

I was mesmerized. "Oh, I hear an accent," I said, as I leaned closer to him.

"Yah," he said, "It is Arabic accent."

"Where are you from?"

"Alexandria, Egypt," he said. "Do you know about Alexandria?"

I couldn't keep my eyes off him. He looked like a model in a fashion magazine. His dark eyes seemed gentle and kind. His hair was thick and curly with gray running through it. His mustache was very thick, well groomed and also going gray. His perfectly shaped lips seemed sensual. He looked distinguished, to me.

He took another sip of his drink and suggested that I find my girlfriend and come back. His accent sounded thick and intriguing. His smile captivated me.

"Ok," I responded without hesitating, "I'll go get her."

He looked like a young Omar Sharif. Even the space between his front teeth was like Sharif.

Could I have ever envisioned this man, I wondered?

I smiled and went to get Leah across the crowded dance floor. I couldn't help wishing I was better at seeing the future. I knew what I wanted to do with this man. I was never a woman who would look for a one night stand.

But this man, I was thinking, *could put his shoes under my bed any time.*

As I neared Leah, my mind was still whirling with the image of this magnificent looking guy. I didn't notice she had found a table for us.

"Oh my God, Leah," I gushed. "I just met the most yummy looking man I have ever seen in my life!"

Leah was caught up in the music. She paid no attention to what I was saying. I waited for the song to end so that I could tell her about him.

Another man approached us and asked me to dance. I accepted and as the music was playing, I couldn't help searching with my eyes to find this "Omar" I had met. When that dance was over, the fellow who had asked me to dance walked me back to my seat and thanked me.

Then, I realized I had not heard a word of the song I had danced to. I smiled but all I could think was how I would get back to that Omar-twin who had crossed my path.

Before I spoke to Leah, the song "Pretty Woman," by Roy Orbison, started playing. That song tears at my heart. The music flooded my thoughts with a memory from many years prior.

My high school sweetheart, Ajax, used to sing that song to me while gazing at me with his piercing, aqua blue eyes. I could always recall him doing the growl from that song. He frequently gave me yellow roses, sometimes for no particular reason. When we went to school dances, the corsage I wore was always yellow roses. To this day, I feel Ajax's presence around me, as if he had never gone far away. Yellow roses became the symbol of our love.

My dreams about Ajax made him seem to remain ever-present, protecting me or telling me what is to come. He kisses me so gently in those dreams, always telling me how much he loves me, as he warns me about the future.

Thank God, I thought. *I'm glad they didn't play "Georgia On My Mind."*

After more than forty-five years, that song still brings tears to my eyes. So often, he and I would listen to it on the car radio. It was his favorite. My mind drifted back to the time of his death. Fighting tears, I shook myself and returned to the present. Then the music paused long enough for me come back to reality, take a deep breath, and tell Leah about the man who I had just met.

Getting up my nerve, I walked back over to that Middle Eastern hunk. I smiled as I told him my friend had found a table. He looked at me, smiled, and put his drink down as he asked me to dance. My heart was beating so fast I thought it was going to jump right out of my chest. We danced two fast dances. We could not look away from each other.

When they played a slow song, he pulled me into his arms and we danced.

He is such a smooth dancer, I thought. I leaned back, looking into his eyes.

"You look just like Omar Sharif," I remarked.

"He is my Uncle," he said, with a straight face.

I almost believed him.

His voice was so serious as he said, "Everyone tells me I look like him."

I didn't want to waste the moment by talking so I snuggled and felt the warmth of his body next to mine. We fit well into each others arms. As the song ended, he walked me back to my table.

"I will go to get my drink," he said in his Arabic accent.

Like a young school girl, I asked Leah if she had ever seen such a gorgeous man.

"I prefer the Nordic look; tall, thin and blond," she said, in her matter-of-fact voice.

She looked at me with happiness.

"Look at you," she said. "You are smitten. I was beginning to wonder about you."

"Smitten?" I asked.

"Yes, smitten," she responded. "All these months we've gone out dancing and you've never given anybody a second look."

As we laughed, he arrived at our table.

"Look at Omar Sharif now," he said, pointing to the photo on his phone. "He lives in France and he's really getting old."

The picture took me by surprise. I remember him so young and handsome. This new "Omar" had another picture on his phone, of a much younger Sharif.

That's the one, I thought.

I took his phone and held it next to his face. I could not believe my eyes. He was the perfect image of the actor.

I mentioned Dr. Zhivago was one of my favorite movies; that I had watched it a dozen times; that I was drawn to his looks; and that I wished I was the blonde that Sharif loved in that movie. The present Omar told me he had seen the movie when he was in Egypt, that his father had taken him to see it. He laughed at my excitement. He kept showing me more photos. I felt quite surprised to be sitting with a Sharif look-alike.

We danced all night, one dance after another, even trying to dance *salsa* style. Two total strangers from different parts of the world and yet it seemed as if we had known each other forever.

While taking a break, I commented that the music reminded me of high school. A very serious expression appeared on his face.

"I do not believe that," he said.

"I am older than you are," I said. "In fact, I am going to have a birthday in a few days."

"No! you are not older than I am," he said.

I dug into my purse and for my driver's license. He tried to read my birthday on it but could not see the small writing.

I offered him my glasses. "Here, maybe these will help."

"I do not think that you are older than me," he said, "but since it is your birthday, I would like to take you out to dinner."

"But I don't know you," I said, concealing my excitement.

With that, he pulled his license out of his wallet. "See, this is me," he said, while handing me the card.

"Oh, a Scorpio," I said, noticing his birthday. "Scorpio men are supposed to be wonderful lovers."

I noticed his birth year.

Oh my gosh, I thought, *he is so young.*

He was eight years younger than me.

He didn't seem to mind at all.

"I always date women older than me."

Nice line, I thought.

But at that point, I didn't care. I was infatuated with him. As he talked, all I could think of was his wonderful accent and that I could listen to it forever. When he spoke, his accent was so strong that I had to follow word-for-word to be sure I understood what he was saying. He was so happy and so interested in me. I felt somehow safe with him. It didn't matter where he was from. He captured my heart. We continued to dance until my feet were numb.

"What kind food do you like?" he asked. "I will take you somewhere nice."

"But I don't know you," I replied again.

"Okay, Okay. Will you give me your phone number so I can call you and then you know me?"

I laughed and thought how adorable this man was. I willingly agreed and gave him my number hoping he really would call.

I thought, *So many times I have given a man a wrong number because I just wasn't interested and now I'm interested and I'm giving the correct number. Now, he probably won't call.*

Having dinner with this beautiful man would be a wonderful way to spend my birthday. I had been through a lot in the previous eight years. This handsome Middle Eastern guy was like a breath of fresh air. So cute, so full of life and drop-dead gorgeous.

As he walked Leah and me out to my car, Omar kept asking if I gave him my real phone number.

"Yes, that's my real phone number," I said, as I looked into his eyes.

"Leah, is this really her phone number?" he asked. She laughed about his insecurity.

I was sitting in my car with Leah. One more time, "Omar" leaned into my car and presented Leah with the piece of paper.

He asked, "You sure this is the real number? I'm going to take her somewhere special for her birthday."

"Can I have your glasses for a minute?" Leah asked me.

I handed them to her.

She looked at the little piece of paper and laughed as she said "Yes, that's her number." Leah spoke with disbelief, laughing. "She gave you the right number."

Then he showed us his bright, beautiful, warm smile.

"I gonna call you soon, Desiree." Omar leaned over again and kissed me. The kiss caught me off guard and then he leaned in again and kissed me two more times.

"I gonna call soon—you will see." Then Omar walked away.

I looked at Leah who seemed bewildered.

"I can't believe you let him kiss you," she said.

"I did, didn't I?" I said, in near disbelief myself.

"He didn't realize how lucky he is," she said. "I'm surprised you didn't knock his head off."

I laughed and turned around to see where he went, but he was gone. Leah and I drove home with me jabbering like a Chatty Cathy doll all the way. I must have asked Leah three times if she thought he would really call me and take me out to dinner. She just laughed and said she was surprised how taken with him I felt.

When we reached my house, Leah got out. She decided not to come inside. It was almost two-thirty in the morning. That was much later than we usually stayed out. We said goodbye and she got into her own car and drove away.

I went into the house with my mind whirling as I replayed the entire evening. Still smelling his cologne on my face, I let my two Boston Terriers go outside. I called them "my Boys."

Omar's cologne smelled so good to me. Exactly the kind of scent I like. A little musky, yet not strong. As that winter night's breeze blew my hair around, his scent was all around me, as if he was there, in spirit.

Gosh, I hope he calls me, I thought.

I still could not believe that I had casually given this new Omar my phone number. That was something I had never done before. I stood outside for a minute, taking in his scent, when I realized my Boys were ready to go back in.

They were standing at the door looking at me as if to say "Earth to Mom. We're ready."

I went inside and began undressing. Then the phone rang.

"Hallo," he said. "I wanted to see if this is really your phone number."

I laughed at how cute he sounded on the phone.

"I just walked in the door," I said. "You have wonderful timing."

"Yah, me too," he said, and there was that accent again.

It was already three a.m. and I would normally be sound asleep. To my amazement, I was wide awake and ready to talk.

He said, "I want, for sure, to take you to dinner on your birthday and I want to know how you can know me, so I can take you."

On the phone, his accent was much more pronounced and harder to understand than in person. I wanted to talk all night because I was enjoying him so much. He must have been feeling the same because we talked until four-thirty. Sleep was the farthest thing from my mind, as I enjoyed each and every word. He was charming and his sense of humor was dryly amusing.

We decided to meet on the following Tuesday for coffee at a Starbucks halfway between us. I felt safe with that plan. I was quite eager to meet again. The entire time we talked, I kept remembering what he looked like and how taken I was with him. As I laid in bed talking, once again I could smell his cologne.

I am going to enjoy seeing you again, I thought.

When we realized we had been talking for an hour and a half, we decided to hang up.

"I will call you tomorrow if that is okay," he said.

"That would be great," I said. "I look forward to hearing from you again."

Then we said, "Good night."

I had a hard time going to sleep. I mentally replayed the evening and Omar. My thoughts drifted back to the song *Pretty Woman* and how, after all these years, my heart still aches for the feeling of love I had enjoyed with Ajax. I had put up a shield for years after his death to protect myself from ever again giving my heart so completely. I had tried so hard to forgive myself for leaving *that* beautiful man. I was afraid he might make a young widow of me— and with good reason.

Such guilt I carried all those years for not staying with him and not giving him my love until he no longer needed it. I guess God had another plan for us. As I laid there, I wondered if I had stayed with him, would my children have had blond hair and big, aqua eyes. I wondered if somehow he could have survived the war. They say time heals all wounds but these wounds had remained for over forty years.

I went on with my life and raised four children but never felt the same love Ajax and I had shared. I thought about all the times he came to me in my dreams and how, when I awakened, I could almost feel his kisses on my lips. I had so many dreams, received so many warnings about what might come and I remembered so much heartfelt love. I never feared for my safety or my children's safety because he always seemed to warn me somehow, telling me he was there and always would be.

My dreams about him were intensely vivid. Sometimes, when I awakened, I felt my dreams were real and that he was there, telling me what would come or what I should do. And when he kissed me, I felt his lips on mine as if he was alive and had never left this world. Such love, I never allowed myself to feel again.

As I laid in bed awake, my thoughts were scattered. I reviewed the night before. I still couldn't believe how taken I was with this man who I did not even know. My little fur babies were still sleeping in their beds when I decided to get up and start a new day. As my feet hit the carpet, I thanked God once again for giving me another day.

I had faced cancer and survived. That gave me a new perspective on life and the joys at my fingertips. That old saying, "Take time to smell the roses," became a part of my life. I lived by that saying after my major illness. As time passed, I realized more and more just how suddenly one's life can end.

"Come on Boys, lets go outside," I yelled.

How cute they were. One can't deny the love a pet gives. It's completely unconditional. "Amoree," my first dog, was a Mothers' Day gift from my two daughters. My little granddaughter, Angela, who was only four, carried him to my front door and rang the bell.

"Here Nana … look what I brought you," she said, giggling.

Quite surprised, of course I fell in love with him. He is so sweet and mild mannered. Yet "Levi," my other Boston Terrier, is actually natured more like my departed husband, Titus, who brought the little dog home to me after a trip to Texas.

It was hard to accept my husband's passing eight years prior. He was difficult to live with but he was an honorable man and devoted to his country. He would have given me the world if he could have but I was never able to give him my heart freely. I loved him in my own way but I could never let go to give him all of me.

Twenty years was a long time to stay with a man and not really let him into my heart. Even so, after a husband's death, no woman should have to go through what I endured. I never got over how our entire shared life comprised total deception.

While Titus was alive, he would get upset with me. He could sense that I could not give him my heart without reservation. Many times, he said he was living with a dead man in the house and sharing me with him. He said he didn't know how to compete with that.

Somehow, I simply couldn't let go of my fear and give in to love again. I remember dreaming of Ajax the night before I took Titus into the hospital for what was supposed to be removal of a gallbladder stone:

> As he usually did in my dreams, Ajax appeared coming through a door, straight to me and kissing me. Standing in front of me he said, "I love you and I always will." Then he stepped back and told me, "You need to be strong. Everything will be alright. Never forget Titus loved you very dearly."
>
> As I stood there in his arms, I asked him, "What's going to happen?"
>
> "I'll be there, guiding you. Remember that he truly loves you. Be strong. You'll be alright. I'll be with you the whole way, always remember that."
>
> He would kiss my lips so softly and then a cloud of whiteness would engulf him as he slowly disappeared.

The next morning, when I took Titus to the hospital, I knew something tragic was about to happen.

Thankfully, the phone rang. That jarred me from my deep reverie.

"Hi Leah," I said. "Why are you up so early?"

"Well," she said, "I'm checking on you, to see how you're doing after last night."

"I feel all warm and fuzzy. I still can't get over last night. And you will not believe who I talked to until four-thirty this morning."

"My God! I knew he would call but I didn't think he would call that soon."

"Yes, he did, and was he ever cute on the phone. His accent is even stronger then. We had a ball talking. He's going to call me back today or tomorrow when he sees how his schedule is going to be, so we can meet. He still wants to take me to dinner on my birthday. Isn't this the strangest thing, how I met him?"

"Especially since you just told me you didn't care if you ever met anyone special."

"You're right."

"See? When you least expect it, someone drops out of the sky. Is he taking you out Wednesday on your birthday?"

"I'm not sure, maybe not until the weekend. We didn't decide that yet. Besides, I want to meet him somewhere before I get into his car. You know me, I'm always leery."

"Yes. The history."

"That last guy I went out with, who met me somewhere six times before I allowed him to come to the house or take me out. Boy, that situation was a disaster. I should never have gone out with him. But Omar sure got my motor running, I must admit."

"What's his real name?"

"I don't remember, but I'm going to call him Omar for now. He laughs, so Omar it will be. Hey, another call is coming through. Let me take it and I will call you back later."

"Okay, talk to you later. Bye."

As I clicked through to the next call, I heard this wonderful "Hallo, how are you this morning?"

My heart started beating faster as I answered, "Hi. I'm fine, and how are you?"

"Good. I did not wake you, did I?"

"No, I've been up for a few hours."

"I check my schedule and I can meet you on Tuesday afternoon. Is that okay with you?"

"Yes that will work great. We could meet for coffee."

"Okay."

"How about Starbucks by the mall? That would be half way for both of us."

"Good. How about one o'clock? Then I can work until noon."

"Perfect."

"Thank you for such a good time last night, I really enjoyed meeting you. Your smile is so beautiful."

It had been a long time since someone had given me a sincere compliment or even a kind word.

I felt silly and laughed but I managed to say "Thank you, I really am glad you had a good time because I did, too … and speaking of smiles, I still can't get over how much you look like Omar Sharif. It was fun dancing with you."

He laughed and said, "It was nice."

I asked, "Are you tired today from all the dancing we did?" "Yah, we did a lot of dances but I am okay now. Where would you like that I take you to?"

Gosh, this man is charming. Typical Scorpio, I thought.

"Where would you like to go for your birthday?"

"Wherever you want to take me," was my response as I thought to myself, *Anywhere with you will be a treat.*

"I take you somewhere very, very nice. You will see and then we go dancing."

Yes! I thought, as I replied, "That will be great."

I felt so happy inside. I couldn't believe this gorgeous man wanted to take me out for my birthday and then dancing. We confirmed our meeting place and time, said our goodbyes and hung up. Just two days more and we were to meet again.

I thought, *Yes, I can hardly wait.*

Then I called Leah back. I told her "You will not believe who that call was from."

"Bet I can, just from the excitement in your voice."

"Yes, it was Omar. He checked his schedule and we are going to meet on Tuesday, at one, at Starbucks by the mall. Can you believe I just told Kelly that I was going to meet a man with an accent? Just a few weeks later, here he is."

"Like I said, I like the Nordic type. But it's very obvious you are taken with this Middle Eastern man. Well, I wish you luck on Tuesday and keep me posted."

We chatted for another half hour and then hung up.

I called Kelly, my daughter, to tell her what happened the night before. She was every woman's dream of a daughter. From the time she was born she was my sidekick. We had more than a mother-daughter bond. It ran deeper. We were closer than we might have been had her father not departed when she was very young.

I told her the whole story about meeting Omar and about him calling me that morning. She got a kick out of hearing me so excited.

"You just told me a few weeks ago that you thought you would meet a man who spoke with an accent. Wow, Mom, you hit that one on the head. Good for you."

"He's going to take me out for dinner on my birthday."

"I'm so happy for you. You deserve it."

We talked for about an hour. My heart was aching for her at that time in her life. I related well to the situation she was facing. She too, had four children and was now facing a troubled marriage. Reflecting back, I wondered how I was able to hold it all together and raise four children.

Without Titus, I never would have made it. He raised my children as if they were his own. He took on the total responsibility, something their natural father never did. I thought how much their father lost throughout the years we lived in Florida. Kelly was only seven when we left, leaving him behind, cut out of our lives.

Tuesday morning finally came. I was showering when I heard the phone. Reaching out of the shower door, I grabbed the cordless phone and said "Hello."

"Hallo, how are you this morning?" It was Omar.

"I'm fine, in the shower," I said. "Are we still going to meet at one?"

"Yah yah, one is good," he replied. I will let you to take shower and I will see you then, at one."

I thought to myself, *This is not the time to show my crazy personality by saying something off the wall.*

So I simply said "I'm looking forward to seeing you."

Wow, I thought, *did he think perhaps I would not be there? A team of wild horses couldn't have pulled me away from our date.*

I stepped back into the shower, washed my hair, shaved my legs and soon got out. There was plenty of time to get ready but I found myself hurrying as if I were in a rush.

Trying to find the right thing to wear proved more difficult than usual. I didn't want something sexy yet I wanted to show off my figure.

How fortunate to be sixty-five and still wear a size six, I thought.

I always was so lucky that what I ate never went to my hips or thighs. My business developing topical creams and gels for so many years helped me to stay young-looking. I hadn't aged as rapidly as some women do.

Rain was forecasted for later that day but the sun was shining.

What a beautiful day to meet, I thought.

I continued to get ready by finding the right clothes. Soon it was time to leave. I would drive twenty minutes to our meeting place.

As I pulled into the parking lot, I could see Omar waiting for me, outside Starbucks. I parked my car and got out but waited for just a minute, taking in the sight of the man who was waiting.

Wow, what a body, I thought.

Today he was wearing a different black, long-sleeved tee shirt and blue jeans.

Oh, nice butt, I thought.

Just as I was smiling about his butt, he spotted me and smiled as broadly as if he had just seen the most important person in the world.

As I walked toward him, he raised his eyebrows as if he were pleased with what he was seeing. That made me feel good inside. I hadn't felt like that in years. It seemed to take forever to arrive where he was standing yet it was only a hundred feet. As I approached him, I took it all in. I sighed about what I was seeing as we reached out to each other and hugged.

The air was chilly so we decided to go inside for coffee instead of sitting outside.

I chuckled to myself as I thought, *I would sit on the sidewalk if I had to, just to have a cup of coffee with this man.*

Still not knowing what drew me to him, I decided to enjoy rather than analyze.

"What would you like to drink?" he asked, as we approached the counter.

"Just regular coffee with cream, please," I replied.

He ordered our coffee. I went to get a seat. I found one by the window so the sun would be shining in on us. He came back with our coffee and sat in the seat across from me. Once again, our eyes locked on each other just as they had on Saturday night. I felt warm and lost in the moment.

"How are you?" he asked.

I wanted to tell him how crazy and young I felt inside but chose my words more carefully.

"I'm really happy today," I responded, "and you?"

"I am good. I worked today, half day, was good."

"You are so cute," I blurted.

He laughed and said, "You are crazy."

That was the first of many times he would tell me I was crazy or refer to me as the "crazy blonde."

I frequently said things that amused him. I loved to hear him laugh. For some reason, that day, I sensed some sadness in him. Making him laugh brought me a feeling of accomplishment. Whatever sadness he was feeling quickly vanished.

We talked for hours, over many cups of coffee. At one point, I reached across the table to hold his hands but quickly pulled my hands back.

"No, no, please, it is okay," he said, as he reached across the table to hold my hands. "Here, give me your hands."

It felt so good to feel the warmth of his hands around mine. I remembered dancing with him and the warmth of his body next to mine. Now, here I was sitting across from him at a table holding his hands, learning about him. He had very sincere eyes and seemed to have a big, warm heart.

"Where are you from in Egypt?" I asked again.

"Alexandria," he said, "but I have been in the States almost forty year now."

I thought, *what a different life he must have experienced since he left his country at age seventeen, moving across the world to study.*

"What do you do?" I asked.

"I am structural engineer with my own business for twenty-nine years."

He looks successful, I thought. *He is very distinguished and classy looking. You can tell he's a professional man.*

"And you, what is it you do?" he asked.

"I owned my own business developing creams and gels with silver or copper in them."

"Wow," he said, his eyes opening widely. "You do that? You develop them? Are you chemist?"

"No, but I worked with chemists while I owned my own business for about twelve years. My youngest son, Craig, was in business with me."

"How many children do you have?"

"Four. Two boys and two girls."

"Really? Wow, you look too good to have four children."

"Thank you."

We learned a lot about each other that afternoon.

I could not help thinking, *here we are, two people from different parts of the world, from different cultures, yet enjoying each other.*

We couldn't have been more different. I was raised Catholic and he was raised Muslim although neither one of us still practiced the religion we grew up in. He was raised by two parents. My mother raised me alone, without my father. He adored his father who had passed away in Egypt the previous year. I never really knew my father. He is dark-haired, about five feet, eight inches tall with an olive complexion but I'm tall, at five feet, five inches, with long blond hair and a fair complexion. So different, and yet so attracted to each other. They say opposites attract and we were that.

We never looked away from each other as we talked for hours. He told me about where he was from. I enjoyed listening to him.

"Do you have email address?" he asked.

"Sure do," I said.

"If you give me your email address, I will send you something about where I am from and you can see it."

I opened my purse and got a piece of paper to write down my email address for him. I laughed as I looked at my watch. I realized we had been talking for four hours.

"I have not eaten," I said, "so if you want to continue talking you will have to feed me."

"Okay, where can we go to eat?" he asked.

It had started to rain. I suggested we go next door to a restaurant. We both got up at the same time. He helped me put on my red leather jacket.

Hmmm, also a gentleman, I thought. We didn't have to fight the elements. We went out one door and into the next.

The restaurant is busy for a Tuesday, I thought, but then I remembered it was almost dinner time.

The hostess seated us in a booth where it was not noisy.

Good, I thought, *because I am enjoying his conversation so much that I don't want to miss anything he says.*

Breaking my thought, he said, "You get whatever you want, it does not matter, whatever you want."

"Thank you," I replied.

"What is good to to eat here?"

"This restaurant has wonderful food, everything is good. Do you like seafood? They have delicious salmon."

"Yah, that is good. I like Salmon."

So we both ordered salmon.

We toasted the occasion with our drinks as I whispered, "To happiness."

"Yah, to happiness."

We each took sips of our drinks.

Looking into his eyes, I saw a sadness that I could not put my finger on. He hadn't spoken of anything sad or unhappy, yet I saw it in his eyes. We laughed a lot during the afternoon. There was no overt reason for him to feel sadness, but there it was.

Our meal came and we both savored every bite, although I'm not sure whether it was the salmon or that we enjoyed our dinner together.

Omar kept asking me where I would like to go for my birthday. I didn't want to admit the truth that I really didn't care, as long as I was with him. With the meal behind us, we ordered a dessert to share. The chocolate was rich, but again, sharing it with him was the best part. I wanted the day to last forever but I soon realized it would be coming to an end.

With dinner over, we went outside to leave. He walked me to my car, opened my door, and helped me get in. He closed the door, then came around the other side to get in, since it had started to rain. His cologne overtook my senses once again. Neither of us was ready to say goodbye. It was dark outside. Soft rain was falling.

"I have an umbrella in the car. Would you like to walk around the shopping center?" I asked.

"Sure," he said, but he decided to kiss me first.

Feeling the warmth of his perfectly shaped lips on mine, my only thought was, *I want more.*

I tilted my head back. He kissed me again, this time devouring me passionately. I never gave a thought to whether he would be a good kisser though I noticed his lips the first night we met, how perfectly shaped they were. He held my face with his hand as he kissed me. Each time, I felt I was about to melt into his very being.

"I like kissing you," he said.

I managed to say, "You make me feel so alive."

"Good."

I reached into the back seat, grabbed the umbrella and suggested we'd better go for a walk.

He laughed and said, "Yah, we need cold shower."

We got out of the car. He put the umbrella up and held it over us. We walked slowly as the rain fell around us.

How romantic, I thought.

I could never have dreamed of a better day with someone I had just met. The rain against the roof of the building sounded so soft and gentle. We could almost hear each drop as it fell. Chuckling to myself, I thought of how much I loved rain after moving to Florida. Rain is warm there and I absolutely loved the feeling of rain on my face and the sound of it on a roof. The smell of the rain that night was light and clean. I took a moment to come back down to earth and take a deep breath.

The scent of his cologne was refreshing and intoxicating. That shopping center was expansive but we took our time. I was sure neither one of us wanted to leave. We walked arm-in-arm, savoring the experience. I had never walked in the rain with anyone before, and I did not remember ever being kissed in a car with the sound of rain on the roof as we just did. His kisses were absolutely magical. They sent quivers down my body. Maybe there is something to be said about a Scorpio man. Whatever it was, I would soon live for his kisses. His skin looked radiant in the dimly lit night. I kept thinking I did not want that night to end.

As we walked, we talked more about things we liked to do. He told me he lived on the beach in a condo after I told him how much I like to walk on the beach. Once we reached the car we just looked at each other.

I said "Want to walk around one more time?"

"Yah," he said.

The rain had turned to a mist, causing a foggy atmosphere. I was enjoying the evening.

What a priceless, one-and-only man, I thought.

I could not have imagined doing this with my deceased husband Titus. He would have thought I was nuts but as I looked at this Middle Eastern man, I realized we had both found something very special in each other. There were no words yet to describe the unique connection we were feeling, a connection that rarely happens in a lifetime, something distinctive.

When we had returned to the car, we decided we had better stop walking in the rain before we both got sick. The dampness was chilling as the night air got cooler. Neither of us had dressed warm enough to be walking in that weather. Many cars had left; the parking lot was almost empty.

I got into my car and started it, turning on the heater to take the chill out. Omar closed the umbrella and got in on the passenger side. My thoughts went to his kisses. I wanted more. As if he had read my mind, he reached over with his hand on my face and pulled me to him until his lips touched mine. Over and over he kissed me, each kiss more passionate than the one before it.

We looked into each others' eyes, as if we both wondered, *Where have you been all my life?*

"Wow," I said, "You are a true Scorpio man.

"What is that?" he asked.

I started to tell him the little bit of knowledge I had about Scorpio men. Since I had never dated one, my information was academic but I said they are very sexy and sensual.

"Yeah?" he asked.

"Yes," I replied, "they really know how to treat a woman and they are supposed to be the best lovers."

"Yeah." Only this time, his reply was more in affirmation as he smiled and very coyly said, "Would you like to see if that is true now, right here in the car?"

We both laughed.

"Look at the windows, they are all fogged up," I said, and laughed again.

"Yeah, we better say 'good night,' or I gonna to make love to you right here in this car."

I laughed, knowing that was not going to happen. As he was about to leave, he said, "Remember, I gonna send you information about Alexandria. You look for it."

"Okay, I will. That will be interesting."

He gave me one more passionate kiss and stepped out of the car. All the way home, I could not get the thought of his kisses out of my mind. I never enjoyed kissing Titus, it seemed so mechanical but this man I could kiss all night.

Poor Titus, I thought, *I never let my guard down with him, to allow myself to feel. He always said he was competing against a dead man who no longer exists.*

I never acknowledged his remarks because, in a very real sense, they were true. No one could ever complete me like my first love.

My little dogs had been home all day alone. Thank goodness my neighbor called me to see if I wanted her to let them out. When I got home, they were happy to see me.

What a day to remember! One of those days that only comes once in a lifetime. Two people meeting the way we did was so unlikely, but meant to be.

I learned so much about him, but couldn't shake that bluesy aura of sadness around him. Although there was something sad in his eyes that I just could not put my finger on, I felt a calming feeling that I have not experienced in a very long time. A real sense that he is an honest man with no agenda.

Except to make love to me in the car, I thought, as I laughed. It's been a long time since I have felt so at ease with someone that I had just met.

That day replayed over and over again in my head. I felt such respect for him. He had been so young to travel clear across the world for an education. It's hard enough for most seventeen-year-olds to go to another State to attend college much less going so far and not even knowing our language. He seemed like a very modest man who didn't brag at all about himself.

I came away from our afternoon and evening together feeling comfortable with him, feeling I could tell him my most closely-kept secrets and I would not be judged. He made me feel so much at ease. I looked forward to going out again with him. I gave him my email address so he could send me that documentary about Alexandria.

That would be interesting, I thought.

I had traveled to many parts of the world with Titus, although at the time, I didn't know what he was doing. I was oblivious to it all. That, I guess, was exactly what he wanted.

Sleep was hard to come by that night. All I could think of was Omar and what we had talked about. I fell asleep feeling good about the day and for a change, about myself. I had not felt that in quite a while.

The next morning, I awoke with those conversations still whirling in my head. As I sat down to my computer, I saw an email from Omar. I hurriedly opened it, feeling so anxious inside that my fingers could hardly open it fast enough.

He wrote:

Desiree,

Hello, Good Morning. I want to tell you I enjoy yesterday with you. I am glad we can get to know each other. I want to take you somewhere special for your birthday. It was nice seeing your smile.

Omar

I replied:

Good Morning, Omar,

It was my pleasure, believe me. I really enjoyed walking in the rain with you. You are quite charming and I am really looking forward to spending my birthday with you.

Anywhere you want to go will be fine with me.

Desiree

The day was quite uneventful. I found myself counting down the days until I would get to see Omar again. Then, about seven-thirty p.m., my phone rang. I saw his caller ID.

I got butterflies in my stomach as I said "Hello."

"Hallo, how are you tonight?" he said.

"Perfect, how about you?

That started our conversation which lasted about thirty minutes. When he asked me where I would like to go for dinner, I suggested we go somewhere close to where I live instead of traveling an additional hour to somewhere else. He would drive close to an hour, just to get to where I lived. Then there was the additional drive back home. I thought that was time wasted in driving.

He seemed a little surprised about my consideration for him.

He replied, "Thank you for your thoughts."

We agreed on going out somewhere closer.

He asked, "Could you find somewhere nice to go since I am not used to your area?"

"Sure, I will," I responded.

We decided on Saturday at seven p.m.

"Oh, I can hardly wait," I said.

He laughed at my silliness.

"Crazy blonde he said," with a chuckle.

I love making him laugh, I thought, and then said, "Do you think you can handle me another evening?"

"Yah. Yah, I can," he said.

This time, we both laughed. We talked a while longer and then said our goodbyes.

Jeez, I thought, *I'm so happy when I'm talking to this man. Maybe there'll be happiness for me after all. He's fun to be with. Those kisses are to die for. And what yummy eye candy he is.*

Like a young girl, I called Leah right away when I hung up with Omar. I needed to talk about this with someone. I couldn't understand the happiness I was feeling about a man who I had really just met.

"What do you think, Leah? I just can't understand why I am so attracted to this man. I can't remember when I felt like this."

"I don't understand it either. As I said, I like blond men."

We laughed at her repeating the same thing she said that night at the dance.

"Just enjoy it. Don't try to question it," she said. "You know, Desiree … if it feels good, do it."

With that, I really giggled.

"I can hardly wait to do it."

"Well now, lets not go into details."

"Here it is, Friday. One more day and I will see Omar."

"Got to go, Lucky Woman,"

We hung up and immediately, my phone rang again. When I saw it was my friend Laura, I felt happy.

I hadn't talked to Laura for days because she was working late hours. In this call, there was so much to catch up on that I really didn't know where to begin. Laura and I became friends when I first moved to Florida thirty years earlier. We had been really close ever since. Both of us were going through quite a lot. We were always there for each other. She was the friend I turned to with everything.

If it hadn't been for Laura, I don't know what I would have done when Titus died. She was my rock, guiding me and keeping me sane. She knew first-hand everything I discovered after his death. She grew close to my children, too, having lived a few doors down from us for a time.

Those few years when we were neighbors were wonderful. We spent a lot of time together by the pool and in each others' homes. Titus was always out of town for some reason, for days on end, so that gave Laura and me a lot of time together. We formed a strong bond. We could sit for hours telling each other about our lives and what we did in our younger days.

I was no match for her. She lived life to the fullest and enjoyed every minute. Trip, my oldest son, was already in the military when I married Titus. Lilly, my oldest daughter, would soon be going to Paris to model.

Laura grew especially close to Kelly, my youngest daughter, and to Craig, my second son. Kelly would seek refuge at Laura's house when she felt Mom was being too strict, which in Kelly's mind, was often. Actually, it was good for Laura too. It took her mind off the troubles she had with her husband, back then. We lost touch with each other for a few years while she lived in California but when she returned, we soon picked up where we had left off and we remained very close, thereafter.

I picked up the phone and said, "Laura, I am so happy you called. You will not believe what has happened. But first, tell me how everything is with you. I bet you're exhausted from working so much."

"I am," she said "but I do need to make money."

Laura remarried after the days when I lived in the townhouse. She found a wonderful husband who treated her well. Phil really loved her and was so willing to say so. He was such a good friend to me, I really liked him. He even came up to the hospital to sit with me one afternoon when Titus was hospitalized terminally. He stayed for hours talking so calmly to me. He had soothing ways in both personality and voice.

"You sound excited about something," she said, "what's going on?"

"Laura, you will not believe what happened the other night when Leah and I went out. I met this awesome-looking man who is originally from the Middle East and is he ever gorgeous to look at. You should hear him talk! He has this wonderful accent. Oh, how I love to listen to him talk."

"Good for you! And how did you meet him?"

"At the dance. He is gorgeous, and he is going to take me out to dinner for my birthday."

"Whoa, slow down Girl. Tell me all about him."

I started from the beginning, telling her about the whole evening and about meeting him for coffee.

"I am so happy for you, you sound so excited and happy for a change."

Once again, I felt like a schoolgirl telling her how wonderfully he kisses.

"Laura, it was like he was going to eat me up! I've never been kissed like that in my life. Ooo, he's good!"

"I'm really happy for you. I'd love to meet him. Where are you going for your birthday?"

"*Bon Appétit.* He asked me to decide where we could go since he lives down in Indian Rocks Beach and I live way over here. It's about thrity miles each way, so I suggested *Bon Appétit.*"

"I love it there. It's so peaceful, enjoying dinner and looking out on the water. It really is such a nice place. Well, good for you, My Dear, it's wonderful to hear you so happy. I hate to cut this short but I need to go start dinner. Phil will be home any minute, but keep me posted. I'm really happy for you. Let me know how your birthday dinner goes."

"Okay," I replied," and we hung up.

Chapter Two

By Saturday, I was so excited that I simply couldn't wait for seven p.m. to come. I made my usual morning coffee and sat down at the table to drink it. It was still too hot, so I put the cup down on the table. I felt a warmly soothing sensation come over me. This feeling, I was all too familiar with. I had felt it many times during the years after my true love, Ajax, had died. I'd learned to welcome the feeling and take comfort in knowing he was around me, guiding and protecting me.

The sensation was nearly indescribable. It felt overwhelming and warm, as if he were standing so close to me that I could feel his body next to mine. I learned to welcome dreams of him and to realize he was still there, guiding me. Days before something was about to happen, something sudden, tragic or out of control, he would appear in my dreams to let me know everything will be alright. He continually prepared or warned me.

Even though sometimes I didn't understand what he was saying or why he appeared, in the end, I responded as I should. Afterward, I'd go back and think about the dream and what he said to me, marveling at his message.

And then there were the yellow roses to wonder about. They appeared out of nowhere. Even when it had been a while since I had dreamed of him, I took comfort in feeling his presence, knowing he was always there for me.

I took a sip of my coffee and thought about how peaceful my home was after Titus. I used to call him "Hurricane." And that he was. He'd be away for a whole week and when he came home he would make his presence known. I hated him being gone so much but I hated even more the chaos he created at home. I never got used to him traveling so much but I never had a choice. Choosing to think happier thoughts, I finished my coffee and cleaned up the kitchen, eagerly awaiting the big evening that was coming. Gosh, I could hardly wait.

The day went by quickly. It was soon time to start getting ready. As I stood in the shower, feeling hot water run down by body, I thought of many previous dates throughout my life. Somehow, none of them seemed as exciting as the upcoming evening. Something about Omar made me tingle all over. He made me feel so alive the night when we danced, a feeling I haven't felt in so long. Stepping out of the shower, I wrapped my hair in a towel.

Listening to the weather report seemed less than satisfying. They predicted light rain later in the evening. Once again, the effort of curling my hair would be lost. Even so, I dried and curled my hair, then put my makeup on. I have been blessed all my life with never needing all the makeup many women take pride in wearing. Having finished with the final touches, it was time to wait 'til he arrived.

I went to the front door in anticipation and there he was, driving past my house, then pulling into the driveway next door. I chuckled to myself, thinking about the two nosy women who lived next door. They watched me like hawks. If he went to their door, they will surely come over, asking questions. I stepped out the front door and went to the sidewalk to tell him that he was parking at the wrong house. I saw him spray cologne on his face. I hoped it was the same one he wore the night we met.

I could still close my eyes and recall that scent. He then reached down as if to pick something up. By then, I had his attention. I motioned to him to come next door, which he did. Oh, was I ever happy to see him! It seemed to take forever for this evening to come. He reached down again to retrieve something more. When he stepped out of his truck, he looked absolutely adorable. He approached me with roses in one hand and a bottle of Champagne in the other.

He kissed me gently, and with his accent in full swing, he said "Happy Birthday," as he handed me beautiful, long-stemmed white roses. I brought them to my nose to inhale their fragrance. Either my imagination was in play or they were the most awesome-smelling roses I had ever sniffed. They had a clean scent, and a little spicy. I gazed at them thinking how beautiful they were and how thoughtful he was to bring me something. I looked up and saw him smiling from ear to ear, pleased with himself.

"Thank you so much," I said, as I fought back tears of joy, "This is so sweet of you."

"Yah," he said.

We both laughed at his innocent happiness with himself for bringing me these roses.

"I am glad you like them," he said.

He carried the champagne into the house. As we approached the kitchen, he put it on the counter.

I smelled the roses again and said "Let me put them in a vase with water. They are so perfect and beautiful."

He looked at me seriously and said, "I am glad you like them."

Like them? I thought. *That is to say the least.*

I hadn't expected anything. I went into my curio cabinet and found the perfect, tall, lead crystal vase. I filled it with water. As I arraigned the roses, I noticed two of them had a yellowish cast and had started to open into big, beautiful splendor.

Throughout the years, I had received many red roses for various occasions from Titus but no other color. Titus never knew what a yellow rose meant to me or what they stood for. So many things, I never shared with him or anyone else. It was a sacred secret that I never repeated. So meaningful, yet kept so deep inside.

I finished arranging the roses and placed them on the coffee table for good visibility. Still surprised and pleased, I leaned over to smell them again. By then, Omar was looking around at my home.

"You have beautiful home," he said, "I like it." Being a structural engineer, he noticed everything, the ledges that surround the rooms and the rounded corners.

"I designed the home myself," I replied. "My husband was a builder at one point, so he was able to draw exactly what I wanted."

"Wow, you do good job," he said.

"Thank you. I really enjoyed doing it and seeing how the final product turned out," I answered. I wanted a home that looked big and open but wasn't so large I would spend all my time cleaning.

"This is *nice*," he said.

I couldn't stand it any longer. I wanted to reach out and touch him, so I did.

I took a step toward him and gave him a hug as I quietly said, "Thank you again for the beautiful roses and champagne."

He smiled broadly.

As he hugged me back, he said, "You are very welcome."

I hated to let go. I could have just hugged him all night, he looked so handsome standing there with that beautiful smile on his face.

"We better go so we are not late," he said.

Then I took my Bostons out one more time before we left.

"Is something wrong with the one's eyes?"

"Yes," I replied, "Levi has cataracts. He's ten years old. He was my deceased husband's little guy."

I looked at Levi and thought about how much Titus loved him. That little guy was Titus's pride and joy. Titus was almost selfish with him, wanting the dog to constantly be in his lap. When Titus died, Levi somehow knew. He howled for hours when I came home.

"Aww, poor little thing, I feel sorry for him," Omar said.

It was time to go. A certain feeling of pride came over me as he opened the door and I entered in his truck. I felt so special.

I went into a reverie: *Out of all the women in the world, Omar has chosen me to date. I'm smitten with him in every respect. I want to let go now, to feel what I have not allowed myself to feel for so long. It's time to knock down the walls I've hidden behind these past forty years, never allowing emotions, never trusting anyone with my heart. It's time to let myself feel love again.*

After my last surgery, I asked God to let me to feel love one more time before I die, with my heart bursting from the joy that only love can bring.

At the restaurant, the valet opened my door, helping me out of the truck. I felt proud as I walked around the truck approaching my gorgeous man.

Wow, I thought, *I still can't get over how incredibly handsome he is.*
He broke into my thoughts by asking, "Are you hungry?"
"Yes. I. Am!" I said, as we started up the stairs into the restaurant.
"Good. So am I."

Omar excused himself, leaving me in the lobby for a bit. As he walked away, my thought was, *Wow, nice butt.*

I remembered noticing that before but in jeans he really looked incredible for a fifty-seven year old man. I laughed at myself for even noticing that. I don't remember noticing a man's butt previously, but I sure noticed his that night. He soon returned.

As the waiter led us to our seats, he told us about the *Torte au Chou* special they offered that evening. He took our order for drinks.

I looked at Omar. "Now it's my turn to excuse myself."

Omar stood up as I left the table.

While returning to the table, I noticed the wide view from the picture window where we were sitting, a brilliant sunset panorama. Little did I know, that was the first of many sunsets we would enjoy together.

When our drinks came, Omar toasted me, saying, "Happy Birthday to a beautiful blonde. I am so happy I am able to take you out to dinner tonight."

"Thank you," I replied. As I touched his glass with mine, I smiled and declared "Happiness!"

"Yah, happiness!" he said. We sipped from our drinks. The meal tasted wonderful, as only *Bon Appétit* could achieve.

We laughed and enjoyed each other as we were meant to, as if we had always been together. I loved to make him laugh, to see the sadness leave his eyes, if only for a moment. I wondered what his sadness was about as I watched him take another sip from his cocktail. This time, when he looked back at me, his face lit up. I knew he liked what he was seeing.

Because it was my birthday, the waiter brought us a coupon for a free bottle of wine the next time we ate there. Along with the coupon, the waiter brought me a cup of chocolate mousse with a candle. As the waiter sat the mouse down, Omar took out his phone.

He said, "Smile, so I can take your picture."

He snapped pictures as I blew out the candle and made my wish. It's easy to guess what my wish was. I shared the mouse with Omar as I told him how much I love chocolate.

"All women like chocolate," he said. "Enjoy it!"

He took one more picture. We dallied with coffee. I don't usually drink coffee in the evening but I thought, *Tonight will be a long night so I don't need to worry about not being able to sleep.*

After he paid the bill, we went into the bar for another drink. It was a pleasure to sit at the bar beside him. The conversation flowed, and then suddenly Omar took my hand and asked if I would like to go dancing. I could hardly say yes fast enough. We finished our drinks and out the door we went like two people on a mission.

"Is there anywhere special you would like to go?" he asked. Feeling stupid, and hating to admit it had been years since I had gone dancing, I just smiled and said, "You pick somewhere."

"Okay then, I know where we can go. Have you been to Shepard's, on the Beach?" he asked.

"No, but it sounds like fun," I replied.

"Okay then, let's go to Shepard's."

The drive was about fifteen minutes. There wasn't much silence, we laughed and enjoyed each other all the way. At Shepard's, we pulled up to the valet station and of course, once again, they opened the door for me and helped me out.

With my arm through this gorgeous man's arm, I was in Heaven. Little did I know just how much I would grow to love this place. It was cool out. They had Tiki lights burning that produced a beautiful ambiance of color and heat. The dance floor and the band were outside. As the Tiki lights glowed, we could hear the Gulf of Mexico surf roll in. Stopping, I took in the beautiful, romantic atmosphere. Never having been there before, I couldn't believe my eyes. The music was loud and the dance floor was filled with couples dancing to the beat.

Omar took my hand. We walked over to the bar to get a drink. I felt like a young girl just let out of a cage. I just couldn't stop my feet from dancing.

He laughed at me and said, "We will dance in a minute. Let me get us a drink. What would you like?" he asked.

"A Margarita," I responded.

"Oh, a Margarita for the lady," he said. He ordered himself one, also.

We toasted again. This time I said, louder than before, "Happiness!" as I smiled at him. I could hardly wait to get out onto the dance floor with this wonderful Prince Charming.

After a few minutes, he took my hand. "Come, lets dance."

We set our drinks on a table near the dance floor. We danced and danced until a slow number started. He pulled me close as we began. A slight mist of rain had started. As we danced, I could feel the rain ever so slightly on my hand that was on his shoulder. Once again, I could feel the heat from his body against mine. I leaned back to feel the mist on my face. I looked up at the stars.

I thought, *if I live to be a hundred, I can never again capture this feeling as we dance body to body tonight.*

The Tiki torches produced enough light to see the mist in the air and the glow of the stars. The scent of his cologne was all around me. As I took it all in, I wanted that night and those feelings to never end. We danced until the music ended. Neither of us wanted to stop but with the evening almost over, we headed back to the valet area to wait for his truck. Omar was holding my hand as we stood close to each other. After we were inside the truck, he kissed me, so beautifully, so tenderly, that I wanted more. On the way home, we talked and talked. Again, we laughed together.

Once home, I asked him to come in for another cup of coffee or another drink. It didn't take long for him to agree. The rest of the evening began to unfold.

I had to let my Bostons out, so Omar came out into the lanai with me.

"Wow, this is big lanai," he said.

I went into a big explanation of how I wanted to pay cash for the house, so we put the pool in after the house was built. "I didn't want a house payment," I said, "so we built the house first to make sure we had enough money, and then about nine months later, we put in the pool. It worked out well because I was able to live with the size of the lanai at first and knew that I wanted to put the pool out farther in the yard to give us more room for the lanai.

"That was good idea," he said.

"I just love listening to you talk," I said. "I could listen to you all night."

Back inside, he sat down on my butter-yellow leather sofa. At first, I sat in the recliner but soon got up to get us something to drink and then sat down next to him. We talked quietly together, never taking our eyes off each other. It was so peaceful and I felt so contented. I felt him lean closer to me. Then, with his hand, he guided my face to his until our lips met. He kissed me with such passion it took my breath away.

"I love kissing you," I said. "I don't think I have ever in my life been kissed so beautifully." He looked into my eyes. He kissed me again, this time pulling me even closer. There was no denying that I wanted to kiss him as much as he wanted to kiss me.

"You kiss good," he said, as he once again reached for my face, holding it tightly and kissing me. All the while, I kept thinking how long it had been since I felt so alive, so completely present. We kissed each other, neither one wanting to stop. Then I did something I had never done previously in my life.

I stood up and took his hand, saying, "Come with me."

I led him into my bedroom, feeling for the first time in my life, free. Free to feel. Free to enjoy. Free to make love with this man.

It had been years since I had made love. I wondered what it would be like to do that again. We undressed in the dim night light, both moving quickly to get our clothes off. As we went to lie next to each other, I started to laugh.

I said, "Oh my God Omar! What in the world am I going to do with all that?"

"Where will you put it all?" he said. "It be ok, you will see." This time, when he kissed me it was feverish with passion. I felt as if my body would melt into his. Making love proved more difficult than he anticipated although he was so gentle and so loving it only left me wanting more.

We fell asleep that night both feeling complete. The next morning, I was awakened at four a.m. by this wonderfully sexy man who thought the outside lanai lights shining through the vertical blinds meant it was morning. At least that was the story I heard.

He was just as warm and loving in the morning as he was the night before. To my surprise, it was just as difficult as it was the night before but he was so patient and loving, reassuring me with that awesome accent.

"It will be okay, just go slow," he whispered.

It had been so long since I was in someone's arms. Never had I felt so much into the moment.

I looked up at Omar, thinking, *Here I am with a man who I really don't know well, yet I feel my body completely becoming one with his.*

We laid in each others arms, holding each other tightly. As sleep once again overtook us, we never moved, never let go of each other. We woke up again around seven-thirty. As I opened my eyes, I saw he had already been wake and was watching me. I laid next to him feeling so at home in his arms and so contented.

"Would you like a cup of coffee?" I whispered.

"No," he said with a sweet smile. "I gonna take you out to breakfast."

"I can make breakfast."

"No, I saw a sign close to where we went last night. It said 'breakfast' so I gonna take you there."

With that decided, we both settled in. We continued to hold each other and talk.

"Thank you for a wonderful time last night," I said.

I laid close to him, and drank in the feeling of his presence next to me.

"You are very welcome," he said. "Be still. Let me rest for one minute. Then we go."

A few minutes stretched into an hour before we decided it was time to get up and go for breakfast.

My little Bostons needed to go out, and then to be fed, before I could think of anything else. Omar followed me as I went to the glass sliding door in the family room.

"They are so good and quiet," he said. "Wow, my daughter's dog would not be so good. He is bad but he loves my daughter. What kind dog are these?"

I laughed at his adorable Arabic accent that I soon grew to love, and answered, "They're Boston Terriers. The smaller one was my deceased husbands dog. His name is Levi. The bigger one my daughters bought for me on Mother's day. His name is Amoree."

I added, "I don't know what I would have done without these little guys, they have comforted me through so many hard times."

"Yah?" he said, as he looked into my eyes.

Feeding his curiosity, I responded, "When my husband died, I discovered so much that I was unaware of. I went through so much heartache. These little guys brought me comfort just being next to me. Sometimes, when I would get so frustrated that I would sit and cry, they would come to me, as if to say, 'Don't cry, Mom. We're here for you.' Just having their presence around me made me feel better. When they would run and play it would bring joy to my heart."

He explained to me that in Egypt, people don't have dogs in the house; that if you touch them, you have to wash your hands before you pray.

"Didn't you have pets when you grew up?" I asked.

"Not in the house but my father loved all animal," he said. "He was a good man. I loved him so much. He just die one year ago in November."

I could feel the pain in his voice. I asked if his father lived in the United States or in Egypt.

"Egypt. But he and Mother, they were here a lot."

I didn't ask anymore questions because I could see pain in his eyes. We went inside. I fed my little guys which brought more laughter from Omar.

"Wow," he said, look how fast he eats.

"Amoree eats like it is his last meal," I replied.

"Look, the other one, he eat slow and nice, wow, how different they eat."

I could see he had not been around dogs very much since it all seemed to fascinate him.

"Now I have to let them out one more time and then we can go," I said.

I was excited to go to breakfast with him.

I said, "Just give me one minute and I will be ready."

When I came out of the living room into the family room he looked up and I could tell he liked what he was seeing.

"That was fast," he said, "Are you ready? I am hungry."

I laughed this time at the way he said hungry.

"What," he said "you are not hungry?"

"Yes, I am," I said and laughed. "Where are we going?"

"I show you." he replied, as we went out the door and got into his pickup truck.

As I got in, I looked around and saw a hard hat and could not keep from imagining how ruggedly masculine he would look in that hat. Masculine looking like the old television commercial with the Marlboro Man.

We arrived sooner than I would have liked because I was enjoying every minute with this adorable Omar. The little outside restaurant was near the water with a wonderful view.

"Let's go, he said. "I am very hungry."

He parked the truck in a nearby parking lot,

Walking up to the open, outdoor restaurant, I felt so happy that morning. I had a wonderfully strange feeling of pride to be walking next to this man. Not only was he gorgeous, but also my sixth sense told me that he was as beautiful inside as he was on the outside.

We reached the restaurant and chose a Bristol table. It was chilly outside. We both seemed to get a chill at the same time.

"I am glad I wore my jacket, it is cool this morning," he said, with a little shudder. "Can we have two coffee please?"

"Of course," said the waitress, "I will bring you a menu."

He looked at me and smiled like a little boy with a new toy. I sat at the high table. He walked over to the railing and looked out at the water. Within a minute, he was back at the table, smiling again from ear to ear. There was a definite chill in the air but I was so happy I barely felt it. The waitress brought our coffee and menus.

"I just made coffee. These are the first two cups out of the pot," she eagerly told us.

"Good. I can not drink coffee that is not fresh. It make my stomach upset," he said. He looked at me and said, "What looks good on the menu?"

I named a few things that appealed to me and we decided on a croissant sandwich with eggs and sausage. I think anything would have tasted wonderful that morning. I was floating on a cloud, and felt that he was, as well. We sat by the water, eating our croissants, just taking in the moment.

Although the air was cool, I kept thinking how wonderful I felt and how lucky I was to be alive. After you face the possibility of death as I did, you think differently; each new day is another blessing. Not a day went by when I didn't thank God for answering my prayers, allowing me to survive. At the time, I thanked God for my wonderful children but selfishly prayed to see my grandchildren grow into adults. The thought of not dancing with my granddaughter at her wedding tore my heart out, she is so special to me there are no words to describe it. During that time, the thought of her gave me strength. That morning, I was exceptionally thankful. I simply felt completely happy inside.

I looked across the table at Omar and felt overwhelmed again with that feeling of sadness. His eyes couldn't hide the hurt and pain that was inside him. I wanted to reach out and touch his face but somehow I held back.

Instead, I said, "Isn't this a wonderful morning?" hoping somehow to make his pain to go away. He looked at me as if he read my mind and knew what I was thinking.

"Yah, it is. It is beautiful," he said.

Then the sadness once again left his face. Those dark brown eyes surely were the windows to his soul. They spoke volumes when they were happy. Once again, he smiled with that warm, beautiful smile.

We finished our breakfast. Although the sun was shining, the cool breeze made it impossible for us to stay for another cup of coffee. I was disappointed but happy that we were heading back to the truck. I chuckled to myself and thought if Titus would have wanted to sit outside and have breakfast with the air so chilly, I would have told him "No way," and flatly refused. But there I was with this man who I just met, loving every minute of it, not even mentioning I was chilled to the bone. We laughed like kids when we ran to the truck.

What an adorable man, I thought.

"I will turn on the heater for you," he said, as he started the truck.

"I didn't realize how chilly it is until we came back to the warm truck," I said. "I got goose bumps all over."

"Yah, it is not a warm day."

"Thank you for breakfast and thank you for a wonderful birthday. That was so thoughtful of you. I really enjoyed myself." Then I laughed as I looked at him.

"What is it? Why are you laughing?"

That just made me laugh harder.

"What?" he asked again.

"I was just thinking about last night," I said. "I really didn't think we were going to be able to make love."

He laughed and reassured me, "I will make it work." Then he laughed again. "Are you okay?"

Again I laughed, and said, "I feel like a young bride on the morning after her wedding."

With a reassuring voice, he said so sweetly, "It be okay, you will see."

As I sat there, feeling like that young bride, I reassured myself that he's right, it will get better.

We spent the rest of the day having fun. I made him laugh all day with my crazy, off-the-wall remarks. I was enjoying myself. I felt so alive. He made me feel so happy.

Later in the day, we made our way back to the house. "I love to watch football, do you?" I said.

"Yah, really? You like football? Wow, that is unusual for a woman to like to watch sports on TV. Do you like basketball?"

"Yes I do. I like most sports." I looked at him. "What is your favorite sport to watch?"

"I like basketball, they are such good game. That is a skill game. You have to be good to play good basketball."

We watched a football game that day. Omar got a glimpse of how I get into the games. He laughed at me. It was so nice to see him laughing and enjoying himself. During the game, I made us the first of many salads that I would make for us. As I was preparing the salad in the kitchen, I could see him sitting in the family room. Again, the thought of two people from two different parts of the world enjoying each other crossed my mind.

"Omar, do you like avocados? I asked.

"Yah, I do.

"What about yellow and orange peppers"

"Yah." He spoke with a swing to his voice.

"Okay, one salad coming up."

I already knew he liked turkey. So I put together turkey, cranberries and tomatoes along with a mix of fresh greens. I had thrown a loaf of French bread into the oven so I was prepared. As soon as the bread was hot, I put the salad in huge wooden salad bowls and brought them to the family room so we could continue to watch the game and eat.

I think I surprised him with all that because he had a really pleased look on his face.

"Wow, you made this so fast," he said. Then, "Oh, looks good," as he reached for the bowl.

"I hope you like it. Can I get you something to drink?"

"No, not now." As he took his first bite, I knew he liked it from the noise he made.

"I like this, you make salad and it is healthy for you."

You are cute, I thought. *Really cute!*

The day went so fast. I hated to see it come to an end. We moved from the reclining chairs to the couch. I couldn't help laughing about what I had done the night before. I was still surprised with myself, but I had no regrets. Except for the bride-like feeling, all was well with me about what I did.

After the game, we watched TV between the times when we talked. I enjoyed talking with Omar. I liked looking at him even more. But like all good things, the day did come to an end. Then it was time for us to say goodbye. As he hugged me he gave me a kiss.

He smiled big and said, "Alrighty now, I gotta go.

I walked with him to the driveway.

"Thank you once again, I really did enjoy going out with you," I said. "Bye now." Then I tuned and walked back into the house.

A few hours later, Leah called. She asked, "How did your birthday dinner go?"

"Oh my Gosh, Leah, he is truly yummy. We had a wonderful dinner at *Bon Apétit.* Then we went dancing at a wonderful bar on the Beach. I have been all over the world but I swear, nothing, not even Las Vegas, can compare to dancing at this place."

"What is the place called?" she asked.

"Shepard's. It is so neat out there. The water is so close you hear the waves. They have neat Tiki lights all along the sidewalk. We sat at a Bristol table. There were outdoor propane heaters everywhere. The atmosphere was unreal. Oh, Leah, I had such a wonderful time. At one point, later into the night, it started to rain a light mist. I could feel it on my face when I leaned back in his arms as we danced. It was surreal, magical. Leah, I have not felt so captivated by a man as I feel with him, in forty-some years. With the rain lightly falling on my face, I felt so alive and just plain happy. We had such a wonderful time. He wore that same cologne. Grr, I like it."

"Down girl" she said, and laughed. "It's good to hear you so happy. After all you have been through, you deserve happiness."

"Leah you won't believe what I did."

"It must be good. Wait, let me get a cigarette, I'll be right back." When she returned, she said "Ok what did you do?"

"Well …" I paused. Then I laughed.

"Ok, tell me already" she said.

I continued to tell her the whole story. "When we got home, I made us something to snack on, along with a drink. We were kissing on the couch and I just threw fate to the wind and took his hand as I stood up. He got a real serious look on his face and asked "What is it?" as if he had done something wrong. I just lifted his hand to get him to stand up and then I just quietly said, "Come with me."

"Oh Lord! Good for you, Desiree," she said. "But what took you so long? I thought you two were going to make love on the dance floor the first night you met." Then she laughed.

"Leah, that is the first time in my life I have gone to bed with someone on the first date. I don't regret it, I really don't. There is something so special about him, I just can't even explain it. He and I are going to be really good friends, I feel it."

"Well, you're off to a good start, Girl. Did he ever send you the email about Egypt?"

"No, not yet, but he told me he was looking for it and as soon as he finds it, he would send it."

"Well, was he worth the wait?" Then she giggled,

"Leah, are you asking if he was good in bed? Let's put it this way, after we made love the first time, he woke up at four a.m. and saw the lanai lights shining through the vertical blinds, thinking it was already morning and the sun was coming up…

"And…"

"And, I didn't refuse."

"So I guess that is a yes. You go, Girl."

Some things are best left unsaid so I didn't go into details about wondering where I was going to put it all or that I felt like a young bride.

"We went out to breakfast this morning down on the beach near *Bon Apétit*," I said.

"Wasn't it cool down by the water?" she asked.

"Yes, it was but we went anyway. He just left a little while ago. I could listen to him talk all day. I love his accent. I really got the feeling that he is a sincere man who can be trusted. Boy, Leah, I don't know what it is, but, you know how I am about trusting men."

"Ah yes, I do. Well hopefully you are right about him."

"I hope so too. Mmm, I can smell his cologne on the pillow as I lay here talking to you. I love it. He said his daughter bought it for him. She has good taste. I am beat. I need some sleep."

We agreed to meet at the gym the next morning and we said goodbye.

The next morning, I went to the gym feeling so good inside. A few of my friends were waiting for me to come in so they could ask how the weekend went. Steve was being his obnoxious self. He loves the "shock approach" to things, and does it quite well. He is quite a great looking ladies' man, although once he opens his mouth, they run. We have been friends for over a year now and I appreciate his friendship even though he is a little rough around the edges.

"Well, Hell, it's about time you came in," he said, "Did you have a good time?"

"I did", I said.

"You must have gotten laid from that smile on your face."

"I really had a wonderful time, Steve, I really did. I like this man. He is so adorable."

"Aw, Hell, just be careful. You know he is from a different culture and they don't respect women."

I thought, *Okay, Steve, think what you want to think.*

"You know I am your friend and I don't want you hurt," he said.

"Jeez, Steve, I just went out with him. I'm not marrying him."

"I know, I know. Just be careful."

"Okay, will do."

I worked out, making my way around the gym to the treadmills.

I thought, *How glad I am to get away from Steve.*

I looked up and saw William coming toward me. William and Steve are good friends but about as opposite as they can possibly be. I really like William. He and I can get into some quite deep conversations.

"Hey, William!" I yelled, "what's happening?"

"Nothing much. Just wondered how your weekend went."

"Ooo, he's yummy! I had an awesome weekend, really awesome."

"Good for you, Lady. Let's have coffee after you finish working out."

"OK, that sounds good."

William dated a Muslim woman about two years prior and wanted to marry her. He studied the religion and was going to convert but even though he went along with all the Muslim customs, there was one thing he could not accept. That was how her children treated her with such disrespect. It is the custom that when a woman divorces, or becomes a widow, children do not accept a different man into their family.

Omar and I discussed the Muslim faith because I was interested in hearing about it and about his childhood although he said that he hadn't practiced religion since he moved to the States.

I worked out feverishly that day but could not explain why I felt so good and so alive. When I finished my routine, I checked to see if William had finished. He was ready to talk. I could hardly wait.

There was something special about his understanding and accepting manner. He never judged anyone. He always had a kind word, no matter how bad a situation was. I really liked his friendship and trusted his judgment. Steve, on the other hand, was quite judgmental. He only saw black and white. Obviously, someone from Egypt was not within his scope of acceptance.

As I approached the table, William smiled broadly and said, "Well, look at you today, with that big smile that says, 'I'm happy.'"

I laughed and said, "William, for the first time in years, I feel so good, so happy, so alive. It's not because I was out with a gorgeous man, it's because he made me realize there is still happiness out there. I silently existed with no emotions for over forty years. Then I met this man who caused me to realize I need to take down that horrible wall that has been my anesthetic."

"Good to hear," he said. He took a sip of his coffee, then continued. "Sometimes, we think we are protecting ourselves when, in fact, we are doing just the opposite. I'm happy to hear you had a good birthday. Tell me about it."

I told him about the night, with a few exceptions, of course, and that Omar brought me beautiful roses and champagne.

"Wow, aren't we special" he said with a chuckle and smile. I asked William if he would someday explain what he knows about the Egyptian culture and the Muslim faith.

"Of course I will, I would be happy to…"

I cut off his response with, "Who knows, I may never see him again but I really would love to know a little about it all."

Steve made his way back to us, so our conversation stopped. All William quietly said was that he would give me a call. It went over Steve's head because he doesn't hear well. He probably didn't even hear William. We all chatted for about half an hour. Then I decided I should leave. I can only take Steve for just so long when he is "in rare form" and that was one of those days. I finished my smoothie, said my goodbyes and left. Leah was late. She was still finishing her workout when I departed.

The rest of the day went slowly but I kept myself busy. I went over the events of the weekend, thinking what a lucky lady I am. I needed to call Laura later to fill her in.

During those trying years after Titus' death, I realized what it means to have a true friend. Her friendship never faltered. She was always there for me. I thought of our trip to London and what an unbelievable experience that was.

When the phone rang later, it was my attorney. I wished I had all the money I'd spent on attorneys after Titus's death. I would've been rich.

I got side tracked into cleaning up the kitchen. When the doorbell rang, I figured it was my neighbor and went to the door. I was right. She needed to talk. Her husband had left her a few months earlier. She was beside herself with fear over how she would take care of herself if he decided to divorce her.

She drove me nuts but I pitied her. She was not playing cards with a full deck. She had no true friends. After I made her a cup of coffee and listened to her non-stop bitching for an hour she asked me how my weekend went.

"I saw him the other night when he picked you up," she said. "He looks Middle Eastern. Is he?"

There was my opening. I told her a little but did not go into detail. "He is absolutely the sexiest man I have ever met. I really enjoyed myself. I love his accent, I could listen to him talk all night long."

"Where is he from" she asked. "Well, originally from Egypt but he has been here almost forty years," I replied.

That was the wrong thing to tell her. She was a political nut-case. She went off like a rocket, lecturing me on why I should never see him again. Thank goodness the phone rang.

This time it was Laura. I indicated it was someone who I needed to talk to. I whispered aside to my neighbor that I would have to take this call and that it would take a while. She scooted out the door, to my relief.

I couldn't wait to tell Laura all about my weekend. Laura had been a rock, too, like Leah. She never judged anyone, although with her history, almost anything I would do could not compare with the fun she had enjoyed.

We talked and talked like two girls in high school. She was so happy for me. She kept saying, "Good for you... good for you."

We talked for over half an hour before we realized how long we had been chatting. After hanging up, I made some dinner and decided to call it an evening.

I had talked to Mother earlier that morning so that obligation was handled. Sometimes, I had a very hard time talking with her. At age eighty-six, she had her own way of thinking. We never did see eye to eye on much. That became even harder as she aged. Our personalities were never compatible, in the least. She thinks acting mean and hateful gets you what you want. I prefer "the honey approach." I try to be a good daughter but find that can be quite difficult, sometimes.

I woke up early Tuesday morning and laid in bed thinking positive thoughts. I had a few errands to take care of. Also, I was going to have lunch with Kelly. We enjoyed doing things with her children, together.

My husband, Titus, used to say, "You take care of the house and grandchildren and let me worry about everything else."

I received everything from Titus that any woman could want except for the fundamental emotion. I was empty inside. His being absent so much didn't help matters, either. I loved him, in my own way, and had grown to accept that I would never truly love again. Not as I had loved Ajax. Always staying positive though, looking at the bright side, I realized how lucky I was to once have that wonderful love that Ajax gave me. That was a love not everyone is privileged to receive. I kept the memory of it tucked away, deep in my heart, for safekeeping, where nobody could affect it.

I didn't sleep well that night. I woke up each hour, on the hour, it seemed. How well I remember not sleeping soundly, night after night, during the months after Titus died.

I must have asked a thousand times after his death, "Why, Titus? Why couldn't you have prepared me for what I was going to face? Is that why you said over and over, as you passed, 'I'm sorry, I'm so sorry?'"

As I drank a cup of coffee that morning, I tried to convince myself that I had energy for the gym. I chuckled and thought, when all else fails, have another cup of coffee. My second cup was almost finished when the phone rang. I picked the phone up thinking it was Mother calling.

I felt surprised when I heard the voice of Omar, saying, "Hallo. How are you?"

"I'm fine. How are you doing?" I said, feeling happy to hear his voice.

"I was wondering if you would like to come over here and I will make you dinner." The sound of his accent makes me happy every time.

Wow, all these firsts, I thought. No man had ever invited me over to make me dinner. "Sure! I would love that. Sounds great," I said, smiling.

"Let me tell you where I live," he said. He told me how to find his condo, then he asked, "Is six o'clock good for you?"

"Sure, I will be there at six," I said.

"All righty now, I see you then, Goodbye," he said.

I was smiling from ear to ear as I said, "Goodbye."

Talk about energy; I had just received a huge bolt of it. I went to the gym for a wonderful workout. I felt eager to talk to William. As I finished my workout, I saw him sitting with a cup of coffee, so I went to him.

With a huge smile on my face, I said, "William, you will not believe who called me this morning."

How could he have not known, given my smile?

"Ah, let me guess," he said. "Would that happen to be Omar?"

"Yep, it would. He asked me to come over to his condo so he could cook "deener" for us.

"Well, isn't that wonderful? I'm so happy for you."

"Can you believe, William, this is the first time in my life a man asked me to come over so he could cook dinner for me? Honest. The first time. I am so tickled, this man just makes me tingle all over."

"Well that's so good to hear. I'm so happy for you."

"You know, I need you to pinch me because this is all so surreal. A few weeks ago I was just existing and now I am living. I don't want this feeling to ever end. I wonder what he will cook. I hope it's an Egyptian dish. Do you think he really enjoys my company?"

"I would think so, Desiree, why wouldn't he?"

"Well, he is younger than me and he is so handsome. I imagine he can get any woman he wants."

With a smile as big as mine, William said, "He *did* get the woman he wants."

We laughed, as I fully realized that I didn't call him, *he* called *me* for dinner.

"I'm excited, I really am, William. I just can't believe I met someone who I so thoroughly enjoy being with."

"Good for you, I'm so happy for you," he said again.

"Well, I better get going, there are a few things I need to do yet today and I won't be late for my 'deener.'"

I giggled. I did have a few things I needed to do that day but they were no longer as important as they seemed before the invitation. I ran my errands and came home to my little Boys. I really don't know what I would have done without my little Bostons. They truly had been there for me through so many tears that I cried those past years. It's hard to fathom what it would have been like without them. They say dogs have unconditional love. It's so true in my case.

I called my neighbor Penny to tell her the good news about my "deener" invitation. She was happy for me but once again she tried to rain on my parade. "Are you sure you want to go to his place? Desiree, he's Egyptian, you need to be careful."

There she goes again, I thought, *with her political craziness.* "Penny, he has been here for thirty-nine years. He's a structural engineer, so I rather doubt I need to worry. Besides, it's just dinner. Anyway, would you please come over about eight thirty and let the Boys out so I don't have to worry about getting back early?"

"Sure I will," she agreed, "but I want you to be careful. I don't think you realize what you are dealing with."

I thought, *God bless her but she really is ridiculous.*

I ended with, "Come on over later, for some coffee, if you have a chance. I'm not going anywhere today. I need to paint my toenails and fingernails."

She liked that idea. *Great* I thought, *I was hoping she would say she was going to be busy and couldn't come today. She wears me out with all her political rhetoric and now the pending divorce.*

"See ya later," she said.

That day, I tried to straighten up the house but wasn't interested. I decided to pamper myself with a long, hot bubble bath, and a pedicure and manicure. Before I married Titus, I was a licensed manicurist, experienced doing nails, so that wouldn't take long. I thought back about all the money I earned doing nails. Wow, it's hard to believe what women will pay to have nice nails.

My doorbell rang as I got out of the bubble bath. I knew who it was and what I was in store for. I put my robe on and went to the door.

"Hi Penny, come on in," I said. "Let me put a pot of coffee on." We had coffee and a conversation so pleasant that I was relieved. She agreed to come over and let my little guys out around nine p.m., since she would be gone to her AA meeting 'til then.

That's perfect, I thought.

It was about four p.m., so I politely said "I need to get ready but I'll call you in the morning to let you know how the "deener" was." She laughed at my trying to say "dinner" the way Omar says it. She departed as I started getting ready.

It was an hour's drive to Omar's condo. "Hallo," he said, as he stood back for me to come in.

"Hi," I said. "This was easy to find. You gave me good directions."

"Good, I am glad you found me easy."

I gave him a hug and walked into his spacious great room. The view of the Gulf was spectacular and the sound of the waves was soothing. "Wow," I said," as I whirled around to look at him, "this is awesome."

"Yah, I like it too." He smiled. "I like the Intercoastal better. This is like black hole at night, you do not see anything. I like the intercoastal where there is lights."

He asked me if I would like a drink, which I gladly accepted, thinking it would calm my nerves a little. I couldn't understand why I felt nervous, but I did. He made drinks. We went out on the balcony. He sat on his chaise lounge. I took the end of it, facing the water and him. I was living in the moment.

What a beautiful view, and what a beautiful man I am enjoying it with, I mused.

We talked and talked. That was the first of our many marathon conversations. He went into the kitchen for more drinks.

I thought to myself, *Okay now, two drinks on an empty stomach, this should be interesting.*

When he came back, he brought our drinks and something that looked like seeds, or small nuts. He handed me my drink, and said, "Here, taste these, they are from Egypt they are good for you."

I loved the way he said "Egypt," it was like he twisted his tongue, somehow. I tasted the seeds, and to my surprise, they were delicious, although at that hungry moment, I would have thought anything was delicious. Omar wanted to know all about me but I noticed he offered very little information about himself. Once again, as I looked into his eyes they revealed such sadness. I felt it to my bones.

I seem to feel their sadness when someone is hurting, and that night, I was overwhelmed with that feeling. I leaned over, gently kissed his lips, looked into his eyes and kissed him again.

"Wow," he whispered, "I like that."

We finished our drinks while quietly enjoying the evening.

Eventually, Omar announced it was time to start cooking.

"Come with me," he said, "you can help me."

I asked what he was going to cook and although he told me, I didn't recognize the dish. I was excited about him making something from his country. He made a chicken dish with curry and served it over rice. His rice was different from the rice I am used to. I welcomed the chance to try it.

He slowly explained, "When the rice is cooked, you drain the rice and put a little olive oil in a pan. When the oil gets hot, you put the rice back in and let it cook. It gets hard, and – how you say – crisp."

He put some crisp rice on my plate and said, "Here, try it."

I found I liked the crunchiness. He explained so much to me that night. I felt like a sponge trying to absorb it all.

After dinner, we sat on the couch to digest our food.

Omar asked, "Would you like some tea?"

I accepted. He was happy with my answer. He told me he has tea from Egypt, excellent tea, not like tea from the US.

"What kind tea you like?" he asked. "Surprise me," I said. "I like all kinds of tea." He decided to make red tea.

He went to the kitchen.

I like this great service, I thought.

He came back to the room, sat on the floor next to the couch, and told me we needed to wait a few minutes until the tea would be done.

"You like Honey?" he said.

"Wow this is like a restaurant" I replied.

He laughed. "No, not like restaurant."

In a few minutes our tea was ready. When he brought it into the room, I sat on the floor with the coffee table before me. He put the tea down and joined me. I was happy that Omar was so casual and easy to be comfortable with. We drank our tea side by side. I felt like royalty. I relaxed in Omar's company, knowing there was no need for pretense.

Although he had movie star looks, he was so down to earth. *This was a wonderfully relaxing evening,* I thought. I listened to the waves on the sand as they rolled in.

"You told me you like the Intercostal better," I said, "But gosh, this is stunning here, listening to the waves."

He kissed my lips, then said, "But after a while you do not hear the water. I do not even hear it anymore."

"Do you walk on the beach often?"

"No, not really. I used to, when I first came here."

"How long have you lived here?"

"About two years now." He smiled and went on, "I got this condo so Mother could enjoy her visits and watch the water while I was at work. Mother was here about six months. In November, a year ago, my father died. I loved my father very much. I always loved my father. When he died, I had to take Mother home on airplane for twenty-four hours without telling her he had died."

My heart ached for him. I could see the his own pain in his eyes.

I said, "That had to be hard, to be on a plane for so many hours and not show emotion."

"I go to the bathroom," he said, "and I cry, then I come back out and sit down."

He told me their custom of going back on the anniversary of someone's death and holding a service. I was interested to hear about another culture's customs. I could perceive the love he had for his father from the way he talked about him. He told me many stories about his father; how he helped so many young people. He sounded like a wonderful man. Not really knowing my own father, there was nothing I could add to the conversation except to say, "My dad died when I was twenty-three."

"Wow, he was young man when he die," he said.

Explaining how Mother tried, in every way she could, to alienate me from my father would have been hard that night. So I left it alone, figuring I would explain that another time. Somehow, I knew, this was just the first of many visits, and I sensed his need to talk. And talk we did. For hours and hours. We talked about everything that was tugging at his heart. It was fun listening to him trying to explain things to me that were important to him, things he wanted me to understand. I listened intently, never turning my eyes away from him.

Not wanting to overstay my welcome, I thought maybe I should leave. He definitely did not agree. He let me know I should stay longer. Not really wanting to go, I was happy to stay. There was something so special about this man and it wasn't just his looks. The more we talked, the more I realized how enormously deep his soul was. He was so sensitive and yet, still so virile. I love a man who can show emotions and not be afraid of seeming weak.

We talked into the wee hours and kissed until neither of us could stop. Making love that night seemed so natural, so... inevitable. As he looked at me, I melted ever more into his arms, feeling the intensity of his touch, and the gentle manliness of his heart.

I drove home slowly that night, going over our conversation mentally and wondering what caused the sadness his eyes. What could have happened to trouble him that deeply? I just couldn't put my finger on it but I knew something was there. Some pain was tearing his heart out, but he said nothing about it. My thoughts were diffuse.

Of course, my fur babies, Levi and Amoree, were happy to see me when I got home. I let them out again. And again, I caught the subtle scent of Omar's cologne. Oh, how I liked his cologne. I was exhausted. Sleep came easy for a change.

The next few days passed quickly. I thought about Omar often, still not understanding that feeling I was picking up, but simply enjoying the thought of him.

On Friday, my phone rang and again.

I heard him say, "Hallo, how are you today?"

This time, he didn't give me a chance to answer.

He said, "Maybe you would like to go dancing at Sheppard tonight?"

It didn't take long for me to say, "I'd love to!"

"Would your friend Leah like to go along?"

"I'll ask her and let you know."

"Okay. I gotta go now but I will call you back later."

"That will work."

"Bye, I call you later." Then he hung up.

I could hardly contain myself. I was so excited when I called Leah to find out if she wanted to go along. After I asked her if she wanted to, she chuckled about the excitement in my voice.

"Sure I'd like to go," she answered. She said that she would drive, so she could leave if she decided not to stay late.

When Omar called back, I told him, "Leah has decided to drive, herself."

"That's alright, I meet you there nine o'clock, if she want to go early, I will bring you home or you can come here. It is going to be cold, be sure wear jacket," he said all of that, in one, long sentence.

I said that I would and then, after a few more words, I heard his usual closing remark: "I gotta go now, I will see you tonight, you can stay here if you want."

We arrived at Sheppard's promptly at nine o'clock. Since valet parking is the only option, we pulled up to the valet station and got out of her car.

"Ooo! Listen Leah... listen to the music," I said, as I danced a little.

She looked at me with her are-you-kidding-me look and said "Oh, Lord, what did I get myself into?"

By now, my whole body was moving to the beat of some music that we heard from the hotel building. The band was behind the hotel but one would think the band was right there beside us. Leah likes music that is more mellow, but I like it all. We got our valet slip and walked through the entrance to the bar area.

"This music is awfully loud, don't you think?" she said.

I laughed and said, "You'll get used to it." Then I laughed harder when I saw the incredulous expression on her face.

"The atmosphere is awesome," I shouted, when we approached the entrance and the band sounded quite loud.

"You have got to be kidding," she said, as she made a face like she was going to get even with me.

"It's really neat, you'll see," I said.

"You might think that," she joked. "Okey dokey," she added. "I'm glad I drove."

"We can sit in the back," I suggested. "That way, because it's so open, it won't sound so loud. "

"Yah, right. Okay. If you say so," she said, with a mocking laugh. The look on her face was astonishment.

As we arrived at the back, the band was about to take a break and the volume wasn't quite so intense. The DJ started to play music but it wasn't nearly as loud. Looking around, I didn't see Omar but before I could say something to Leah, he appeared, standing behind me. It was as if he came out of nowhere.

Ooo, what a pleasant surprise, I thought.

He stood behind me and placed his hands on my shoulders, then skimmed them up and down my arms. Of course, he looked smashingly dapper in his black sweater.

"How're you?" he said?

"I'm good, I replied, and how are you?"

He answered, "Good," with a big smile.

"How are you, Leah?" he said.

"Well… I am here," she almost shouted, to be heard above the music. He asked us each what we would like to drink. Leah decided on a diet coke. I asked for a Margarita. He went to the bar. Leah and I looked for a seat. We found a few extra chairs at a high table where a couple was sitting. We asked if we could have them.

"Sure. Why not join us?" the woman suggested.

By the time Omar brought our drinks, we were sitting at a table beside a big propane heater. The heaters created both ambiance and warmth we appreciated because the air felt chilly.

"Wow, you got table quick," he said. He handed us our drinks. Since there were but two chairs, Leah and I sat, and Omar stood behind me. Before long, Omar and I started dancing. I was in seventh heaven. Though the air was cool and crisp, all the heaters, combined, produced enough warmth to feel pleasant, even outside.

"Your friend. She not happy?" he asked.

I chuckled, then told him, "I didn't mention how loud the band is. I think she's ready to kill me."

He nodded his head that he understood. Next thing I knew, the song "Sweet Alabama" came on. Omar's face lit up like a full August moon.

"Ooo, I like this song," he said. He sang, "I love it."

His feet moved in time with the music as he reached for me. He held me close as he moved his head back and forth singing into each of my ears, in turn.

The chemistry between us is undeniable, I thought. I so enjoyed feeling his body next to mine.

"Let's go back to the table by your friend," he suggested. When we returned, Leah gave me that look of hers, an expression that only she could assume. It comically suggested, "You owe me *big time*," as she raised one eyebrow and squinted with the other eye.

"Come on Leah," I urged her, "lets dance."

She uttered some mock-evil laughter, glared at me, and then said, "Dance? I don't want to get one inch closer to that band. But you go ahead… dance your fool feet off."

And that I did. Dancing with Omar was pure delight. He was quite a good dancer, so easy to follow. Although slow dances were spaced apart, when one appeared, it was welcomed.

Leah decided she "had enough of the loud music," as she put it, around midnight. When she was about to leave, Omar tried to convince her to dance with him but she sweetly refused.

He looked at me and asked, "Are you going to stay? I will take you home or you can come to my condo and I take you home tomorrow."

He didn't have to ask me twice. I brought a change of clothes with me, so I went with Leah to get her car. I got my big purse that held my clothes.

"I'm sorry you didn't enjoy the music, Leah," I said, "but isn't the atmosphere awesome?"

"Yeah, it really is," she said. "I liked all the Tiki lights and the glow of the heaters, but that music was awful."

"Aw, come on Leah," I joked. "Think young."

"Think young? Really, I couldn't think at all, with music that loud. I prefer music that's mellow, music that I understand. Not that overly-amplified stuff."

"Anyway," I said, "I'm sorry you didn't enjoy it but I'm glad you came."

"No worries, go have a great time," she said, while getting into her car.

After I returned to Omar, we danced until around one-thirty a.m. When we left, I almost didn't want the evening to end, but I looked forward to being in Omar's arms, and to making love with him.

Morning seemed to come too quickly. As I laid there watching him sleep, many thoughts ran through my head. This was the first of many mornings when I would lay quietly and watch Omar sleep. Once awake, we both laid there, not wanting to move. I then realized what I had been missing for so many years.

Although our relationship was quite new, I felt uniquely different with Omar. I can't deny that I still felt like a moth drawn to a flame, just as I did the first night I saw him standing alone in the dance hall. It's such an unexplainable feeling, one that I have longed for, so much. Instead of analyzing, I laid in his arms, simply enjoying the moment, realizing how fortunate I was to feel love again.

Suddenly, Omar cracked a childlike smile, as he rolled on his side and kissed me gently. It wasn't coffee he had in mind.

I giggled, then said, "You remind me of the Energizer Bunny on TV."

He laughed. "Yah, it is true. I am 'ever ready.'" We both laughed, but soon we became quiet as we looked into each others eyes while we made love.

Later, lying side by side with a fulfilled feeling, I raised up on an elbow and coyly remarked, "Now, *for sure*, I need a cup of coffee."

He laughed and agreed. I made a move. He held on to give me one more little kiss.

"What? You want more?" I said.

He laughed and came back with, "You crazy blonde. Get up."

After we were up, Omar decided to make breakfast. He offered eggs, which I eagerly accepted. It was a beautiful morning. We opened the sliding glass doors. I could hear the waves rolling onto the beach. I felt I needed a pinch to assure I really was present there, enjoying breakfast with this beautiful man, while listening to the waves. I sat on the floor, as I had done the other night, just looking out at the water. He came back into the room, bringing breakfast to me.

Wow, service with a smile, I thought, as I accepted my plate of eggs and flatbread toast.

After we ate, he brewed more coffee. The first cup of coffee eventually became three as we talked and talked.

During this visit, I discovered what the sadness in his eyes was about; that sadness I had been noticing ever since meeting him that first time. He began with "My father died one year ago, in November. It is our custom to go back where loved ones are buried on the one-year anniversary of their deaths."

I asked if he had gone back during the previous November.

He said, "Yah, I did."

Then he spoke about his father. Tears welled up in his eyes as he revealed such love for a parent that I could hardly fathom it. Not being close to my father or even knowing him very well, made it difficult for me to understand. He mentioned words he and his father had exchanged, some months prior to his father's death and how he wished he had simply granted to his father's request to give his younger brother some money.

"I dreamed of my father at least once a week," he told me. "I always love him so much. My father loved my oldest brother best. My oldest brother was his favorite. He could not do anything wrong. Mother feels the same.

"Oh, Omar," I responded, "you are so beautiful inside and out, I think your parents would be so proud of you and what you have achieved. I can't imagine such feelings because I'm an only child. I never had to share my Mother with siblings."

We sat for hours, talking about what he had been through during the previous forty years. All the heartache he had experienced in the past year made my own heart resonate with pain as I tried to say things to him to somehow help him heal.

Weeks went by as we continued to enjoy each other's company. He would regularly make dinner for me. I stayed at his condo ever more often as the weeks passed. I helped him with marketing his business, first by making brochures, and then setting appointments to meet potential new clients.

Soon, I began bringing my Boys with me so that I didn't have to worry about them being home alone for long periods. On the weekends that followed, I learned more and more about Omar, about his life and all he had endured since coming to the USA alone. One Sunday morning we sat as usual, on the floor, drinking coffee, when Omar decided to show me a movie of Egypt. He had purchased it at the airport the last time he was there.

I couldn't believe how beautiful his country was. All we Americans saw on television seemed to be rocks and sand. The city he was from is called "The City of Roses."

"We have roses everywhere," he told me. "Everywhere, it is so beautiful."

He described these scenes that appeared in detail, one by one. I sat with him, like a child receiving a story, taking it all in. We viewed columns hundreds of years old, still standing, and a market with beautiful rugs hanging all around. His photos were so artfully chosen and colorful they resembled illustrations from a magazine feature story. There was even some jewelry displayed out in the open.

I was excited to see it all and by imagining a visit to shop for a beautiful rug. That was the first of many times I would ask him to take me to see the market where they buy tea and vegetables. I wanted to experience, first hand, this land where he grew up. I longed to take in the beauty of it, not only through his particular viewpoint, but with my very own eyes. He played Egyptian music during the show and the atmosphere made it even more compelling.

He got excited showing me those photos and seeing me enjoy them so much. We probably went through his collection three times before he said "enough." But I could have watched it one more time.

"I will send another collection for you to see. I have to find it," he said.

I tried to start calling him by his given name because I was doing some marketing for him but he was happy with "Omar," so I continued using it. What a wonderful team we were, seeming to feed off each other's energies. I saw him as a brilliant man with deep experience and solid common sense. When I began to market for him, I marveled at all the projects he had devised throughout the years, the numerous hotels and condominiums, those great complexes with so many buildings, projects located in so many different counties and states. He created so many, while making a new life in another country, far from his home. I felt so proud to know this honest, brilliant man.

During meetings, he spoke eloquently, and with such professionalism, that he would captivate his audience. On many occasions, he awed listeners with his command of engineering. He would tell me I needed to talk more but it was not me they wanted to hear. Meeting after meeting, he never faltered, always keeping the meeting controlled, never leaving any doubt about his capabilities. I loved working with him. I was proud to be part of his team.

One Saturday night, we sat on his balcony having a beer, as we had done so many times before. Once again, as our conversation flowed, his heartache surfaced and I heard it all. Only then did I realize the true nature of that sadness I felt when I first met him months previously, that sadness he always bore silently behind those luminous, brown eyes.

I sat quietly listening, not wanting to misunderstand a word of what he told me. My eyes filled with tears as my heart ached for him. He told me his whole, gut-wrenching story. The depth of his ability to love was second to none. The discipline, loyalty and devotion he commanded; I imagined that any woman would die to have those forces directed toward her. His voice, cracking as he told the story, burdened my heart. I fought back tears. I wondered how he would ever heal.

As we laid in each others arms that night, I tried to understand how women who claimed to love him could be so cruel. I could feel his relief in sharing what had happened with someone safe. I came away that weekend with an aching heart and a mind whirling with wonder. How could all that have happened to him? I wanted to reach out and help, but I felt unsure if I could.

On my long drive home, Sunday night, my thoughts went to Ajax for guidance. I asked if this relationship was meant to be; if Omar's shattered heart would ever heal. So many times, Ajax had guided me. I found myself hoping somehow he would do so again.

Though I wanted so much to help him, as I thought through the situation, I realized his healing would have to come from within, that all I could do was be there for him and bear witness to his heartbreak. I asked Ajax for some insight about something I could do to help the man I was growing to love. I felt a bond with Omar beyond description. The feelings I had kept so deeply buried surfaced easily with him. I was too afraid to even think of how much I cared for him.

On Monday, I worked from home, setting more business development appointments. I had a talent for motivating architects to meet Omar to discuss his qualifications and decide if they wanted to engage his engineering skills. I made numerous calls that day. The appointments were set for the following week. He would always get so excited when I set the appointments.

He'd say, "Good job! Wow, you do all that!"

I wanted to please him more than I had wanted to please anyone else. Hearing happiness in his voice made my heart sing. As the day wore on, I tried not to dwell on what I had heard but instead, to think of the right words for the next time we would get together.

By Wednesday, I had set enough appointments to last a few weeks. That morning, to my surprise, there was an email from my Middle Eastern guy on my computer. It was the email he had promised me months earlier, the one about Alexandria.

My phone rang and I heard him say "Hallo."

I said "Good Morning, how are you this morning?"

"Good Morning, I am good, how are you?

He called me early that morning before I had time to open the email. He seemed so proud and said "You gonna like this, it is good."

We talked a few minutes and I told him that as soon as I was finished watching his video, I would give him a call.

I made myself a cup of coffee and decided to call my daughter before I opened the documentary. I knew Kelly would be calling me. I wanted to watch the program without the phone ringing. Kelly and I chatted for about twenty minutes before we hung up. By then, I needed a refill of my coffee.

Having filled my cup with more fresh coffee, I was finally ready to sit and view what I had waited so many months to see. My computer had shut down, so I had to put in my password again and wait for the screen to reappear. Then I went to email and clicked on the message I had received that morning. I felt excited to see this. I hoped it would include that inspiring market where all those gorgeous rugs hung. Like a typical woman, I was always looking to shop.

After getting comfortable and taking a sip of my coffee, I went to my email.

He wrote:

Re: Alexandria History.

Hi, Good Morning, Desiree,

Here are some short story about Alexandria. I hope you like it.

Omar

I tapped on the link he had forwarded. As the page loaded, the screen filled completely with a single, gorgeous yellow rose. A perfect long-stemmed rose, with yellow hues so vivid and so striking I could almost smell it.

Oh my God, a yellow rose! I thought,

The words Alexandria, Egypt, appeared next.

By now, my heart was beating so fast, I felt tingling all over my body. As I took a deep breath, an aerial view of Alexandria appeared, then the sound of Ray Charles' voice filled the air.

He was singing:

> *Georgia, Georgia*
> *The whole day through*
> *Just an old sweet song*
> *Keeps Georgia on my mind...*

I slumped back in my chair, so overcome I could barely move. How could Ray Charles be singing on a video about Alexandria, Egypt? I frantically reached for the red X at the top top of the screen, shutting down the website.

Then I sat there, perfectly still, weeping.

Chapter Three

I decided it was time to make my debut into the world during a blizzard that crippled our town. Entering in the midst of that storm seemed to foretell my future. Since that day when I was born, my life had been one storm after another.

My parents divorced when I was a bit past two. After the split, I lived with a mother who was bitter and self-centered. The words "I love you" were never spoken in our home. Nor did Mother ever tell me or show me that she even cared about me. I was in the way of what she called happiness, and she reminded me on a regular basis. If the reminder wasn't verbal it took the form of action.

She said repeatedly that men in her life would have married her if it wasn't for me.

"Nobody wants to raise a kid," she would say.

Anything negative, she blamed on me. When she fought with her boyfriend, somehow, it was my fault and I would get the brunt of it. Fights were frequent in our home, even on a holiday. God forbid she should fight with her boyfriend on Christmas Eve. That would surely affect when I would open my presents from Santa. Sometimes, not until late afternoon.

I spent most of my younger life on the phone trying to find a member of my father's family who would let me spend the weekend with them. With me gone for the weekend, Mother could go out and do her own thing. If everyone, including my paternal grandmother was busy, then I would be left home alone until late at night. My maternal grandmother lived only a few doors from us but she wasn't into grandchildren. She resented watching me.

Mother's boyfriend used to bribe me with cash to not cry when they went out. My crying probably spoiled their rides to the local night club, though I'm sure I was soon forgotten. Her boyfriend seemed more concerned about me than she ever was. His money bribes taught me early in life that money does not buy happiness. Somehow putting a few coins into my piggy bank didn't take away the fear I felt when I heard a noise outside during the long hours they would be absent.

When I was six, my father brought me a Chihuahua puppy. I treasured that little fellow and enjoyed him almost twenty years. When he passed he had no teeth and arthritis, but I still loved him to the very end. He was the only dog Mother didn't give away. When a puppy would grow up so it was no longer cute and cuddly, she would give it away. Or worse: have my grandfather drive out of town and just drop it off. She carried on with that even years later when she remarried. As a young girl, I sometimes worried that she would give me away when I wasn't little anymore.

On weekend nights when I was left alone, I would crawl under the bed with my blanket and dog to sleep because I was so afraid. I knew I was there alone for the the night so I resigned myself to crawling into my pseudo-safe haven. I remember wrapping the blanket around my legs before I scooted under the bed so they would not contact the bare, cold hardwood floor. Often, my hair would get caught in the bed springs above me. I learned to be careful to not lift my head up much. Sleeping that way must have felt like the lesser of two evils because many nights, I slept there under the bed with my tiny little dog until she came home.

Soon I learned it didn't do any good to cry. My tears only made matters worse. Sometimes my crying caused her to lash out at me with those cutting words, "If it wasn't for you I would be happy." I never figured out why I was born. I just accepted that I was a mistake.

As a small child, the only true love I felt came from my paternal grandmother. I found my Grandma's love such a comfort. I knew without a doubt that she adored me. She spent time with me. She taught me everything from cooking to folding towels. We would spend hour after hour together as I learned to cook and bake. My little fingers were into everything. I wanted to absorb it all, like a sponge.

I spent much of my young life with Grandma and my grandfather. They both showed me much love. By their example, I learned how decent people lived. With them, I felt happy, safe and secure. I felt like I was recharging my batteries. So I never wanted to leave them. I would fake getting sick on Sunday mornings when I knew Mother would be pick me up later in the afternoon.

At bedtime, my Grandma would tuck me in with a hug and kiss that felt wonderful. She always said "I love you, Desiree Kay." I never got that at home. When I close my eyes, I can still recall the clean smell of the sheets, so fresh. My Grandma always took such care with me. She saw to it that was I clean when I went home with clean clothes, folded in my suitcase.

She knew those same clothes would be in my suitcase the next time I came over. I had four pairs of underwear and certain other clothes that I was not allowed to wear at home. Those items, I wore during visits to my father or his family. Mother made sure others thought I had everything I needed. I didn't care if I could only wear those clothes when I went away. I was happy to save them for visits.

Even though things were never smooth or loving at home, I always thought I was lucky to have a wonderful family on my father's side, folks who cared for me in a way that was impossible for Mother. Looking on the bright side, I was happy with the good. The special clothes pretense continued for years but I never told anyone because I was afraid that if I did, I would not be allowed to go away. Grandma never mentioned the special clothes either, but I'm certain she knew what was happening because she washed them at the end of each visit.

At home, I recall waking up many nights to the aroma of frying bacon at two-thirty in the morning. Mother's boyfriend liked BLT sandwiches but the bars closed at two a.m., so he might arrive drunk and hungry around two-thirty a.m. It didn't matter if I had school the next morning or not. The smell of bacon would fill our tiny, one-bedroom house.

But the bacon odor wasn't the worst part. He also liked to sing when drunk and was usually three sheets to the wind by the time he arrived, singing operatically. I used to pray he would continue drinking and get drunk enough to pass out. Then I could get back to sleep. Getting up in the morning was already difficult enough without him singing 'til all hours of the night. He continued like this from the time I was six until I graduated from high school and moved out of the house. Why she stayed with that man all those years was beyond me. In retrospect, maybe the drunken sex was good.

There was a lock on the outside of my bedroom door. That was installed after I wandered outside my bedroom more than a dozen times, catching them in some quite awkward situations. Strangely, I would be the one who got punished, as if I were the one bent over the kitchen table with no underwear. I was so little, I simply didn't understand. By the time I was old enough to realize what was going on, the noises they made disgusted me.

My fathers' family was wonderful: all decent people who treated me with caring. My father had one brother and three sisters. When he was only seventeen, his brother Nick moved from Pennsylvania to live with us. He loved playing with me. His name was the first word I spoke. Years later, I learned that I really loved him. I would squeal with delight and reach out to him when he walked through the door.

By the time my parents divorced, my paternal grandparents had moved close by us, from Pennsylvania. Then Nick moved in with them. He was the kindest and most gentle man. As I grew older, I used to wish he was my father. I spent a lot of time with him after he married and started to have children of his own. His wife was beautiful and so kind to me. He called her "Lovie." That was the perfect name for her because what she gave me was lots of love. I remember their wedding and how proud I felt when I danced with her during the bridal dance. In my mind, I was dancing with a princess.

They made me feel so welcome in their home. I spent a lot of time with them through the years. They took me along with them as if I belonged to them wherever they went. One time, when Aunt Lovie was pregnant with their second child, we were spending the day away from home. As we were going to the car, she jokingly started to count to see if we were all together.

She pointed to their boy first and said, "One…" then she pointed to me and said, "Two…" and then she pointed to her belly and said, "Three." I never forgot that short scene. The way they treated me, I felt I was part of their family. Although this was a simple thing, I have replayed that head count scene over and over, mentally.

I adored my father's sister and her husband; Aunt Sarah and Uncle Joel. They took in foster babies when the baby was a few days old. They took care of them until the mother was able, or deemed responsible by the court to care for her baby.

I loved spending weekends with them. Whenever I had to start making the weekend phone calls, she was the first I would call. They had a son who was born about two weeks after me. We got along quite well. He and his buddies would take me everywhere as if I was a buddy, too, but staying in and helping with the babies was a pleasure for me. If motherhood doesn't come naturally, then I would say that is how I learned my childcare skills. From that early time onward, I loved babies. I always knew I wanted to have a large family. Possibly being an only child helped me develop that attitude, but I always knew that I definitely wanted children. Many summers, I stayed with them, sometimes for weeks at a time.

Years later, after I had my own family, on a Thanksgiving, I composed a letter to Aunt Sarah and Uncle Joel.

I told them, "This Thanksgiving, I'm most thankful for having spent so much time with you throughout the years. Without your care and guidance, I would not have become who I am, with my learned values and morals. Nor would I have this rich store of wonderful memories."

Saying that felt good. They didn't need another child to be responsible for, but they did that readily, lovingly and frequently.

When I was ten, I asked my Aunt and Uncle if I could come to live with them. They seemed shocked but they agreed that I could. I'm not certain what took place but I do remember Mother saying she didn't care, if I wanted to go, I could.

Then her boyfriend, Author, started fighting with her. He told her that if she could let me go so easily, he wanted no part of her. Of course, there was the old pattern again: she blamed me for him not wanting her.

I begged her to let me go. I was so unhappy because I felt so unwanted. I couldn't understand how a mother could be so cold.

Author put his foot down. He talked her out of letting me go. I hated him for that. Although I don't know whether or not there were any legal papers prepared, I do know I wanted to move on, and the sooner the better.

When I was older, Mother allowed me to spend a few Christmases with my father's family. I was in my glory being a part of them and their way of celebrating. They sang Christmas carols, sat down at a table big enough for everyone and simply enjoyed the traditional festivities for the holiday.

Mother's family didn't get together for holidays. I don't recall my maternal grandmother ever coming over to our house, even to only see my presents. Nor did we go to her place.

Things were typically so happy at my father's family gatherings. I'm sure, as with other families, there would be ups and downs but nothing like the continual dysfunction I lived through daily. I had cousins on my father's side who I could play with and being the only granddaughter, until I was eleven or so, made me think I was special.

Christmas Season was a joy to my father. He always brought me such wonderful gifts. He tried to compensate for not being there for me. He knew what kind of life I was living. My father always assured that every year I had a new winter coat, hat, gloves, scarf and boots. That was a given until I was at least sixteen or seventeen.

He paid child support but realized, early on, where most of the money went. Another thing he assured was that I had a bicycle. One year, he brought me a pink one. I thought I was the luckiest girl in the world. I was so excited about that bicycle.

Through the years, the most exciting gifts were my rings. I loved rings. My father would often bring me one. I treasured them all. I never lost or misplaced them. Once I had a new ring, it went on my finger and never came off until I started to outgrow it. Even after all these years, I have some of them in my jewelry box.

Being Mother's ex-husband was a challenge. I imagine what hurt my father most was that I stayed distant from him, never allowing him to give me a hug or kiss. My father really never had a chance to get close to me. No matter what he did, Mother found fault in it, and would use it to drive a wedge between us. She embedded such a fear of him in me that I never even gave him a chance to prove he wasn't the monster she made him out to be.

He died when I was twenty-three. As I stood at his casket, I realized I didn't even know the man. The man lying in the coffin was a total stranger, a forty-six year old man who died much too young. The poor man only had one daughter, to whom he was never able to get close. We were lost to each other.

After their divorce, my father lived with his parents for quite some time. That was how my weekends with paternal grandparents got started. Mother remarried when I was about three. We lived with her new husband and his mother about twenty minutes from my maternal grandparent's home. That marriage didn't last but it did last long enough for me to suffer consequences. Years later, I heard what happened from someone who I knew was telling me the truth.

Mother worked. I was left with her new husband's mother during the day. Somehow, no one noticed I was losing a lot of weight. As the story goes, I fell down the basement stairs and was knocked unconscious. I was taken to my pediatrician, who noticed the weight loss. He ordered blood work. The tests showed that I was anemic and terribly malnourished. He prescribed medication and special liquids to get my weight back to a healthy level.

How my condition went unnoticed is beyond me. Mother discovered my caretaker was not feeding me all day. I was being locked out of the house so I couldn't even get something to eat on my own. At the age of three, I was being locked out of the house all day. My own pediatrician, who later took care of all my children, told me all this one day when I took one of my children to his office. He told me how worried he had felt about me and how proud he felt about the mother I had become.

I remembered falling down the steps and a fight between Mother and her husband of that time, but I didn't remember any details of why they were fighting. I vividly recall them fighting and Mother running out of the house, yelling that she was going to kill herself.

There were busy railroad tracks a block away from that house. I remember running after her crying because I thought she was on her way to kill herself. He husband ran after her, leaving me trailing behind. As I neared the tracks, I could see Mother standing on the back of a railroad car. Her husband was yelling and she was yelling back at him. Suddenly, a train came roaring past between me and her. As young as I was, I thought the train had run over Mother.

My stepfather had picked me up. I was shaking and sobbing from fear as he held me in his arms. Then I fought, pounding on him with my tiny fists, trying to escape so I could go to her. It seemed like forever until that train between us passed.

When I finally saw her standing there, I could see she had not died, after all. Although I had been terrified, there she stood, as if everything was okay; as if scaring me that way didn't matter; as if all that mattered was her starring role in a personal drama.

I went limp with relief from my intense fear but kept sobbing for a time. I don't recall Mother coming across the tracks to comfort me. All I recall is, the man carried me home, telling me everything would be okay.

That marriage only lasted a short time. We moved back to the neighborhood where I was born, one house apart from my maternal grandparents. My grandfather built a one bedroom house for us. I lived there until I graduated from high school.

Even after my father remarried, I would mostly stay at my grandparent's home instead of his. That worked out well because he lived only a few blocks away. Mother never found fault with my grandparents and never said anything bad about them to me. She would have been cutting off her nose to spite her face if she had done so, because she pawned me off to them most of the time.

When I went away for the weekend, she would drive up to the curb in front of their house leaving her car running, get out of the car, put my suitcase on the grass, open the car door for me and as soon as I was out of the car, standing in the grass, she would get back into the car and leave. She would literally drop me off and not even wait for someone to come out for me. No hug. Not even a wave goodbye.

When I would look up at my grandparent's home, I thought, *What a lucky girl I am to have such wonderful grandparents.*

What I didn't have in my home life during the week, I had tenfold with them on weekends.

I would go to the door to let them know I was there. My grandfather would rush out to pick up my suitcase and bring it in for me. My heart sang because I was there for the weekend. They never said anything to me about the way Mother dropped me off but I am certain they thought about it. If they knew what time I would be coming my grandfather would be waiting on the porch for me. He would come down the steps to greet me right away.

Even if he was waiting for me outside, Mother said very little and just left in a hurry. Not a single time did I ever get a hug, much less a kiss from her, but I didn't care. I was where I wanted to be. When she would pick me up after the weekend, she never asked if I had a good time or what I did, she only asked me if my father asked me any questions and if I kept my mouth shut. I was afraid that she would not let me go there again if I ever told my father's parents anything that went on at our house.

Much later in life, I found out that my grandparents had paid a neighbor of ours to watch out for me and to call them if Mother abused me. They kept quiet so she wouldn't keep me away from them. They understood what she was like.

Something funny about Mother's paranoia is that, despite all she badgered me about not repeating, many years later my father showed me that he knew about them all, regardless. Many times the police went to our house at the request of a wife who wanted her husband to come back home. We even had cat fights in our front yard between Mother and her lover's wives. Her shenanigans were reported in the local newspaper. There must have been six or seven articles about her. I was quite surprised to see the stories. Between our nosy neighbor and the newspaper, my father and grandparents knew about it all.

Before my father died, he brought out those newspaper clippings he collected and showed them to me. The poor man. He just wanted me to realize he wasn't a bad person. He wanted the truth to be known. There was never enough evidence for him to get custody of me. His great fear was that Mother would keep me from seeing him, if he wasn't successful in getting custody. Behind Mother's back, he tried, but I was being fed and clothed. At that time, that's all the law required. She never really wanted me but I was her pawn and she played chess well.

During the work week, from the time I was about seven years old until I was about eleven or so, Mother dropped me off at the YMCA to swim. I would often have to wait for a long time until Mother picked me up. It didn't seem to matter to her if she was late, rain or snow. I felt afraid I would not see Mother pull up if I stood inside. So I usually waited on the steps, whatever the weather.

The women who worked in the YMCA office saw me outside one night with wet hair, shivering. It was snowing. The temperature had dropped below freezing. They came to the door and told me to come inside. One woman brought me into the office and let me stand by the window where there was a heater. It was so warm in there that I soon stopped shivering. From that day onward, the two women took me into the office with them. One of those woman was so sweet. She would brush my hair. I recall her often cutting and cleaning my fingernails.

When I would see Mother's car coming down the street I would panic, put my coat on, and run out the door so Mother wouldn't know I had been waiting in the office. She was always late. I was so happy the women allowed me to wait inside, out of the cold, snow and rain. I never told Mother about the two women. And certainly not that someone brushed my hair and cut my fingernails. I was terrified she would get mad and yell at me for allowing the women to see my unkempt condition. Within a few weeks of being invited inside, I started to go in on my own.

One day, I overheard the two women talking about how sweet I was and what a shame it was that Mother didn't keep me clean. Their kindness was my secret though I felt ashamed. I pretended I didn't hear them. From that day onward, I took care of myself better. I bathed daily and washed my own hair. Mother rarely paid much attention to me, so she never even noticed that those women painted my fingernails a soft pink. I felt so proud of those pink nails though my hair and nails went unnoticed.

Things like painting my nails, or even just talking to me, would not have happened unless Mother thought someone was watching or that someone would hear about it. She had very little time for me. Her world revolved around herself and her boyfriends. I don't recall why I stopped going to the YMCA but I do remember going three days each week, for years. I became quite a good swimmer and diver. The chlorinated odor of the water was almost a comfort scent to me. When I walked into the pool area, I felt at home.

I never missed a day when her boyfriend was working days. He would be coming to our house after work, around three-thirty in the afternoon. He worked rotating shifts, so my attendance at the "Y" would vary according to his work schedule. When he worked second shift, she wasn't as eager to drive me to the "Y." There wasn't any need to get me out of the house then and she needed to rest, which meant not driving me back and forth.

While in second grade, I once walked a mile coming home from school in a blizzard. When I tried to get into the house, the door had frozen shut. There was no way I could open it. I was afraid to go to my friend's house across the street. I knew that would make Mother quite angry. My grandparents lived close by, but they weren't home. I sat down on the steps and started to cry. I tried the door again three or four times but it was frozen solid. I couldn't get in. I was freezing cold. The wind blew the snow so hard that I sat on the step and tried to hide my face. By then, I was crying hard. I was chilled to the bone. I fell asleep on the steps.

When Mother came home, she yelled at me, accusing me of trying to get attention. She had a hard time getting the door open. When she did, my feet were so cold I could hardly feel them. All Mother was concerned about was whether or not I went to the neighbors house and told them I could not get into the house. I had been sleeping outside in that horrible weather for almost two hours.

Mother was a hard-working woman. I will give her credit for that. That day she was working, but she never made arrangements for situations like those I encountered. I was expected to take care of myself. Sometimes, she even took extra jobs but I was the one who suffered, being left home alone, and so young, for even longer times.

Being very quiet during the early evening was a regular requirement in our house. Coloring and drawing became my passion. Her priority was to be up and cooking when her boyfriend Author arrived after the bars closed. His work week was four or five days straight on one shift, then two days off, then he went to a different shift. She would have to work in the morning so she would sleep earlier so she would be able to stay up with him after he arrived and then go to her work.

There was very little communication between us other than her screaming or yelling at me when things didn't go her way. Most of my evenings were spent behind a large, living room chair, coloring in my coloring books or drawing. I found comfort in that little space and was clearly out of her way. Knowing I could never do anything right, in her eyes, I found safe refuge behind that chair and would sometimes fall asleep there.

When I was seven, Mother came home from work one day and I hadn't cleaned the house the way she thought I should have. She yelled at me and, of course, I started to cry. She grabbed my hair and started pulling it and then started slapping my face. I pulled loose from her and ran out the back door, over to my maternal grandmother's house. Thank goodness she only lived one house away from us.

By the time I arrived there, I was out of breath. My face was red and welted from her hitting me. I ran into my grandmother's house crying. Although she was not a very loving woman, she took a look at my face and told me to go upstairs and wait in her bedroom. Just as I got to the stairs, Mother came in the back door yelling for me to come to her. She worked her way deeper into the house.

She came upon my grandma, who asked her, "Have you lost your mind? What in the world are you doing, hitting her face like that?"

"It's none of your business. Where is she?" Mother yelled. Normally my grandmother was mild mannered but this really did not sit well with her.

Grandma yelled as loud as she could at Mother, "If I ever see you hitting that girl again like that, I will kill you, do you understand?"

Of course, being a bulldog, Mother tried to just cut her off, demanding, "Where is she?"

That was the wrong thing to say because Grandma threw Mother out of the house, repeating her threat, "Do you understand me? I will kill you! Have you completely lost your mind?" she yelled.

Mother didn't respond. She just stormed out of the house. I didn't go home for hours. I was scared to death of even going near my house. My grandma took me home and once again warned Mother, in a tone that was not at all tolerant. I remember being especially quiet that night, simply going behind "the chair," then coloring in my coloring book.

I basically became invisible. Mother treated me coldly for a while after that incident though she thought twice before ever hitting my face again. In later life, I summed up my Mother as a "tempest in a fine china teacup."

There were birthday parties but everything Mother did was for show. Life in Mother's home was always a challenge. I knew it was best to stay quiet and remain in my room. Sometimes that was next to impossible. In her eyes, I could never do anything right.

I couldn't even smile "right" for my First Holy Communion pictures. After the photo session, I felt so happy but then all Hell broke loose. She yelled at me, saying that she was "paying all this money for pictures, but I wasn't smiling right" that I "spread my nostrils like a freak." When I started to cry that fueled the fire. Strangely, the photography studio used those photos for promotions. They enlarged two of them to sixteen by twenty inches. Apparently, my nostrils weren't too freaky for them. There was no pleasing her, at least not for me.

I had only the minimum of shoes and clothes but Mother never did without anything she wanted. She had many beautiful dresses and dancing gowns. I was not even allowed to touch them. She would say my hands were dirty, that I would make her dresses dirty. I felt as if I had leprosy. She never touched me. Nor was I allowed to touch her or anything that was hers.

I continued to visit my Grandma every weekend when I could, even when I was sixteen. My grandparents were first to meet Ajax, the young man who would love me into eternity. My grandmother fell in love with Ajax's gentleness, his platinum blond hair and aqua blue eyes. He looked so handsome. I would visit my grandparents for the weekend and he would come over there to see me. He often stayed for hours with the four of us chatting.

Unlike my house, it was always peaceful at Grandma's. She baked cakes and pies. I often helped to bake those goodies. A feeling of pride in accomplishment used to come over me when the four of us would sit down at the table enjoying the conversation and pastries. It was a feeling of self-worth; that I was part of a family; that someone I loved also found me lovable. At last, I felt worthy to live, as if I were a part their very flesh. I felt ashamed of Mother's actions. My home life with her, I kept to myself.

Mother had one sister and one brother. Her brother was killed, at the age of twenty-three, in a car accident. He was home on leave from the military. He went out drinking and partying with friends. They were drunk when their car stalled on a railroad track and a train hit them.

My maternal grandmother never got over her son's death. She prayed for revenge on the young man who drove the car. It didn't matter to her that he was her nephew, her sister's son. When he was older and had a son of his own, my grandmother wished he would lose his own son so he would feel the pain she felt when she lost hers. Like a curse come true, she got her wish. Her nephew's son, also at twenty-three, died in a boating accident. Yet I didn't see that his death ever soothed her pain. She had lost her only son. It wouldn't have mattered to her if her son had been driving the car. She would have held everyone else at fault.

Mother's sister served in the Marines. Beatrice rarely came home to visit. When she would try to visit, there would be a fight. Consequently, I wasn't allowed to talk to this aunt or her children, my two cousins.

Mother's mother loved one of Beatrice's twins because that grandma raised the girl from birth until she was about five. I heard the twins were premature, that the girl was too weak to travel, so she was left with grandmother for five years. I never did figure that out.

Grandmother filed custody papers so the girl could go to school. At that point, Beatrice took the girl back with her to California. Grandmother never recovered from that loss. She missed her little girl. Because I was only a few months younger, I became her constant reminder of what she had lost.

Soon after Aunt Beatrice took her daughter back, she placed both her children in an orphanage after their father was killed in an electrical accident. I suppose motherhood instinct didn't run in Mother's family. Later, after she remarried, Beatrice reclaimed her twins after they had been institutionalized for years.

I went to Catholic school from the third grade until I went to high school in the ninth grade. I felt that environment ruined me. The nuns treated me badly and with tremendous prejudice. They knew Mother's reputation. I was never chosen for any special events. They pushed me aside in everything that happened.

It annoyed them that I was left handed. From the first day of third grade, they tried to force me to write with my right hand only. After I came home repeatedly with my knuckles bleeding, Mother went to the school and threatened the teacher. Then the teacher was rough on me for the rest of that year. I made it through all that continuing to write with my left hand.

Life at that school was miserable. The nuns shunned me and ignored me. Even knowing this, Mother continued to send me there despite how they treated me as an outcast. Eventually, during recess, I would sit by myself and read a book or just watch the activities. It seems the parents of some of the children didn't want their kids to associate with me.

Mother had amassed a reputation as a divorced and wickedly licentious woman. Because of her behavior, I was also considered wicked. That was the typical witch-hunting mentality of those times. Being ostracized and shunned while the other kids played together felt very painful. That didn't last long, though. Soon, some of the kids let me join them. These kids had parents who were more sensible.

I sang in the choir all through grade school but had never been chosen to sing a solo before eighth grade. My teacher of that year treated me the same as all my classmates. This kind mentor liked my voice. At Christmas time, she chose me to sing solo. I felt so proud but didn't want to tell Mother. She came to church with me for midnight mass. The choir sang from the choir loft, above and behind the congregation.

When it was time for my performance, the music teacher brought me to the front of the group. She smiled at me and started the music. The song she had chosen for me was perfect for my soprano voice. When I started to sing, I looked down. The whole congregation turned around when they heard me. They looked up at me. The look of shock on Mother's face was priceless. I sang that song with bright enthusiasm and nailed every high note.

As my song ended, the congregation applauded. Tears welled up my eyes. My teacher hugged me. She told me how proud she was of me, that she knew I would sing that song better than anyone else. In my moment of personal triumph, I felt as if I glowed. All the pain of my former ostracism ceased to exist. The devil that had tormented me was, at last, exorcised from my heart.

I managed to grow into my teens and become an independent person. There was actually a single positive outcome from all my Mother's abusiveness: I was very self-sufficient. I had been cooking dinner for Mother and myself from the time I was very young. I made sure my clothes were washed, ironed and put away. The two women at the "Y" had taught me personal hygiene. From an early age, thanks to them, I took proper care of myself.

We were able to add a second bedroom after we lived in a one bedroom home for many years. That new room became my refuge and thereafter, I lived there. Then I finally had my own closet to hang my clothes in. Mother's boyfriend, Author, helped build the addition and put in new kitchen cabinets. He did a wonderful job. I felt proud of our house for the first time.

Due to my early childhood experiences, I matured at an early age. By the time the addition was complete, I was in high school and I had many friends. I was always the one teasing and joking. Everyone was my friend. I danced to the beat of my own drum. I was closest to my girlfriend, Julie. She and I were "best buds." Julie came from a family of six children. I used to love going over to her house after school. Her parents were wonderful to me. There was always a generous amount of food on the stove. Her family made me feel welcome to eat with them. She and I would serve our plates with food and then go and hide somewhere to talk, as if what we were talking about was some special secret to share.

It seems no matter how large the family may be there is always enough room for one more. Her mother would ask us how our day went, showing genuine interest. Julie's father was quite a ruggedly handsome looking man. I recall when he would pick us up after one of the house parties, one mother in particular would go to the door to talk with him. She was taken with his good looks, and even as kids, we realized he was attractive, with his rugged, Marlboro look. He was strict, and fiercely protective of his family, and we all respected him. I certainly never wanted to cross him.

One night when we were sixteen, Julie and I decided to sneak into a club that younger adults went to. We weren't old enough, but got in anyway and we danced. When a fight broke out, everything went to Hell in a hand basket.

Fists were flying and everyone was jumping into the action. Suddenly, a table went airborne and the beer glasses from that table went flying. I dodged just in time but Julie got caught in the cross-fire. She was soaked with beer. It was all over her clothes and her hair was drenched. We didn't drink any alcohol but she sure smelled like she had some.

She panicked and so did I. Both of us were thinking about the wrath of her father. I knew the police would be coming soon. They closed the front door and weren't letting anyone pass. I had an idea and I told Julie to come with me. We went into the restroom and crawled out the window. We got out of there in a hurry and made our way to the car. I was driving that night. Mother would have killed me if I had been arrested.

Thinking quickly, as teenagers often do, we went to see a girl who went to school with us. She happened to live right down the street from Julie. In a panic, Julie asked if we could come in and borrow clothes for her to change into. It worked out perfectly because the girl's parents weren't home and she was the same size as Julie. That was a close call and we made it our secret, something we never mentioned. Julie and I remained friends for many years to come. We even married a couple of brothers.

I never really liked school. I wanted to fast-forward my life until I was old enough to be out of Mother's house and on my own. None of my girlfriends liked Mother. Most of them weren't allowed to spend the night at my house. Their parents didn't like how we would frequently have to step over Author, sleeping on the floor, to get out the door on our way to school in the morning.

It bothered me at first but there was nothing I could do about it. Trying to talk to Mother was out of the question. *As long as I am happy,* she thought, *To hell with anyone else.* It was a normal situation to me but I understood where those parents were coming from. I did stay at my girlfriend's often and tried to stay away from Mother's house as much as I could. I kept my grades average, which is a miracle in itself, because there were many nights when I lost sleep. Even though Author liked to sing loudly and he was the main cause of total disruption in my life, he was good to me in many ways. He put a stop to Mother's violent outbursts. If she would start screaming at me, he would shut her up, by pointing out that she caused their troubles, not me.

I started working, as many young girls do, by babysitting. Then I moved on to a part time job in a department store. I got the job before I had a car. I would walk to the shopping center after school. It was maybe a mile and a half but I was making some money so I didn't care. When the weather was bad I, walked as fast as I could. Mother would pick me up after work since that was much too far to walk at night.

Author bought my first car for me when I was seventeen. The fan belt occasionally slipped off but that would never have stopped me. I got really good at lifting the hood and putting it back on. Oh, did I ever think I was special. A car meant freedom to me. I was seldom home much after that. I would have some sort of job so I could buy gas and whatever else I needed.

At home, I still kept myself invisible. There was so little communication that I really don't think Mother ever noticed how I stayed out of the way. Life became a lot easier for me after the room addition was on the house. I stayed in my own room. I also stayed busy with after-school activities. I was always working on some project. For school dances and proms, I did a lot of artwork and designing. "Creative" was my middle name and I loved it.

Chapter Four

As I entered my sophomore year of high school, I met the young man who became the love of my life. He would watch over me, guide and protect me, forever. I was smitten at first sight. I knew he would be the love who I would never forget. His looks were unique: natural platinum hair, aqua blue eyes, and a smile that made everyone smile with him.

After mutual friends introduced us, we quickly became close. Hardly a day would go by without us seeing each other. When we weren't together we were on the phone. His nickname was Ajax because of his platinum blond hair. He was the youngest of five children and also the only boy, so he was well loved. Because I was an only child, I loved his family from the moment I met them and they seemed to genuinely like me.

One night, when the phone rang, I heard this wonderful voice as I picked it up, saying "Hi, Desiree. This is Ajax."

I had given him my phone number but still I was surprised to hear his voice.

"Hi, gosh, I'm happy you called," I said.

"How was school today?" he asked.

"Good, how are you doing?"

I tried to calm down, to not act as excited as I was feeling.

"It was okay," he soberly said, "but I think I blew my History test. My dad said I can take the car this weekend. Would you like to go somewhere?"

Without hesitation, I blurted out "Sure, what did you have in mind?" perhaps too enthusiastically.

So began our eternal love.

Friday after school Ajax was waiting for me. As the bell rang, I dashed from the classroom, ran down the hall to my locker, then out the door. I had tried on my whole wardrobe the night before trying to find just the right outfit. Being picked up after school made me feel so special. I wanted to look my best.

His family's car was a huge, pink Buick sedan that we soon nick named "Our Pink Pig." We put a lot of miles on that car and spend a lot of hours in it. Our big thing was to drive down to the beach, which was about thirty five minutes from my house, and go to the drive-in for hamburgers and fries.

All the teens from all the local high schools would gather there to circle around and around until lucky enough to get a parking space. Once parked near the intercom speaker, we could place our order.

"Desiree, what would you like?" he would ask, as if I ever changed my order. It was always, "I'll take a hamburger, french-fries and a root beer." And he would order the same. Somehow those hamburgers and french-fries tasted better than anywhere else. The server girls would bring out our order. We would roll down the window so she could attach our tray. That ritual was all-important to us. We never tired of circling around, waiting for a parking space or tasting the same flavors every time we went there.

Our school's schedule was posted on the lobby bulletin board Monday morning. The Cotillion Dance, a big event, was scheduled on it. I already knew about that dance. I had been planning for it, for months. Making my dress in sewing class was a challenge for me. I chose a dress that would fit the theme of the dance perfectly. Being on the decorating committee, I knew ahead of time what the theme would be.

That night, when the phone rang I was so excited I didn't even wait for it to ring a second time. I grabbed it and hoped the right person was at the other end. Sure enough, it was Ajax.

"Hi, Pretty Woman," he said.

"Guess what?" I replied quickly.

"You sound so excited. What is it?"

I talked so fast he had to slow me down. "The schedule came out today and the Cotillion Dance is on it, do you still want to go?"

"Of course. I'll take you. I wouldn't turn down a chance to take the prettiest girl in the school to the dance," he said.

"Aww, you're so sweet to me. Thank you for saying that, you always make me feel so good."

He laughed and said "You deserve every compliment, plus more."

"So you'll take me?" I asked again with a chuckle.

"Umm, let me think about it," he responded this time. We both laughed.

I continued sewing the dress I was making, constantly praying that not only would I get it done in time, but that it would be sewn well enough to wear. To my surprise, not only did I get it done in time for the dance, but also, it was sewn so well that I received an "A." I was so proud of that dress.

The theme of the dance was "Blue Velvet," after a song by Bobby Vinton. I chose an aqua blue velvet top with a white brocade bottom. I had my shoes died the same aqua blue as the top of the dress. I felt so proud at how well it all turned out.

When time until the dance grew short, during one of our nightly calls, Ajax said, "What is the color of your dress? I want to order your flowers."

I replied by telling him the color and also that I had made it myself.

He was always so sweet to me and so thoughtful. "Do you want any special flowers or any special color?"

"No, I want you to pick the flowers and the color."

Decorating for dances was so much fun for me. I always looked forward to it. I didn't know who chose "Blue Velvet" to be the theme for the dance. It was a popular song, so I imagined that was why they chose it. The name was a little difficult to decorate for, given our budget, but we got creative. We decorated the hall and surrounding area well enough to take some pictures.

When the day finally arrived, I was so excited I could hardly contain myself. I stayed in my room most of the day, taking my time to paint my finger nails and talk to my girlfriends about the night to come. Soon it was time to get ready. I put my makeup on meticulously, making sure every single eyelash was coated with mascara perfectly. When time came to put my dress on, I looked in the mirror and felt quite pleased with my reflection. I donned crystal earrings and a crystal bracelet that one of my aunts gave me for this occasion. After one more look in the mirror came the waiting for my Prince Charming.

I listened for his knock on the door. When it came, I ran to let him in. There he stood, looking more handsome than ever before.

"Wow, Desiree! Did you really make your dress?" he asked.

I took a step back and whirled around so he could see all of it.

"Do you like it?"

"I am the luckiest guy in town. Just look at you. You are so beautiful... Oh, gosh, I almost forgot... your flowers."

He handed them to me. I looked at my flowers and couldn't have been more pleased. The wrist corsage was beautiful, with perfect yellow roses and a soft yellow ribbon to match. The corsage covered my wrist. I slipped it on that night, having absolutely no notion what yellow roses would come to represent in my life. We danced the night away with me sniffing my corsage every change I got.

While dancing to the song "Blue Velvet," I told Ajax "I want these yellow roses to last forever, they are so beautiful, I really love them."

He told me, "Don't worry about the roses lasting. I promise I will send you yellow roses forever and ever." And he was destined to keep that promise.

We continued to go for hamburgers in our "Pink Pig" of a car. We logged many hours riding around, listening to music. Ajax was especially close to one of his sisters. Though he loved them all, we went to visit his favorite frequently. Being only sixteen, I looked up to her. I loved visiting with her and her family. She and I became really good friends. I tried to hide the kind of home life I lived, for fear that Ajax's family would not accept me. Soon, I realized they were down to earth and they loved their brother so much that my home life was not an issue. They took me under their wings and treated me wonderfully.

Laura was quite pretty, with big blue eyes and dark hair. She and her husband had two darling girls. Michaelene was almost three and Dee Dee was only a few months old when I entered their lives. Laura's husband played baseball on a local team, so Ajax and I got to babysit often that summer. I loved every moment of being there. I often imagined those two girls were ours. I grew especially fond of Michaelene, who I thought was the most gorgeous girl I had ever seen. Her face was like an angel's, with large aqua eyes. Her hair was dark. She became very attached to me. Soon, Ajax and I were taking her with us everywhere. I truly adored that child.

The following May, Ajax and I took Michaelene and Dee Dee to have their picture taken by a photographer who set up a temporary studio in a discount store. We had the photo taken as Laura's Mother's Day gift. We felt pleased that we could accomplish that without Michaelene telling her mother. We framed the picture and surprised her with it. She felt thrilled with our gift and thanked us repeatedly. Whenever I looked at that picture sitting on their end table, I would recall the fun we had with the girls as it was taken.

Ajax and I had a serene and happy relationship. There were no angry words between us. We seemed to mesh naturally. Our ideas and goals were very much the same. Life was good when we were together. I told him things that I would have never told anyone else. Things that happened to me as a little girl, things I had to tolerate in order to survive my unorthodox home life. Somehow, he always understood, never criticizing. Instead, he offered to be there for me, no matter what. Like his promise to send me yellow roses, he kept his word. He was always there for me.

When I was in the tenth grade, I got my first modeling job for a clothing store. I was quite pleased with how they paid me. I would model on Saturdays from nine a.m. until about five-thirty or six p.m., then return Sunday at noon and model until around six p.m. Not only was I paid hourly, but I also kept one outfit that I modeled each weekend. After a few months, I had a wonderful wardrobe to be proud of. I was well-dressed, to say the least.

The store managers liked the way I mingled with the customers and how they would purchase the outfits I was modeling. It was exciting for me to come into the store Saturday morning and have all these new clothes hanging on a rack, just waiting for me to wear. Being tall and thin, I seemed able to wear about anything and they seemed to know just what to pick for me.

Often, Ajax would come to the store during my break and take me out for lunch or a soda. I would look up and see him standing behind a display smiling from ear to ear. He was always so proud of me and that I was his girl. There were many restaurants in the downtown area. We always had choices about where to go. Most were within walking distance, so if the weather was nice we would walk. He never failed to hold my hand or open a door for me. He always showed respected and caring for me.

As the months marched onward, Mother allowed me to go more and more places with him. Not wanting to give her any reason to ground me, we always managed to get home a little before the time I was told to be in the house. I used to hate walking into the house, given I never knew what to expect. I usually didn't ask Ajax to come in when we got me home. He would walk me up to the door. We'd say goodnight and I would go straight to my room.

There was never pleasant conversation as I came in, such as "Did you have a good time?" or "How was your evening?" Because I never knew what mood Mother might be in, it was best to just make a beeline for my room. Mother had a habit of taking everything out on me so I avoided her as much as I could. Once closed into my room, I was alone with my pleasant thoughts instead of her ranting over some paltry concern. After having a wonderful time, I didn't want to ruin my evening, or go to bed upset. I controlled the situation the only way I could.

Author often aggravated Mother and then the fights would begin. If I came home during a fight, all Hell would brake loose. She would lash out at me over some thin pretext. When she did that, Author would get angrier and the fight would escalate. The next day, I would get yelled at because Author would lash out at her for yelling at me. I would get caught in the middle of this vicious circle, without even saying a word. It all goes back to Mother's fundamental neurotic delusion: "If it wasn't for you, I would be happy."

Thanksgiving was not pleasant at our house. Author's family would have a big gathering but his family judged Mother negatively so we were never invited. One year, this nonsense was even worse because Author's family decided to have their dinner in the evening instead of early afternoon. So he would not be coming over to see her at all. Not only were we not invited but she was also angry about him not coming over. They had a big fight the night before so Mother decided she was going to stay in bed all day and not cook a Thanksgiving dinner for her and me. Our small turkey was in the refrigerator along with the rest of the dinner but I was not allowed to cook it. This was another example of her lashing out at me because she was unhappy.

When Ajax called me, I was feeling low. "Why is she such a witch?" I asked. "Why can't she have Thanksgiving with me?"

He listened, and then said, "I'll be there in a few minutes. How about making me a cup of coffee?"

"Okay," I said, "but don't knock on the back door. I'll wait for you and let you in. God forbid we should wake her up," I whispered.

"Alright. Just watch for me," he said. When he arrived, I quietly opened the door and held onto the dog so he would not bark. I had started some coffee so it was just about ready when he got there. She had her bedroom door closed. I closed the kitchen door, hoping she would not hear us. We sat together and whispered quietly so as not to wake her. He hugged me when he got there. He felt genuinely disgusted with what was happening in my home.

Now, as we sat at the table talking, he asked me "Do you think she will let you go to Laura's and have Thanksgiving with us?" Afraid of even asking, I decided to wait until we drank our coffee and he was ready to go. He must have touched my hand a dozen times that day trying to somehow help me feel better.

He told me "No matter who her child is, she would have to blame them because she is so mean and hateful she probably can't stand herself."

He promised me that day that he would take me away from all that as soon as he could. I sat at the table with tears streaming down my face, counting the years before I would escape from that miserable house. When we had finished our coffee and it was time for him to leave, I went to her bedroom door and slowly opened it up to ask if it was alright if I went with Ajax to have Thanksgiving with his family. One would have thought I had asked for a million dollars.

She sat up and yelled as loud as she could, "No! You will just stay right here. You are not going anywhere." I started crying but knew better than to say another word.

I closed the door and went back into the kitchen.

Ajax stood up and hugged me. He said "She is evil."

He decided to wait. He asked for another cup of coffee.

Then we heard her shriek, at maximum volume, "Desiree! Come here."

I went to the bedroom door and opened it. She said, in her hateful tone of voice, "If you say one word to him, he will never be allowed to come over here again. Do you hear me?"

I reassured her I had said nothing and closed the door. Of course, he heard what she said but when I came back out he just shook his head and didn't say anything.

I made another cup of coffee for us and put an ice cube in his to cool it off so that he could drink it. He always put an ice cube on top of his coffee and sipped at the coffee that the ice cooled. I would laugh at his trying to sip the cooled coffee around the ice without getting any of the hot coffee underneath. Jokingly, he would say that was his challenge for the day.

We sat speaking very softly, not wanting to ruffle Mother's feathers which might cause her to make him leave. He tried so hard to comfort me. As he did, all I kept thinking was what a precious person he is. We drank our coffee and since he was already late, he hugged me and left, but not before telling me how beautiful I was and how much he loved me.

On Monday at school, I listened to everyone talking about their Thanksgiving Holiday. When asked about mine, I did my usual thing. I made light of it and only spoke of the positive side. That positive thing being, someone important to me showed me they care. Ajaxs family cared enough to open their home to me so that I could enjoy Thanksgiving with them. That was all I needed.

The Christmas holiday was a little easier. I had someone of my own to share it with. We managed to spend some time together. Christmas break made that a little easier, given there was no school. No matter what we did, it was always fun, pleasant and easy.

We truly got along very well together. The snow was quite beautiful that year. What a wonderful white Christmas we had. Laura was slow getting her tree set up so she let Ajax and me help decorate it. I was so excited to do that with them. At home, we always had a metallic silver tree with a light that revolved, creating different colors as the wheel turned. Sitting by the tree for hours just watching it by myself gave me much peace and pleasure.

I vowed that I would make Christmas for my children happy; that I would never put my children through miserable holidays like the ones I endured. To me, the sad thing was that this was all because of a boyfriend, not even a husband. A boyfriend who never cared enough to marry her. He never even brought me a single Christmas present during all those years. Not even one.

How pathetic, I thought! To put your own child through all that and to trash my father to the point that I feared him.

Ajax brought me a beautiful necklace that year. Was I ever happy that he gave me a present! It was an oval, diamond-cut pendant with a single pearl. I thought it was something wonderful to get that necklace, and I vowed I would never take it off. Soon, I would be posing for my graduation pictures. I planned to wear it then. My hands trembled while opening his present because I was so delighted that he had thought to bring me something.

When time came for us to get graduation pictures taken, I chose one of the tops I earned modeling. Ajax's necklace looked outstanding on this long-sleeved, red cashmere sweater. Ajax knew when I had my picture. He wanted an eight by ten enlargement to take to college. I ordered one for him along with prints for my father and grandparents. After school one day, about three weeks after taking the pictures, Ajax called me.

He sounded excited as he told me, "Desiree, the photo studio enlarged your and Julie's graduation photos to twenty by twenty-four and they put them on display in the front window. Your picture looks beautiful," he said.

I had not told him that I had been wearing the necklace he gave me for Christmas or what color my sweater was. I drove down to the studio to see the picture. I was taken aback with the blue color that they put on my sweater instead of the red. I felt a little disappointed because I'm not blue color-compatible. I had to admit the enlargement made me feel proud but it didn't make Mother proud. When she saw it, she insisted they redo the picture with the sweater red. She caused such a scene that I felt embarrassed when they called me about that the next day. I felt so proud of my picture being in their window that I went down there right away and smoothed things over.

I said I liked the color; that since it was my picture, please leave it as it was. Nothing ever pleased that woman. If I had been crowned Miss America, she would have said I didn't walk down the runway right.

The school year was over. *Only one more year to go,* I thought. That summer, Ajax and I were inseparable. We spent every moment we could together.

His mother was not happy with him seeing one girl exclusively and she made that well known. One day, at his house, he pulled me down on his lap and said to his mother "Mom, I am going to marry this girl, I love her so much."

His mother who had been drinking beer, looked at me with such resentment I felt uncomfortable. I tried to get up but he held me tighter and said, "Yep. Mom, this is going to be your daughter in law."

She said, "You're going to college first."

"Why?" he asked. "Why can't I do both?"

With another dirty look she went into the next room. We had never discussed marriage so his remark was a surprise. I had one more year of school, myself. Thinking that far ahead had not even entered my mind. I had often wondered how I would adjust to him being away at college. Without his encouraging support, life would be tough.

Deep inside me, his words were music to my soul. It felt so soothing to know he was thinking of me as his future wife. As the summer continued, we became anxious about being apart, with him in college and me left to finish high school. We both realized our future depended on the next few years.

Toward the end of summer, we decided to go to the amusement park in our area to spend the day walking around and on the rides. There was so much to see and ever so much to do there. On the way to the park, we stopped for breakfast and, of course, coffee with an ice cube. We entered the park that day with excitement and enthusiasm about how the day would unfold for us.

We arrived in early morning as the park opened. We planned to stay until it closed, at midnight. As we were walking in, Ajax took my hand and started singing the song "Pretty Woman" to me, loudly. I looked at him with love and adoration and as he did that growl in the song, as Roy Orbison did. It startled me and I burst into laughter.

"You are what keeps me going" I said, smiling at him.

"And you, my love, are the very air I breathe," he replied.

The day was hot and humid but we didn't seem to feel the heat. Around noon, we decided it was time to eat. Finding somewhere cool was not as easy as we thought it might be, but we found a place with good food and cool ambience.

We sat across from each other, enjoying lunch and discussing what to do next. There was so much, yet we seriously thought we could pack it all into one day. We wanted an A for effort, and to see the wax museum for sure, so we planned that for after lunch. It was even more realistic than we had heard and we liked that. We wandered from area to area. Eventually, we got hungry again, only to discover it was already six thirty p.m. We figured we would wait a little longer and hopefully the crowds would thin out.

Our thoughts proved accurate. We found this wonderful little restaurant that would seat us right away. We were winding down. We took our time eating dinner and just relaxing. I wanted to see the glass blowers and candle makers so Ajax suggested we head toward the shops. As we entered the area, we picked up a list of shops and attractions. I could not believe there were so many things to see. I was glad to see the glassblowing demonstration was nearby and scheduled to begin shortly. We chose front row seats and waited.

I mused about what a wonderful day it had been and how much fun we were having. I left everything else behind to just be there, in the moment. We sat close together, not caring that we were both perspiring or that we were sweating as we held hands. We had such love and respect for each other it seemed as if the outer world did not exist and there was only the two of us.

The glassblowing demonstration was about to begin. We thought it was hot in the covered area before the demonstration began, but it was much hotter after they started. It lasted about forty minutes with the audience melting about as much as the glass. It was quite a great show. The items they crafted were so beautiful. I was taken with it all but I was happy when it was over so we could find a cooler place.

We watched artisans make candles and toured more exhibits. There were many souvenir shops. We slowly wandered through them. We didn't skip around because we didn't want to miss anything. We moved on down the "Make Believe Street," where a woman stood outside her one room cottage. She asked us if we would like our fortune told. I looked at Ajax and he looked at me and we both said "Sure, why not?" I had never seen anything like this. It scared me some. The woman came to me first.

In an accent that I didn't recognize, she said, "Come in. Let me see what your future holds."

When I was inside, the woman closed the door.

"Hello," she said, "What is your name?

"Desiree" I responded.

"What a beautiful name. It's okay, Honey, just relax. I will tell you everything I see."

So it began, and the world as I knew it would never be the same again.

"I see you have had a rough childhood," she said. "Your mother has not been good to you."

"That's true," I said.

Then she asked me, "Is the young man outside your boyfriend?"

"Yes."

"Oh, Honey" she said, as she frowned and looked straight into my eyes. "You want to marry him?"

"Yes," I answered, "he is going to go to college this year. When we are both out of school we plan on getting married."

"He is good to you?"

"Yes, he is the reason I am able to survive all the crap that goes on at my house. Mother hates me. She has always told me that if it wasn't for me, she could have happiness."

"Your mother will never find true happiness because she's a very troubled woman. Honey, all the wrong she has done you will only bring her more karma to pay back. But back to you. I see four children in your future, two boys and two girls. You will travel the world and see more things than most people. Are you following me?

"Yes, I want many children and so does my boyfriend."

"Honey you will have a choice to make. There will be two men for you to choose from. Another man will enter your life and you will care for him very much. If you choose the young man outside, you will be widowed very young. If you choose the other man, you will have many marriages."

As she spoke, my mind went blank. As tears welled up in my eyes, I asked her why she would tell me something like that.

"I am telling you what I see. You've had a rough childhood and been through a lot. If you marry this man outside, you'll be a widow soon after."

"He's so good and decent. I love him so much."

"I know, Honey, but you will have to choose. It is tragic, what is going to happen to him but I must tell you, he will not live long."

I do not remember much of what she said after that. I really didn't know how to react. As she finished, I wiped my tears away. I stood there for a minute before walking to the door.

"Honey, when you go outside, please tell your friend that I will not be able to read him today. I cannot read him, it's so tragic. Please Honey, tell him I must stop now."

I approached the door I looked back at the woman.

I must have looked desperate because she said "You will make the right decision, Honey. Don't be afraid."

I took a deep breath trying to control myself before I opened the door to face Ajax.

I put a smile on my face and opened up the door.

Ajax was standing there, about twenty feet from where I was. He started to walk toward me. I told him that the woman said she was unable to do any more reading and that she was sorry. He seemed okay with that. He didn't question her decision. He wanted to know what she told me, and as I walked with him I became like a stone. That enabled me to tell him everything except the part about him.

He was happy to hear about four children, thinking they would be his. Right away, he wanted to know if she saw whether they would be boys or girls. I told him what she had said. He was pleased, quickly saying, "I hope the girls look just like you."

I continued to tell him about the traveling and all the positive things she said. Then, to my relief, we never discussed that again.

That night, I laid in bed, totally disbelieving what she had told me. *Surely she had to be wrong,* I thought. Ajax was my everything. I leaned on him for emotional support. How could I exist without him? The fortune teller's words never left my mind. They ate at me. As fear took hold of me I kept wondering, *What if she is right?*

Toward the middle of summer Ajax's parents became more and more resentful toward me. They feared he would not go on to graduate from college if he had me on his mind. We played it cool and his parents soon stopped nagging him about me. We just kept thinking it was only temporary and soon we would be together. Many nights, we would go to the the beach at a nearby lake, park the car, listen to music, and talk. We had our life planned.

A constant breeze rolled off the lake which made it pleasant to sit in the car with the windows down. There was parking for as far as our eyes could see. We were usually lucky enough to get parking with a great view of the lake and boats on the water. The most popular song on the radio was Ray Charles, singing "Georgia On My Mind." That was Ajax's favorite song. If we weren't listening to it on the car radio, we would listen to it over and over again at his house, sitting in the living room. I had the forty-five RPM record of that song. So, of course, every night I would listen to it in my bedroom. It became part of our lives. Both of us knew the words forward an backward.

I dreaded summer ending, which meant me going back to school and Ajax going off to college. I knew it would mean months between times we could see each other. There was no way he could come home on weekends and I couldn't drive there for a weekend. How would I explain being gone for two days? That simply wouldn't happen.

The months dragged on. As events came up at school, I was left without a date. He kept telling me to ask someone to take me to dances but my heart wasn't in it. It became time for my prom and he was not going to come home that weekend because he had exams. For months, he kept telling me to ask someone to take me. Finally, I agreed.

Three different guys asked to take me to school proms that year. Instead of accepting a date from one of the guys who had asked me to go to their dance, I invited Wade, an older fellow I had met that summer while going to the beach with Mother. He was a few years past me but I had seen him quite a few times and he always asked me to dance with him. He was happy that I asked him and he accepted. It wasn't the same excitement that I would have felt with Ajax but sometimes you can't have everything you want.

Once again, instead of being proud for me that I had been invited to three school proms, Mother was upset because she didn't want to buy the dresses. That was no problem for me though. I borrowed dresses from my girlfriends and bought a new one for my own prom. Surprisingly, it happened the proms were scheduled on different nights. That worked out well. The three of us were with dates from different schools so one knew that I had borrowed dresses. It was fun going to all those proms. My prom was fun and I was proud walking in with Wade who was exceptionally handsome but my heart wasn't really in it. He brought me the most beautiful orchid corsage but again, it wasn't the yellow roses that I loved.

Mother never figured out that she couldn't control me with her nasty attitude. I became a rebel. I blocked my ears against her screaming demands. She never knew where I was or what I was doing. I didn't get into trouble but it was by the skin of my teeth that I stayed out of jams. Although I never drank, I was always sneaking into places where I shouldn't have gone. I loved to dance so I found places where I could.

Having my own car and work gave me gas money to go where I wanted. Once, during my senior year of high school, I was trying to crawl into a window of a hot spot on the beach. With my hands still on the floor and my butt in the air, I was just about in when my hands came upon a set of men's feet. I looked up to see it was the owner of the place who knew Mother. Knowing I was grounded for sure, I decided I better have a good time that night. I smiled sweetly and backed out of the window. I waited until the owner left and then I went back in.

Surely enough, the next day, the owner of that place told Mother he had caught me sneaking into his beach bar, and as I knew would happen, I was grounded. Summer was on its way and the school year would soon be over. I was delighted to graduate from high school and move forward in my life.

I wasn't sure how much more I could take at home. Author had assumed a different attitude with Mother as well. A few years earlier, he had gone to Spain for about six months, leaving her behind. After he returned, he seemed to act indifferent toward her. I'm certain she realized it but she acted as if it wasn't happening. Total denial.

Although Wade had asked me out quite a few times and I really enjoyed his attention, I could hardly wait until Ajax came home. I had missed him so much. That first night, we couldn't seem to talk fast enough to catch up on everything. In between bits of talking, he kept singing to me and laughing when he growled during his rendition of "Pretty Woman." We laughed a lot that night as we enjoyed our reunion.

Ajax got a job working at a shoe store for the summer. I worked in a television repair shop. My first choice for continued education was to attend dental hygienist school but there were none close enough. My second choice was enrolling in the business college courses that started in the fall. Going away to college was out of the question. I had to settle for something local. Being open about what to do, I knew I wanted something that would involve only a few years of school before I could get a decent job. I did not want to be in school any longer than I had to.

Wanting so desperately to move out on my own and have some peace, I didn't care much what I took on. I knew I would be stuck making a meager wage without some higher education. I chose the business college. I thought it wouldn't be long before I could take a keypunch course. With that training, I could make enough money to take care of myself and get away. I was looking forward to starting. It couldn't come soon enough as far as I was concerned. Even though Ajax and I saw each other often, it seemed the summer dragged on and on. Wade still took me out to dinner on occasion but my heart was still with Ajax.

Time came for college to begin for him and for me to start business school. I was particularly happy that I didn't have to take English and history classes that academic colleges required. This school jumped right into practical courses I needed for business. I did quite well and aced all my classes. It came easily to me. I seemed to have an unmistakable flair for business. I excelled in all aspects of the courses. I had chosen a privately-owned school. The owners took me under their wing, helping me to choose courses that would benefit me most in the least time.

In October that year, I noticed Ajax talking about a girl he studied with too much for my comfort. My heart was fearful about what this could potentially mean. Although I had gone out with Wade, that wasn't anything serious but I was afraid I was losing Ajax. I was trying so hard to get good grades myself, that I pushed it aside and hoped everything would be okay.

My hopes didn't work out as well as I wanted. I began to realize we were drifting apart. I was hearing less and less from him. Still in the self-preservation mode, I studied feverishly, taking more classes than required, trying to finish early even while working a full-time job.

Wade realized what a difficult time I had at home. He began calling me more often to encourage me. He tried to comfort me when he would hear the fighting in the background, always encouraging me to come out and get away from it all. Going out more often with Wade became important to me.

Although I never lost sight of the freedom that more schooling would eventually bring me, I met more and more people who became good friends. Always having a wonderful time, yet most importantly, keeping my grades high, I came to realize that other man the psychic had predicted was right in front of me. He was tall, dark, and handsome, and ready to settle down. He and I started out just being friends, dancing together and having a good time but soon it became more. I found myself starting to care for him.

I received fewer and fewer letters from Ajax and with less love in them. I kept writing to him but his letters just weren't the same. Feelings of guilt would come over me as I danced or went out for a soda with Wade, but also I realized Ajax's relationship with me was not what it used to be; that the plans we made weren't meant to be. My heart ached as our love slipped away. There was nothing I could do to stop it.

At first, the words the psychic spoke replayed in my head, over and over. As time passed, I thought she was a fake, that nothing she told me would come true. When I started to go out with Wade more and more, she reappeared in my mind. I did wonder if he was the other choice she told me I would make. His gentleness was refreshing but my heart longed to be with Ajax. Yet my relationship with Wade deepened. Soon we found ourselves truly caring for each other.

When Ajax came home the next time, I was almost scared to see him for fear of the unknown. Unfortunately, that unknown did not turn out well. Ajax decided we should see other people for a while longer and see what happens. Although I knew this could be the end, I also knew that if there was any hope, it would be to set him free and pray he comes back. To be truthful with myself, I also had mixed feelings. I was also drifting away from him.

With the visit behind us and both of us back in school, I concentrated on doing well and taking as many courses as I could manage. Wade became more and more a part of my life. He was an outgoing guy. He accepted my feelings about remaining a virgin until I married. I received criticism about that, but I was not giving in.

Sometimes, even I thought, *Oh, to heck with it.*

But I was able to hold my own and wait for my wedding night. With Ajax out of the picture, I looked at Wade differently and began to care in a different way. Wade loved me more than I cared for him at first, and his "wanting to settle down" feelings were beginning to show. My main concerns were staying focused on business school and doing all I could to improve my chances of taking care of myself. I knew that some day I wanted to get married but as far as I was concerned, that was for the future. Wade, on the other hand, thought differently.

Life at home was still the same, with Author coming over drunk and the two of them fighting continually. I played music at high volume so I could concentrate on studying. That became a way of life for me. You do what you have to do to survive. That's exactly what I did to study. It's a wonder I could study at all given the volume of the records, but I managed.

With another semester almost finished, Wade called me, as usual on Tuesday nights. Instead of talking, he asked me, "Would you like to get something to eat?"

"Give me about half an hour to finish my final assignment," I said "and I'd love to go."

"Wear something warm, it's damp and cold out."

"Ok, I will."

I hurried to finish my assignment and got ready. He was right on time. After I was in his car, I sensed he was a little nervous.

"Is everything okay," I asked?

"Sure. Why do you ask?" he said.

"You seem a little nervous or troubled. Are you sure everything is alright?"

"No problem, I'm fine" he reassured me.

Somehow I just didn't believe him but I said no more about it.

After eating, we left the restaurant and started for the beach to watch the water. He reached for me and took me into his arms, kissing me ever so gently.

He then pulled back and said "I have something to ask you." Before I could say another word, he kissed me again.

Then he said "Desiree, I want to marry you. Will you marry me?"

I was dumfounded. I could hardly answer. I started to say something but he cut me off, saying "I have loved you from the day I met you at the beach and I want nothing more than for you to be my wife. Let's just go away and get married."

I smiled. All I could say was "please give me some time to think, I really didn't expect this so soon. I have just a few months of school left, let me get through that first" I said.

He agreed to give me time but I could see disappointment in his eyes. That night, my mind was whirling with whether or not I wanted to get married at all, or right then. I knew I loved him. How could I not love a man who treats me so wonderfully? Ajax was no longer an ache in my heart, although I thought about him often and wondered how he was. I had settled my mind, thinking that we would never be husband and wife; that some things are not meant to be.

Always lurking in the back of my mind were the horrifying words that psychic spoken, "If you choose the man outside, you'll be a widow very young." She destroyed a certain innocence within me with her harsh prediction. I was not able to forget those words. They haunted me for years after she spoke them.

All through high school, I had taken classes geared toward family life, such as cooking, sewing and even child psychology. Hating math,

I steered away from Algebra and Geometry. I always loved children but I knew, early on, that I didn't want to become a teacher. I modeled quite a lot for different agencies but I was not quite comfortable in the spotlight. Modeling was not a career I would choose. I only did it for the good money I made.

My home life left me feeling empty. I became attached to the proverbial image of home, the white picket fence with the husband, children and puppy. Somehow, I thought having many children would ease the pain of loneliness I felt while growing up.

When I went home that night, hearing Mother and Author fighting felt horrible.

All I could think of was, "Why am I here? What have I done to experience this misery so regularly?"

I thought long and hard that night about what Wade asked me. I made the decision the psychic woman alluded to. The following night, when the phone rang, I answered it quickly and quietly, knowing it was Wade.

"Let's go for a ride," I said, "can you?"

He asked if everything was alright since he could tell by the tone of my voice that something was wrong. Reassuring him I was fine, I agreed to a time when he would pick me up. I sat back on my bed and prayed that the decision I had made was the right decision and that my marriage would be a happy one with lots of children.

I made an excuse to Mother the following week. I told her I was going with one of my girlfriends to see another friend of ours at College; that we were going to stay for a few days. She agreed, because she and Author had made peace. Things were fine between them for the time being.

I left with Wade. We were married in a little chapel in Michigan. I was happy. I felt my life would soon be calm and peaceful. We decided not to tell anyone until I finished school that year. The plan was, by then we would have enough money for a place to live.

Author's drinking, and the fighting with Mother increased more and more, to the point that our house became total chaos. I tried to study during the day, between classes, because I knew studying at home was next to impossible.

Mother left for work one morning with Author still sleeping. I was at the kitchen table studying when he woke up. I made him a cup of coffee. He sat down to drink it, apologizing for all the arguing they had done recently. He told me he was worried about me and wondered how much longer I had to go in school and what would happen to me if he just left, unexpectedly.

Reassuring him that I would be okay, I confided in him what I had done. I told him that I would be leaving shortly, anyway. Never thinking he would tell Mother, I figured my secret was safe.

What a mistake. He felt guilty. He blamed himself for my actions, telling her what they had done to me. One would think Mother would feel remorse. Absolutely not. She turned into a monster. She said that I will never shame her by running off to get married; that I will either have a big wedding at the church or she will file charges against Wade and he will go to jail.

Because he was over twenty-one and I was only nineteen, the law stood against us. She could have filed charges against him. I could not believe Author did that to me but he did. Thinking Mother's threat would go away was wrong, because it didn't. In fact, she was soon laying down the law about a list of things that Wade and I would have to do if I didn't want her to file charges against him. She had the most evil look on her face. Of course, I feared her wrath, so reluctantly, I went along with what she said.

Mother seemed excited, as if she were planning her own wedding. At the same time, I hated her for what she was forcing me to do.

When the Catholic prenuptial classes finished, Wade and I were married "In the Church" that June. Our wedding was beautiful. My little love, Michaelene, was my flower girl. She was beautiful in her long yellow flower girl dress. Her long, dark, curls hung down on her shoulders as she walked down the aisle, dropping flower pedals. She smiled the entire time. One would have thought she was my daughter, I was so proud of her.

I had remained friends with Laura. I asked her if she would allow her daughter to be my flower girl. She had no problem with that but I was unaware that Laura had to sit near the door of the hall to assure Ajax didn't get drunk and barge in. I was told later that he was devastated. He had realized he had lost, as he put it, "the Love of his life."

During the wedding reception, I took pictures with a crowd of people. Grandma and Grandfather were the first ones I wanted to pose with. Then everyone else followed, including my father and his family, and my maternal grandparents. I had so many friends present that the hall was filled to capacity. I felt happy and knew in my heart I had made the right decision.

Within only a few months, I got pregnant. I felt so thrilled I could hardly wait to get home that night to tell Wade what the doctor had said. We rented a small two bedroom, one bath house. I was the happiest woman alive. Morning sickness did not become me but it became my morning ritual.

One night, Wade came home from work and sat me down looking very serious. Soon I was to learn my whole world was about to come to an end.

Coming in late from work, Wade announced he wasn't ready to have children yet. He demanded that I abort the baby. I cried, not believing my ears because we had agreed that we wanted to start a family right away and also, that we both wanted a large family. He became very serious and asked me to sit down so he could continue to talk.

With tears rolling down my cheeks, he said, in a matter-of-fact tone, "I do not want this baby. I am not ready and I don't know I will ever be ready."

By then, I was crying so hard I could hardly speak but I managed to ask him why he lied to the priest about having children, and most of all, why did he now feel like this?

All he would say was, "I don't think I ever wanted children but I knew I had to go through with the wedding at the church or go to jail. Desiree, please end this pregnancy or I will be forced to leave."

I was numb.

I stood up and very quietly said, "This is my baby, too. I will not harm it."

This was never discussed again. I simply continued onward, as if the conversation never existed. Mother still tried to boss me around and become a part of my life but I was trying to distance myself from her negativity. I wasn't mean about it but I had enough of her tying to suddenly become a mother.

I chose to keep the baby, and the pregnancy went as well as it could with Wade coming home late, consistently, smelling of alcohol. I delivered a beautiful, eight-pound, healthy baby boy. I named him Trip. That was a name I had chosen when I was in high school.

Wade's father's name was Author. He passed away the night of our wedding shower, we decided on Trip Author. Then I had the family I had so desired. I treasured that little guy. Being a mother came very naturally to me. Wade didn't want me to work, though. He felt I should be a stay-at-home mom and take care of Trip, full time.

I sensed Wade withdrawing gradually from us. I thought perhaps he was missing my undivided attention, so I tried to shower him with all the attention I could. That didn't seem to work. He only became more distant. We didn't argue or get short-tempered with each other, I just felt something was eating at him. I feared he really had been serious in his statements that he didn't want to be a parent.

On a Saturday morning, when Trip was only a few weeks old, I got a call from Mother. She wanted me to come over. I went to her place and I was shocked to see her house was trashed. Apparently, Mother and Author had gotten into a fight and Author smashed up the entire house.

Author's violence shocked me. He had never done anything this extreme before. He broke all the dishes and glasses and smashed up the lamps and furniture and everything else that was within an arm's reach. I had to climb over all the broken glass and smashed furniture throughout the house to get into the kitchen. Not only could I not believe what he had done, most of all, I could not believe that he had been pushed to such a point. When I asked what happened, Mother told me Author had come in late, drunk. It wasn't until about a week later that I would hear Author's side of the story.

One morning Author appeared at my front door. He asked if he could come in. He looked tired, as if he had not slept for a week. As we started to talk, he suddenly leaned his head forward into his folded arms on the table.

"Desiree, I need to tell you about what happened," he said. Then the real story about the smashed-up furniture began.

He told me he was never so angry in all his life as he was Friday night when he got to Mother's house and saw a man leaving her home.

He said that he waited outside until the man left because he did not recognize the car.

Sorrowfully, he said "I shouldn't have busted up the entire house but I couldn't control my anger. That was the only way for me not not hit her, instead of the furniture."

I sat very quietly, listening but was in no way prepared for what he was about to tell me. He asked how Wade and I are getting along. I started to cry. I told him about Wade wanting me to abort the pregnancy when we first found out I was pregnant but that I insisted on keeping the baby. Then everything poured out, the whole story.

He listened with intense emotion showing on his face. When I was finished, he asked me to please hear him out.

What could it be, I thought. *Why is he so serious?*

Then, he told me the man leaving Mother's house at three a.m. was Wade.

To say I was shocked would be to put things too mildly.

I wondered, *Was this man making something out of nothing or did my husband really leave Mother's house at three a.m.?*

I did not want to believe him. I lived in denial for weeks to come, not knowing what to think or how to feel.

When Trip was about three months old, the world as I knew it came crashing down, yet again. Wade came home from work exceptionally drunk. He was abusive, pushing me and yelling that he never wanted a kid; that I had forced him into being a father; and that Mother had forced him into an elaborate wedding that he detested.

I had taken Trip to the doctor that day with an ear infection. For some reason, I had put a knit hat on his head, pulling it over his ears, and then I swaddled him in his blanket.

The volume of Wade's voice kept escalating. I was getting scared. I went into the kitchen to warm the baby's bottle. Suddenly, Wade came after me. He said that it was all my fault entirely and he was going to teach me a lesson.

I went into the bedroom. He followed me, pushing me down on the bed. I kneed him so hard that he rolled off me. I ran into Trip's room, grabbed him, and ran out the back door. I hid behind a rambling, climbing rose bush near the corner of the house. I noticed a thorn had scratched my baby's face. He was starting to whimper. I put my finger in his mouth. In his sleep, he thought it was his bottle. He started to suck on it. Wade came to the door and looked around. He saw I was gone. He went back into the house to go out the front door. That gave me a chance to run across the neighbors' yards, up onto the main road. Then I ran to Mother's house.

I ran all that way. I could hardly breathe. I banged on the door, waking her up. I had marks on my throat and bruises on my legs where he had grabbed me. Mother called the police. This was the second time he had been violent with me. Once, during my pregnancy, he came after me but he did not hit me that time, he shoved me into a wall.

I knew I could not live like that. I realized he was serious when he said he did not want children. I filed for a divorce and moved back into Mother's home. I was so broken I could hardly function but gazing at my beautiful baby son kept me going.

Life went on. The weeks passed. What a beautiful little boy Trip was. I had his picture taken at a studio. They entered it into a baby contest that included the whole United States. One afternoon, the phone rang, and to my surprise, the voice at the other end was telling me that my son had won second place in that baby contest. Next thing I knew, the local newspaper contacted me. They wanted me to bring Trip in for a photo. They wanted to put his picture in the newspaper. I was so proud of my little boy that no words could describe my feelings.

Sometimes I would lay in bed, letting my mind wander, asking over and over, *Why me? Why me?*

As the days passed, Wade would call reassuring me that I didn't do anything wrong, that he loved me with all his heart, it was just something within him. Over and over, he kept reassuring me that I was a perfect wife, it was just that he didn't want to be a father. After about six months passed, I noticed there was some fight in Wade's voice. He didn't want to be responsible in any way for our child.

I was lost. The man who I thought would be with me forever didn't want his own son. The decision I had made a few years prior, to keep my baby, had become my decision and my responsibility. I would look at Trip and wonder how he could not want this precious little boy. I loved him so much that I would sometimes pick him up after he was asleep, hold him, and look at his little face. I was so proud of him. I knew in my heart Wade would never change his mind. He really did not want children.

Soon, Author started coming back to the house to see Mother. He had replaced everything in the house after he destroyed it that night. She wasn't happy with what he bought. That didn't surprise me because nothing ever pleased her. I never said anything about what Author told me because it was easier to deny Mother could be unfaithful with my husband. I justified it, thinking, *There's no proof anything happened.* She gave Trip and me a home until I could find a job to support myself and my son, so I never mentioned it.

My maternal grandparents were not healthy. They took up a lot of Mother's time. Every morning, my grandmother needed an insulin shot. She was afraid to give it to herself so that left it to one of us, usually, Mother. Then she would leave for work. She built a little two bedroom house for them, beside their big house. The big one had stairs that were getting hard for them to climb every day.

Author would spend hours playing with Trip. He brought things for my boy. I noticed Author was coming over often when Mother was working during the day but I just thought he was enjoying the baby so I didn't think much of it, at first.

I would soon be twenty one, legal age to go into all the places I had sneaked into, when I was younger. I laughed at that thought. The divorce was not final yet, so I made no special plans, although all of my friends wanted to celebrate. Mother and Author ended up taking me out to dinner. We toasted my twenty-first birthday. Not much excitement for a life milestone.

Right after that, Author again failed to get along with Mother. She made me feel so "in the way" that I was uncomfortable. During this time, Author decided he wanted to take care of Trip and me. He wanted me to go away to Spain with him. He felt remorse for what he put me through all those years.

I was stunned. I rejected his advances firmly and with a look of disgust on my face. He wouldn't take no for an answer. He continued with those antics. One day, he came a little too close to me. I felt scared. I started to cry. As he reached to grab me, I whirled around. I fell. He realized he had gone too far and he apologized.

When my divorce was final, I moved out of Mother's home into an apartment with a girlfriend who had a baby girl the same age as Trip. She worked nights and I worked days, so it was a good arrangement. One of us was always there to watch the little ones. Sometimes, I would leave Trip with Mother while I worked. Her father was very ill with cancer and Trip was like a breath of fresh air to him.

My grandfather adored my child. Trip would spend time pushing the button on the hospital bed so that "Papa" could go up and down. At first, we would try to stop Trip but soon, we realized my grandfather loved the attention Trip was giving him. Then we let them play like that together. Trip looked a lot like Mother's brother. I wondered if that brought my grandfather comfort.

Author was more respectful after I threatened to call the police. He would come to the apartment and bang on my door for what seemed like forever but I never let him in. I wanted no part of that man. As far as I was concerned, he made my life miserable. That episode in Mother's kitchen was the straw that broke the camel's back.

Days turned into weeks and weeks merged into months. I tried to make a normal life for Trip and myself. Reading the daily newspaper occupied my mind. It kept me informed on the local news. I read that many of my friends were shipping out to Viet Nam. I would go out with my girlfriends, but as far as seeing a man was concerned, I wasn't interested.

Then, one day when I least expected it, my phone rang. I nearly fainted when I heard the voice on the other end.

"Hi, Pretty Woman" the voice said.

"Oh my Gosh" I replied. "I heard you were drafted in between semesters at school."

"True. But how are you?"

"I'm sure by now you have heard about Wade."

"Yes, I did, is he crazy, or what?"

"I'm not sure what he is thinking. He has been gone many months now. But tell me about you, how are you?"

"I'm okay, I'm home on leave for a few days. Could I come to see you?"

"Jeez, Ajax, I don't know if that would be a good idea, or not."

Before I could say anything else, he said, "I'm only home for ten days. Please say yes. I'd like to take you out for dinner, could we do that?"

As I thought about it, I thought, *Why not, it is just an innocent dinner.*
I asked him, "When would you like to go?"
With a chuckle, he replied "Tonight."

I told him that I would ask Mother if she would watch Trip; and that he should call me back in about an hour and I would let him know.

I called Mother. I told her Ajax had called and asked me to go to dinner with him. She had known he was drafted between semesters and he had gone to boot camp. When I asked her if she would watch Trip, she agreed to watch him, to my surprise. I thanked her, and off I went.

I felt like a little girl while waiting for his call. When it came, I nearly dropped the phone from excitement. This time, he started the conversation with "Please say you can go."

I said, "Yes, what time are you picking me up?"

With excitement, he told me his plans. "I just got in today. I haven't seen my father yet. As soon as he comes home, I'll visit with him for a few minutes and then be on my way. Let's say, about an hour and a half, how's that?"

"That will work. I'll see you then" I said. With our plans made, we said goodbye.

I got Trip ready first and took him to Mother's. To my surprise, she said, "Have a good time and be careful."

"I don't know how long I'll be but I'll come and get Trip as soon as I get back," I said.

"No, just let him sleep here, until morning. He'll be fine." Wow, I felt shocked. I managed to say "Thank you so much." I then left to go and get ready.

I showered and got ready so fast. I couldn't believe that I had a few minutes to spare. When the doorbell rang, I froze. I got so choked up I couldn't move. My heart was beating so fast I almost couldn't breathe. Finding my composure, I realized the door bell rang a second time.

My apartment was large. It seemed forever before I reached the door to open it. There he stood, the Love of My Life. As he brought his hand around from his back he held out a dozen beautiful yellow roses. "For you my love," he said.

I couldn't move. All I could do was cry. Stepping back, so he could come in, I reached out for the roses. As he handed them to me, he reached out with his other hand and pulled me close to him. We stood there hugging for what seemed like forever.

As I sobbed in his arms, he held me and begged me, "Please forgive me for what I have done to us."

He wiped my tears with his fingers. Then kissed my lips.

He whispered, "I am so sorry, I will never leave you again, I promise."

My heart was aching so, I couldn't stop crying as he held me in his arms, trying so hard to sooth me, all the while pleading with me to somehow forgive him. He kept telling me, over and over again, "I will never leave your side or hurt you again, I promise."

Composing myself, I put the roses into a vase with water.

"They are so beautiful," I told him, "and their fragrance is so delicate. I haven't received yellow roses since you brought them to me the last time. Thank you so much. They are absolutely gorgeous." I once again brought them to my face so that I could smell their fragrance.

We went out to dinner at one of the finest restaurants in town. Although I felt nervous, I managed to calm down and enjoy the evening. Here I was, already a wife and mother of a little boy, yet it was as if time stood still and nothing changed. It was just as if we were still young and innocent and so in love. Some things, even time can't change.

Ajax reached across the table and held my hand while he talked to me, telling me, "I was so foolish to have ever thought the grass was greener on the other side, because it wasn't. Nobody can compare to you," he said, "Nobody."

I made us coffee once we were back home. Not waiting for him to ask for an ice cube, I automatically put one into the cup of hot coffee. When I put the cup on the table, he looked at the coffee and he sipped. "You didn't forget did you?"

"Some things you never forget."

We talked and talked that night, neither of us wanting the evening to end.

"Can I come back and see you again?"

"Of course you can," I eagerly reassured him. "How long are you going to be home?"

"Not long enough."

"Well … let me know when you'd like to come over. I only work days, so an evening could work."

"Could I see you again soon, since I am not home for long?"

I said, "Sure, just give me a call. The sooner the better." Then I giggled.

And then I saw his familiar smile. His smile was so beautiful and warm it would melt anyone's heart.

It was two a.m. when we decided to call it a night. I needed to get up early because my little boy was an early bird. I took parenting very seriously. I never dropped my son off at Mother's just because I needed sleep or time to myself. I never forgot about my boy's needs. I always assured he didn't suffer because I wasn't rested enough to take of him.

Saying goodbye that evening was not as emotional as when I first saw him standing outside my front door. We decided he would call me the next day so we would talk about when we could get together again.

I found it hard to fall asleep that night. My mind was whirling. I never expected to see Ajax again, especially never to be in his arms again, nestled into his familiar hug. I had to get back out of bed and go back into the living room to look at my beautiful yellow roses once again before I went to sleep. I had been stunned when he handed that bouquet to me. I had thought he would never give me yellow roses again.

As I laid back into bed, I asked God, "Why did all this happen to us?"

We were so much in love. Such a wonderful, innocent love we shared. Suddenly, that horrible psychic's words replayed in my mind. It had been years since that carnival, yet it was as if she was standing before me, saying those very words that would change my life and haunt me ever after. My eyes flooded with tears at the thought of something happening to Ajax. Wondering why God would only allow him a short life, I tried not to think about that fortune teller or her words. It had to be impossible, my mind insisted.

As I went to work the next morning, I couldn't help thinking about the night before. I felt as if time had stood still and yet I had experienced so much since the last time I talked with Ajax. I was happy about seeing him and although I was looking forward to seeing him again, I felt guilty and I was scared to death. All those months, I could never understand how Wade could not want Trip. The day seemed to drag by and thoughts flowed in my head, nonstop.

When I got home that evening, Mother wanted to know all about how my evening went. I started to tell her everything that had happened and what was said. Suddenly, I started to cry. I told Mother "I'm not sure if I'm crying because I feel sad or if I am happy to see him."

"I imagine it is a little bit of each. Just don't do anything you will regret," she said.

She had consistently acted cold before, never sweet and loving. Now Mother was stranded at home ever since she had to quit her job to take care of her father. So she was lonesome and wanted to talk whenever I had a chance. Now, she had cooked my grandfather some chicken. I stayed and ate with her.

Often, I thought, *Where were you when I was little and lonely,* but I never said anything like that.

It wouldn't have done any good. She was always right in her own mind and with my life in turmoil I didn't need any more pressure. She told me to just be careful seeing Ajax. She realized I had loved him deeply until he decided to be free in college.

After I ate, I took Trip home. My apartment was a blessing. I didn't have anything to put up with there. I was my own boss with an easygoing roommate.

Mother had built a small house next to hers for my maternal grandparents so they would be close by, making it easier for her to care for them. My grandmother only lived there a short time before she eventually succumbed to her illness. After she passed, Grandpa, her husband, became ill. Mother decided she should move in with him to take care of him but he didn't want to live in that small house any more.

He wanted to live where he and my Grandma had lived all of their married life. Mother didn't care much which house they lived in. She loved that big house where she was raised so they moved into it. As soon as Mother was living with my Grandpa in the big house, she sold the smaller house where I had grown up in. Then she talked to me about moving into the little house which was now vacant, so she would have someone she trusts living next door and I could help her with Grandpa. That sounded good to me because I would still be on my own, in a safe haven but I would not have to pay rent. I would only be responsible for the upkeep. That would be a win-win situation, I thought.

After talking with Mother, I gave Trip a bath and put his pajamas on him so he could play for awhile before going to bed. The phone rang around seven p.m. Before I could answer it, my heart was beating so fast I could hardly breathe.

I heard those old, familiar words, "Hello, Pretty Woman."

"Hi there," I said.

"Are you up for a little company this evening?" Ajax asked.

"I'll put Trip to bed in a little bit, but sure, you can come over," I said with excitement.

"Can I come now while Trip is up? I'd like to meet this little guy who his Mommy adores."

"Sure."

After hanging up, I realized how much I had talked about Trip at dinner the previous night.

I laughed to myself and thought, *Oh well, I guess I am just a proud Mommy.*

My son was indeed a beautiful little boy. I felt eager for Ajax to meet him. Trip was playing with his trucks when Ajax arrived. My boy ran to the door to greet him. Ajax picked him up and asked to see his trucks. Trip gladly obliged. After playing with trucks for a while, Trip was getting sleepy, so I put him to bed. Ajax asked for a hug and a kiss goodnight. To my surprise, Trip reached his little arms out to give him a hug and kiss.

I tucked Trip into bed and came back into the living room to find that Ajax had picked up all the trucks and cars that he and Trip had been playing with. I sat down on the sofa. Ajax sat down next to me.

He reached over and took my hand as he said, "That little boy should have been mine. I will never forgive myself for being so stupid. Can you, ever, forgive me?" he asked.

"Forgive? I forgave you a long time ago. It happened, so I guess it was meant to be."

He looked into my eyes and said "I was such a fool. If I ever get the chance to be in your life I will never hurt you again. I want you to know I would never take anything out on that little boy. He is innocent and I would love him like he was my own. Please give me another chance to prove myself to you."

I sat there motionless, listening but not believing what I was hearing. "I want to see you again and again, please let me see you again."

I was thinking, *As long as we keep it innocent it should be alright.* But in the next moment, I also thought, *I am merely justifying it.*

My heart was filled with love. I didn't know how to control it. I didn't answer Ajax. Instead, I got up and asked him if he would like a glass of wine. He welcomed it, so at least for a few minutes I was alone in the kitchen getting the wine. I got a few things to snack on and came back into the living room with the wine and snacks. This seemed to buy me time in answering. He toasted us both, to have a long, happy life. To my relief, he seemed to drop the subject of seeing me. The rest of the evening felt happy and light just like it used to be years before. We laughed together and enjoyed each other's company.

At one point in this evening, we were laughing so hard that tears streamed down my face. This felt so familiar and so comfortable, being with him.

As we laughed, he said, "You always had such a prodigious appetite for life. I admire that in you. No matter how bad things got, you were always shining bright with a zest for happiness. Desiree, there could never be anyone who could take your place in my heat, never," he said.

Not knowing what to say, I laughed and said "Wow, big words, did you learn them in college?"

"I don't know how else to describe you. You have such a lust for life and happiness. It's who you are."

I almost cried to hear him talk like that, but managed to utter the words "Thank you. I do want to be happy and right now I am very happy sitting here talking with you."

As I choked up, wanting to cry, I said, "I didn't think I would ever be sitting on a sofa like this, just talking to you again. It's wonderful."

The next moment, I was in his arms and he was passionately kissing me. I couldn't fight my feelings. My heart was melting from the warmth of his lips on mine and the gentle touch of his hand as he held my face close to his.

"I promise, I will never leave you, just give me a chance to come back into your life. I'll raise Trip as my own, I swear to it," he said.

I whispered, "Ajax, please don't do this to me right now. Let's take things one at a time and just enjoy our evening together, okay?" He gently kissed me, this time nibbling on my upper lip as he whispered, "Okay."

The roses he brought the night before had opened fully. They were beautiful and so fragrant that they filled that small room with their scent. Before he left, he walked over to the roses were and sniffed them.

"I will never be like a man, who over the years, forgets to send his wife flowers. Just give me a chance and you will always receive roses and all the love I can give."

I smiled and reassured him, "Please, for now, let's just enjoy what we have."

"Okay, can we enjoy this again *soon*?" He laughed.

"Yes, we can, call me, I am here every night with my boy, just give me a call," I said.

I pinched his arm and led him to the door. We said good night and he left, leaving me so emotionally confused that I could not sleep, once again.

Seeing Ajax during his leave left me drained, confused and so torn. Although seeing Ajax was not Wade's fault, I blamed Wade for putting me in this situation. If he hadn't come home drunk, if he hadn't decided he didn't want a child, I would not have been living there. I would probably have not even known that Ajax was home on leave. I knew he only had a few days left before he had to go back and already I was dreading his departure.

During his leave, he asked me to go over to his sister Laura's house with him. He said she wanted to see me and that I was welcome to come with him. I felt nervous, since I had not seen her in quite a while, but I said I would love to go.

I could hardly wait to see her daughter, Michaelene. I still had such caring for that little girl. I wondered if Laura knew what had happened the last time I had gone to their house to see her and the girls.

I doubted Ajax's mother would tell her how she treated me, how she told me, "If you truly love this little girl, then go away and never come back. She cries every time you leave and that is not fair."

Somehow, I thought if Laura knew, she would have apologized for her mother. She would have been angry about what her mother said. But I saw no sense in telling her about her mother's comments. Instead, chose to keep it to myself.

After we arrived, I knew for sure that Laura could not have been aware of what happened. She welcomed me with open arms. Michaelene ran to me screaming with delight.

As I wrapped my arms around her, she said, "Don't let Grandma make you leave anymore, please."

I reassured her I wouldn't and quietly prayed nothing about that would be mentioned around Ajax. I knew he would get upset if he knew what his mother had done. I didn't want anything to ruin his leave, especially involving me. We all sat and talked as we used to. Laura and Ajax were so close. I wished that I had such a brother, one who would be my true friend.

The evening was wonderful. During the course of conversation, Ajax asked Laura, "I'd like Desiree to go to the airport with me when I leave. Can she ride with you?"

"Of course she can," Laura said. Then she followed with "she will have to bring her own tissues, though."

We all laughed. He had not asked me to go to the airport to see him off. I wondered if he thought I might refuse, and that was why he invited me in Laura's presence. I would never have refused but it would have been nice if he had asked me while we were alone.

When we left Laura's house, in the car, Ajax told me he was worried about leaving us; that he thought if I was there, Laura would have someone to go home with instead of driving alone.

I sarcastically joked, "Oh, so you want me to go to the airport to see you off so Laura will have someone to drive home with."

"No, I was just afraid you wouldn't go to see me off."

"You could have asked. But yes, I'll go. A wild horses couldn't keep me from seeing you off."

"Thank you, that means a lot to me."

It was a short ride home, and not wanting to leave me yet, he pulled into a drive-through restaurant and ordered us each a root beer float. As we sat talking, I couldn't help but notice his crystal clear, aqua blue eyes again. They were beautiful beyond words. I wanted my children to have his eyes and light hair.

In that moment, my thoughts wandered. I wondered, for the millionth time, how Wade could absolutely refuse to ever be a parent. My first obligation was my son and although I did love Wade in my own way, I always knew Ajax was my one true love, just as I always knew my heart could never love another man as I loved him. He was special in so many ways. I did not allow myself to be intimate with Ajax, although I wanted to. It was difficult for me, when he would reach to hug or kiss me.

Now his kisses felt so familiar, so warm and so loving, with such meaning, I found it harder and harder to resist him. Saying goodnight became almost impossible but I had to think of my son. I never wanted him to experience what I experienced when I was that young, with the bedroom door being locked from the outside so that I could not come out, or even worse, that he might wake up and wander into the kitchen and witness what I had seen. My love for my child was so strong I would have never considered treating him as I was treated. Never.

Mother approached me again about moving into the little house she had build for her parents. This time, I said yes. I would wait until after Ajax left and then start packing for the move.

The time soon came to see Ajax off at the airport. Not knowing where he was going or how long it would be until I saw him again was extremely difficult. I was so very confused. All the way to the airport, he held my hand and kept squeezing it. He looked at me and whispered "I love you so much." My heart was aching. Michaelene sat next to me and wanted to hold my other hand.

This could have been my family. If we had married as we wanted to, all this would not have been happening. Had Ajax been married, the government could not have taken him when he got sick in-between semesters and had to stay out of college. Being married, and in college, would have made him exempt. But that was not the case. I now wondered what his mother was going through, knowing that because of her choices, he son was in the military, and we are going to the airport to see him off to fly into some unknown fate.

When we arrived, butterflies were flying around in my stomach. I never was good with goodbyes. This one would be very difficult. We arrived early, so we had plenty of time to wait until he had to board the plane. We went to the boarding section of the airport to wait until it was time for him to get on the plane. There were little snack bars there. Although I could not even think of eating, I did get something to drink. My mouth was like cotton from my nerves.

We all made light conversation and tried to be happy-go-lucky but all our hearts were heavy. The hours seemed to fly by so quickly. When it was time for him to board, as we stood up, my knees felt weak but I tried to act like everything was just peachy. We went to the gate and he hugged everyone goodbye.

My thoughts once again drifted, but soon reality shook my foundation as he reached for me.

My heart ached, as I thought, *Oh my God, I love this man so much, please God please keep him safe.*

I looked at Ajax and smiled and then hugged him, whispering, "I do love you so much, please be safe."

He was surprised by my loving words.

He hugged me again as he whispered "I have waited so long to hear those words from you. Please wait for me. I'll be back."

I nodded my head and said, "I'll be here when you return."

As he approached the door way to the boarding ramp, he looked back at me and loudly declared, "I love you Desiree, I do love you." Then, he was out of sight.

I stood at the glass, looking out at the airplane that would soon take off, when suddenly I saw him looking out the window where he was seated.

I said, "Look Michaelene, there's Uncle Johnny." That was the name his family used. "Look Honey, he's waving at you."

As young as she was, she looked at me with her beautiful little face and said "No, Desiree. He is waving at you."

I started to cry. Not wanting him to see me cry was the hardest part. I stood there as we looked at each other through thick windows, each saying "I love you," until the plane started engines and pulled away.

One last time, he said "I love you" and blew me a kiss.

I looked at his face, framed in the plane window so clearly and wondered why our world had to be at war; why we couldn't all live our lives in harmony. I realized just how much I did love this man and my heart ached with the thought of him leaving. I prayed he would be assigned a position in the States rather then going off to war in Vietnam. That prayer I would say over and over again during the months to come.

When his plane was out of sight, we turned to walk back to the car. Michaelene, still holding my hand, walked silently with me. I had never in my life felt so completely empty. As I walked down the hallways to the exit, my heart was heavy. I tried to wipe my tears and smile for this gorgeous little angel walking next to me but that was next to impossible.

I had gained control over my emotions when we reached the car. I asked Michaelene if I could come back to the airport with her when her uncle comes back.

She giggled so innocently and sweetly, than asked her mother, "Is it was okay if Desiree comes with us when we come back to get Uncle Johnny?"

"Absolutely," Laura said, as she also wiped tears from her face. Laura and I looked at each other as our eyes once again filled with tears. Two different kinds of love, but both for the same man.

The ride home was only about forty-five minutes but it seemed endless as my mind drifted from one focus to another.

When we reached Laura's house, she asked, "Would you like to come in and have a cup of coffee?"

I looked at her as my tears once again started to well up, this time causing me to choke up so I could not speak. I just nodded my head for yes and tried to smile about her kind gesture. This woman was so special to me. I truly wished she was my sister on more than one occasion.

Once inside, Laura's husband handed her their baby and left to run some errands. Privately, I felt amused, because it seemed like he wanted to run out of the house to avoid two crying women. We talked and talked that day. As I left, I hugged Michaelene tightly and then reached for Laura to give her a hug and thank her for letting me ride with her to the airport.

"We both love him" she said, with a smile.

Once home, I really realized Ajax was facing a whole new world compared to us. I was scared for him.

My little one came running to me yelling "Mommy, Mommy."

As I wrapped my arms around him, I once again returned to reality. I loved this little guy more than life. There we were again, just the two of us, together.

I went back to work as usual and continued to come straight home. I started to pack, which really made my roommate angry. I had to do what was best for me and Trip. Wade never gave me anything for the baby nor did he ever buy him anything. I was on my own and he was off making a new life for himself. It had been many months since he had even seen Trip but I didn't push it. I realized there is no way to make someone have feelings that just aren't there. I often did not even receive the tiny "child support" he was supposed to send us.

To my surprise, a few days after my highly emotional trip to the airport, a letter came from Ajax. I took it inside to read it. As I opened it, I felt my heart fill with joy.

Dear Pretty Woman,

I made it back safe and sound. I hope you and Trip are doing well. I never knew what it was like to feel such love in my heart as I feel for you. I am so sorry for hurting you the way I did while I was in college, you didn't deserve that. I can't even tell you what it was like seeing you open that door for me the first night I came to see you. You are so beautiful and all I want is for you to be mine, really mine.

I had such a wonderful time visiting with you, it was as if we had never been apart. I promise you, if you give me a second chance, you'll never want for anything the rest of your life. I also promise I will raise Trip as if he were mine. He is so innocent in all of this. I know that in time he would grow to love me because I would love him. He is a part of you and I so desperately want all of you.

Please wait for me. I love you with all my heart and soul and will love you forever. Please write to me to let me know how you and Trip are doing. I hope to hear from you soon.

I love you with all my heart and always will.

Ajax

I read and reread his letter a dozen times. I couldn't believe what he was saying nor could I believe he had taped a picture of a yellow rose on the letter. I wondered where he found the picture.

Silly man, I thought, as I laughed to myself.

After dinner that night, I played trucks with Trip until it was time for his bath. Afterwards, with his snack eaten, it was time for him to go to bed. As usual, I read him a story and then tucked him in for the night. As I kissed him good night, I thought about him growing up and one day, becoming a man. I wondered if there would be a war and if he would have to face what I feared Ajax was about to face. I looked at this adorable child laying in his bed, so young, and so handsome. Yet he was a male child who would grow into a man and possibly have to defend our country, some day. That thought scared me. As I quickly pushed it out of my mind, I wondered if Ajax's mother ever looked at her son when he was a baby and felt the same fear I was feeling.

When Trip fell asleep, I started a letter back to Ajax but as I began to write, I burst into tears. I felt so many different emotions I didn't know where to begin. This beautiful man was professing his love for me. This was a dream come true, but I was so scared. Along with all this, I have a tiny son, sound asleep in the other room. He needed me to provide a stable future.

I thought, *This is like a soap opera, with me as one a main character. All I ever wanted was a normal life with a loving husband and six children but so far, it hasn't been that way...*

I gathered my strength and dried my tears because, at that point, my hands were shaking so badly I could hardly write. I was not ready to make any major decisions although I knew darn well where my heart belonged. As I continued to sit at the table, I asked God to guide me in the right direction for my son and for myself.

I managed to write the letter. I sent it off the next day. It wasn't filled with the love that was in the letter I received but it was warm and caring. As the days passed, more and more letters came. Each one was filled with such love and devotion. My heart ached with each letter I received.

Packing everything for the move while working full time kept my mind busy. The move itself went well since I had a few friends who helped me. I truly appreciated how Mother let me live in the her rental house with Trip and not pay anything. Her life at that time was so restricted due to my grandfather's grave illness that I'm sure Trip and I at least brought her some joy by living so close. Even the Ice Queen, as cold as the Arctic night, had some feelings. Whatever the reason, I really was happy to have an appealing, clean place to live with my son.

Days turned into months. Eventually, I received the letter that I had been dreading:

My Beautiful Desiree,

I have received my orders. I have been deployed to Vietnam. I knew I would be going but hoped somehow they would change my orders and send me somewhere else. We were given a leave to come home first, for a few weeks. I can hardly wait to see you and Trip.

I will be coming home next Tuesday at five thirty p.m. Do you think you can pick me up from the airport? If not, I will understand. I will call you Monday night about nine, your time, to see if you can get me. I hope you will be able to spend time with me while I am home. I really am looking forward to seeing you.

I'm going to cut this letter short so I can get it into the mail today. Life is throwing us a lot of curves, isn't it? But at least we will have a few weeks to spend time together before I leave.

Talk to you soon, Pretty Woman. Remember, I love you with all my heart and soul.

Ajax

After reading the letter, I sat down on the couch to compose myself. I felt my heart was going to break. I looked at Trip, who was playing with his toys. I wondered, with fear, if Ajax would be safe and if our lives were meant to be spent together.

I was so confused that I could hardly think straight. Being raised a Catholic, I believed in God but at that moment I didn't know if I should pray or cry. Suddenly, the psychic's face appeared in my thoughts. There was no way to erase the horrible words she had said. What she had told me was becoming more and more vivid.

The week went fast. Soon, it was already Monday night, the night Ajax was supposed to call me. I waited with my heart in my throat, not knowing what to say. When the phone rang, I jumped for it, so it would not wake Trip up.

"Hi, Pretty Woman," Ajax yelled into the phone.

"Hi, how are you?" I replied.

He laughed and then said "Well, if you tell me you can pick me up at the airport, I'm great. If you say you can't, then I'm not so great."

We both laughed, although weakly, realizing the seriousness of his visit. "Yes, I can come to get you," I answered. "What airline are you coming in on?"

"Continental," he said, so happily that he seemed the happiest man alive.

He then told me about getting his orders and how long he would be gone.

I felt numb. I could barely keep up the happy voice but managed to tell him "God will keep you safe."

We talked about fifteen minutes more and then he had to feed more change into the pay phone. Then we had a few more minutes before he had to hang up. I really acted upbeat and happy but inside I was aching. When the time was running out on the pay phone, we said goodbye.

As he said his goodbye, he slipped in, "I love you Desiree, I want you to believe that."

The phone went dead. I felt a sharp pain as if my heart was being pulled from my chest. I couldn't stop my tears as I hung up.

How will I "put on a happy face" when he gets home, I wondered?

Chapter Five

The week dragged on until it was time to go to the airport to pick Ajax up. I could hardly work that day because I was trying to process my anticipation of what the next few weeks would bring. My heart was pulling one way yet my mind was going in another direction because I was so confused and fearful.

I asked Mother if she would watch Trip for me while I went to the airport. To my great surprise, she didn't deliver a long sermon but instead she simply said, "Just be careful of your feelings." I started to cry and just let it all out. Everything that had been bottled up for months came gushing out. I was at a major crossroad in my life. I didn't quite know how to handle it. For the first time in years, I felt as if I was Mother's daughter, not the child who had "ruined her life." Though she didn't reach out to hug me, she did talk to me, clearly trying to sooth me. For her, that was big.

As I drank a cup of tea, I poured my heart out. For the first time, I shared the story about the psychic with someone. I couldn't hold it inside anymore. The psychic had taken a lot away from me that day. I knew I could never get it back. I told Mother about that horrible woman and what she had said. Then, I felt shocked by how Mother comforted me. She didn't tell me, straight out, to disbelieve what the woman said, though.

She said, "Things change. Maybe the woman felt something at that time but some time has passed now and things could be different. Besides, she could be wrong. Maybe he will live to be a hundred."

Mother told me about an experience she had with a psychic, how some predictions came true and other things didn't.

So Mother added, "Just put that out of your mind. Forget about what she said. Life can't be always be predicted. Psychics aren't always right."

We talked and talked that day, something we hadn't done in a long time. I wanted so much to have a healthy relationship, as other mothers and daughters do but I had to deal with her typically difficult way of being in the world. At that point, my son and I had a roof over our heads. Although I rarely went anywhere, if I had needed her help, she would have at least taken care of Trip for me.

Having finished my tea, I dried my eyes. I got up to go get ready for my trip to the airport. My head was spinning with scattered thoughts as I left to go next door, to the little house I had moved into that felt so comforting.

I started to get ready. My stomach was in knots. I could hardly calm down my nerves. So much to consider; lives at stake; and it was all on my shoulders.

Even though this tugged at my heart strings, *My main concern is always Trip,* I thought. Although at that moment, I really didn't know what was best for Trip.

I knew in my heart I had to put him first. He was so tiny and he needed a secure home life. How well I knew that, being raised as I was, not knowing from one day to the next where I would be sleeping. How lucky I was that my father's family never denied me when I made my weekly calls.

Having taken one more look in the mirror, I was ready to leave. I took a deep breath and left. The ride to the airport seemed to take forever. Although I left in plenty of time, I thought I had to hurry. I felt relieved at the arriving flights gate, knowing I was there on time with a few minutes to spare.

They announced the arrival of his flight. My knees felt weak. *Could I really be standing there waiting for Ajax to get off the plane?,* I wondered.

I looked up and saw passengers who were coming into the terminal. I watched with my heart in my throat as each person came through. Then, there he was with his wonderful smile. As I went to meet him, I started to cry. We hugged each other. I didn't want to let go. He pulled a bunch of yellow roses from his duffel bag.

"For my Pretty Woman," he said.

I couldn't believe he had brought them such a distance for me. They were pretty and again, so fragrant.

"Thank you so much," were the only words I could manage.

"I told you, I would always give you yellow roses. See, I keep my word", he said.

"Yes you do, don't you?" I replied.

We walked down the hall way to the baggage area. When his bags came around on the conveyer, we gathered them and left.

"Have you eaten yet?" he asked. I just smiled in a way that he knew I hadn't.

"Let's get something to eat. I'm starving," he said.

I asked him if he wanted to see his family before we went to eat.

He said, "No. You are the only one I want to see, now and forever."

"Oh I think you would get tired of me eventually," I said, and laughed.

"No I won't. I have waited for this moment for a long time," he whispered as he kissed my cheek.

After we put his luggage in the car, he opened my door but changed his mind about getting into the car. Instead, he put his arms around me and, holding me, he kissed me. I didn't know what to do. I wanted so much to simply kiss him back but I felt so torn. There I stood with the man I adored and yet I was filled with fear.

He sensed my hesitation.

He asked, "Are you okay?"

All I could do was shake my head yes and reassure him that I was great. I made up my mind in that moment that we were going to enjoy the few weeks we had together, no matter what.

With a big smile, I leaned into him, kissed his lips softly, and said "Let's see how much fun we can have in the next few weeks, okay?"

"Absolutely. Let's see how much fun we can have," he agreed. We both laughed and got into the car.

There was a beautiful restaurant near the airport called the Atrium. He chose to eat there. This was the most impressive restaurant décor

I had ever seen. It had huge glass panels in the roof, at least thirty feet high. The entire restaurant was glass with a lush presence of large plants all around. Ferns were hung from the glass ceiling by chains in containers that were carved in gold and cream colors. There were beds of greenery all throughout the restaurant.

I was happy I had dressed up to meet him because this restaurant was uniquely elegant and everyone there was well dressed. We ordered wine and sat there taking it all in. I felt special for the first time in a long while. With Ajax, I felt I was the only woman in the world who mattered. Sitting across from me in his uniform, he looked so dashing and handsome. I wanted to sit back and take it all in. The glass of wine calmed me down so I was able to relax.

I excused myself and went to the ladies room, just needing a moment alone to collect my thoughts.

When I came back, he stood up to pull my chair out for me. "Wow," I said, "you are going to spoil me."

"You have no idea," he replied.

I smiled and sat down just as the waiter brought us another round of wine.

"This one is on the house" the waiter remarked, "for our appreciation of the soldier and his lovely date."

We both thanked him and picked up our glasses for a toast.

Ajax touched his glass to mine and said, "To the most beautiful woman and for the next few weeks, she's all mine."

I smiled, touched my glass to his, and said "to the man who makes me feel so special. Happiness!"

We sipped our wine and ordered our meals. Everything was completely delicious and the atmosphere looked dreamlike. Candles burned all around us, some in free-standing, six foot, carved medal candlesticks. Some were in sconces on the wooden beams. They created such a romantic ambiance. One could see the candles sparkling brightly, reflected by the glass windows that surrounded the entire, round room. I wanted that evening to last forever.

After our meal, we sipped coffee, and of course, he put ice in his and sipped cooled coffee before I even began to take a sip. He laughed and asked me when I was going to start putting ice in my coffee.

As we laughed, I said "Now" and put a cube in my cup. Sitting there with him was such a pleasure. We really were a compatible couple. I fought the feeling but I was so in love with him.

We left the restaurant and headed toward his house. "Can I get my car and come back to visit with you?" he asked.

"Of course you can," I said, "But won't your parents want to spend some time with you?"

"They can, tomorrow," he answered. So I drove down the road to his parents' house, about ten minutes from my place. I didn't want to go into the house with him but he insisted. His mother was so sweet to me it took me by surprise. I suppose she didn't want me to tell him what she had said to me that day when I went to Laura's house.

When I thought about her words, it seemed cold and cruel to tell me. She said, "If you really do love Michaelene, you will stay away from here and not upset her."

As if I could help her crying when I would leave. Oh well, that had happened a long time in the past.

It didn't take long for Ajax to ask his Dad if he could take the car for a while. Of course, his father had no problem with that. "I'll just see you in the morning then" his father said, and we departed.

Ajax walked me to my car and said, "See you in a few minutes."

"Okay" I replied. He looked at me and growled like Roy Orbison does in the song "Pretty Woman," then he closed my car door.

Silly man, I thought but I had to admit after all these years, hearing him growl like that still made me laugh. I loved it!

He followed me home. When we entered my driveway, I got butterflies in my stomach like a school girl on her first date. We got out of our cars simultaneously and walked to the door. I had those latest roses in my hand.

I was sniffing them when he asked "Are you okay with me coming over? I don't want you to feel uncomfortable."

"Yes, I'm okay," I said.

I didn't want to tell him what I had decided at the airport; that I basically just wanted to enjoy his visit. After all the tears I shed at Mother's house, I was certain she wouldn't say anything to me.

"Come on in," I jokingly said.

This being the first evening of his extended leave before going to Vietnam, I felt weak. It scared me seriously but I was determined to make this leave a wonderful experience for both of us. One that neither of us would ever forget.

Once inside, we decided on more coffee. I got another laugh when, as usual, he went to the freezer for an ice cube.

I looked at him and shook my head as I said, "No one else in the world puts an ice cube in their coffee. Nope, just you."

He moved his lips to a spot where the ice had melted and sipped the coffee. Then he smiled. We sat in my kitchen and talked for hours. Then, suddenly, we both realized it was four a.m.

"Oh, my gosh, I said, and then sighed. Am I ever glad I don't have to work tomorrow."

"Good," he said, "Then maybe you and Trip can go with me to the mall. I need to get a few things."

I was a little apprehensive about going to the mall but told him to give me a call and I would see how things were going with us. Because we had two cups of coffee, I wondered how I would fall asleep, but I figured I would deal with that when the time came.

I walked him to the door, sorry that it was time for the evening to end. When we reached the door, I stepped back a little. He asked if it was alright if he called at noon the next day.

"Sure," I said softly, "that will be fine."

He reached out to me and pulled me close in a hug. I responded in kind.

With a sweet kiss, he whispered, "Talk to you tomorrow," and he left.

I had put those yellow roses into a vase when we first arrived at home. Now I looked at them, thinking about the evening we had just shared. I closed my eyes and continued to think about the restaurant and how proud I felt sitting there with him. No matter what, this man would always have my heart. There was no way around it and no way to deny it, regardless of all my fears.

To my surprise, I fell asleep quickly, although morning seemed to come far too soon. I went next door at about eight-thirty a.m. to get Trip. He was happily playing with Grandpa.

Poor man, I thought.

Trip was pushing the button on Grandpa's hospital bed, causing it to go up and down. When I was about to stop him, Grandpa shook his hand to say, "Leave him alone." Trip thought it was great fun. That seemed to be all that mattered to his "Papa." The poor man had cancer of the larynx. He was hanging on to life tenuously. Trip provided the bright spot in his day. Actually, Trip was the bright spot in everyone's day. He had such a cute, outgoing personality, and his face was so handsome. Sometimes I would look at him and just thank God for giving me such a winsome son. He looked very much like Mother's brother who had passed away, and he was an attractive man. Sometimes I wondered if that wasn't why Grandpa loved Trip so much. Trip was the image of the son he had lost.

Mother had a thousand questions that morning. Since I didn't have to go to work, I visited with her for a while. I told her about Ajax wanting me and Trip to go to the mall with him. To my surprise, Mother told me to do whatever makes me happy because Wade hadn't been a very good father. I wasn't sure about going that way. In the back of my mind, I was afraid of how I would feel when Ajax returned to the military: lost and alone once again.

I ate breakfast with her, talking away. Mother was lonely and it showed. Author was still coming around to see her since she was stranded at the house. I wondered if perhaps he used that to his advantage sometimes. I'll bet he didn't come at midnight and sing until all hours of the night any more or bust up the whole house. My Grandpa would have thrown him out even being so sick. Why Mother tolerated Author all those years was beyond me. But she did and now that she was stranded full-time in the house, he's better than nobody at all. At least he talks with my Grandpa. They seem to enjoy each other.

The rest of the day went smoothly. My errands were completed in less time than I estimated. Trip was his happy-go-lucky self, tolerating running around and riding in the car rather well.

He's such a good boy, I thought.

I wished things were perfect, for his sake but unfortunately, they weren't.

"You're a sleepy little boy," I whispered as I hugged and kissed him.

I got him ready for bed and gave him his snack. He was rubbing his eyes a bit after eight p.m. He fell asleep quickly after all the running around. I was pleased. It gave me time to sit by myself and think.

When Ajax called, I bowed out graciously. I asked him to give me a call later if he had time. I told him I put Trip to bed; that anytime later would work fine. We didn't talk long but those few minutes were pleasant. I think he understood my need without me getting explicit because he eagerly said, "Okay, I'll call you later then."

On the couch, I looked over at my beautiful roses. I wondered exactly where my life was heading. The phone rang. Though I jumped to answer, it was only a wrong number.

I closed my eyes and prayed that somehow I would have the strength to do the right thing for my son and myself. I laid my head back praying and I fell asleep. Though sound asleep, I dreamed I heard a phone ring. Suddenly, I awakened enough to realize the phone really was ringing.

When I reached for it, I heard "Desiree... Desiree, are you there?" I felt relief that I wasn't dreaming, that it was Ajax.

"Mmm... Sorry, I must have fallen asleep," I said, in a drowsy voice.

"I wish I was there with you," he replied.

"Come on over. I'll make us some coffee," I suggested.

"That's what I wanted to hear. I'll be over in a few minutes."

Within fifteen minutes, there was a quiet knock at the front door. I hurried to the door. There he stood, with the biggest smile on his face.

He said "I was hoping you would invite me over. I hated to waste the rest of the night sleeping."

"Come on in," I said as I gestured with my arm.

Another evening of coffee and conversation began. This time, the conversation took a serious turn. He told me how he counted days until he could come home again. Then he asked me how I felt about seeing him again. My eyes welled up with tears but I held them back and sipped my coffee.

I had gotten a second wind from my short snooze. I jabbered away like a Chatty Cathy doll. It felt fabulous to look across the table and see Ajax. It was like a dream that I didn't want to wake up from. Once again, we talked the night away. Before we knew it, the clock showed two a.m. Though I hated to see him leave, I knew that early in the morning, Trip would be wide awake, full of energy. There would be no keeping up with that child. Given that he fell asleep early, I felt certain he would be up earlier than usual.

Before Ajax left, he asked me if I had plans for the next day. I didn't, but wondered why he asked.

"I'd like to take you and Trip to Cedar Point one of the days while I'm home. Tomorrow would be perfect for me if you could go."

I thought for a moment and then threw fate to the wind.

I said "I would love to go. What time should we be ready?"

"Really, that's great, I've been wanting to go back there with you. How about eight thirty in the morning?"

I smiled and said, "That'll work fine. We'll be ready."

He hugged me tightly. It felt so good. He kissed me, ever so lightly, and went out the door.

The next morning, Trip was up early as I had predicted, at the crack of dawn. He was as full of energy as I had thought he would be. I fed him breakfast and told him where we were going that day. He got excited so I started to laugh. He really had no idea what Cedar Point was about. He was too young to know what an amusement park is.

Promptly at eight thirty, we heard a knock on the front door. Trip went running. He was starting to put words together in sentences. He tried so hard to tell Ajax where he was going. Ajax laughed at his excitement. We left quickly because he wanted to stop on the way and have breakfast.

In the restaurant, Trip climbed into the booth insisting that he would sit beside Ajax.

Bless his little heart, I thought, *he has no clue what's happening.*

After breakfast as we left the restaurant, I was excited to see what Trip would think of the park and all the rides.

The day was perfect, the weather was perfect and everything else was perfect. Trip was so well behaved, I was really proud of him. Since I really didn't sleep well I was dragging as evening came. Trip was content riding in his stroller and taking in everything there was to see. That was good, at least I didn't have to worry about him falling and hurting himself.

What a wonderful day we had, the kind of day that stays in your memory forever. I was so tired by the time we left the park I just wanted to lay my head down and go to sleep. Trip fell asleep in the car. I carried him inside and put him to bed for the night.

"Thank you for the most wonderful day," I said, as I came out of the bedroom. "You are so sweet and I truly appreciate you taking us, that was so thoughtful," I said.

He looked at me and started to say something and then stopped.

"What is it," I asked?

He said, "You can't possibly know what today has meant to me. Thank you for going with me."

I walked over to him and hugged him, only this time, I welcomed his kisses. At that moment, I wanted his arms around me and I wanted his kisses more than ever. I was still so in love with him that my heart ached. In that moment, I knew I had never stopped loving him and never would.

I had to go to work the next day. I definitely needed more sleep than I was getting, so I politely called it an evening.

"Are you throwing me out," he asked?

"Yep I am, unless you want to go to work for me tomorrow morning," I replied.

I sat down on the couch. He sat down next to me.

"I'll go in a minute," he said, as he put his arm around me. "Just let me sit here with you for one more minute, okay?" he asked.

I snuggled into his arms and that was it, I was sound asleep in one minute. I woke up a while later and saw he was watching me sleep.

I looked up and smiled and asked "How long have you been watching me sleep?"

"About an hour he answered. "You are so beautiful, and I love you with all my heart. I could sit here forever and just watch you sleep."

"Silly man" I whispered in a sleepy voice. "Go home."

"Only if I can come back again soon. "Deal?"

"Yep, it's a deal. Now let me go to bed."

We both laughed and he got up to leave.

"Thank you for a wonderful day. I mean that," he said. Then he left.

I could barely get my clothes off quickly enough, I was so tired. Surely didn't have to worry about falling asleep that night. I was out and didn't hear a thing until the alarm sounded in the morning.

Trip usually got me up before the alarm but on this morning he was sound asleep, after the busy day before. I hurried into the kitchen to make myself some coffee and tried to wake up so my day could begin. After I got some coffee down, things started to come alive and my brain was functioning. I went over the day before in my mind and felt overwhelmed with joy about the way it all worked out. I went to work that day a happy woman.

I received a call that night from Ajax but I really needed some sleep, so I quietly refused his offer of a pizza.

"I think you better spend some time with your family or they will begin to hate me," I said.

He laughed, then said that his sisters were a little upset with him but he would go ahead and spend time with them since I was refusing his offer for a pizza.

"I visited with Laura today," he said. "So I'll try to visit with the rest of them tonight. See you maybe tomorrow?"

"Sure, give me a call," I said.

All I could think was that things were working as they were supposed to. I thought of the French saying "Que sera, sera," whatever will be, will be. For then, that was what I needed to think to stay sane.

The next day when I returned home, there was a message on my phone from Wade. He knew I was working. This was his way of avoiding me.

His message was, "I'm sorry that I won't be able to take Trip for a visit Saturday. I know I haven't seen him in a while but something came up and I can't take him."

I erased the message. It didn't impress me one bit. Wade had found a new girlfriend immediately after I left him. Daddy wasn't exactly his favorite name. He had only seen Trip once in over five months. I wasn't sure why he even called. The last time he took Trip for a few hours, my boy came back with bruises all over his face. Wade told me that he fell. They were serious bruises, so I took a picture of them.

I felt relieved that he wasn't coming around. I needed a soak in a long, hot bath. That's exactly what I did. When Trip was asleep, I filled the tub with a soothing, scented bubble bath, sat in it and relaxed. It couldn't possibly take away all my heartache but it was calming.

I went to bed early thinking I would not hear from Ajax. While sound asleep, once again, I thought I heard the phone but I couldn't tell if I was dreaming or if it was really ringing. I jumped a foot high on the bed and grabbed the phone. My heart was beating so fast that I was out of breath when I answered it.

"Hello," I mumbled.

To my delight, I heard this adorable growl.

"You crazy man," I said and laughed. "Only you could wake me up from a deep sleep, growl into the phone, and get a laugh."

"I figured I better give you a break from me but I can't sleep so I had to call. Is it alright that I called?"

I laughed. "Well, it's a little late to ask, now that I'm awake." Then we both laughed. We talked for over an hour. It was a warm conversation. We both whispered, so we wouldn't wake anyone. I was surprised that Trip slept through the call.

He might wake up if he hears me talking, I thought, so I kept my voice low.

Lying there, I felt happy, as if all my problems had disappeared. We talked and talked like we used to when we were still in school. That seemed like a previous lifetime but it was only a few years earlier.

So many things happen in only a few short years, I thought as I laid down in bed again, trying to go back to sleep.

Work was easy the next day. Time seemed to fly. Before I knew it, it was time to go home. Trip was so excited when he saw me.

I loved the way he came running, yelling "Mommy, Mommy."

I swooped him up in my arms and hugged him. I whispered in his ear "I love you so much," and listened to him giggle with delight.

What a precious child, I thought, *and he is mine.*

We ate dinner and played with Trip's cars and trucks until time for Trip to go to bed. I loved playing with him and noting his imagination as he "drove" the trucks all into one area and moved the cars into another. I thanked God for the precious gift this child was. He had spread his cars all over the living room before I knew it. He didn't want to go to bed and didn't want to put his toys away but soon he gave in and helped pick them all up.

Ajax called. It really wasn't a surprise. I thought he might at least call if he didn't appear at my door. My surprise in this was that I was hoping he would call.

The instant I heard Ajax's voice, I said, "I was hoping you would call. Do you want to come over and have a drink or some coffee?"

He laughed, and whispered "I'd like to come over and have you."

I felt my stomach contract.

I mustered the courage to say, "Then come on over."

He must have sprouted wings. He was there in a flash.

As he walked in the door, he leaned over and kissed me on the cheek and said, "I was hoping you would let me come over. My mother is driving me nuts and I just wanted to see you so badly."

"Well, then I am glad I wanted to see you, too." I replied.

That evening, spent quietly in my kitchen, made me realize more and more just where my heart was heading. Although it was heading in another direction, I reminded myself that I did have to think about my son, and what was ultimately the best for him, also. I had baked some cookies for Trip so I put them out on a plate for us to snack on.

I always had cheese and other snacks in the house. It was easy to serve a plate of appetizers, so that's what I quickly did. We decided to go into the living room with our finger foods. It was so pleasantly heartwarming to sit on the floor, feeling completely at ease with someone comfortable. My girlfriends kept telling me I should date, but that was not something even remotely interesting. Time with Ajax felt so natural and so right.

We talked and laughed for some time before I noticed the atmosphere getting serious. His facial expression changed from laughter to a solemn, intense look.

He looked me in the eyes and asked. "How will I leave? How will I leave you and go off to Vietnam after spending time with you and Trip? What if I don't come back? What if something happens to me and I am no longer whole? For three years now, I dreamed of having these moments with you, seeing you laugh, hearing your voice, and most of all, kissing your lips. I've longed for your touch and hated myself for the misery I caused" he said.

Then he really broke my heart. "If I die, I want you to go onward and be happy. Promise me you will, even though the thought of you loving someone else tears me up. I know in my heart that what went wrong with us before is all my fault. I don't want you to suffer because of what I stupidly did. Promise me, that no matter what, you'll find happiness in your life."

I started crying because I realized what a truly wonderful, loving man he was. I feared, deep down in my heart, that he might not come back; that these next few weeks would be our last. He reached out to hug me. I melted into his very being. I sobbed because I couldn't control my fear of his death any more.

He kissed me and wiped my tears. He whispered, "I love you. I swear, I will always love you no matter what happens. You are so sweet and decent. I'm the one who tore us apart. I don't know how I will forgive myself," he said.

I looked into his eyes and said, "You can forgive yourself by coming back so that our love can grow and we can be together. Deal?"

"I will do my best to come home to you and make up for the pain I caused you. Please stop crying. It breaks my heart to see you cry."

He took my hands and lifted me up from the floor where we had been sitting together. As I arose, he wrapped his arms around me as if he would never let go. He stared into my eyes and again whispered, "I love you with all my heart."

His intensely passionate kisses were full of love. He respected my desire to keep us from going too far, though he lost himself in our kisses. He found it very difficult to not follow his passionate feelings into physical intimacy. In those few moments, I wanted to make love to his so badly. Try as I would, it became more and more difficult to say no.

His words echoed in my brain, "What if I don't come back? Or if I do come back, but I'm not whole?"

All I could do was reassure him he would come back and that he would be whole when he did. We held tightly onto each other for a long time, wanting to never let go.

"Please tell me you will spend the day with me tomorrow," he asked.

Because I had to work, that was impossible but I promised I would ask Mother to watch Trip in the evening on Saturday. Then we could be with him during the day. Also, we two could go out together in the evening. He agreed. He asked if he could take Trip and me out to eat the following evening, after I got out of work.

"Not having to cook was just what the doctor ordered," I said. "We'd love to go somewhere."

He asked where I would like to go. I told him to surprise me. It was very difficult for me to sleep that night. Those terrible words he spoke were like a tape loop that kept repeating, again and again. I simply couldn't get those words out of my mind.

After I did manage to fall asleep, Trip had a bad dream. Quickly, I went into his bedroom to comfort him. As I took that beautiful little boy into my arms the full force of fear for my loved ones struck me. Tears welled up in my eyes. I wondered what I would do if my own son were going off to war. How would I function in that situation? Trip soon was sound asleep in my arms.

I laid my boy back into his bed and whispered to God, "Please, never take my son into war, please."

Once back in bed, I finally fell into a deep sleep. I woke up in the same position the following morning.

The next day, as I was making Trip and myself ready to go out for dinner, I thought long and hard about my foolish mistake in marrying Wade. But it was too late to erase all that happened during those past few years. And of course, I would never want to change having my handsome son. I never knew how a mother's love would feel in my heart until Trip. Now that he was with me, I was overwhelmed with the power of the love and devotion I felt for my child.

Ajax took us to a special restaurant that was made to entertain children with rides and games.

"I thought we could go here first and let Trip play, then go to another restaurant to eat," he said. "How does that sound?" he asked.

"Perfect," I replied.

So began our evening and what an evening it became. I laughed so hard at the look on Trip's face when he saw all the little rides that were just his size. His eyes were so big and bright-looking naturally but when he saw all those little cars and trucks he could ride, they brightened even more and he squealed with delight. This proved to be a very good idea. It gave Trip something to with all his excess energy, causing him to become quite mellow by the time we went into the restaurant. On the whole, that evening was superb.

When we returned home, Trip was ready to sleep. Being absolutely exhausted, I wanted to sleep, myself. Once I sat down on the couch next to Ajax, who was so considerate he even thought of taking Trip somewhere he would enjoy, I could hardly keep my eyes open. I suggested making us some coffee, but I really didn't have a desire for a cup, I only wanted to close my eyes.

"No, don't make coffee," he decided, "just close your eyes and let me hold you. Go to sleep, I'm not going anywhere."

That was all I needed to hear. I was sound asleep in his lap, pronto. With us both asleep, the hours flew past. We ended up sleeping on the couch until morning. I woke up right before Trip and started a pot of coffee. While brushing my teeth, Trip decided to go to the living room and climb on top of Ajax to roughhouse. My heart melted. Once we were all awake, going out to breakfast became an option that I quickly took. The day went well. We didn't return until late afternoon around four p.m.

Ajax went home to shower. I took care of feeding Trip and getting him ready for a night with Mother. I was concerned when I took him over there. I feared I would get the third degree, especially since Ajax stayed all night.

To my surprise, she only said, "Be careful. You don't need another child."

I laughed and I reassured her that you must have sex to get pregnant and it has been a very long time since I've had sex. Her comment almost made me angry but I let it go. I just considered the source.

I left as soon as Trip started playing with the button on Grandpa's bed. It worked out well. He didn't see me leave so he didn't cry to go with me.

As I entered my front door, I drank in the wonderful sense of home I felt in this little house, even more intensely. Taking a long bath was so relaxing. Bubble baths were almost a thing of the past. With all I had to do, it became the last thing on my mind. There's nothing like a scented bubble bath. It felt so good that I hated to get out. I relaxed a few more minutes. The phone rang as I got out of the tub. I paused before I answered it. Getting a second breath, I picked up the phone. It was Ajax.

"Let's go to dinner and then dancing, how does that sound?" he said.

"Great, I'll put my dancing shoes on," I said, with a laugh. "Okay, I'll see you in a half an hour," was all I heard. Then the phone went dead.

"That was strange," I thought. But I didn't have much time to think. I only had a few minutes to get ready.

Hmmm, I thought. *He sure hung up fast.*

Everything went perfectly that evening. I was ready on time. My hair and my sparse eye makeup all went perfectly.

I closed my eyes for a second to take in the moment. *I'm really getting ready to go out to dinner and dancing with the man of my life. Gosh I can hardly wait for him to get here.*

Just as my thoughts completed, he rang the door bell. There he was, with his magnificent aqua blue eyes and pearly white smile. As he walked in, his cologne filled the air. It was the same cologne that he used to wear when we were younger. He smelled so good and so familiar that all I wanted was to eat him up. Memories, wonderful memories, surrounded me as I reached my arms out to give him the biggest, tightest hug.

He looked at me and smiled broadly as he asked, "What was *that* for?"

"For you", I said. "Just… for you."

We left right after he arrived. In the car, I noticed from his demeanor that something was amiss. Asking if something was wrong opened up Pandora's box. He told me how his mother had been acting the last couple days. Concerned that she might be upset that he was spending a lot of time with me, I asked him what the arguing was about.

"I'm not sure, but I know I don't need to review all that, right now," he answered.

What followed surprised me. He said, "It's bad enough going to Vietnam knowing I might not return. To be in constant turmoil is more than I can take."

Trying to come to her defense was difficult for me. I thought that if somehow it would make things easier on him, I could swallow my pride and stick up for her.

So I said, "I'm not sure just how I would act if my son was going off to war. Maybe she can't handle the emotions that go with that."

"No. it's not that. She's been hitting the beer a lot lately. She's almost impossible to deal with when she drinks. I can't take her anymore and I won't. I think I'll check into a hotel tomorrow for the rest of my leave."

Astonished by his remarks, I was at a loss for words.

When I looked at him, all I could say was "Please don't do anything impulsive that you will regret later. Let's try to forget the rest of the world exists and please only ourselves tonight. Okay?"

He gave me the biggest smile and said, "Okay."

When he asked where I would like to go for dinner, I recalled the wonderful glass restaurant where we had dinner the first night he came home, but my answer was, "Wherever you would like to go."

We were going dancing in another direction so we decided on a place that was right on the water. I really didn't care as long as we had a nice evening. We were seated beside a window so we could look out at the water. I felt queasy when I looked at him, knowing he was currently upset with his home situation.

How unfair and selfish, I thought.

Although his mother was not my favorite person, I pitied her for all the emotion she was processing but I quickly brought my thoughts back to our night together. I was determined not to allow anyone to ruin the few days we had left.

"This restaurant is really cool," I remarked, as I sat looking out the window. "You definitely are spoiling me," I added.

Our wine appeared and once again, we toasted each other and sipped. I tried to act casually but he was in deep thought and needed to make up his mind what he was going to do. He came back to reality quickly and picked up his glass again to make another toast. This time, it was a serious thought that choked me up.

"Here's to me coming home safe and to you being at the airport with open arms," he said, as he clinked my glass.

I fought back some tears but replied, "To you coming home safe."

As we took a second sip of wine, our salads came out. I felt relieved that his thoughts were distracted. I started to eat my salad. Shortly after that, they brought our main course. Everything was perfect. The atmosphere at our table became jovial as we finished our meal. I looked out the window and noticed the water looked darker. By then the sun had set.

I could hardly wait for the dancing. I welcomed the music as we arrived on the scene. It wasn't far from the restaurant where we had just eaten but the route we took made it seem farther. There was a line of people waiting outside to be admitted. I was glad it only took a few minutes for us to get in.

This was one of my favorite places to dance. How well I remembered trying to sneak in there, back in high school. Now, I could come in the front door instead of trying to crawl in a window. I was way too full to get a drink but went to the bar with Ajax. The music was moving my feet as my body swayed with the beat. Ajax looked at me enjoying the music and just laughed.

"What?" I said. "I love to dance. I will still be dancing when I'm ninety."

He leaned over and kissed my cheek to agree with me. His eyes looked sad. I wasn't sure how to make him forget all the nonsense at home, to only live in the moment. The band was excellent. The dance floor was packed as the band announced they were going to slow it down a bit for the lovers. Just as Ajax took my hand to lead me out onto the dance floor, the band started to play "Georgia on My Mind."

How appropriate, I thought, *there couldn't be a better song to play.*

As he took me into his arms, my heart felt heavy. I felt weepy but so much at home in his arms, as if that was where I belonged. We danced as we held each other tightly. I remembered the school dances we went to at both schools, the few that fell on college weekends, and now here we were, dancing what could actually become our last dance.

As the song ended, the band's front man announced, "How about one more for road?" The crowd cheered as they continued to play another slow song. I didn't want the song to end. That weepy sentiment I had going on simply wouldn't leave me. I put on a brave front as the song ended, knowing darn well that he was feeling every emotion I was, and possibly more.

That evening, many people came to us to wish Ajax luck with his trip overseas. By this date, we had already lost some of our friends to that war and the government was nowhere near ending it. It seemed like our local newspaper showed a picture of a serviceman who had lost his life, each day. As I looked at these pictures, I always thought about how that man had a mother and father who loved them. I put myself in the parent's place, thinking how difficult it would be to let them go, yet we had no choice in this. It broke my heart to think of so many fallen soldiers.

We really had a wonderful time that night. I sure was happy that Mother was keeping Trip all night since I knew I would be home late. This was the first I had asked Mother to watch Trip so many times within one week. Although I had never asked her to watch him while I went out before, she seemed to understand, and she was willing to help me.

My Grandma had told me that Mother married at seventeen and that her husband was killed in the war. Grandma said he was such a good man; that he loved Mother deeply. He tragically died right after receiving a typical "Dear John" letter from Mother, who never talked about him; nor did she ever so much as acknowledge him, even in later years.

Maybe that's why she was so willing to help me with Trip during Ajax's leave. She never discussed it with me but I assume Grandma told the truth. Whatever the reason, I greatly appreciated her watching him. I had never left him with a hired babysitter. Perhaps I was an over-protective mother. Whatever the reason, I hadn't left him with anyone else before.

Once back home, I started making some coffee. I was certain he would not want to leave. He eagerly accepted the coffee, with his ice cube floating on top. I chuckled. I told him that I loved to watch him put ice in his coffee so he can sip it sooner. He laughed, and said, "I'm probably the only man you will ever see doing this, but it works."

We laughed. I felt tired so I suggested we sit on the couch with our coffee, which he readily agreed to. When his cup was empty, he got up and poured himself another cup. He asked me if I would like more.

"No thank you, I've had enough," I said from the couch, "but you have all you want." Just as I said that, I heard the ice clink against the side of the cup as he sipped. When he came back into the living room he had the biggest grin on his face, sort of like a little boy who just got away with something he shouldn't do. I was slowly fading. I had been up really early that morning. I laid my head down and that was all she wrote. I woke up about three hours later. He was lying beside me on the couch. It felt so good to feel the warmth of his body next to mine, so I just closed my eyes.

That morning, he left about seven-thirty. I went next door to get my son. Mother always had a pot of coffee going. Though this morning seemed no different, she wanted to talk.

What I thought was: *There she goes again, with her dirty mind, thinking everyone is evil, and I have not slept with Ajax, I have barely even kissed him.*

What I actually said, in a tone that left "The Ice Queen" stunned, was this: "I have not done anything wrong, at least not yet, but I am thinking about it, so just stop, and don't say another thing, please."

Then I sat and drank my coffee.

"Just be careful. I know how much you love him," is all she said.

At about eleven a.m., I was again home with Trip and washing the laundry when the phone rang.

It was Ajax. "Hello Pretty Woman," he said.

"My gosh, where are you?" I said.

"Remember, last night I told you I couldn't take it anymore? That I was going to get a room for the rest of my leave?"

"Yes."

"Well, when I woke up this morning, she started in, so I left," he said, in a matter-of-fact tone.

"Okay... are you sure about this?" I asked?

"Yes, just trust me, I cannot take another day with her."

"Well, I'm home for the day. Come on over and I'll make you lunch, but no coffee, I'm coffee'd out" I said, with a giggle.

He responded happily, "Okay, soon as I shower, I'll come." When I hung up I felt stunned. I couldn't believe his mother drove him to such a point. Not long after hanging up, Laura called me. She asked if I knew where her brother was.

I told her "No, but I will be seeing him soon and will tell him to call you then."

"Thank you Desiree, I knew you would know what is going on," she added.

"Laura, he's upset with your mother's drinking and yelling, please understand, this has nothing to do with me."

"I know Desiree, thanks for telling him to call me. I know it isn't you."

Then we only talked for a few minutes more.

Gosh what a mess, I thought, *this is all so sad.* Then my thoughts shifted to, *How dare she act out at a time like this? What in the world is she thinking?*

My feelings of pity for her, concerning her son going off to war, left me in that moment. All I could think of was Ajax and what he was feeling. I knew it wasn't me that caused the problem. I was positive he didn't let them know he was seeing me all that often. That was important, because I would hate to think the rift was my fault.

Trip broke my train of thought by wanting me to work a puzzle with him. As I sat on the floor helping him put the pieces together, I stared at him, thinking and praying that this would never happen to Trip and me. I would just die if my son was facing war and I drove him out of my home because of my actions. I knew we can't choose who our children love but we can choose to not drive them out of the house into a hotel room.

While I was sitting on the floor the door bell rang multiple times in rapid succession.

Wow, I thought, *someone wants in quickly.*

Ha! As if I didn't know who it was.

"I'm coming," I yelled from the floor.

Trip went running to the door with excitement. I wondered if he thought it was his father, but when I opened the door, his excitement continued. He went running to the puzzles on the floor. In his baby gibberish, mixed with half-understandable language, he convinced Ajax to sit on the floor with him to work on his puzzles.

Ajax called his sister Laura. I took Trip for a walk so he could talk in private. I didn't want to be any part of that mess, not even hearing what was going on. I had my own troubles. I had a hard enough time coping with what was on my own plate. I returned about twenty minutes later and didn't ask questions.

Ajax said "I'm not going back. I'm simply not going back."

I tried to convince him, that for the sake of his family, he should go back. But that notion fell on deaf ears. I decided to leave it alone.

It was Saturday. I had many things to do. Ajax offered his "special chauffeur service." I took him up on it. The three of us had a wonderful day. I got all my running around done far more quickly than I would have, normally. After one of the stops, I slid back into the car laughing as I told him how I liked being spoiled.

I got the same response as before, when he said, "This is only the beginning of how I'm going to spoil you."

I looked at him and hoped it would come true, that he would come home safe and sound, and he would be with me to do just that.

After dinner, we sat on the couch with coffee and talked while Trip played with his toys. Ajax was leaving in only a few days. I already knew what it would be like to feel that void. The first few months, I felt utterly alone after I left Wade. It never really got better. I simply learned to accept it.

I didn't know how I could ever accept being comfortable in my own home while Ajax was lying on the ground somewhere, listening to bullets whiz over his head. My eyes welled with tears as I wondered how I would say goodbye. I tried to hide my tears but they rolled down my cheeks. He caught me trying to discreetly wipe them away. He wanted to know why I was crying. By then, I was crying hard. I leaned into his chest for comfort.

"How am I going to say goodbye to you, now that I have you here with me? Where will I get the strength?" I asked, between my sobs. "I prayed so hard for you to come back and now you are here and in a few days, you have to leave for a year. It just isn't fair!"

I forced a smile as I tried to lighten the moment.

I said, "Let's run away to Canada or somewhere the government can't take you."

He smiled and answered "Wish we would have thought of that when I first came home."

Then he said, with a laugh, "I can just see us going to the Canadian border and telling them, 'We're back together now. So I can't go to Vietnam. Let us stay here until the war is over.'"

We both laughed, but deep down inside I think we both wished it could be true.

With Trip asleep, I sat next to Ajax on the couch. I snuggled up next to him. He lifted my face up with his hand so he could kiss me. This time, I wanted those kisses as desperately as he did. As we continued to kiss, he whispered to me "I want you so much! I want to make love to you."

In my heart, I wanted the same but I knew, as long as Trip was around, I would never take the chance he might wake up and walk in on us. "I can't, I'm sorry, but as badly as I want you too, I won't let it happen with Trip here."

"Then take off work tomorrow and come to my room. No one will know," he said softly.

I reassured him that I would try and that I would call him if I could pull it off. We kept talking, holding on to each other for the rest of the night, knowing we had come full circle, that we had discovered what we both always believed was indeed true, that the undying love we felt for each other was real.

Going out the door, Ajax reminded me that he would be waiting for my call the next morning. When morning came, I got ready for work as usual, but this morning was different. I knew darn well that somehow, some way, I would go to a hotel room to make love to the man who I had always loved. I believed if I went to work and acted sick, they would tell me to go home, so that was how I handled it. By nine thirty, my boss had told me to go home and get better.

Oh my gosh, I did it, I thought.

Leaving, I couldn't wait to get to a pay phone to make the call.

"I did it!" I shouted into the phone when Ajax answered.

"For real?" he said.

"Yep, I'll be there in a few minutes. See you soon."

It seemed like forever going just a few miles to him. Once there, I had butterflies in my stomach. I started second-guessing my decision. But as soon as he opened the door, all my doubts and fears vanished. I could not wait to make love. That idea and the sensations of our embrace filled my whole being.

Music softly played on the radio. Some coffee and rolls he had ordered were waiting for us to devour yet the only thing I wanted to devour was him. Somehow, I felt no shame or remorse. I never gave anything or anyone a second thought. This was something I had ached for so long, nothing would be allowed to ruin it.

We leaned back on the bed, slowly drank our coffee, and I felt only joy in my heart. Here I was, finally alone with the man who I have loved all my life. We reached a point where the rest of the world did not exist. It was only him and me, alone in this room together, ready to express our love for each other. I put my cup down on the night stand. I put my head on his bare chest and listened to his heart. The two of us lying side by side, body to body, was the most wonderful feeling I had ever experienced. As he lifted my face with his hand, I kissed his lips. As we made love softly, I sighed into the feeling of being one with him. He was gentle and so loving that I melted into his body. I looked up at him. I saw tears in his eyes.

He quietly told me that he had never thought we might never make love; that now, he felt his heart could burst with love. We gazed into each others' eyes.

He ever so softly said, "I have never stopped loving you and I never will."

"Shh," I whispered, "don't talk. Let's enjoy this feeling."

Becoming as one, we floated together among the stars.

Afterwards, we laid in each other's arms quietly, neither of us wanting to move, both of us ecstatic, fulfilled even deeper than our desire had anticipated. What we both had thought would never be, finally happened.

"I will remember this moment for the rest of my life." I whispered, in nearly inaudible tones, "I love you Ajax, I never stopped loving you, either. I secretly prayed that somehow our paths would cross and we would be together again."

The feeling of his body next to mine was intoxicating. As he kissed me passionately, my body throbbed with anticipation of him inside me once again…

That evening, I could think of nothing besides that wonderful day. That day will be with me for my lifetime. My phone rang at eight thirty.

It felt like I jumped a foot in the air. I thought for sure it was Ajax, but to my surprise it was Wade.

I acted abruptly, to the point when I told him he should just leave us alone.

I said to him: "You say you're going to come, then you either don't show or you call with some lame excuse for why you won't be here. Listen, I'm done with altering my life for you to have a visit only to see you not care enough to come over."

Then I hung up the phone. My attitude had surprised him. He seemed taken aback.

My mind was whirling with so many thoughts. I was at my wits' end. I needed to use my head so that Trip would not suffer because of all this. Wade should have some responsibility toward this child. What had happened left me feeling sick inside.

I tried to calm myself but try as I might it wasn't working. I even tried to say a prayer that God would guide me but I couldn't even finish the prayer without my mind wandering into another, happier, warmer place. Then I thought maybe all this was supposed to happen because somehow, Ajax and I were supposed to have a life together.

I felt a restless anger set in. I thought of the psychic, her words, and the fear she induced in me. I was also angry with myself for even believing her for one minute.

I shouldn't blame her, I thought, *I was the stupid one, for believing her. No matter who was to blame, I was young and naive to even listen to that garbage.*

I vowed that evening that I would never listen to a psychic again as long as I lived. Nor would I ever wait and wait again for Wade to visit his son, only to have him not show up.

There was a quiet knock at the front door. My heart skipped a beat. I couldn't imagine who it could be at that hour. I went to the door and asked who it was without opening it.

"It's me," I heard Ajax say. I opened up the door. I felt surprised that he came without calling. He apologized for coming unannounced but he was visibly upset.

I grabbed his arm and pulled him in and said "Come on in, Orphan. Would you like a drink?"

He wanted a cup of coffee, so coffee it was. He talked and talked about how he tried to go home, to settle matters but there was no reasoning with his mother and all his efforts went nowhere.

"So... back to the hotel I go," he said, then he laughed. Oh, the thought of another day in his arms was awe-inspiring but I wanted to hear what he had to say first.

When he was finished, I shrugged my shoulders in a coy gesture and said "I'll be there a few minutes after nine."

His face lit up like a country church on Christmas. He stood up at the table, came over to my chair and lifted me up and into his arms.

"I adore you Desiree, I absolutely adore you," he vowed.

His piercing aqua eyes stared at me for a second. Then he kissed me. I wanted to linger in his arms forever.

"How will I let you get on that plane?" I whispered. "My heart will break. I wish I could go with you."

"You *are* going with me, because I will have you tucked into my heart for safekeeping. I'm not going to live another day without you. You are my everything. I love you so much."

He feverishly kissed me and then kissed me again.

Then, he repeated, "Not one more day without you. You're mine."

The next morning, I knocked on his door, as I had said I would.

"I hoped you were telling me the truth about you coming this morning," he said, with a broad smile.

He had ordered room service again. This time, he ordered a full breakfast for us. He told me he wanted to make sure I ate a good breakfast so that I would have enough energy to spend the day with him.

"Silly man," I thought, "being with you is pure pleasure and so natural."

We spent the day together, knowing our days were limited. Soon, he would be gone. I didn't know how I would get through those final days but I kept praying for the strength I would need and the ability to put my emotions aside to make those precious few days happy for him.

I went home at the same time I would have arrived home from work, so I would not have to explain where I had been. I didn't need any negative talk. I knew that was exactly what I would get. I only wanted to be happy, not to answer questions about anything. This was all hard for me to grasp. Also, it was hard to face him leaving and to accept that I would not see him for almost a year. I was a total, emotional wreck. All this was causing my head to spin. The last thing I needed was a lecture from someone who only sees a cup half empty and never half full.

I intended to make dinner for the three of us that evening. I stopped at a store to pick up the few things we needed. We had been eating out a lot, so I thought he would enjoy a good home-cooked meal. Trip would love it, I was certain, because he seemed to gravitate to Ajax. I was not bragging to say that I'm a good cook. Who wouldn't be a good cook with all the experience I had? I had started cooking simple dinners when I was seven years old. By the time I was nine or ten, I was expected to make dinner every day.

That is one issue I can easily forgive Mother for, because I learned young there's nothing that I can't cook. I used to make dinner for Ajax when we were in high school. Watching his face as he took his first bite was so rewarding to me.

Standing in my little kitchen, I thought, *We were so close and so in love. I still can't believe he's back in my life... Our lives have taken such a turn. I feel so eager and enthusiastic about us, yet so scared... During this whole military leave, I have tried to walk in his shoes, to feel what he is feeling, yet it's almost impossible... I'm not the one leaving everyone I know behind, moving into an unknown future...*

The dinner and evening went well. At one point, Trip took a flying leap across the couch and landed in Ajaxs lap. He giggled so sweetly that I couldn't help but laugh. Then the house erupted with boyish play. Trip took off running with Ajax behind. At that moment, my heart sang. I had seen Ajax play with his nieces and nephews but this was my own son he was playing with now.

I felt so happy to see Trip enjoying himself that much. It didn't surprise me; it thrilled me. This child was my whole world. The love of my life was playing with Trip as if he was his own child. If there had ever been any doubts in my mind, they were erased in those few minutes.

Trip jumped into Ajaxs lap and wrapped his little arms around his neck. Then, just as quickly, he looked into Ajax's face. He said "kiss" and kissed Ajax. Then Ajax surprised me. As he kissed Trip, he looked back at me and said, "See? He's already my son."

Trying to laugh didn't seem to work for me because, even though I wished Trip were Ajax's son, he really wasn't.

After Trip went to sleep, the house got quiet and mellow. With the radio playing softly, I sat down for a relaxing evening. We talked and talked

Suddenly, "Georgia On My Mind" played on the radio. Ajax stood up and took my hand. He guided me into his arms and danced with me.

He looked into my eyes and said, "Every time you hear this song, just close your eyes, and feel me holding you, because I will be dancing with you."

My heart was aching. My eyes filled with tears knowing we had such a short time left to be together.

I looked back into his eyes and said "It's a deal, as long as you promise me you will be careful and that you will come home to me."

He didn't answer me in words. He only pulled me closer and continued to dance. It was difficult to say goodnight. I felt like my heart was breaking. Once in bed, I prayed more sincerely than I had ever prayed before. Soon, sleep overcame me.

Going to work was harder than I expected. I found it difficult to concentrate. My boss asked me what was wrong. He could tell I was a mess. I tried to explain without going into detail but that led into confusion, with me in tears. He was the best guy to work for. He understood because his son was serving in the military.

When it was time for lunch, he came back and pulled me aside. My heart was beating fast. I was afraid he had figured out the real reason I didn't come into work on those two days. To my surprise, he asked me when Ajax was leaving. When I told him, he turned his body so nobody else could hear what he was saying.

"Desiree," he said, "you are the best secretary I've ever had. I know what it's like to have only a few days with a loved one. Go ahead and take those days off, with pay. Spend them with this fella who means so much to you."

I was stunned. I must have shown it because he continued, "I mean it, with pay. Just come back on Monday, okay?"

I wanted to hug him but didn't. I squeezed his hand as I thanked him, over and over.

"Now go," he said. "I'll see you on Monday. And this is between you and me. No one here needs to know about this."

Though I couldn't believe my ears, I did leave quickly. I went to the first pay phone I saw, to call Ajax and tell him the good news. He was astonished, as I had been, but now I felt elation.

"Can you come over now" he asked?

"I'm on my way," I said. And hung up the phone.

Going down the hall to Ajax's room gave me a minute to collect myself and realize what my boss had just given us: more precious time together.

What a great guy, I thought.

I had barely knocked on Ajax's door when it swung open. There stood my man, with his gorgeous aqua blue eyes, smiling like his face would split.

"Welcome, My Love," he said.

"Thank you," I said.

Then he stepped through the door into the hall. He picked me up and carried me into his room. "I've always wanted to carry you across the threshold. Now I can thank your boss for making it happen," he said.

He continued to hold me in his arms. He kissed me.

"I love you, Pretty Woman," he said. Then he growled at me.

"Are you going to put me down?" I asked.

He laughed, then shook his head as he said "Never!"

We talked and talked, as usual. We always had a great ability to communicate. We could talk about anything and never get upset with each other. I used to think it wasn't normal because my girlfriends would tell me how they couldn't bring up so many things with their mates. We could discuss everything and we did. I knew it was a blessing to have that much trust and such secure feelings between us.

Until then, we hadn't discussed my situation concerning Wade. But that day, Ajax was asking questions. Word had gotten out around town that Wade never wanted his child and that he had been violent with me, forcing me to call the police. I reassured Ajax there was no sense in going over what had happened. It was in the past and I was with him, thereafter.

The respect Ajax had for me showed in everything he said and did. His actions left no doubt. The magnetism we felt for each other was beyond words. He knew how I felt about being intimate in my home while my son was asleep in the other room. Never once did he try to convince me, or to entice me, to do something I was clearly not comfortable with. This man was one-in-a-million, as far as I was concerned. I thought I was so lucky that I was the one he loved.

While saying "Good night" that evening, I felt sick in the pit of my stomach. I knew we only had two more evenings to spend together before he would leave. I felt selfish. I wanted him to spend that time with me but I knew his family also wanted to visit with him. I said nothing as he left because I didn't want to pressure him to spend all his time with me. It felt so hard to let go. I wanted to cry when I thought of going to the airport to say goodbye in a few days.

As he was leaving, he stepped back inside. He asked me to go with him the next day to see his sisters. I wanted to do whatever made him happy but felt hesitant about this.

"Please, go with me. It will be alright," he said.

I gave in. I asked what time I should be ready.

"In half an hour," he said, with a laugh. "I don't want to be without you any longer than that."

I laughed, too, and assured him that I was positive his sisters loved him very much but visitors at three thirty in the morning would really be a little too much. We both laughed then. He told me he would call me in the morning.

I looked over at my yellow roses. They were wilting but to me, they were still beautiful.

It will be a long time before I get more roses, I thought; *Vietnam is too far away for ordering flowers.*

I checked on Trip before going to bed. He looked so beautiful and he was sleeping so peacefully. When I sat on his bed, just looking at him, a thousand thoughts went through my mind. I wanted only the best life for him but somehow, it wasn't working out as I had imagined. The positive thing in our whole mess was my undying devotion to my son. I provided him with the best possible life I could create. Even though his father never wanted him, I made the decision to keep him because *I wanted him.*

He stirred, and I watched him with such pride.

Falling asleep was difficult for me that night. I laid in bed and wondered, *What am I going to do? Our last night is approaching so fast.*

Morning came too soon. I wasn't ready to get up but I knew for sure that I should get out of bed before Trip. He could get into trouble in a minute. When Trip was awake, there was no time for just a few more minutes of sleep. So I got out of bed to face another day.

Around ten a.m., the phone rang.

I answered it with a cheery "Good morning."

"Wow aren't we happy this morning," Ajax said.

"I'm happy because I'm talking to the man I truly love and we've had a wonderful time on his furlough."

"Well, that's music to my ears," he said.

We went on to discuss the time when he would pick us up, me and Trip. I didn't tell him that I was going to ask Mother to watch Trip, because I wasn't sure if she would. I simply said, "I'll be ready."

After I hung up, I went next door to see what Mother thought about me leaving Trip with her. I didn't think it was a good idea to take him along, although I knew he would behave.

To my surprise, she agreed with me. She said, "just bring him here. You know Grandpa loves that little boy. He lights up when he see Trip."

I thanked her emphatically and told her I would bring him over when ready. But Trip didn't want to stay home. He started to cry, so there went my plans. I sat down to have a cup of tea and to chat a few minutes with Mother. When I noticed he was pushing buttons on the hospital bed, I figured he would be happy to stay, and he was.

Ajax and I went from one sister's house to the other. We really enjoyed the visits. When he was in the bathroom, one of his sisters made snide remarks about whether I went to visit her brother at the hotel. I tried ignoring her intrusions, at first, but I responded to her second remark.

I fired back, with "Whether or not I went to his room is not at issue. The concern should be that your brother was forced to go to a hotel because of conditions at home." Then I sternly said, "Please don't ruin his visit, any more than it has already been ruined, by letting him hear you talk to me like that. Talk to the person who caused him to go to the hotel in the first place."

We saw he was coming back into the room, so his sister didn't say anything more. I felt angry that she tried to make me look bad. I wasn't going to stand for that. Of course, we waited to visit his sister Laura last because she was the sister he felt closest to.

I still didn't know what was going to happen with him going to the airport. I didn't ask because I wanted to do whatever made him happy. I waited for him to bring it up. We had only a few nights left. I wanted to make the most of them. Walking in his shoes was next to impossible for me. I'm not good with goodbyes. I don't know how I would react, in his position.

With the family visits finished, we had some time to do whatever we wanted. Of course, when he asked me, I turned it over to him. I replied "Whatever puts a smile on your face is what I want to do. So you tell me."

"Tomorrow, and tomorrow evening, I would like to spend with both you and Trip. But would it be okay if we spent this evening alone together?" he asked.

I looked into his unbelievably beautiful eyes and smiled, as I said, "Absolutely. But I need to go home first and make sure it's alright with Mother."

Then we headed back to my house. I suggested he come in with me. Mother always liked Ajax. She was worried about him going off to war. She invited us to stay for dinner but Ajax said that he would like to take me somewhere special since we were going to spend tomorrow together with Trip. She was happy with that and offered us some coffee. I was delighted that he accepted and sat down with a look of feeling right at home on his face.

We talked for over an hour and then he asked Mother, "If it's okay with you, I would like to take Desiree out for a wonderful dinner." She laughed at the way he so innocently asked permission. She answered, "Sure. Enjoy. I'll feed Trip, so you just go ahead."

Wow, I thought, *she has really been nice these past few weeks.* I stood up and lifted my son. I kissed him all over his face. He giggled so sweetly. As I stood there with him in my arms, I felt like such a proud mama. I loved that child so much. He didn't even ask to come with us. He was perfectly happy when we left him there.

As we left, Ajax gave Mother a hug. He thanked her for understanding.

"You're welcome," she said, "I'll see you when you return."

In the car, I sat silently, not knowing what to say. Tears filled my eyes as I looked at him.

I asked, "How will I say goodbye, after the wonderful time we've had?"

He looked at me with love and whispered, "Let's not talk about that now. I just want to have a wonderful dinner with a bottle of good champagne."

Gosh, I thought to myself, as I dried my tears, *I'm such a cry baby.*

"Let's stop and get a glass of wine first, okay?" he asked. We went to the pleasant lounge in the hotel where he was staying. After a few minutes, he excused himself to go to the men's room. When he returned, he said he had a surprise for me. I requested that we go to a restaurant where it would be quiet so we could enjoy our evening and not be hearing a lot of loud talking.

A smile spread across his face as if he had just won a door prize. That aroused my curiosity but when I asked him what the surprise was, he said that it wouldn't be a surprise if he told me. I left it alone, figuring he was tickled with whatever it was and that I could wait to find out. The glass of wine went down easily. Though we didn't order another round, the waiter came to the table with an additional glass of wine for each of us.

I must have looked surprised because the waiter followed up with, "Compliments of the house. Please enjoy this one on us."

The first round had already relaxed me. I was happy to reach for the second one. We stayed at the lounge for another forty-five minutes.

Then he asked, "Ready for dinner?"

I smiled and said, "Yes."

I lightly kissed his cheek. He wanted to go to his room to get some money. So we took the elevator. Before entering the room, he put his arms around me and kissed me. I kissed him back and giggled. Nothing he could have said to me would have prepared me for what I was about to experience.

He put the key in the door and opened it slowly. Total shock is the only way to describe how I felt when I saw how the hotel staff had transformed his room into an elegant paradise, leaving no detail unattended. They embellished the entire room, strewing yellow rose petals on the floor, in a path leading to the bed, which was blanketed with those beautifully-scented petals. A glow from candles and the scent of roses greeted us at the doorway with such intensity that it took my breath away. I was so overcome that I could not speak.

Ajax took my hand. He led me into this spectacular room. There were so many candles, all positioned to give the room a golden glow. I stepped inside slowly. I needed some time to take it in. I had never so much as imagined anything like this, much less experienced it. The glow made me feel like I had walked into a castle where I was the princess. Beside a beautifully decorated table sat an ice bucket where a bottle of champagne was chilling. A single yellow rose was placed across the middle of my plate.

Slowly turning, I took in all the beauty this room had been transformed with. I could not find words to fully express my feelings about what he had done for me. This was breathtaking, as beautiful as a scene from the movies.

He broke the silence by saying "I wanted something special that you will remember for years to come."

Still dumbfounded, I looked into his eyes and repeated, "*You*, Ajax. It's you who is so special."

I reached out and hugged him. Sweet joy filled my heart as I held him. We paused, hugging, neither of us wanting to let go. When we eventually parted, he went behind my chair and pulled it out for me to sit. With our eyes fixed on each other's, I walked to the chair and sat.

"Wow, what a gentleman," I said, as he pushed my chair in.

The cork in the champagne bottle popped with sudden force. I flinched in my chair. As he poured the champagne, I noticed the glasses were beautifully etched, making the bubbly champagne appear even more sparkly. Everything was tastefully done. With each glance around the room, there was something new to notice.

He sat across from me. With the champagne poured, he lifted his glass to make a toast. "To the most beautiful woman in the world...

Thank you for making this furlough as wonderful as it has been. I love you, Pretty Woman… I really do."

We clinked our glasses together and took a sip. As I took another sip, I wondered, *Why did it surprise me that the champagne tasted so good?*

Looking around again, I felt astonished by the effort that went into the room's transformation. It truly was gorgeous. I couldn't believe he had done all this only for us.

He called down to the kitchen to tell them we were ready for appetizers. Within a few minutes, there was a soft knock at the door. The waiter who brought our appetizers was dressed in a butler's uniform. That added to the elegance of our meal. Ajax asked him to give us about half an hour before bringing our salad. He acknowledged the request and quietly left. I took another sip of the champagne before starting my shrimp cocktail.

I watched Ajax eat his shrimp. My heart ached at the thought of him crouching in some foxhole in Vietnam, fighting for my freedom, while I was home, safe and comfortable. But I said nothing about what I was thinking. I smiled and continued leisurely enjoyment of our food. As requested, our salad arrived right on time. The waiter quietly asked when we would like our main course.

"Give us a little longer, this time," Ajax requested.

"Yes, Sir," the waiter answered, and left once again.

The salad was creatively plated. Dressing was presented in a three-cup silver service so we had a choice. They included a loaf of freshly-baked, pumpernickel bread with honey butter. It was all delicious and perfectly served. We talked quietly as we ate, absorbing these wonders all evening.

After salad, Ajax turned on the radio. As soft music filled the room, I was taken with the whole experience.

I smiled again and told him, "This is the most beautiful day of my life, because of you and all the effort you put into this intimate, elegant dinner on my behalf. Ajax, I'll remember this evening for the rest of my life."

He picked up his champagne glass and reached across to mine. When I picked mine up, he tapped my glass with his, and repeated "I just want you to be happy. That's all that matters. I love you so much."

We heard the soft knock on our door. The waiter brought in our main course: steak and lobster. A beautiful butter warmer was placed before each of us.

I said "Ooo. Another candle!"

We both laughed. The meal was delicious. Everything, from the baked potato, to the green beans, the lobster and the steak… all was perfection. My steak was done exactly as I like it. We took our time eating and enjoying each other and the experience. I was so happy that everything turned out well because it pleased him so thoroughly.

When we were finished, he placed another call. Within a few minutes, the waiter was back in our room, clearing up the dishes.

When the table was cleared, the waiter brought in a beautifully decorated cake that said, "Happy Birthday, Desiree" on it. I looked at him, puzzled because my birthday wasn't until a few months later. Again, he lifted his champagne glass.

He said, "I know I won't be here for your birthday. I wanted to make sure we celebrated it together." I was stunned speechless, as I realized he had turned this wonderful night into something totally special *for me*, not for himself.

"Happy Birthday Desiree," he whispered. "Happiness."

I got up from my seat and went to kiss him and thank him for the fantastic, surprise evening. When I got close, he stood up and hugged me.

"What a sweetheart you are," I said.

We were both stuffed from the meal. We decided to wait for desert, if the cake could be called desert. He opened more champagne from the refrigerator, then topped off our glasses. We sat on the rose-petal blanket that was spread on the bed. The aroma filled the air. I leaned back on the head board. He kissed my hair and told me he adored me and wanted this night to be all about me and not about him leaving.

I lifted my glass and said, "Deal."

I understood where he was coming from, though I needed to digest how he transformed the room into something special, just for me.

We quietly discussed many things that he needed to tell me about, including how he felt about me moving on in my life if something should happen to him. I didn't want to hear anything sad like that, so I begged him to stop. He did, but not before he made it clear that his love was never-ending; that my happiness was paramount to him. Then he gently kissed my lips. Our hearts were aching as we tried to kiss away the pain of the coming separation.

Making love with Ajax felt fulfilling beyond what we thought we would ever experience. His gentleness left me trembling with desire and yet ultimately satisfied. Once again, we soared among the infinite stars together.

I hated to go home to an empty bed but I knew that was right. At home, I cried from the emptiness I already felt when I thought of him far away and in danger.

I faced the big day ahead. I tried to sleep in, during the morning hours, but sleep eluded me. Surrendering, I got up and looked out the window to see if Mother was up yet. I should have known she would be awake because the woman never slept. I dressed, brushed my teeth and went next door to have a cup of coffee with her.

As I told her about our evening, Trip woke up. He came and crawled into my lap. I kissed his sleepy head and realized what a comfort this little boy was to me. At that moment, I realized what Ajax's mother must have been going through. I couldn't imagine life without my son. As I walked in her shoes, I thought of the anger I would be feeling toward the government for sending my son to war. How scared she must have felt was probably beyond words.

I continued telling Mother about the night before and all the beauty that surrounded us. She was enthralled with the details and delighted about the birthday cake.

She had tears in her eyes as she said "It's a shame you two didn't marry. He would have made you one Hell of a good husband." She didn't say anything negative about Wade, but then, there was no need to.

I looked at Trip lying back in my lap and said "Can you imagine if Ajax was his father and Trip had blond hair and aqua blue eyes?"

Trip looked up at me with his huge, dark eyes and black, curly hair and said "Eyes." He blinked his eyes at me. He thought he was being cute. We both laughed.

I finished my coffee and told Mother that Ajax wanted to spend the day and evening with Trip and me. Also, that I would let her know what time I would be going to the airport the next day. She was okay with all that, as I left.

Not long after I got home, my phone rang. I thought it might be Wade since he had left a message for me the night before but it wasn't him. It was one of my girlfriends wanting to know how my evening went the night before. I dished her the whole story. She couldn't believe what I was telling her. When I got to the part about the birthday cake, her voice choked up as she told me how lucky I was that he is back into my life. As she said that, my mind drifted from Wade to Ajax.

She interrupted my thoughts: "What in the world are you going to do when he leaves?"

I talked with her for some time, then said I would call her after I returned from the airport the next day. I started to make some tea. The phone rang, and this time, I got excited when I heard the voice on the other end.

"Hello, Pretty Woman," he said, "how are you this morning?"

"I'm great", I said. I thanked him again for the wonderful early birthday surprise.

He said it was his pleasure; that it had been the most wonderful evening he ever experienced; then, "I want more of those evenings, many more."

Suddenly switching to considering the future, I went numb with fear for what it might bring. As I talked to him, I realized just how much I cared for him. It was frightening because I didn't know how I could handle what I was facing.

"When are you coming over?" I asked.

"In about two hours," he said, with a chuckle.

Oh, my gosh, I thought, *now what does he have up his sleeve?* We talked for a few more minutes and then we said our goodbyes.

About an hour later, my door bell rang. Trip went running to see who was there. To my complete surprise, it was a delivery of yellow roses. The driver handed me the flowers in a beautifully carved, crystal vase. I looked at him, speechless. There were two dozen roses in that vase. Baby's Breath was scattered throughout them. All was bound with the prettiest yellow bow. They looked like a picture for a florist's ad. Each rose was picture-perfect. I sighed as he handed the vase to me. Ajax had given me beautiful roses before but nothing like these.

Tucked inside the bouquet, I could see a card. I thanked the delivery man and closed the door. Placing the vase on the coffee table, I pulled out the card. Nothing could have prepared me for what I was about to read:

To My Precious Desiree,

Being with you these few weeks has given me inner peace. My only prayer has been answered. Holding you in my arms was all I prayed for. You are the love of my life. You have brought me happiness I never thought was possible. No matter what happens, I will always be with you, walking beside you, guiding you and loving you. This I Promise.

I love you with all my heart and I always will.

Ajax

With tears streaming down my face, I thought of the agony this man was experiencing, knowing he was leaving everything familiar and everyone he loved, the very next morning. I habitually tried to think positively, no matter what, but today I was faced with an unavoidable truth: that our collective future depended on someone in the jungle of Vietnam, fighting for his own life, and in that process, possibly taking the life of someone I love.

I looked at the roses on my coffee table. I couldn't believe how beautiful they were. So perfectly arranged in one of the most stunning vases I had seen. I went over to sniff them and said a prayer. Not a prayer for myself, or for my future, but a prayer that somehow, Ajax would always be guided in the right direction, to safety.

Such a small, special prayer, I thought.

Then I considered all the women who have prayed for the very same thing throughout the ages.

When Ajax arrived, Trip was in rare form, running throughout the house in a fit of jubilance. He was an active little guy with so much energy that it was hard to keep up with him. He had on the red cowboy hat he loved to wear and his toy cowboy guns. He thought that outfit was the cat's meow. He really thought he was special when he wore it.

Ajax played with him for a while, so I could make coffee. We quietly enjoyed it in the kitchen. I had made up my mind I was going to make this day and evening happy, not some sad memory.

No tears, I thought, *absolutely no tears.*

I had a superb dinner planned. I felt quite happy that we would eat at home, in my little house, just the three of us. I definitely wasn't into a crowd at a restaurant, where the waitress comes to interrupt you every five minutes, asking if there is anything else she can get for you. My nerves felt frazzled. Peace and quiet would be fine with me.

I had made Trip some hot chocolate so he could join us at the table but that was short-lived. He was soon playing, leaving us with our coffee and, of course, Ajax's ice cube. I looked at the ice floating in his cup and chuckled, knowing how much my renewed love had grown in these few weeks.

Mother called. She wanted me to ask what time we were going to the airport so she could take Trip.

As I asked Ajax, the only answer I got was, "We'll talk about that later."

I didn't push for an answer. Mother told me to just let her know. I agreed, and ended that conversation.

"I need to talk to you about tomorrow morning," Ajax had said, "but let's not talk about it right now, okay?"

"Absolutely," I responded.

"I've been thinking about it. I know what I want to do. I'd like to discuss it with you and see what you think, but again, let's talk later."

I smiled and leaned on the table. I whispered, "Your wish is my command." We both laughed. His ice cube shrank smaller and smaller. As I watched it disappear, my heart began to ache again. I wanted to hold him and never let go. Blinking, so as not to let any tears well up in my eyes, I decided I'd better get up and make myself busy.

"I'll take another cup of coffee if you have some," he said. "Certainly, I do," I said, as I reached for the pot.

Trip came running into the kitchen for another sip of his hot chocolate, which by now had cooled. He didn't care. He drank it down and went running into the other room again.

So cute, I thought. *Not a care in the world.*

I felt nervous, so I was doing this and that in the kitchen. Then I realized, *I just need to calm myself for Ajax's sake; to simply sit my butt down and be there for him.*

With those thoughts running in my mind, I took a deep breath and calmed myself down enough to enjoy the moments we had left together. We talked about so much that day, the many things that were on his mind that he wanted to share. I listened with ease, knowing he wanted to make sure I knew where he was at in his life and what he wanted for his future, which included me and my son. I felt proud that I was such an important force in his life. Although at times during that conversation it was difficult to stay focused, and to not cry, I mustered the strength to do what I should.

After we finished our coffee, I asked him if he would see Laura and the girls one more time before he left.

"I just don't want to leave you," he responded, "come with me."

This time, I stood firm. I said no, but that if he wanted to go, I would be there when he returned. Also, that I thought Laura would love it, even if only for a few minutes. He seemed to change his mind, thinking he might go after dinner for a few minutes. Seeing how torn he was, I suggested that he go after we ate. That way, I would then have time to clean up the kitchen while he was gone. He seemed to like that suggestion.

The dinner turned out wonderful. Nothing could have tasted better. Just the three of us sitting at that small table seemed so cozy and relaxed. I was happy it turned out well given that would be his last home-cooked meal until came home to the States. I didn't know how to match the flavor of that delicious birthday cake we enjoyed the night before. I had to think carefully about what I could make for desert. He used to love the custard pies my Grandma made for us. I decided on that.

Praying the whole way, I worried it would not come out right, but it was perfect. When he saw what I had made, he smiled broadly. Looking at him triggered my memory of a boyhood picture that his sister Laura had shared. It was a precious photo, taken at about two years old, sitting on the running board of an old car. He sat so still, looking at a bird on the ground in front of him. The expression on his face was so innocent. That bird didn't seem afraid of him.

The vulnerable innocence of a little boy looking at a wild bird reminded me of his innocence as a man trusting our government about that horrible Vietnam war. His family had no thoughts of him going to war when that picture was taken. There he was then, the young boy of yesteryear grown into a fine young man facing battlefields in steaming jungles, so far away from home. He and the rest of the trusting, fine young men, all willing to die for their country. And for what? To make the powerful invincible, and the rich even richer, while the mothers and families mourned their loss deeply and without end.

We decided to wait and have our desert when he returned from his visit. Though he kept procrastinating, I convinced him to go ahead so that he could visit with his folks for a while, then spend the rest of the evening with me. As he left, approaching the front door, he turned back and grabbed me with such emotion that I was startled.

"How, Oh God, *how* am I going to leave you, now that I have you back in my life?" he whispered urgently into my ear.

He was squeezing me so tightly that I could hardly breathe. All I kept thinking was, *Please, come home safe.*

As he left the driveway, Mother called me to see what had happened. She thought perhaps we had some harsh words, and that he then left. When I told her what was happening, she suggested that Trip should stay at her house. That way, we could spend some time together without distractions. I told her I thought Ajax wanted to spend the evening with Trip and me both but I greatly appreciated her offer. As we talked, the more I thought about her offer, the more I thought it made sense, given I would be delivering Trip into her care early in the morning, anyway.

Before I hung up, I suggested I could get Trip ready for bed and let him play with Ajax for a while, then call her to come over and take Trip. That way, she could say goodbye to Ajax and I wouldn't have to get Trip ready in the morning. This would be best since I still didn't know what time I was going to the airport. We agreed on this plan. I hung up then, so I could clean my kitchen and bathe Trip.

It seemed as if, in no time at all, Ajax returned. I barely had Trip dried off when the doorbell rang. I opened the door. Our eyes met. I could see his pain. I tried to joke with him and although he laughed, I knew in my heart this was no joking matter.

He shook off his discomfort and put a smile on his face. Within a minute, we went from having our eyes fixed on each other's faces, to him dancing me around the room while singing "Pretty Woman" in my ear. I laughed, and played along with the dancing.

Suddenly, he stopped.

He said "Desiree, I love you. Please take good care of yourself and Trip until I come home and do that myself."

I looked into his big, aqua eyes and told him I loved him, too; that until he returned, I would assure nothing happened to either of us. I didn't dare tell him what I was really thinking for fear I would burst into tears. I couldn't imagine what wives who had to say goodbye on a regular basis did to hide their feelings. It was next to impossible to appear happy, knowing the void I would feel as I watched his plane pull away from the departing gate.

I stared into his eyes and felt the love that flowed between us. Trip was running around, playing, not noticing the pain we both felt. He was in his pajamas already. Soon I would call Mother to come over for him. I was glad she offered to take him because I really didn't want him to know what pain I was going through.

I told Ajax that Mother offered to take Trip; that she would be come over to get him and she would say goodbye then. He was pleased that he would be able to say goodbye to her. He asked me if I remembered that time when we were younger when Mother refused to cook Thanksgiving dinner but wouldn't let me go with him to Laura's house.

We laughed, recalling that day and how we tried so hard to be quiet so she wouldn't get mad and throw him out.

"Has she mellowed any?" he asked.

I thought for a second, then replied, "Hell, no. But now she's so isolated with my grandfather that she's not so inclined to act that hatefully."

"Boy, she was somethin' else, wasn't she?" he said. "We never knew what to expect. You're so different from that. Thank God, I wouldn't be around if you were much like her."

I went to the phone to call Mother but Ajax suggested we take Trip over there instead, so we did. Trip wasn't happy about going but after we were there, he settled down and got into pushing the button on his Papa's bed. We all laughed. That made Trip laugh because he thought he was doing something cute. It never ceased to amaze me how my Grandpa would let Trip push that button so many times that I lost count.

Bless his heart I thought to myself, he loves that little boy so much that he really doesn't care.

Trip really resembled my grandfather's son. Maybe that's part of it. Walking back after saying goodbye only took a minute. Mother's house was so close that we shared a double driveway. Back in my house, I turned on the radio to break the silence.

We decided to try the custard pie. With coffee brewing, I sliced the pie and put some on plates. I couldn't believe it had turned out just like Grandma made. Watching him taste the pie, I felt some satisfaction knowing how pleased he felt.

He and I would both recall, for the rest of our lives, that we were able to make his leave memorable. We talked for hours about his hopes and dreams; about how I had become the center of his universe; and about a shared future. At some point, it became difficult for me because, although I wanted the same outcome, I feared it would not be realized.

Closing the living room curtains helped me feel I was closing out the world; that there was only the two of us. I turned, and there he was standing behind me, reaching out. We embraced each other, feeling our love-connection. He whispered in my ear, "I want to make love to you one more time." This brought me to tears.

I broke down crying in his arms as my heart felt like it was being ripped right out of my chest. I looked up at him with tears running down my face. He kissed me softly and then he kissed me with such passion that I melted into his arms. Lifting me up, he carried me to the bedroom and laid me gently on the bed. We held each other as he repeatedly kissed my lips. I responded each and every time. We laid in each other's arms until he again whispered, "One more time... I want to make love one more time."

We kissed again, then both undressed. Lying next to him, feeling him beside me, I realized what a bond we had and that nothing, neither time nor even death, could ever change that. We were hopelessly in love. At that moment, nothing could have stopped me from expressing our love. I looked into those unbelievably beautiful eyes and I could no longer hold back. I felt the love between us like fire that welded us into one.

Making love, feeling him inside me, felt so magical, so pure. He kissed me sensually until neither of us could no longer wait. As I felt him pulsating and me exploding, I finally knew the true meaning of making love.

We laid in each other's arms for a long time, not saying a word, only feeling each other's warmth. He reached his hand out and turned my face to his, as he gently kissed me again.

"I love you. I love you so much. I promise I will never hurt you. I will adore you forever," he said.

Then, as our kisses turned to liquid fire and with unbridled passion, we made love as we soared among the stars, yet again.

In the warm, soft light of afterglow, morning drew near. We wanted a glass of wine. As I poured, from the kitchen I asked him when his flight would leave. He said, "Very early. I have to be at the airport by five." The clock on the stove said it was already two a.m.

Knowing he wouldn't get much sleep, I asked him if he thought he could nap on the flight. It didn't seem to matter to him.

His only answer was, "I'm not sure I would be able to sleep anyway."

I was at a loss for words. I sat quietly next to him on the couch.

"Let's toast to continued happiness when you return," I said. He looked at me and answered, "I'll drink to that, and to me never leaving your side, no matter what happens."

He took another sip of the wine and said, "I can't imagine saying goodbye to you at the airport. If you're there, I won't be able to get on that airplane and leave. I just can't. I can't hug you and kiss you, then turn around and walk down the hallway to the plane. So I have a favor to ask of you. Tonight, I want to tuck you into bed, kiss you good night, and leave. That way, I'll have a memory of you here, in your bed. Please simply stay in bed. Don't come to the door. I'll lock it as I leave. Can you do that for me, please? If something should happen to me, I want to be able to close my eyes and envision peacefully lying here next to you. Please forgive me, I just can't say goodbye and leave you standing there at the airport. I'm so sorry, it's not that I don't want you there. It's just me. I don't think I could handle it."

I was sobbing as he took me into his arms. He begged me to not cry. With tears running down his own face, he looked into my eyes and repeated, "I have loved you since the day I met you. No one can ever take your place in my heart. I will love you until the day I die and onward, into eternity. That I promise."

We held each other with all our strength as we both cried, for quite a while. Eventually, we felt ready to release each other physically but somehow, we remained connected and touching. We both felt our bond yet neither of us needed to speak of it.

He leaned back and said, "I used to dream of what it would be like to make love to you. Now, I can simply close my eyes and relive it. I want nothing but the best for you. Please promise me if something should happen to me you will keep me tightly secured in a small part of your heart until we can one day be together again. I am so in love with you. I mean what I said. No matter what happens, I will always be with you, loving you, protecting you and guiding you. Like those yellow roses sitting on the table, to me, you are the most beautiful rose of all. To me, you represent everything any man could want, and I truly love you."

My heart was breaking. I couldn't stop crying because I had such fear in the depth of my soul that he would not be coming back. It was already three-thirty a.m. In only a few hours, he would be on a plane, out of my sight.

Never out of my heart, I thought, *only out of sight.*

I fought so hard to stop crying. He kissed my lips gently. I didn't want to let go. Total fear came over me as I sobbed in his arms.

"Please take care of yourself. What would I do without you?" I said.

"I will. I promise," he said, "now put on your pajamas so I can tuck you in. I really do have to go."

I went into my bedroom and put on my yellow, baby doll pajamas, then went back to the living room. He smiled brightly and growled like he always did when he saw me. He came over and hugged me.

He said, as always, "I love you Pretty Woman, I truly do."

He took my hand and led me into the bedroom where we had made love just hours before. I laid down on the bed and looked up at him. He laid down next to me and put his arms around me. After a few delicious moments, he got up, pulled the covers up, over my shoulders, and tucked them around me.

Kissing me one last time, he whispered, "Good night, my love." He turned and looked at me one more time, mouthing the words, "I love you."

In the next moment, he was gone. I heard the front door latch click closed. I laid there frozen, unable to move. My heart was beating so fast that I thought it would jump out of my chest.

He's gone, I thought. *He is gone.*

Chapter Six

For days after Ajax departed, I felt and acted as if something had ripped my heart out of my chest and burned my soul to ash. That absolute inner void, and the black agony of it, are nearly indescribable. And the nights… they were beyond bearing. Yet somehow, I survived this personal holocaust, the aftermath of love perfected and then snatched from me by the cruelest of fates.

I had to learn to live all over again and even to consent to stay alive. My mind kept drifting back to questions that had no answers. Nor did anyone have a way to populate my now-vacant universe. If it wasn't for Trip, I would have crumbled. His need for care helped me to cope and move on.

I didn't talk to Ajax's sister Laura. I thought that was best. I would probably cry and make her own loss feel worse. I hoped she didn't think I refused to go to the airport. Then again, how could I possibly explain his wish for me to not go along to say goodbye, but rather, to say our goodbyes right there in my bedroom? His wishes were between him and me. They concerned no one else. It was his way of making it possible to handle his situation. Truly, it was the wisest decision.

Work was also part of my salvation. Routine lent simple structure to follow as I began to heal my lacerated soul. I had to get up, get ready, leave the house and go somewhere; to focus on something mundane and familiar. Though devastated by Ajax's departure and my assumption of his impending death, I felt grateful to spend so much time with him during his last home furlough.

Wade called five times in as many days. I hadn't been able to answer his call so he left messages. All he wanted to do was change his visitation times yet again. Even if I changed them, he just canceled, anyway. I was calling my friends instead of letting them call me. That way, I don't pick up a call and hear Wade. I am not much that kind of person but enough is enough. Wade wronged both me and our son. Nothing he could say would change my mind. He wanted to see Trip so he could disrupt my life. He didn't want his son before. Why would he now suddenly wanting to start seeing him? I had tolerated his cruel game more than long enough.

My boss was an angel to me when I returned to work. He took me into his office that day, when no one was around. He asked how I was doing and if there was anything I needed. What a beautiful person to work for. I couldn't have wanted a better boss.

When he asked if Ajax got going safe and sound, my eyes filled with tears. I had a hard time talking about it. I didn't go into details.

Instead, I only said, "It was so hard saying goodbye."

He reassured me that it was never easy saying goodbye to someone when there is so much uncertainty surrounding our world situation. He told me to be strong and my man would come home sooner than I thought.

That evening, being unable to think straight, I couldn't even decide what to make for dinner. Going directly from my car into Mother's house to get Trip, I was relieved to see she had made dinner and Trip was already eating. She could see I was having a hard time with all the situations I faced. Somehow, I think even she actually may have felt sorry for me. She asked me to sit down and have something to eat. She made me a cup of tea. Her gentleness and sincere caring took me by surprise but I warmly welcomed it. We talked for a long while before I went home.

There was another message on my phone from Wade. This time he was not kind. He demanded to know why I was not answering his calls.

As if he has any right to demand anything from me, I thought.

He left me with no choice but to run away with my boy. My head was spinning with all the "what-if's." It really didn't do any good to second-guess them.

I chose not to return Wade's sarcastic call, rather to enjoy the rest of my evening with Trip. He loved it when I get down on the floor to play with trucks, so that was exactly what I did. After getting him ready for bed, I let him pick out a book that he wanted me to read to him at bedtime. The house seemed exceptionally quiet that evening, even with the TV sound. I kept glancing over to my roses as if they could disappear if I didn't keep looking at them. They were still beautiful. They still had such a pleasant, spicy fragrance. I couldn't believe that just a few days before, our little house was happy and alive. The silence was deafening.

I went to bed early trying to sort this whole mess out. As I laid there thinking, I came to the conclusion that no matter what the outcome may be, I would not trade those few weeks with Ajax for anything. After lying there for what seemed like forever, I decided to get up and make myself a cup of hot tea.

I was soaked in deep emotions. As I left the bedroom, I burst into tears. The audacity of Wade's behavior angered me. He used Trip as a pawn to hurt me.

Everyone is responsible for their own behavior, I thought and that included me.

Wade's attitude, shown in the messages he left, was that I had to tolerate his behavior and simply change my schedule, so he could still cancel in the end. He acted as if it's okay that he hadn't seen Trip in months. He acted entitled, as if I should jump whenever he called. Well, that was not going to happen, no matter what. I remained above all of the nonsense.

Sitting in the living room, drinking my hot tea, I glanced at the yellow roses that were starting to show their age. They weren't perfect any more but the love they represented was the most sublime that anyone could experience. I would not have traded those last few weeks for anything. Finishing my tea, I concluded there was no way I could solve all my problems that night, even if I tried. I would have to stay strong. Hopefully, the mess would turn in the right direction. I went back to bed and soon, I was asleep.

My day went well at work. It was over before I knew it. Looking forward to a relaxing weekend, I was happy that Friday was done and my weekend was about to begin. Trip was running around the house, playing. I sat quietly again, thinking of all that had happened, still trying to figure out what might have caused Wade to call so much. I was deep in thought when the doorbell rang.

It startled me. For a moment, I hoped it was Ajax and that they changed their mind about him going overseas. The door bell sounded off again, this time, with multiple rings. I jumped up from the couch and almost dumped my tea. I found a dapper man who I had met through mutual friends a few months earlier was at my door. He stood there looking at my face. It must have reflected the emotional week I had just endured.

He quickly asked, "Can I come in?"

I couldn't believe my eyes. I had been in his company a few times but I never thought much of it. We met in a group that went out dancing. He and I had some conversation but nothing special. His name was Dane.

"Please, could I come in?" he asked again.

As he came in, Dane chuckled, then said, "You look as if you saw a ghost."

I laughed and apologized, explaining that I had just been through a few rough days. He had heard about Ajax coming home on leave. He stopped by to see if I wanted to talk. Dane's words sounded so sincere and kind that they surprised me.

Not knowing what to say next, I offered him a cup of coffee. He gladly accepted. The coffee I had been brewing was ready. I poured a cup for each of us and asked him if he would like to sit in the kitchen. I silently prayed that he would not ask for an ice cube in his coffee. That would have been the end of my dry eyes, for sure. We talked while Trip played with his toys. He told me his whole life story that evening. I welcomed his gentle kindness.

Dane had been discharged from the Army a few months earlier. He was studying electronics at a local steel mill. I asked him if he was hungry.

In a humble tone of voice, he said, "Please, anything would be great. I haven't eaten all day." I opened the refrigerator and reheated leftovers from the dinner Trip and I ate the night before. He was obviously hungry although he took time to eat slowly.

When I looked at him, I thought, *what a nice looking man.* My thoughts again went to the ice cubes that Ajax would put into his coffee, how he would sip around them, to get cooled coffee.

"What is it?" he asked. "You look like you just saw another ghost." Panic shot through my nerves. I wondered if somehow he could read my thoughts.

"Nothing," I responded. "Nothing," and I smiled.

We talked for a very long time, each avoiding the subject of Ajax's departure. I had baked a batch of Trip's favorite cookies when I got home from work.

When I poured Dane's second cup of coffee, I put a few cookies on his saucer.

He looked at the cookies and said, "Wow you can bake, too."

Not knowing what his plans were, I waited until he finished his second cup of coffee. Then I suggested we end our visit so I could get some rest. He asked if he could come over another time, then stood up, acknowledging my request.

I chuckled and asked him, "Was it the cookies?"

We both stood there laughing, briefly. Than I walked him to the door. He told me that if I needed someone to talk to, I should let him know because he's a good listener.

As I laid in bed that night, many things occupied my thoughts. I didn't think I would be able to sleep at all. Morning did come much too soon. Trip was full or energy. He kept asking where that man was. It broke my heart to hear his sweet little voice asking me that over and over again.

So innocent, I thought, each time he asked.

Around eight a.m., the phone rang. I took a deep breath before answering it. It was Mother, wanting me to come over and help her with Grandpa again. Not even thinking twice, I gathered Trip and a few toys and we went out the door.

Grandpa hadn't had a good night. Lack of sleep showed on Mother's face. After we finished with him, she put on a pot of coffee. I felt sorry for her, given the position she was in. Constantly taking care of my Grandpa wasn't much of a life for her. That was something that had to be done, though, and someone had to do it.

While drinking coffee, I looked at Mother, wondering just how long she could sustain the caregiver role she was faced with. Her face looked so worn and tired. I tried to visit and talk with her often but sometimes, I just couldn't. Today was one of those days.

When she asked about the car she had seen in our driveway the night before, I got a sick feeling in my stomach. I really wasn't up to talking about much of anything. Trip heard her mention a car in the driveway.

He came running, saying "Man come."

I felt like a doe in headlights. I just stared ahead and didn't know what to say. She could see pain in my face and asked if something had gone wrong.

My eyes filled with tears as I told her about the man I had met a few months ago. I told her that he seemed kind and that he had just come home from the military; that Dane had heard about Ajax leaving for Viet Nam, so he thought he would stop by to see if I needed someone to talk to.

Then I told her, "He's is calm and soft spoken. He talked and talked, relating his whole life story."

After telling about his visit, I had to leave for work.

When I got back home that evening, there was a message from Dane on the phone, thanking me for dinner and the wonderful conversation. He sounded appreciative, rather like he needed the conversation as much as I did. He left his phone number and told me to call him any time I need to talk or get out a little. Remembering the evening when I was out with my girlfriends took me back to when I first met Dane and how he kept asking me to dance.

He is a wonderful dancer, I thought, *but I don't need to complicate my life by getting involved with someone new.*

When I was starting to clean up the supper dishes, the phone rang again. I wasn't sure I should answer it.

My second thought was, *What the heck. This is my little abode. I shouldn't be afraid to answer the phone in my own home.*

It was one of my girlfriends wanting to chat. I tried to make small talk but found that difficult.

So I spoke freely and said "Guess who came to my house last night?"

She was surprised to hear about Dane and, of course, she wanted to know all the details. Being one of my best friends, she reassured me she was there for me no matter what time of day or night I would need to talk. I knew I could trust her but couldn't go through it all again. Understanding the strain on me, she changed the subject. She asked me if I would like to come over for dinner the next night. I thanked her but couldn't think straight enough to give her an answer. Our conversation lasted about half an hour. Then I went back to my dishes. Trip played well on his own, almost as if he knew I was a total wreck.

The next morning when the phone rang and my gut told me it was Dane. Sure enough, it was him. He talked a while and then asked if he could repay the dinner I gave him by taking Trip and me out for dinner.

"No strings attached" he said, "just dinner."

I declined, saying I had already accepted an invitation to my friend's house. Dane was very understanding, but then, as I thought about it later, I realized he had no choice but to be understanding. I told him I would call him, maybe the next day, and maybe we could do something in the afternoon.

What a nice person, I thought. He quickly agreed to my suggestion.

Vegetating wasn't on the list of things I would be able to do. Mother called again to ask if I would come over and help her with my grandfather. For the second time in a day, I grabbed Trip and went over to help. Grandpa's face lit up when he saw my little guy. It seemed some of his pain eased up.

Trip went straight for the control button on the bed.

Grandpa shook his finger at me as if to say, "Leave him alone, he's fine."

He had just choked on his food. Mother then needed to suction out his trachea, which she was just finishing when I arrived. Everything seemed okay. Of course, Grandpa was in seventh heaven, taking his ride up and down in his hospital bed.

Because he was so young at that time, I wondered just how much Trip would remember of his Papa a few years later. That old man absolutely idolized my little guy. Although Grandpa couldn't talk, they seemed to understand each other. I wondered how much longer Grandpa could linger, given his condition. Without the care Mother gave him, he would have been long gone. The doctors had said he had about two months. It had been fourteen months since then. He was still going strong. I have to give Mother credit for that. She gave her father better care than she ever gave me when I was as young as Trip.

I wondered about this as I looked at Trip. I would have given my life for my precious son but Mother didn't care about me.

So strange, I thought. I went to the kitchen and gave Trip a little snack. I could see Mother really needed some company. I put a kettle of water on the stove so I could make some tea. She started to cry once she was out of Grandpa's sight. He was hard of hearing so she knew he could not hear her. She told me about how bad it was this time, that he turned blue from lack of oxygen. By then, she was crying hard. She spoke of her fear that he would die from choking; that she would not be able to do anything to save him; and how helpless she felt. I didn't know how to console her. Since she wasn't the hugging type, I just listened.

When she finished, I reassured her of what a wonderful job she did on a daily basis. I told her that sometimes we have no control over what happens. It didn't ease her pain but at least she had someone to talk to. I didn't go over there too often in the evening because I'm usually busy with dinner and straightening up and Trip requires my time and attention. By the end of the day, I'm tired, ready to lie down and relax. I'm pretty sure that, being a single mother, she can relate to all that.

The next day was Sunday. I knew Dane would be waiting for my call. I tried to think of something we could do that Trip would enjoy, something away from the house. When an idea came to me, I gave him a call. He was very happy with what I suggested. He asked me what time he should pick us up. We would be going to a park where coyotes were kept. I figured one p.m. would be good.

I could tell by the tone of his voice that Dane was happy that I had called. The timing was perfect for me. It gave me time to relax and collect my thoughts, although with Trip, that could be difficult. He was all wound up when we left. I could hardly wait to see his face when he saw those coyotes. I figured I would take my camera to get some pictures with coyotes in the background.

I tried to explain to Trip where we were going to go but he didn't get it. Although he didn't grasp what we were going to see, he did understand that he was going to a park.

Such a handsome little boy, I thought.

Soon, Dane was at my door. I was ready. Trip was so excited he went wild, screaming and running. Dane picked him up and squeezed him. I could see Trip's little arms wrapped around Dane's neck.

All I could think was, *Wow, what a kind man to take time to hug Trip.*

The day went quite well. It seemed we all enjoyed the coyotes. Trip thought they were puppies so we just let him say "puppy" over and over. He was so excited that I hated to keep correcting him.

I love this park, I thought. *It's so different from typical parks.* This one was deep inside a valley. You could see it was protected on all sides. Every year, for as long as I could remember, the park managers brought in coyotes. Visitors would watch these animals' coats change with the seasons. They looked magnificent, almost regal. You couldn't get very close to them but you could approach within a few feet of their enclosure. I think I enjoyed the day just as much as Trip did.

One thing I had to say about Dane was that we enjoyed the same types of family outings and similar entertainment. I thought to myself, as I looked at him, he seems to be a family man.

Leaving the park turned into a challenge. Trip did not want to leave. He started to cry. Dane picked him up and quietly asked him if he would like to get some ice cream. That worked well. Once we were in the car, Dane asked me if there was anywhere special where I would like to eat, but I said no. I asked him to pick somewhere.

Within a few minutes, Trip was sound asleep. I reassured Dane he didn't have to take us out to eat but that comment fell on deaf ears. He drove to a restaurant. We sat in the parking lot for a few minutes for Trip to sleep as we talked. We went inside and ordered some food. To my surprise, Trip was like an angel as he ate all his food.

"I guess running around gave him an appetite," Dane said, "and it gave me one."

When we arrived back home, Trip had fallen asleep again in the car. I carried him inside and put him to bed for the night. I asked Dane if I could get him a drink since he had already made himself at home on the couch. We decided on a glass of wine and then sat and talked for hours. This time it was me who opened up. I told him all about my life up until then. He listened carefully, seeming to find special meaning in every word I spoke. I told him how Mother insisted on my wedding in the Church by threatening me and how I cried profusely because I simply didn't want that. I couldn't believe how much I opened up to him and how comfortable I felt. He was easy to talk to. He seemed to be kind and gentle. He left that night thanking me as if I was the one who took him and his son to the park instead of the other way around.

I waited for letters from Ajax. When they came, I read and reread them. It had been three months since he left yet my pain was as vivid as if he had flown away the previous day. I wrote as often as I could but on some evenings, I would feel so tired that I would go to bed early and be sound asleep by nine-thirty or ten.

Dane came over on weekends and we would talk and talk. I looked forward to him coming over and Trip was growing very fond of him. By that time, Wade didn't come around any more, nor did he even call, so I didn't feel nervous about answering the phone any more. Sometimes Dane would call to ask how I was doing or if I needed anything, all the while knowing that I was still numb from what I had endured. He would compliment me on what an outstanding mother I was. He always seemed complimentary about everything I did.

I could tell he was starting to truly care about us although he kept his feelings to himself. He never made any passes at me. We seemed to become good friends. He was quite effective with Trip. Having matured during his time in the Army, Dane wanted to settle down and father a family. I felt increasingly comfortable with him around us. I looked forward to his calls and visits. We often talked about Ajax. He would not try to stop me when I would discuss my fears; instead, he reassured me that everything would work out, in time. In his typically calm, collected manner, he would tell me that I could count on him. That no matter what, he was there for me. When he said such things, I realized he was trying to win me over with his gentle kindness.

Starting to become confused, I backed off answering the phone. Then, one day he appeared at my door.

"I was worried that you didn't answer my phone call for the last few days," he said.

Trying to get out of it, I said that Grandpa had been having a hard time the last few days; that I had been helping Mother with him. Uncertain whether he believed me, I followed up with a supporting fact, that Grandpa was getting worse by the day. Dane didn't press matters. Instead, he asked if he could stay and talk for a little while.

Dane and Ajax were exact opposites. Ajax was about five feet, nine inches tall with large, aqua blue eyes and platinum blond hair. Dane was six feet tall, with black hair and piercing, dark eyes. But both were exceptionally attractive and both had an easygoing personality. And in the moment when I compared them, I looked at Dane and I realized: they both care for the very same woman.

He asked if we would like to grab a bite to eat. I accepted. Dinner was pleasant, but then, Dane was typically pleasant to be with. Trip acted like a big shot, sitting there eating his meal in the booth with the grown-ups instead of in a highchair. He stayed very quiet and well behaved. Our conversation amounted to mostly small talk, only something to help me get through the day. It did feel strange to be sitting across Dane, given all that had happened with Ajax was still so fresh in my mind.

I knew I needed to get past all that and simply enjoy the day, for Trip's sake. Going home felt stressful for me because Dane would want to come in for a while and I knew Trip would want the same. So all that was whirling around in my mind. When we approached our house, I could feel a certain tension in the air. So I asked Trip if he would like to show Dane his new trucks. Of course he did, so the cloud of tension lifted. The rest of the day and that evening went very well. Dane paid a lot of attention to Trip.

After Trip went to bed, Dane asked if we could have a glass of wine. That, I was okay with. We each drank a glass wine and then had another, all the while, talking about nothing special and not about anything that would ruffle my feathers. With the second drink finished, he didn't want another one. He continued to talk. It was all very pleasant. It seemed unfortunate the way the last few months had been.

When I started to yawn, he said "I'll bet you are tired. You really have had a lot on your plate lately. I want to tell you how proud I am of the way you have taken care of everything. You're a special woman and a very special mommy."

I glared at him and said "Thank you... Thanks for all those compliments." I stood up, as if to say, time to go now, and given that gesture he took the hint that it was time to leave. And so continued a glacially slow process: which was Dane trying to become a regular part of our lives.

My nerves were beginning to get the best of me. The entire next day, I felt like I had been sucker-punched in the stomach, so a boring Sunday suited me fine. Trip played as I did laundry and tidied up the house. It may be a small home, but it seems there's always something to clean up or freshen. Slowly, I got everything done and even managed to make a good dinner.

I love to cook. Cooking was not a chore for me. It was a pleasure. Tackling ethnic dinners was never a challenge but instead, always an adventure. Maybe I'm weird but I do enjoy it all. Because I was brought up, in effect, by my Grandma, setting a pleasing table was important to me, as well. I allowed no pots or pans on the table. My grandma would go a step farther, not even putting a jelly jar on the table. Instead, she put jelly in a small dish. That's not an extent I care go to.

When Dane called again, he asked if he could take us out for ice cream later in the day.

I knew my stomach would not take that so I suggested, "Maybe another time."

He wanted to shop at a store near us. So he asked if he could stop by. With plans and a time agreed upon, I brewed a cup of chamomile tea with honey. That seemed to sooth not only my stomach but also my soul.

Trip got excited, and as I saw that, I wondered if he was growing fond of Dane as a person, or if he was generally looking for a father figure that he craved. The latter notion made me feel sad. Mother had always badgered me about my father. That would never happen with my son. I grew up afraid of my father because of the fearful things she instilled in me. She would ask if he touched me in my privates. Although he never did anything even remotely like that, a fear was placed in my mind.

Never! I thought. *Never could I put my child through that.* While absorbed in these deep thoughts, the door bell rang and Trip went running to the door. They seemed so happy to see each other that it made me feel good inside. Dane asked if he could take Trip for some ice cream and, to my own surprise, I said yes.

With the two of them gone, I decided to see if there was anything Mother needed my help with. She mostly needed someone to talk to because she was nearly pulling her hair out from loneliness. We talked on and on, which seemed to be good therapy for her. In many ways it was good for me, as well.

Although no critical world issues were resolved, we both seemed to enjoy our quiet conversation. She helped us in many ways. Most often, that caused me to forgive her for all her hateful behavior toward me when I was younger. My childhood couldn't be erased or "rewound" back to a new start. There really wasn't much sense in hanging onto foul memories, I had decided, a long time previously.

I simply let go of all that misery. When I got pregnant, I didn't want negative emotions lurking around me to linger. I made up my mind then to only think positive thoughts; to accept whatever good was available within an experience and to build upon that. I know I'm the mother I am today because of the mother that my Mother failed to be. I became a better person because of my stressful childhood. I constantly told my son how much I loved him, and readily, with deep, abiding conviction. Mother, on the other hand, couldn't even think about saying those words. That is her loss, not mine; her own failure, not mine.

One bit of good advice that Mother did give me stuck in my mind. I thought of this when we got home that day: to take my time, to not do anything rash that would bite me later. She was right about knowing when to use caution. That advice, I appreciated. I wanted my son to have a good life. Therefore, I was not making key decisions until they were well thought out.

My little guy came back later with Dane in tow.

So cute to see that excitement in Trip, I thought.

He tried to explain to me what he had eaten. The harder he tried to explain it, the more enjoyment I got out of it. He tried to tell me about bananas and chocolate sprinkles but somehow it didn't come out even remotely resembling bananas and chocolate sprinkles. I was laughing hard and the harder I laughed, the cuter he became. Dane was also trying to help him say what he ate, but that didn't work either.

"Would you like a cup of coffee?" I asked, laughing to myself. I was thinking, *as if he would refuse it...*

"Yes that sounds wonderful," he replied. I got up from the couch to put on a pot of coffee. A few hours passed and then it was time for dinner. Knowing Trip would want Dane to eat with him, I just asked him if he was hungry and would like to eat with us.

His answer was a no-brainer, "I would love to. You're a fabulous cook," he said. "Lucky the man who gets you."

I smiled but without responding.

Dinner went well. After the dishes were washed, it was bath time for Trip. He was such a stinker when it came to taking a bath. That child loved to take a bath. He refused every time to get out of the tub. So I would pull the stopper. When the water was gone he had no other choice but to get out.

He didn't fight me over putting his pajamas on, that night, because he was tired from playing all day.

I thought, *This is the way it's supposed to be. Why did all that mess have to happen? Why did his Daddy leave?*

I read Trip a story. He fell asleep so quickly that I wasn't even at the end of his little story book. When I came out of Trip's bedroom, Dane was sleeping on the living room couch. He woke up and smiled as if pleased with what he saw. When he started to talk, his voice choked up.

I looked at him curiously, asking "What is it Dane? Is something wrong?"

He started to say something, but stopped and thought about it, seriously.

In an emotionally charged voice, he said, "These past seven months when I've been seeing you and Trip have meant the world to me. I care deeply, and I want more than a hug when I leave."

I was trembling because I realized just how much I enjoyed him and his gentle kindness with me and my son.

"Please, give me a chance to talk," he begged.

"Really, let's not ruin what we have with words, please," I replied."

He smiled and reached out to hug me. As we hugged each other I knew that I cared more than I wanted to.

The days stretched into weeks and the weeks turned into months. Dane was still coming to see us, continually trying to win me over and to show me how much he loved us. I kept it on a friendly level, not allowing him to touch me or kiss me. As crazy as that may seem, he went along with it.

One Sunday, I was making dinner when he asked me if I was ever going to allow him to kiss me. I laughed and said "Probably not but it is nice having you come and spend time here with Trip and me. That sure makes us happy."

He came up behind me as I was peeling potatoes and reached around me, hugging me and kissing my cheek.

"I want more Desiree," he said, as if it was a request.

I looked at him and stopped what I was doing long enough to study his eyes. Then I added, "Let's just keep things as they are. I'm not ready for anything more, right now."

He looked hurt as he walked into the living room and started playing with Trip.

I sat down at our table and I asked him to sit with me and let me explain what was going on in my head. I started with the heartache I felt when Wade wanted me to abort my pregnancy. Then I went into how I had to fight off Mother's boyfriend when he decided he wanted to take care of Trip and me and he decided he loved me. The surprised look on Dane's face didn't stop me from continuing.

I told Dane how the boyfriend would tell Mother that he wanted to come over to see Trip. Then, unexpectedly, one day Author knocked me down on the couch and tried to kiss me, telling me how sorry he was for causing me to have such an unhappy childhood; that he wanted to make it up to me now by taking care of Trip and me.

I looked Dane in the eyes with tears rolling down my face and I asked him, "How can I tell Mother all this with what she has to handle, huh? Tell me Dane... how?"

His face turned ash white. He asked me how I responded when all this happened. "Well, I moved out, into my own apartment. After the second time he appeared at my door, I threatened him with telling Mother.

Then I said, "If you ever come to this apartment again I will call the police."

Then I had Dane's attention. He could grasp exactly what I went through and why I acted so stand-offish.

"All of this has affected me in ways you can not imagine. And now, when I look at Mother, I pity her because this S.O.B. acts like nothing has happened and she has no clue."

Dane stood up and came over to my chair. I stood up and walked past him. He followed me to the stove, turned me around, and hugged me.

"I need to move on with my life and take care of my son," I replied softly.

Then I went on to explain how Ajax found out about what had happened to me and when he came home on leave, he came to see me. I then started to cry.

I said, "So you see, you're dealing with a very confused woman."

He didn't let me go; instead, he hugged me harder.

He said, "I'm so sorry for what you have gone through. It only makes me respect you even more."

"I've gone through a lot with Author, Mother's boyfriend, and now with Ajax leaving..." I whispered.

All he said was, "Hush now. Please don't talk, just let me hold you." I was sobbing into his chest. I couldn't control my tears.

"It's okay... it's okay," he whispered in my ear.

We stood like that for a long time, holding on to each other, neither one letting go. Trip came into the kitchen.

He said "Mommy cry," and he hugged my leg.

"What a wonderful child," I thought, "and one thing is for sure, he is mine."

That night, after Trip went to bed, we sat on the couch talking in such a low voice one would think we were afraid someone outside might hear us.

"I'm confused, Dane. Seeing Ajax brought back all the feelings for him I had suppressed. I acted like those feelings didn't exist but they did."

Then I went on, telling him, "I simply don't know how I feel any more. I'm so lost and confused. I know my feelings for Ajax never ended. And now I'm faced with conflicting feelings, for you. You've been such a joy to be around. You're so kind and gentle. Trip just loves you… but I feel so torn. There's no way for you to understand how strong my feelings were and what Ajax and I went through those few weeks when he was home. How could anyone understand the depth of my fears and what it was like to say goodbye after a psychic predicted he would make me a widow?"

I still felt heartache just thinking about the click of the front door as he left. I was crying for so many reasons and the ache in my heart was so severe that nothing could make it go away, no matter what words we spoke.

Dane said, "I'm here. I'm not going anywhere. I care for you and your son, so you just take your time to find it in your heart to allow me into your life."

I continued to cry as he held me. While still holding me in his arms, he asked me about Author again. It seemed like he couldn't believe Author would stoop so low. I went through it all again, this time in detail, telling him how I had to fight and hit Author because he kept trying to pin me down and kiss me.

I could see Dane was getting quite upset. After a while, we moved. We sat at the table, continuing to talk. Somehow, I did feel better after finally getting it all out in the open rather than holding it inside. I wanted him to know all of this so I could see if it would make a difference to him or affect his feelings for me.

The next week went by quickly. Soon, Dane was coming over regularly. I still wasn't intimate with him but he didn't seem to mind as long as he was able to be with us. My feelings started to grow for him, more as each day went by. Seeing my son so happy and having Dane around all the time made it seem like he was meant to be there.

I thought about being safe in my house while Ajax was in a jungle somewhere, with no comforts of home. That upset me so much I tried to exclude such thoughts from my mind. His letters were few and far between now. It almost seemed as if he had forgotten me.

I wasn't sure if Ajax's sister knew Dane was coming over frequently. In such a small town, one could only assume she did. She would call me and we talked but nothing was ever mentioned about Dane.

With a weekend approaching, Dane suggested he and I go out for a change. We hadn't gone anywhere for quite a while, so I liked the idea.

I asked Mother if Trip could stay over at her house. Of course, she loved the idea. Author was coming to see her a lot less frequently. She was so lonely that she was glad to have Trip running around, making noise. We set a time and I was eager to go. I took a long bubble bath and just relaxed, with my mind at peace.

Having flawless skin meant I didn't need makeup. That made it easy for me to be ready in just a few minutes. So I knew I had time to soak in the bubbles. With my hair in rollers, I started to put on my mascara. I wondered what it was going to be like going out again. I was looking forward to it. I couldn't have been ready more than two minutes when the door bell rang and there he was.

When I opened the door, he took a look at me, shook his head with satisfaction, and said, "And I am your date this evening. Wow what a lucky guy I am."

Silly man, I thought, but it did feel satisfying to hear a compliment.

Dane was a man who said only what he truly thought, so I welcomed the compliment. First, we went out to dinner and then dancing. This man could really dance. We could take over an entire dance floor and have everyone else standing around, watching.

This is what the doctor ordered, I thought, as he whirled me around. Then suddenly, the band shifted to a slow song. He took me in his arms as if to never to let go. He held me close. As we glided across the floor, I felt like a princess.

As the song ended, he kissed my lips softly and looked me in the eyes and whispered, "This is where you are supposed to be. We were meant for each other." I felt too shocked to reply but my heart was talking to me. My emotional confusion grew worse.

We danced for hours, as we used to when our dance group went out together. I loved every minute of it. On the way home, we talked and talked, as folks do on a date. I asked him if he would like a snack or cup of coffee when we got home. Knowing he would not refuse made me giggle. He laughed, and asked me what was so funny. Although I hated to say it, I replied, simply, "You."

He whirled me around and while hugging me close, he kissed me passionately and this time, I kissed back. We stood in the living room kissing with such emotion neither one of us wanting it to end.

Between kisses, he whispered, "Desiree I love you. Please give me a chance. I need you in my life."

I couldn't answer. I was that dumbstruck and still so confused. Yet I welcomed his carnal kisses. I found myself kissing back with desire as torrid as his. When we made love that night I cried tears of utter confusion, yet my body gave in to the delicious sensations of making love. In the afterglow, we laid in each others arms. He kissed my face in rhythms like those we had danced to, telling me, "I [kiss] feel [kiss] so happy. [kiss] Please, don't ever [kiss] leave me." I only curled up closer to him. I couldn't say anything at all. Soon, we both slept.

When the sun shined through my white, lacy curtains, falling golden upon the wooden furniture and our glowing skin, we got up as if all was well at the start of a typical day. I started a pot of coffee and made some breakfast. We talked about our night and how much fun it was to dance again. Neither of us mentioned making love. I think we both felt our pleasures were best left unspoken and thus unspoiled.

We went on like this for a few weeks before he told me about his parents being upset that he was seeing me so much. I felt torn and didn't know what to say. Nor did I understand why they would be upset. We were both twenty-three, so it wasn't as if we were teenagers. He went on to say they were upset that I was married and that I had a child.

My blood boiled then, as I thought *how dare they criticize me.*

I kept my child. I didn't abort the pregnancy to take the easy way out, nor did I ever take my parental responsibilities lightly. I worked, I took care of my son diligently, and I didn't go out drinking like other women my age.

"I want you to meet them" he said.

I wanted no part of folks who harbored preconceptions about who I was before they even met me. I let that subject fade away. I said we might talk about it later. He left early that night, deciding he would go home to study for the test he had coming.

Dane came over after school the next day. He felt excited that he got a perfect score on his test. We ate dinner. After Trip went to bed we opened his bottle of champagne to celebrate. He left about eleven p.m. and I went to bed.

No sooner did I close my eyes than I heard this quiet knock at my front door. Opening it up, to my surprise Dane had come back. He was quite upset. His parents had confronted him, forcing him to "choose me or them," and in the process, they would not allow him to go upstairs to even get his clothes or his books. There he stood like an orphan with nowhere to go.

I couldn't believe this was happening, all because of his relationship with me. He was the easiest-going man I had ever met. We seemed to mesh together easily.

But I am not ready for where this is going, I thought. I told him he could stay the night but that he needed to make up with his parents because this was not my idea of how to begin a relationship. The next day, Dane came over after work. He asked if I would go with him to meet his parents. He said he had called them from work and told them he was not leaving me, so they would have to adjust their way of thinking.

Going to his parent's house was not my idea of the way to spend a pleasant evening. I felt quite nervous, as if going to be sentenced after a kangaroo trial. Yet I went, knowing this situation had to resolve one way or the other if we wanted to live in peace.

Once inside, with introductions complete, I decided to take the bull by the horns. I revealed what I was feeling, with frankness. I told them that they could treat me any way they wanted; that really did not matter to me. But my son was innocent. They would have to treat him as a faultless little boy because he had no responsibility for anything that adults had done around him.

To my great surprise, Dane's parents backed off entirely and offered us desert. That surprised me. When his father sat down at the table, he told me that he respected me for putting them in their place concerning my son. I could hardly believe my ears.

Dane started staying with us more and more. Soon, life with Dane became easygoing and serene, with no drama at all. I welcomed the tranquil peace in my home because my girlhood had been nothing but drama, nonstop, with spurts of total chaos when Author was drinking. I vowed that I would never live like that and I meant it.

Dane didn't buck and twist about anything and everything that I might suggest could be good. But in my heart, I never quit thinking about Ajax. I simply put my feelings aside and continued to live. I prayed every night that God would watch over him and bring him back safely, in one piece, but in my heart, at the same time, I knew it would not be that way in the end.

That haunting sentence the Cedar Point psychic delivered never left me. Her words played in my mind like a stuck record, leading me away from him, in another direction. It had been at least six months since I had heard from him. In his final letter, he told me to move on in my life because he was needed over there. His words cut like a knife but I could only pray he was making the right decision. He had signed up for another tour of duty.

Soon, Dane was asking me to marry him. We were into the family routine, going to his sisters' and parents' homes for dinners. I was living a home life that I had not experienced before. They all treated me well. I seemed to fit in, effortlessly.

The second time he asked, I said, "Yes." We were married a few weeks later. We chose to quietly go away for a few days. We kept it just the two of us.

As the months passed, we became quite happy together. Dane's parents truly liked me. They felt pleased to see us happy together. One morning, I woke up feeling sick to my stomach but I got dressed as usual and helped us all prepare for the day. Dane had finished his schooling. He now worked as an electronic engineer in the steel mill, making good money. We talked about saving for our own home.

On about the third day of feeling being sick, I realized I was pregnant. I felt happy about that because I always wanted a large family. On the other side of the issue, I knew it meant heartache for Ajax. I still hung onto the hope that he would come back alive. Dane felt as thrilled as he could possibly be. Frankly, the thought of another baby thrilled me as well.

Mother seemed to know right away.

She said, "Your eyes look like you're pregnant."

I wasn't sure, yet. So I didn't respond. I ignored her remark. After missing two periods, I figured I was pregnant for sure, so I went to the doctor. After he confirmed my pregnancy, home I went to give Dane the good news.

I was continually sick with this pregnancy. The doctor advised me to take it easy so that I would not miscarry. The instant Dane heard that, he insisted that I quit my job, stay home, and care for myself and Trip. I hated to quit because we were saving money and my boss was so good to me. He and I had many conversations while the rest of the office had no clue. He had advised me to marry and try to move on in my life. Once, after work, he told me that when his son came back from the war he was never the same. That caused his son's marriage to fail.

To me, he was like the father I never had. He took me under his wing and guided me. He had a good marriage then, though it hadn't been happy in the beginning, so he told me to be strong, to fight for what was good for me and my son. Sometimes, I would go into work on Saturday, get my work done quickly, then he and I would take some time to talk.

He would say I was wise for my years and that Dane was a lucky man to have me. When I told him I was pregnant and the doctor said it was best for me take it easy, to not work, he hugged me. He told me how happy he was for me and that I definitely did the right thing by marrying Dane. I knew he was only my boss but somehow, he was more than that to me. Hearing him say how happy he was and that I did the right thing made me feel even more positive.

The thought of a miscarriage scared me. I knew with this pregnancy my whole life had taken a new direction, that this baby was meant to be. The morning sickness was hard to bear but soon over. Then that wonderful feeling of being pregnant took over. I was one of those crazy women who loved being pregnant. I was normally so thin that by the time I was three months pregnant, I could tell from my clothes. They seemed a little snug. That was fine with me because I had saved all my maternity clothes from my pregnancy with Trip. It didn't matter that I eventually gained sixty pounds. I was in my glory. I lost all that extra weight fast. Within six weeks after the baby came, it was all gone and I was back to my original, slim self.

Mother liked Dane. She was happy that he came into my life. She also loved Ajax, but somehow, she didn't feel positive about his future. I sometimes wondered if that fortune teller had spooked her, also. I stopped dwelling on her words for fear of creating negative experiences from negative thoughts. Mother thought she would move into our small house and let Dane and me live in the big one that she had shared with my Grandpa until he passed on.

Dane and I were happy. We decided we would switch houses but not until we got organized, after another few months. That was fine with me. I loved our cozy little house, although for a while, when I would hear the front door close, I would get chills thinking about Ajax leaving. I was eventually able to put that behind me.

Dane would feel my tummy often to find out if it got any bigger since the day before. He was such a gentle man that I looked forward to his touch and his kisses. Lying in his arms at night was the highlight of my day. I hadn't thought I would be so happy after being so confused. It was almost like a white veil had been cast over me that washed away all my doubts and fears. We were so happy then.

However, I felt on edge all day. I felt weepy and nervous. I had to control myself to not loose patience with Trip. Everything seemed to bother me. I attributed all that to my pregnancy. I decided I better take it easy. I was thinking perhaps my inner feelings were telling me something. I had felt this way one other time, when I was pregnant with Trip and our beautiful dog was hit by a car. She was alright but the whole day before it happened, I was so anxious. I discounted those feelings and tried to ignore them.

I was generally tired with this pregnancy, so I thought I would lock the doors to make sure Trip didn't get out and maybe then, I could rest. That didn't seem to work, though. I was so jittery that I simply couldn't rest. I was happy whenever Dane got home. Then, I would tell him how I had been feeling all day. Being such a calm person, he just hugged me and told me everything was alright and it probably was simply that I was tired.

After dinner one day, I decided to get Trip ready for bed early so that I could take a bubble bath while he played with his daddy. That child was ready to take a bath any time of day. He absolutely loved to play in the water. He was ready whenever I mentioned it. The weather was getting bad. December was upon us. We decided to put our Christmas tree up that weekend which would be about a week before Christmas.

With dishes done, and Trip bathed and ready for bed, I thought, *This is my time to relax.*

I filled the tub high with bubbles and slid down into it. It felt so soothing and relaxing. I just let my thoughts drift. I could hear Trip and Dane playing in the living room. All sounded pleasant, so I continued to relax.

As I laid there, I thought, *How blessed I am. I have a good life with Dane and I know it, his love for me is real.*

I stroked my tummy and wondered what gender this little baby was and how it would change my life.

Some day, I thought, *I will have to tell this little one just how important it's birth was and how happy I am that it came about.*

When I got out of the tub, I put on a warm night gown. Usually feeling cold was a constant frustration. I went to the living room and looked around, thinking about where we could place our Christmas tree. Dane laughed at me because I was always thinking way ahead about what I am going to do. I call it planning. He calls it putting the cart before the horse.

Brrr, it's cold outside, I thought, *we need to move to a warm climate.*

Trip was wound up for some reason. He didn't really want to go to bed. Dane put him to bed for me. That gave me a few extra minutes to relax.

Hmm, I thought, chuckling to myself, *why is he so willing to put him to bed for me tonight. I bet he has some ideas as to how he would like to spend his evening and just hasn't shared those ideas with me yet.*

Dane was a very loving man. He made me feel special. He let me know with every action just how much he loved me. His kisses were to die for. Each and every one of them let you know that he is there with you, not kissing in anticipation of pleasure that may come later. I laid my head back on the couch to rest, for what I thought was going to be only a minute. Dane's gentle touch awakened me about an hour and a half later.

Not one for much sweet talk, he merely said, "Hey, Sleepyhead, time to go to bed."

I smiled, realizing I had been sound asleep and didn't even notice when he came back into the living room after putting Trip in bed.

The next day, I was even worse. I really felt like jumping out of my skin. I would start crying and not even know why. I thought it was all part of being pregnant, but that didn't seem to ease my anxiety. Mother hadn't started to work again yet. Grandpa had died only a few weeks earlier. She tried to convince me that it was all part of the pregnancy and that it would pass. Somehow, I knew she didn't really believe what she was telling me.

Trip was full of energy that day but it was too cold to let him play outside. I had a cup of tea and lunch at Mothers and tried to help her put things away and sort out what needed to be thrown out or given away. She was having a hard time with Grandpa's death, although she took such good care of him that he lived sixteen months longer than they thought he could possibly hang on.

She looked worn. She still wasn't sleeping at night, since that was the worst time of day for him. He had a bell by his bed that he would ring if he needed her while she was sleeping. She said she still jumped in her sleep, thinking she heard the bell. I felt sorry listening to her talk and cry. Death is such a final thing.

My father had died a few months before Dane and I got married. As I stood in front of his casket, I couldn't help thinking that I didn't even know the man who was lying there. He had been a total stranger to me. I never said anything about that to Mother since I knew she would take off on a tangent, claiming he never was a good father. Truth be known, he never had a chance. She instilled such fear of him in me that I completely stayed away from him. Then, one day he was gone.

Leaving Trip with her, at her request, I thought I might lie on the couch and rest if I could. But I tried to no avail. I was a nervous wreck. I didn't remember being so restless during my pregnancy with Trip. I thought it would soon pass. I started dinner and went back over to Mother's house to get my little man.

He came running to me yelling "Mommy, Mommy..." He wrapped his little arms around me as I picked him up.

He was trying to tell me that his Papa wasn't there. I could see tears welled up in Mother's eyes. I felt so sorry for her. Trying to explain to Trip turned out to be very difficult, he just didn't understand. He cried so pitifully it broke my heart. The hospital bed was already gone and he just wanted his Papa. There was an undeniable bond they shared. Even though my grandfather couldn't speak, the communication of the heart passed between them. After calming Trip, I left.

I was home for a few minutes when Dane walked in. Trip was excited to see him. He tried so hard to tell Dane that his Papa wasn't there anymore. Dane handled it much better than I did. Trip was contented then to play with his treasured trucks.

Settling in the kitchen, Dane wanted to know how my day went. He treated me so thoughtfully. He consistently wanted to hear about my day before talking about his. Deep inside, I still was shaky even though he was so sweet and understanding.

I thought, *How lucky, it really seems everything is going to work out. This baby undoubtedly was meant to be.*

I touched my tiny, new baby bump and Dane laughed.

"What are you laughing about?" I asked.

"You," he said. "I can imagine you in a few months. That little bump will have grown into a really big bump."

I tapped his shoulder lightly with my hand and told him that he could carry the next one. We laughed.

He hugged me, whispering, "I'm the luckiest man alive. I have the most beautiful wife and mother of my children."

With relief, I turned to finish our meal. He obviously felt happy with what I had cooked. He came to meals with a huge appetite, which made it fun to cook for him.

I realized that I had done the right thing for both myself and my son as I sat across from him at the kitchen table that night. My love for Ajax was deep and real but despite those emotions, I had found my place where I was meant to be.

With candles lit, we laid in each others arms for hours that night talking about our future and what we wanted from life. We had been surprised to learn that my grandparents wanted their big house to eventually become mine. We were astonished to hear Mother finally admit the truth, and say she intended to carry out their directive that on my fifth wedding anniversary their former home was to be passed down to me. We both found it hard to believe that she had never told me about this legacy before, but then, nothing much about Mother's actions could surprise me. For a good example, her own sister stayed at hotels when coming from California for her parents' funerals. There was no love lost in that sibling relationship.

My mind whirled with all the creative things I could do to the house to make it feel special. As I laid there mulling things over, I realized that paint was all we could afford right then but I was still delighted.

Making love felt natural and delightful with Dane. I felt so fulfilled and loved, each time. Feeling the warmth of our naked bodies touching, we fell asleep in each others arms. I realized how lucky we were.

I had been asleep for hours when I heard Ajax yelling my name, loudly and clearly, and then again, more softly...

"Desiree, Desiree... Desiree."

I felt myself stir. It sounded so vivid and so real. I then heard a gunshot. I could see a bullet hit him. He was shot in the belly. I could see blood gushing.

He called my name one more time, and said, "I love you. I will never leave you, I promise."

Then I felt an unmistakable, heavy warmth flooding over my body, as if someone was lying on top of me. He was silent, lying there next to me with his hand reaching up to my face.

I then saw myself in a funeral home. I was looking down at him in a beautiful casket. I wanted to touch him but couldn't. I knelt at his casket, crying hard because my hand could not reach him. He looked so handsome and so peaceful in his dress uniform with white gloves on his hands. I could see this all plainly and so clearly.

I started screaming in my sleep when I saw beautiful yellow roses in the background at the funeral home as they carried me away from his casket...

By then, Dane was sitting up, shaking me, saying, "Wake up, Desiree, wake up. You had a dream. You were screaming. What is it? Are you alright?"

I was wringing wet with sweat running down my body. I was shaking from what I had just seen in the dream. Struck speechless, at first, I could not find words to describe what I had just felt and witnessed. When I could talk, I reassured him that I just had a crazy dream; that I was okay. I told him to go back to sleep, that I was alright.

I laid there numb, still feeling Ajax's warmth enveloping me. I fought back tears. I glanced at the clock and saw it was three-thirty a.m. I quietly got out of bed when Dane fell asleep again and I went into the living room. Not able to contain myself, I slipped out the back door at about four-fifteen. I stood outside to get some fresh air. Mother came to her window and saw me. She then came to her door.

"What's the matter?" she asked, softly. I fell on my knees in the snow, sobbing uncontrollably. She came outside to get me up, thinking Dane and I had a fight and that was why I was crying. She helped me up, out of the snow, and into her house. I tried to tell her about hearing Ajax call my name twice loudly and then call out again softly. All the details poured out.

I had not told her about the night he left and all that he had told me about wanting to have a vision in his mind so that if anything happened, he could close his eyes and find peace in his vision of himself laying in bed next to me.

By then, she was crying just as hard as me.

"Mom, he's dead, he's dead and he called my name before he came to lay next to me," I cried. She tried to calm me down but I cried uncontrollably, with deep, gut-wrenching sobs that blocked my breathing. I knew that she felt it too. Only she wasn't saying so. She tried to bring me a cup of tea but I couldn't stop crying.

It was so real. "I was at the funeral home," I told her, "And I could see his body so clearly, lying there, but I couldn't touch it. I kept trying but somehow I just couldn't."

"It was a dream, that's all," she kept telling me. But that didn't convince me. I knew better. I knew he was gone.

We put our Christmas tree up that day. I tried to push that dream out of my mind but found myself repeatedly going back to it, trying to touch Ajax but not being able to reach him. Our tree was pretty and Trip felt excited, but my heart was heavy.

Trip understood who Santa was. He couldn't wait until Christmas so he could get more trucks. That made it even sweeter. I tried to concentrate on all the positive things around me; to not dwell on my dream. It was sweet fun watching Trip helping to decorate the tree. My girlfriends often complained about their husbands, that their men don't help much with the trees, but Dane seemed to enjoy it. I made hot chocolate and tried to force myself to leave the dream alone and enjoy the moment. That proved to be difficult.

I had a hard time with putting that dream behind me. I continued to see it no matter what I was doing. A few days later, while enjoying a cup of tea as I read the newspaper, there it was: Ajax's handsome graduation picture on the front page, announcing his death on December nineteenth. I realized that the day he died was the same day I had that dream. Could he really have come to be with me during his final moments? That thought tortured me.

I went outside. Mother had just pulled her car into the driveway. I collapsed in the snow. She came running to me but she already knew from the sound of my hysterical sobs that Ajax was gone and that I saw it in my dream, with him calling my name and coming to lay down beside me. I was inconsolable.

I screamed "He's gone, he's gone..." over and over again. Mother tried to get me up and into the house. She kept reminding me that I was pregnant, that I needed to go inside. I couldn't move. I was out of control as I sat there in the snow, wracked with grief.

Then it struck me: I said, "The psychic, that horrible psychic told me he would die young, Mom. Remember? I told you about that psychic," I cried.

She replied "Come on, Desiree, get up. You have to think about your baby. Sitting here in the snow is no good."

At that point, I was so stricken with grief and couldn't get myself up. I couldn't accept that Ajax was gone.

The next few days were a blur. I wasn't sure how to handle the situation. I knew Dane would not let me go to the funeral home alone but I didn't feel it was fair to Ajax's family that I walk in with a husband. I asked all my friends. They couldn't help me because not one of them could imagine walking in my shoes. Mother kept reminding me to do what Ajax would want; to do what is best for me.

My grief consumed me as I fought to accept what had happened. That dream haunted me. No matter how I tried to find peace in thoughts that he stayed true to his vision by coming to me in his final moments... nothing worked. Absolutely nothing worked. A feeling that he was all around me had not left me. I tried to convince myself that is only my imagination. That didn't work, either.

His obituary appeared in the newspaper with all the details about the funeral home, the time of viewings and the place and time of burial. The only thing I knew for certain was that I was going to send him yellow roses now instead of him sending them to me. As soon as the obituary appeared, I called the same florist who delivered my last roses from him. I requested that same type of yellow roses. They told me they would go into their receipts and find out what he picked. They reassured me they would make up a beautiful arrangement of those same yellow roses that he had sent to me.

This was the first thought or action that brought me any consolation. He would say to me that yellow roses were the most beautiful to him because they reminded him of pure sunshine. I was the sunshine in his life, he would say to me, and to him, the most beautiful woman of all. I used to laugh. But deep inside, it made me feel so very special. Between that, and him singing Pretty Woman, with that Roy Orbison growl, no one could make me feel the way he did. I cried about him never again putting a silly ice cube in his coffee and never sending me another yellow rose. How lucky our world was to have this beautiful soul among its people. He fought for us, giving his life for us. In only a few short years, he brought me fabulous memories for a lifetime.

With the flower order complete, my thoughts focused on getting through the wake. I didn't know how I would be able to stand seeing his still body lying in that casket. That night at dinner, I told Dane about ordering flowers sent to the funeral home. We had discussed this the night before but I wanted to tell him that I thought he was right to say I should put my name only on them. Now I would try to convince him that I should go alone. What I wanted was to go when no one else was there so I could say my final goodbye alone. I knew that was impossible. I felt the next best thing was to just go alone quietly and leave without being noticed, if that was at all possible.

When I mentioned all this, Dane said he would not accept any part of it and he readily told me why. As he started speaking, I felt like a doe in headlights, unable to move.

"I have shared you with him from the day I met you. I knew that, but my love for you was so real and so strong that I overlooked it. Desiree, he is gone and whatever he was to you is now a memory of the past. You are my wife. I will not allow my wife, who is pregnant with my baby, to go to this funeral home without me."

I was numb already with grief and this was the last straw.

All I could say was "Okay. I understand but please know that I must go and say goodbye. I'm so sorry you have always felt as you say, but he truly did have my heart until you came along. Then I realized that with you is where I want to be, with you and our child." I choked back my tears and said "Please forgive me. I do love you so much. Maybe I was God's way to give him happiness before he died."

Then I told Dane that I wanted to go to the afternoon viewing so Mother could watch Trip. He seemed okay with everything I said and with going to the afternoon viewing. Then I said no more about those matters.

On the way to the funeral home, I relived that entire dream but didn't say a word. When we pulled into the parking lot, I was numb with grief. I had to take a deep breath before I could get out of the car. Walking in the front door, I went to the table where visitors signed the guest book and signed my name. In that moment, I wondered what Ajax's mother would think when she later read my name.

I wondered if she would think: *If only I had let them marry, maybe my son would be alive today.*

I turned to face the area where the casket was set up and walked toward it. Dane walked beside me with his hand under my arm. I felt his guidance. As I walked to the casket, it seemed just as it had been in the dream, so beautiful. I approached the casket and I could see he was wearing his dress uniform with the white gloves on his hands. I went closer and knelt before the casket with my eyes closed. I automatically reached out to touch him. My hand stopped against a glass enclosure. Then I realized why I wasn't able to reach him in my dream. I started to cry as my hand reached across that glass. By then, Dane lifted me up to a standing position. All I recall was looking at Ajax and the overwhelming scent of yellow roses.

When I came to, I was lying on a couch in the lower level of the funeral home. The wretched odor of smelling salts waved beneath my nose revived me. I tried to get up but Dane and Reid, Laura's husband, were standing over me. They told me to lie still. I didn't know what had happened, but I started crying again, asking why I couldn't touch Ajax. Reid asked everyone else to leave. He said he wanted to speak with me alone. Although Dane felt reluctant, he left the room.

Reid sat down at the end of the sofa near my feet. I laid there in total silence absorbing every word, longing for truth and the closure it would give me.

He told me, "Do not believe what the family is going to tell you about Ajax being engaged before he died. It's not true. That young man died loving *you and only you*. What the two of you shared before he left for Vietnam was the highlight of his life. I know this with certainty because he confided in me one night when we went out for a beer together, just the two of us."

He went on to say, "I want to tell you about the soldier who accompanied Ajax's body back home. Ajax was killed while trying to save one of his buddies who had been shot. He tried to rescue the man, to pull him back to safety but instead, Ajax was also shot.

"The escort asked us who Desiree is because that was who Ajax called out for as he died. The escort told us Ajax called your name three times before he passed. Ajax said, 'Desiree, move on with your life and be happy.' He knew he was never coming back before he even left. He told me he knew but you gave him what he needed to die in peace. He also told me that he had written you three letters telling you to move on with your life, find love and happiness. Ajax loved you with all his heart and he always will."

I laid there not moving except to breathe.

All I could say was, "Thank you so much, Reid. I promise I won't say anything about all this."

He went on to tell me that when the body came back, his hair was full of orange mud. That the funeral director, who knew Ajax from the time he was just a little boy, sent the men who escorted the body out for lunch. While they were gone, he removed the glass and tried to clean up the mess for the family's sake. He knew the entire family since they lived so close to the funeral home.

Then Reid said something that really shook my foundation, "I wonder how Mama feels now. I bet she feels she should have let you two get married. Maybe her son would be alive today if she had."

Tears streamed down my face as I said "Thank you Reid."

I asked him how I got onto the couch. He told me that I passed out and before Dane could get to me to pick me up, he did.

He said "I did it for Ajax. I loved that kid, and he loved you. Desiree, move on in your life," he said, "that's what he would have wanted."

I asked Reid if he would go back with me so I could say goodbye. He got up and took my hands to help me up. He walked with me back into the room where Ajax's body laid and went with me to the casket, standing there until I was ready to leave.

I went to Laura and Ajax's older sister but I didn't have strength to speak to anyone else or the desire. From them, I heard the story about Ajax being engaged before he died. When I asked where his fiancée was, they said she chose not to come.

I touched the glass one more time and whispered "I love you and always will, no one will ever have my heart as you did, no one ever, as long as I live."

While leaving the room, I went to the yellow roses that I ordered and smelled their wonderful scent. I saw Ajax's father sitting with Ajax's mother. Our eyes met and I merely nodded my head. I'm sure he understood why I didn't go to him because he nodded back.

I didn't attend the funeral but I could hear the twenty-one gun salute from the cemetery. I was in my tiny kitchen sitting with Mother at the same table where Ajax and I sat at during those few months before he left for Viet Nam.

As we heard those twenty-one shots, one by one, they seemed as loud as if we stood beside the casket.

All I could say was, "He's gone. It's really over."

I looked into Mothers eyes and said, "I will never allow myself to love like that again. Never... never. It's simply too painful."

Chapter Seven

With the holidays over, I welcomed taking the tree down. The three of us took the decorations off and put them away neatly so they would not get broken. I loved Christmas, but this one had been tough, one I wanted to quickly forget. I felt happy that I had planned way ahead. All of Trip's gifts from Santa were bought way before Christmas.

Although my heart was not really in it, no one knew that. I covered up my emotions. Mother seemed eager to switch houses or at least that's the signal she sent us. We decided to wait until the weather was a little better. Moving our home in the snow was not something either of us wanted to take on.

Spring came early that year. My little bump was turning into a well-rounded tummy. The baby was due at the end of June. There was plenty of time to get everything situated. Being the kind of person who tackles any project with gusto, I wasn't worried at all. I already had beautiful baby furniture that Author had bought when I was pregnant with Trip. So I figured I was already a step ahead. Mother allowed me to go into the big house anytime I wanted, to paint or decorate. That was great. I was getting bigger steadily, so I wanted to finish what needed to be done before I was too big to deal with much.

The move into the big house was more difficult than I thought because we were moving two houses instead of only one but I was grateful to have a bigger house. My furniture looked quite well in the bigger rooms. I was happy to leave all the memories behind in the little house. Most of the time, I concentrated on the present but sometimes that became impossible. Once in the big house, I was able to tackle all my projects and get everything in order by the time the baby was due.

My second labor and delivery was much easier than the first. When they laid that beautiful baby boy in my arms, I cried and cried as I held him close to me. All the nurses were coming in the room to see him because he was so incredibly beautiful. His features were small and perfect and his little head was covered with silky, jet black hair. The nurses told me they had not seen a baby with that much hair in years. I felt so proud. I decided to name my new little boy Craig.

Dane brought Trip to the hospital the day I went home so he could be a part of it all and not have jealous feelings. He looked at the baby and smiled as he touched his head, although he was more interested in the cherry lollipop that the nurses gave him.

Dane was as proud as a peacock. When he handed the baby to me in the car his face glowed with pride. All the way home, Trip chattered and chattered, telling me about things he did while I was in the hospital. During that ride, I realized what a lucky lady I was and how blessed to have Dane in my life. He was a decent, wonderful man who showed me daily how much he loved me and his family.

There were days when I felt blue and depressed but I handled that to the best of my ability. I was feeling guilty that I was alive with two handsome little boys while Ajax was gone. Nobody knew about my depression or the guilt in my heart. I thought about Ajax a lot in those first few weeks. When I fed Craig his bottle late at night, my thoughts would drift to "what if this" or "what if that." I loved every minute of being a mother. I enjoyed our two little sons to the fullest though I was still troubled over Ajax's death.

I often wondered if I would resolve my guilt and regain my happy-go-lucky personality. Some women go through depression after giving birth but what I was feeling was much deeper. It was something that made me promise that some day I would make my life count by somehow giving back and helping others less fortunate than myself.

Soon I was to discover the true meaning of what Ajax promised me, on that last night we were together, about always loving me and guiding me, and never leaving me. What I was about to experience would help me understand the meaning behind Richard Franklin's famous painting

"To Go Beyond." The painting depicts two human souls reuniting with such adoration for each other that their true and tender love can not be mistaken.

That night after we brought Craig home, when I was sound asleep, Ajax appeared to me. This was the first I had dreamed of him since he died calling my name...

> *There he was in front of me, reaching out to hug me. As I went toward him I felt his arms around me.*
>
> *"Hello, Pretty Woman," he said. Then he kissed me gently and said, "I told you I would love you forever and that I would never leave you."*
>
> *I felt his warm, moist kiss as if he was there in person. He continued to tell me, "Your baby is beautiful and healthy but you must listen to me, you will need to get him medical assistance when he gets sick, do not wait or you could loose him. I was staring into his beautiful eyes and I started to cry, asking him why it had to be this way with him gone and me still there.*
>
> *"Hush now," he said. He kissed me again, and said "Just remember that I love you, and I always will. No harm will ever come to you, I promise. I must go now, I love you."*
>
> *Then a white cloud enveloped us and he was suddenly gone.*

I awakened, feeling tears run down my face. I laid still, quietly digesting what I had dreamed.

It was so real, I thought.

I could even feel his arms around me and his lips kissing mine. Even though I knew this was a dream, I still relived it, over and over, wishing each time that I could be with him again and feel his kisses.

After a few months, the dream was no longer on my mind as much as when it first happened. One night, Craig woke me up crying and pulling on his ear. The next morning, I called the doctor and took Craig to be checked. At the doctor's office, an ear infection was confirmed. He needed medication. The poor little guy was so miserable. I stopped at the drug store on the way home and had his prescription filled. Soon, I was back home. I gave him his medication and rocked him to sleep. Laying him in his crib, I thought of the dream and how Ajax had told me to get him medical assistance right away.

Well, I thought, *that was it. I did get him to a doctor right away.*

Within a few minutes, he woke up crying and throwing up. He was very sick. He couldn't seem to keep much down, so I gave him clear liquids instead of his formula. By then, it was time for his second dose of medicine.

I gave it to him, thinking *when the medicine takes effect he will feel better.*

It was four in the afternoon and he was crying hard, so I called the doctor again, who told me to wait until morning and then, if he was still throwing up, to bring him in.

Nothing I did would calm him down nor did he stop vomiting. It was about ten p.m. and I just couldn't get that last dream out of my mind. I decided to take him to the hospital emergency room. There I learned that the medication I was giving him was spoiled. If I had continued to give it to him all night, it would have poisoned him and he probably would not have survived.

I cried as I held my little baby son, thinking if I had listened to the doctor instead of to Ajax, my boy would have been gone by morning. How do I thank a dead man? Or when asked why I took him to the hospital, how do I tell them about a dream?

They admitted my baby into the hospital with intravenous tubes in his little legs. I refused to leave the hospital. They had to give in and ignored my presence there. They brought me a chair to recline in, and that is where I stayed. Craig was kept in the hospital for three days and I never left him alone. He was such a sick baby. I was filled with rage about the medication being spoiled and causing all of this. But I never told anyone about my dream.

I kept it to myself, and in my own way, I whispered, "Thank you" to Ajax.

With Craig back home, everything seemed to get back to normal except I felt like I was coming down with the flu. I was sick to my stomach and tired. I thought the cause was all that I had gone through with Craig but I soon learned it wasn't any of that. Craig was only six months old when I realized I was three months pregnant.

I was astonished because we had done everything possible to prevent a pregnancy at that point. Dane was happy about the idea of another baby, though. He kept telling me this one would be the little girl who I wanted.

The pregnancy developed with no problems, and of course, my tummy grew and grew. I often wondered how it could possibly go back to being a nice tight tummy, but it did. My labor was long and hard but the moment they put that gorgeous baby girl in my arms I soon forgot what a hard time I had getting her here.

We named her Lilly after a beautiful little girl that we had met at a wedding during my pregnancy. I was so tickled that I had a daughter. She was one of the prettiest babies I had ever seen. Her features were delicate and she had the largest, far-set eyes. Her hair was as dark as the boys' and her eyes just as huge and as black. The day I brought her home from the hospital, Craig looked big next to her. When I left to go to the hospital to deliver her, I hugged him, thinking "my little baby," but when I brought my baby girl home, he looked big.

Having three children was like a dream come true for me. "Proud and contended" are good words to describe how I felt. Dane was such an easygoing man that it was a delight to be married to him. He was a real, hands-on daddy, doing everything from two a.m. feedings to diapers. Although I never took him for granted, I couldn't seem to simply let go and really love him wildly. Not knowing if he sensed that or not, I just went on trying to be a good wife, hoping that would somehow prevent him from feeling the distance in my heart.

Two weeks after I came home with Lilly, I felt beat from being up all night with her and then trying to take care of two very active boys. Craig really loved her. He refused to take his bottle, saying "baby, baby," while gesturing for me to give the bottle to her. I was thinking this would be an easy way to get him off the bottle.

Laundry was a daily chore that I tried desperately to keep up with it. Remembering I had a load of clothes that needed to go into the dryer, I headed toward the basement steps as Craig asked for a drink of water.

I gave give him some water first and then went to the baby to check on her. What I found was a blue baby who could not breathe.

I lifted her out of her crib and gave her mouth to mouth resuscitation until she breathed on her own again. Going to the telephone, I called our doctor to tell him what had happened. He said to bring her in so he could check her. I called a neighbor to stay with my boys and left right away.

Thank goodness Dane was home so he could drive us, because half way there, Lilly stopped breathing again. I had to give her mouth to mouth again, in the car. When the doctor examined her, he found she had newborn pneumonia and put her in the hospital, in an oxygen tent. Once again, there was no dealing with me, so the nurses gave in and brought the same reclining chair back into the room for me. There I stayed until she came home a few days later. As I sat in that chair one night, watching my precious little baby girl sleep, I wondered why I hadn't dreamed of Ajax telling me about this crisis ahead of time, as happened with Craig. Not knowing why I would even think that, I just focused my thoughts elsewhere and soon fell asleep. With the nurses coming in constantly, I didn't get much sleep, but wild horses could not have persuaded me to leave her there in the hospital alone.

When we brought my precious little girl home, and I'm not sure who was more excited, me or Craig. Gosh, was he ever excited when he saw the car pull in the driveway. I was home again with my own family that I had always so disparately wanted. I was exhausted but so happy to be home.

Hearing the door open, I looked up to see Mother was standing there. Without even asking if she could help with anything, she began telling me about her day.

"I saw Bill today and he couldn't believe I'm a grandmother of three," she bragged. Then she said, "He saw you last week and he was surprised that I look so much younger than you do."

I didn't respond. I was too surprised that she would even tell me something like that, knowing what I had been through in the past few weeks. This woman was so mean-spirited and, truth be told, the man probably didn't even say that. She may well have made it up just to bring me down. I never knew why she was compelled to be so hateful to me. But I was so happy to be home that I couldn't be bothered to give her another minute of my time. I went to the kitchen and made a bottle of formula for the baby then fed and rocked her. I wanted the Arctic Queen to go home and leave us alone. She must have read my mind. She left very soon after telling me how much younger she looked than me.

She's something else, I thought, as she closed the door.

Life was good. I had my fabulous family and a wonderful husband who loved me, without doubt. I flourished, I was so happy. It was as if all my dreams were only a heartbeat away. I couldn't have been happier. The ache in my heart seemed to slowly heal. I threw myself into being a good mother. My children were my life as I strived every day to make them healthy and happy. I cooked, baked, even grew a garden and canned, all with the thought in mind that my children would have everything I didn't get.

A hug, a kiss or the words "I love you" were all a part of what I gave my children, daily. I continued to slowly rework the house to fit our needs. I would put the children to bed and tackle one thing after another.

Stripping paint from woodwork and repainting throughout our large house seemed like an endless project. Never before have I seen so many windows with so many layers of paint on them. My Grandpa must have re-painted every year. I stripped all the woodwork and stained it from white to a wood tone. My grandparents must have put ten layers of paint on the window frames, but we slowly stripped them all.

I was a fanatic about my children living in a clean house. I would sometimes scrub the kitchen floor at midnight. Dane worked in the electronics department of the steel mill so he worked a swing shift schedule. On nights when he would be working until eleven o'clock, I would take on a task and work at it until he got home. I reworked that house to a point that it was unrecognizable, compared to what it had been when we moved in.

Dane was a good worker but not with skills to fix things in a house, so that was left to me. I realized I had a good husband, compared to some of my friends, so I didn't complain. I simply took the bull by the horns and did what I could by myself. Lilly was about eighteen months old when, Heidi, our dog, had a litter of puppies. We loved this dog and planned to breed her before we had her spayed. What I didn't expect was a dozen puppies at once and a mother dog who got sick and could not nurse. Just when I thought it couldn't get any worse, when Dane was in the garage he moved the lawn mower and a large wood board hit him on the head, giving him a concussion. It was fairly bad, so the doctor put him in the hospital for a few days.

There I was with a husband in the hospital, three small kids, a dozen puppies who had to be fed every few hours, and a frustrated mother dog. I didn't know which chore to tackle first. When those few days were up, Dane came home from the hospital, and thank goodness, because I was about to scream. I couldn't depend on Mother to help me, with Author gone. She was way too busy in her social life to do anything else. About a week later, I took the little ones outside and brought all the puppies out into the grass so they could play with them. Lilly was pushing her dolly in her buggy on the driveway, so I put some of the puppies in her buggy for her. She was so excited she squealed with delight.

A man came to my fence and told me he was a photographer with the local newspaper. He asked if he could take a picture of Lilly and the buggy full of puppies. Of course, I said yes, and to my surprise, the next day, on the front page of the newspaper, there was a picture of Lilly pushing her buggy full of puppies. Being proud of that picture, I wanted the whole world to know she was my daughter.

Never losing sight of how happy my life was, I tried never to take it all for granted. Dane and I were not a couple who argued or disagreed about how to raise children or how to handle money. Our marriage was quite easy and comfortable. Knowing what some of my friends were going through with their husbands, I made sure to let Dane know he was appreciated. He was such an easygoing man that everything I suggested, he went along with.

Our sex life was good, or at least, I thought it was, and that is half the battle.

Dane told me, "Making love with you is my gift. It's always just as exciting as the first time."

Him saying that made me feel special and even more willing to please him. He wasn't a demanding man but he was a man, and like most men, he thought sex was the be all and end all. He was loving and caring and always wanting to please me. To me, that's important. I felt like we were a good match, but then there were times when I longed for what I felt when I made love with Ajax. There was a total feeling of surrendering to each other with him, a feeling words cannot describe. The world stopped existing and my body responded to his kisses, and to his touch. I cared deeply for Dane but somehow I just couldn't let go.

I never talked about this with anyone, I just tucked it way deep in my heart, knowing no one could understand. As much as I tried, those feelings were one of a kind. They just didn't exist thereafter. Those feelings were buried for a long time but the memories of them were still fresh. As much as I tried to not think about it, it was such a pure, true, deep love. How does one ever forget that?

It was such a blessing that I sold one of my dozen puppies to a woman who became my best friend. We did so many things together. I welcomed someone to have fun with, someone I could trust. Since her husband worked changing shifts, it was fun to have someone to visit with occasionally after the little ones went to bed and my man was working.

I really liked Gigi. I felt so comfortable around her. Most often, she brought her puppy with her, so our dogs could play together. Dane thought Mother was jealous of Gigi but I couldn't imagine why she would feel that way. Gigi is the sweetest woman. She and I had a solid friendship.

I had an innate need to give something back in return for all the good that I was blessed with. I came up with an idea: to make small animal pillows for the unwanted children in a county home. Gigi and I worked for months on these stuffed pillows. In the holiday season, we delivered them. When we gave those poor little handicapped children our pillows, my heart ached for them. I'm not sure which of us cried more when we saw their faces. Our reward far outweighed the work those pillows represented.

Mother wasn't into her grandchildren as much after becoming socially active. Mother seemed to love our kids but they had their place with her. That place was to not to interfere with her dating or with entertaining in her house.

There were no young girls around who could babysit for me. It was easier to stay home. But when New Years Eve was upon us, we decided to go out. Dane and I so rarely went out that this was a treat for us. I bought a new dress and I couldn't wait to dress up and go out dancing.

Dane and I danced out feet off, hardly ever sitting down. Even after three children I am still thin and can dance all night.

When midnight came, Dane took me into his arms and kissed me lightly, whispering "I am so in love with you, you are my world." Then he kissed me with such passion that it took me by surprise. I wondered how the night would unfold for me.

And unfold it truly did. What a night. I couldn't believe the desire, the raw lust, that Dane showed as he whispered how much he loved me.

At one point he said, "Thank you for choosing me."

I went numb, but did not show it.

With the New Years Eve behind us, I happily got up and made breakfast for everyone. Gigi and her husband were coming for New Years Day dinner, so I need to get everything started, ready for me to enjoy conversation with them when they arrived.

Gigi was a wonderful cook most of the time but then there were times when she cooked weird stuff, like fried cow brains and scrambled eggs. She laughs at me because I can't even get that close to to my mouth much less put it into my mouth and eat it. I believe I'll always pass on eating brains.

Mother stopped by before she went to dinner with one of the men she was dating. She didn't behave very friendly but then, what was new about that? I hated how she acted like that but there wasn't much I could do to improve her. Thinking back, I can see why Dane's family never invited her to their houses on a holiday. She just couldn't stop acting hatefully.

"Oh well, her loss," I would think and quickly dismiss it.

I continued to redo our house in my spare time. Gigi and I still made those little pillows for the special needs children. Some nights, I was so tired that I was asleep before my head even hit my pillow.

On one such night, in a dream, I felt a kiss on my lips
and heard the words, "Hello Pretty Woman."
"Oh my God, it's you!" I said. "I miss you so much."

"Let me hold you." he said, as I felt his arms close around me.

"I told you that I would always love you and guide you."

I didn't want to let go, but he moved away and said, "You have to listen to me carefully. Don't wait inside for Dane. You must wait outside for him. Please listen to me."

"What do you mean?" I asked.

"You will know, just wait outside, not inside. I must go," he said, "but let me hold you one more time."

I started to cry and begged him not to go.

He said, "Come with me."

"I can't," I cried, "I have to raise my children."

Once more, he kissed my lips and said, "I love you."

Then, as before, there was a white cloud and he was gone. I awoke with tears streaming down my face.

I laid there, very still, not knowing what to think about what had just happened. Still wet with tears, I buried my face in my pillow and cried even harder. Knowing what took place the last time he warned me, I felt unsettled and scared. I was glad Dane had not come home from work yet, because it was all so real I wondered if I had talked out loud during my dream.

I dried my tears but couldn't go back to sleep.

Dane will soon be home, I thought. *I'd better calm down and go back to sleep.*

When morning came, I thought long and hard about the words Ajax had said that didn't make sense. Again, not wanting to tell anyone about this for fear they would think I'm crazy, I withdrew into my thoughts.

"You're awfully quiet today" Dane said.

I said, "I'm just tired. I didn't sleep well last night."

"Go to bed early tonight. Forget about the house. It will be here tomorrow."

I smiled and agreed.

With spring soon coming, I wanted to concentrate on sprucing up the outside of our home. That's something I had not tackled previously.

We had a beautiful lawn but the landscaping needed some tender loving care to make it look complete.

"Can we go to the Home and Garden Show in Cleveland?" I asked. "It's going on this weekend."

"Okay," Dane replied, "that's a good idea. We might get some inspiration."

We decided to go on Sunday since Dane was off Sunday and Monday that week. Awake early, I had breakfast and was started before anyone else got up. I had made a pot of coffee when I first went downstairs. I was quietly drinking my coffee when Dane came down. The thought of an ice cube in Ajax's coffee was still so fresh in my mind that I thought about it often, as I did on this morning.

When Dane entered the kitchen, he leaned over, kissed me softly and said "Good Morning."

Of course I replied in kind, as I got up and pour him a cup of coffee. We decided to go to the Home and Garden Show in late afternoon and then stop at our favorite pizza restaurant for dinner. Dane had a few things he wanted to do that day so this plan would work well for us. Our little ones were much more content after their nap.

The morning went fast. Soon it was time to get everyone ready for our forty-minute ride into Cleveland. During nap time, I got myself ready and packed the diaper bag with everything I would need for the afternoon. I thank God for the company that produced Cheerios. They come in handy when I need to keep one of the little ones happy and busy. I was really looking forward to the show. With the babies, Dane and I hardly ever got out. That day was a treat for us both.

The Home and Garden Show was held at a big convention center. I knew it would attract many vendors but what I saw was even bigger than I imagined. The main entrance was huge with beautifully polished marble floors that seemed to extend forever. After reaching the right doorway, I put the two little ones in the stroller and we started visiting all the booths and displays. Of course, every vendor was giving away logo swag, so I collected a supply.

When I had to use the rest room, I told Dane I would be right back. I left him with the three children. When I returned, I saw a yellow rose sitting on top of our diaper bag. I picked it up and sniffed it, then asked Dane where he got the rose. Looking around, I realized the garden section was far away, at the other end of the building.

He looked at me blankly and asked, "What rose?"

"This one, Silly, where did you get it?" I said.

Now he was looking at me with a blank stare as he answered "I don't know where it came from. I didn't see anyone put it there and I have been standing here."

Being afraid to speculate, I dropped the subject and put the rose back on the diaper bag. My heart was in my throat. I tried hard to not show it. There was much to see and we both enjoyed getting out so we made our way through the crowd and came to the garden section. Looking around, I didn't see a single rose bush nor did I see any vases with roses. Then, I really wondered where the rose came from. I moved past the rose to enjoy all the displays of landscaping.

The baby was getting fussy. It was the end of the day so we decided to leave. I had Dane take Trip and Craig to the bathroom so they would not have to go in the car when we were half way to the restaurant. When they returned, I took the baby into the women's room and changed her diapers, so we were good to go. By then, it was evening and getting quite dark outside.

Dane told me to wait in the lobby while he went for the car since it was raining. Our car was parked in a parking garage rather far away. He left, but then returned, to tell me which doorway where he would pull up. Trip and Craig were running around on the beautiful marble floors as I stood watching with Lilly in my arms. She was fussy but she was watching them run. I looked down at the stroller to get a pacifier for Lilly because she was starting to cry. Just then, I saw that rose, still sitting on the diaper bag, and the dream that I had before came back to me. I wondered for a minute if this was what Ajax was talking about when he said I should wait for Dane outside and not inside.

I got a panicky feeling inside as I called for the boys to come to me. They weren't very far away so soon they were by my side. I put Lilly back into the stroller, and of course, she started crying but I took Craig's hand, and with Trip following closely, I took my children outside the big doors to wait for Dane. By now, it was raining really hard. It seemed like he was gone forever.

Suddenly, I heard a loud roaring sound of motorcycles inside the convention center. I backed up a little to look into the door. Sure enough, there were a dozen or so motorcycles, all lined up in a row across the floor. I had no idea where they came from or how they even got in there. People were moving out of their way as they rode on those beautiful marble floors.

I pulled Trip and Craig closer to me and picked Lilly up into my arms. The motorcycles roared louder and louder as they made their way back to the entrance. Sudden they were silent. Then a burst of engines roared so loudly it scared the boys. The motor cycles started racing and I could hear people screaming so loudly it scared even me.

Dane pulled up just as the motorcycles left the building through a side entrance. I almost threw the boys into the back seat. Then I hopped in with Lilly in my arms.

Dane asked, "What is it? What was that noise?"

All I said was "Hurry, just hurry, lets get out of here!"

He quickly put the stroller into the trunk and we left.

"What is going on?" he asked?

Trip jumped in. He tried to tell his father all about the big motorcycles and that they were inside the building, riding in the hallway.

After Trip finished, with my voice still quavering, I told Dane about the loud roaring and how the motorcycles went right past the doors where we were standing outside. Then we heard people screaming.

Dane put his hand on my hand and said "It's a good thing you were outside. I didn't expect you to wait outside since it was raining so hard but it's good that you did."

I just let it go. I didn't say anything more about it as we went to the restaurant. Inside the restaurant, I felt safe and tried to relax and enjoy the pizza.

The next day, the newspaper's headline read, "Motorcycles Slay Two at Home Show."

I felt sick to my stomach as I read the article. Two men who had been knifed by those motorcyclists bled to death.

What a horrible sight, I thought.

Dane was off work that day. When I showed him the article, his face blanched, as white as a sheet. He kept saying, over and over, that I had been right there in the lobby, with the children.

Then he looked at me strangely and said, "Just think what might have happened if you had not gone outside to wait for me."

I agreed with him but was far too upset to carry on a conversation.

I silently communicated with Ajax, thanking him for protecting us. I knew in my heart I would not have gone out into the rainy weather if I had not been warned to wait outside. Then I remembered the yellow rose that appeared on my diaper bag. I looked at the sink in our kitchen. There it was, in a small vase, sitting on the counter.

Ajax wanted to remind me of my dream, I thought, *and to make sure I remembered his warning.*

It's hard to fathom such a thing. Maybe, if someone else was telling me all this, I might wonder if that person was crazy. Those dreams were so real and out of my control. I didn't know Craig would get a spoiled prescription. Nor did I know there was going to be a Home and Garden Show, much less motorcycles rampaging on the inside of the building. How blessed I am to have someone love me so much that he continues to watch over me and my loved ones from beyond the grave.

Soon my thoughts of the Home and Garden Show were a distant memory. I continued to work around the house to create a home I could feel proud of. I kept the thought in mind that soon we would own our home with the deed in our name.

Sometimes, as I worked, I mused about my Grandma's stated intent for creating my inheritance. Grandma often said how regretful she felt that I went through so much emotional suffering as a little girl; that to make up for Mother's cruelty, at least partially, she wanted me to have her home after she passed, where I would raise my children in a loving way. She would say that she couldn't imagine what genes Mother inherited because nobody she knew of, in our family, was as selfish and mean-spirited as Mother was.

Hardly a day went by when I didn't spend at least an hour on some improvement. I even painted the basement and fixed it up enough to have birthday and Halloween parties down there. I painted the walls and the floor with two coats so it was quite clean and fresh. There wasn't much that wasn't redone or at least painted. It wasn't as if the house had been neglected but it was old and needed sprucing up.

One day in March, I thought I was coming down with the flu. Then, when I realized just what the problem was, it wasn't the flu. One night when Dane came home from work around midnight I was sitting up waiting for him, crying. Right away, he thought Mother had acted out and showed her colors again. That was not unusual but this time she was innocent. I wasn't sure just how to tell him, so I blurted out the words, "I think I am pregnant; I'm not positive but I'm pretty sure."

Being the calm one between the two of us, he simply said, "Well, make an appointment and go to the doctor to make sure either way."

Then he came to me and wrapped his arms around me.

He said, "I'm not sure about you, but I have plenty of love left for another child. Who knows, maybe it will be another girl. Then we would be complete with two boys and two girls."

He was kissing me sweetly, convincing me not to cry, saying it will all be okay.

You are such a good husband, I thought, as I looked at him standing there, looking down at me.

Then he replied, "Hey, you always wanted six children, so if you're pregnant again, we're on our way to achieving that goal."

I hugged him hard and said, "Well, maybe four would be enough." He laughed, knowing he had calmed me down.

The next day, I made an appointment with the doctor. Sure enough, I was pregnant. While still on the table, I told the doctor to check again to make sure.

"Oh, I'm sure," he said. You're about three months pregnant."

I felt dumbfounded. I could hardly believe my ears.

All the way home, I kept thinking, *Four children, wow! I truly am on my way to having the six children I always wanted.*

Dane was thrilled. He showed it in many ways. This new little one would be born in September.

"Seems that New Years Eve was more fun than we thought," I told Dane that night. He was thrilled about another baby. He was a great daddy and a truly wonderful husband.

With number four on the way, I wanted to work hard to get the house finished. If my calculations were correct, our home would be ours some time in July. I worked feverishly, trying to finish it by then. We decided to spend our savings to have new kitchen cabinets installed along with new carpets. Our furniture was in great shape. Most of it was relatively new, purchased within the last two or three years. Cabinets and carpeting were all that we needed.

I was especially excited about a new kitchen. I worked especially hard to get the old oil cloth off the walls and hang new wallpaper. Everything was falling into place and looking so new. Gigi helped me strip off the oil cloth. That took several days to achieve. By the end of July, I had most of it done. I was ready for the new cabinets and carpeting to be installed. I wondered why Mother hadn't said anything about transferring the title of the house but I didn't say anything to her.

I noticed more frequently that Mother didn't like Gigi being my friend or that we did so much together. One night, both our husbands were working until midnight. Gigi and I continued to make the pillows for special needs children. Mother came over in a lather and seemed to have a burr under her saddle. She didn't say very much but I could see she was unhappy. I didn't know what her problem was but I soon learned.

The next day, she came over before Dane left for work. She screamed, "You're going to ruin you marriage if that bitch Gigi continues to come here. I don't like her and she is not to come here again. Do you hear me?"

I was stunned. I told her she could not control me like that. Then I said "Gigi is my friend. We're not doing anything wrong."

Suddenly, her face flushed and she started to yell again, only this time, she went way out of line.

She said, "If Gigi comes here one more time, you two can pack your bags and get out this house."

Dane told her "Get out of here, Catherine. You have no right to scream at Desiree this way. Get out *now*."

She stormed out, yelling "Pack and get out, *now*."

With her gone, I started crying. I asked Dane what we would do with a baby on the way and nowhere to go. Once again, being the calm one, he told me not to cry. He said that he would see to it that we had somewhere nice to live. I was crying largely because we had just put all our savings into the house. We didn't have much cash.

I called Gigi and told her what had happened. After talking with her for over an hour, I told her I thought it best that she not come around until we could decide what we were going to do. She was not happy with any of it. She said Mother was controlling my life and that I needed to get away from such an evil woman. This wasn't the first time one of my friends referred to her as an evil person but somehow, this time it hit me like a slap in the face.

All my life she had put me down with her harsh words. She never liked any of my friends. Any time she could, she made derogatory remarks about Dane. This man who was so good to her, doing everything and anything for her, she chose to bash when he was not around. I had been overlooking and justifying it by believing she was simply a miserable woman. But this time, I got it. I was through.

I went to Lamaze classes so I could have a natural childbirth with this baby. That proved to be more advantageous than I could have ever imagined. Dane and I met some friendly couples at these classes and thoroughly enjoyed every minute. I felt nervous about our home situation but tried to stay calm for our baby's sake. With only a month or so to go, I was torn between starting to pack up a few things before my due date or simply waiting until we decided what we were going to do. Knowing that after I delivered this baby, my hands would be full with taking care of our little ones, I was confused about how to handle my situation.

It was difficult to live next door to Mother. So was even speaking with her. She stayed away, which suited Dane perfectly. I hated confrontations but this was not something I caused. I was missing Gigi a lot. She and I had done so many projects together. She and her husband were close friends of ours. They didn't have children yet, so they were willing to come to our home to make visits easier for us. They always brought things for us to share and our kids just loved them. This was a sad situation but not one that I could change or fix.

A few weeks after the fight with Mother, I received a phone call from the attorney that was to handle the paperwork for the transfer of the house. When the secretary told me to hold for his call, my heart was beating fast with anticipation. When he came to the phone, he said that he was calling me to see if I knew that Mother had changed her mind about transferring the home to me. She decided to cancel it all.

He told me he thought I probably didn't know, given the way she had handled the changes. I wasn't surprised. She frequently pulled some kind of stunt with me, but what he said next did surprise me. It seems she had directed him to cancel the transfer in January, almost eight months earlier and she had finalized the cancellation, just lately. He apologized for not calling me sooner but said it wasn't his place to inform me. However, he had heard that she was forcing us out of the house. He was more than an attorney to me; he was a friend. I had known him for years. I became acquainted with him through mutual friends.

I then told him he heard right; that we had invested all our money in new kitchen cabinets and carpeting throughout the house and that I was due to deliver our fourth baby anytime now. He sounded sympathetic but there was absolutely nothing he could do about her actions. After hanging up, I sat down, feeling astounded.

What a cold, heartless bitch, I thought.

She had already maneuvered our legacy away from us, months previously, before all the remodeling I did at our own cost and with my own hands. It was, basically, a theft, pure and simple. Not only did she cheat me and Dane, she also did this crooked deed to our little ones as well, because now, most of our savings were gone. I knew we wouldn't be out on the street but I also knew it would be tough moving so soon after delivering a new baby.

When Dane came home from work, I told him about the lawyer calling me. He couldn't believe his ears.

Being very emotionally pregnant, I started to cry and asked, "How could any mother do such a thing to her only child? I'm all she has and she cheated me, royally."

After all I had done for her over the years she did this to me. In the last few years, I even made enough dinner that every day she could eat at my house after coming home from work. She never bought any food or gave me even a little bit of money toward the cost. I did it because I respected my Mother and because she was working. There was always something on my stove for her to eat and she ate that food knowing that behind my back she had taken my house and knowing we were using all our savings to upgrade it. No wonder she had been so happy with the kitchen cabinets and carpeting.

Dane was very angry. He opened up about many things. He and I talked for a while about what we should do. He tried to set my mind at ease, telling me not to worry, that we would be fine.

Then he said that he wasn't happy to be living next door to her; that he felt ashamed of her having men coming and going like her home was a brothel. He didn't like the kind of questions Trip was starting to ask about why Grandma locks the door and doesn't let him in when she has company. Trip was approaching an age where he noticed such things. Being a very bright little guy, he didn't miss much.

I felt so used, abused, and disappointed, because all my life I had been overlooking what she did to me, making excuses for her behavior, and all to no avail, because in the end, she let me know exactly how little she cared for me.

As Dane and I talked that night, we realized that one of the men who used to come to her house must have known something was fishy because he came to our home one night when he knew she was gone. He had played a trick on her to get even with her for cheating on him. He wanted us to know the truth about what was going on. He warned us to be wary, saying she was not truthful and that he knew she had lied to us.

When we asked why he came to us he said he respected us and he had grown to like us, "But do not believe her," he added, "she lies about everything. I wish I could tell you more, but I can't."

Of course, we thanked him for caring enough to warn us, given we had not a clue about the issues he was revealing. Whatever the trouble, it was good to hear that he had grown to respect and care about us.

I never let Mother know that this guy had come to us. Her version of him was in no way even remotely similar to our own perceptions. She tried to paint him as some sex-crazed guy that she had to throw out. It was interesting how all the pieces of this puzzle fit together.

Going into labor a few weeks early didn't surprise me. I delivered a beautiful baby girl. We named her Kelly. I was delighted that I now had two boys and two girls.

What a beautiful family, I thought.

I was sure that Dane told his family about what happened with Mother, but they were such sweet people that they said nothing to me about that. I knew they loved me and thought highly of me, so I assumed they didn't want to hurt me by calling attention to all that. I'm sure they were disappointed that their son had put all his money into a home only to have it taken away, but they thought enough of me not to make an issue of it.

Everyone we knew came to the hospital to see our baby but the conversation was just about the her. She was a pretty baby. She had the tiniest features, a beautiful little mouth, and a complete head of jet black hair. There were no blonds like me anywhere in sight. I was so proud of her. I felt she was my treasure, my perfect baby.

Craig and Lilly were thrilled with her and wouldn't leave her alone. They wanted to hold her and feed her. They continually checked the hospital bassinet to make sure she was okay. Trip, on the other hand, was done with babies. Although he did ask to hold her, he soon lost interest and went about his own business of checking out what he could get into next.

When I came home from the hospital, of course Mother wanted to see the baby. She acted falsely, as if nothing had happened between us. I would never keep the little ones away from her because I felt that would only hurt the innocent. I didn't want to hurt them. Even dismayed by how she acted, I still said nothing.

Dane, being the gentleman that he was, followed my lead and kept things pleasant. I was "over the moon" with another daughter. I wasn't going to allow anything or anyone to destroy my happiness. There were so many people coming in and out of my house within the next week that I lost track of how many came to see our new little bundle. It was a constant flow of all our friends, extended family, and Dane's family. The friend who didn't come was the one who I really wanted to share my happy moment with. Gigi hadn't come over since the day Mother told me to pack my bags and get out.

When Kelly was about six weeks old, we went back to have a reunion with our Lamaze classmates so everyone could see the babies we gave birth to and also to share our experiences during child birth. It felt great to see all the mommies with flat tummies instead of huge baby bumps.

During this reunion the couple who we became friends with, asked us to come to their home for dinner the following weekend. I was pleased that we could meet more people who shared the same interests we did. We soon became very good friends with Luis and Christine. We did many things with them.

During one weekend when they visited our home for dinner, we confided that we were looking for a new home. Of course, they were astonished and sympathetic. The following week, Dane got a call from Luis asking him to meet for lunch. I thought it was slightly odd that he wanted to meet during the day but I felt happy that Dane had another friend. He sorely missed Rich, Gigi's husband. When Dane came back, he was overjoyed with Luis's suggestion. As he walked through our door, he asked me to take a minute and to talk with him.

Luis was supervisor of a large construction company. He wanted to talk to Dane to discover if we were interested in what he was willing to do for us. Then Dane continued to explain it all to me.

I felt overjoyed with Luis's idea to build a house, a new home that nobody could take away from us. With Dane's' permission, he was willing to come back the next night to show us what he could do. With us not having any money to speak of, I didn't see how it could be possible but I was all ears, anyway.

The next night, Luis and Christine came over with blue prints and copious information. They got a babysitter for their children. So as soon as ours were in bed, Luis explained what he had in mind. His company specialized in building homes. The carpenters were familiar with the blueprints that he brought with him. He had already talked to his crew and they were willing to do our home in the evenings and on weekends for substantially less cost. It was to happen entirely with private transactions, passed through Luis.

Dane and I would find land that we wanted to build on. Again, not having any capital, I wasn't sure how this would work but Luis told Dane what to do. We would simply borrow five thousand dollars from someone until we were able to obtain a loan for the house that would include the lot. Dane thought his parents would put that money into an account for us.

He told Luis and Christine that his parents were disgusted about what Mother did to us. Also, that they had told him they would help him in any way they could. This was the first time I had heard this about Dane's parents. It made me happy that they thought enough of us that they wanted to help us. Luis told us not to worry about anything he would guide us all the way.

When we studied the blueprints, to my astonishment, this was a beautiful, spacious home. Luis guided us in choosing a design that was economical to build and also the most spacious for the cost. I felt afraid to get very excited but I couldn't help myself when I saw the plans. Luis would purchase all the lumber, windows, doors and whatever else was needed through his company so we could get a substantial discount. I felt like I was floating on a cloud.

Luis told Dane he could even arrange the banking for us. All we needed to do was pick out a lot, put the five thousand dollar deposit into an account for thirty days and we were good to go.

So began our new home. That night, as I cuddled up against Dane, I once again realized just how lucky I was. He kissed me with passion.

Again, after making love, he whispered to me, "Every time I make love to you is like the first time, all over again. I love you so much."

I loved Dane in my own way but without giving my full self, without complete abandon. My fears still limited me. Holding back was how I protected my torn heart. Somehow, I could not purge my apprehension. Sometimes, after lovemaking, I would wonder if I would be able to give myself completely, ever again; to simply let go of all fear and jump into the yawning abyss with arms spread wide to catch the wind and fly.

Our plan moved along smoothly. We borrowed the five thousand from Dane's parents. We picked out a beautiful lot with woods and a stream behind it. Not being able to believe my eyes about what we found, I kept thinking sometimes things work out in strange ways. I also thought this would put us into a home that we would be proud of, and of course, one that Mother couldn't snatch away from us on a whim.

The new house would be perfect for our family. The plan we chose covered thirty-six hundred square feet with a full basement and a two-and-a-half-car garage. It even had a separate laundry room, and a playroom that was fifteen feet square. Our fireplace covered a whole wall in the family room, which measured sixteen by twenty-six feet. I felt so excited.

We shared the blueprint with Dane's parents. They couldn't believe the huge house we were building for such a cheap amount of money. I didn't share the plans with Mother. She had moved on to another new boyfriend so she really didn't care, anyway. She showed very little interest and frankly, she was not very kind about it, at all. Her only concern was how soon our home would be built so she could move back into the big house.

What a mean slap in the face! I didn't want to make it any more miserable, though, while we still lived next door. Dane seemed to disliked Mother more every day as she acted so hatefully about our new house. She got angry, as if we were leaving her on our own initiative, as if she never threw us out.

She had really better hope Karma isn't a woman, I thought.

With the moving day only a few months away, Mother asked me if she could take our little ones shopping. I really didn't want to go but decided not to provide her an excuse for more unkind words. I agreed to go. Dane told me that I was acting like a saint but the decision was mine.

We tried to save every dollar possible on the cost of the house. We did anything we could possibly do, like painting and staining. I was already a pro with that task. By the time I packed up four children and drove to the new house, an hour and a half was consumed, but I persevered. I did all the painting, while watching four little ones. Dane's parents brought us food, many times. That was greatly appreciated, especially since his mother was such a great cook.

Falling into bed exhausted became my routine. Then, one night after putting the kids to bed, I decided to go to bed early; to not worry about straightening up the house. I closed my eyes and immediately fell sound asleep.

> *Suddenly, I heard, "Hi, Pretty Woman..." and there he was. Ajax stood before me, gazing at me with those gorgeous eyes. I reached out to hug him. I could feel his kiss on my cheek as he hugged me hard.*
>
> *"I miss you," he said. "Come with me."*
>
> *I started to cry. I said, "I can't. I have to raise my children."*

He was holding me so close that I could feel his breath on my face as he whispered, "I love you so much."

Then he leaned back and said, "Remember now, listen to me, I'm always with you. I will never let anything happen to you, never."

I could see him so clearly as he stood holding me so close. He lifting my face so he could kiss my lips. He kissed me one more time.

He then said, "I have to go now. Remember, you are always safe. I am always right there, beside you."

I wanted to continue, to hold on to him, but that white cloud appeared all around us and then he was gone.

Waking from the dream, I laid still, afraid about what this dream might mean.

"What was he trying to tell me?" I thought, and "Why would he say 'Come with me?'"

My heart was beating so fast that I thought it would jump out of my chest. Being certain Dane would not appreciate me dreaming about Ajax, I was happy that, once again, Dane was working when I had this dream. It seemed Ajax would usually appear to me when Dane was working. That was good because I didn't know if I could be heard speaking to him. My heart ached but there was nothing I could do. Loving someone that much, even though he had passed, was heart-wrenching. I was left on this earth for a reason. Although I sometimes wondered why, I do know that whatever the reason, I needed to fulfill my purpose for both our sakes.

Dane planned to install the kitchen cabinets on the weekend and I had a little painting left to do, so our weekend would be filled with tasks at the new house. It was all coming together. I could see how spacious and beautiful it would be. I was so excited that I didn't mind working long hours to get it finished.

On a Wednesday, Mother asked me to go to the mall with her the next morning. Since she was trying to be pleasant, I figured I would go. While shopping, I picked up a few things for the new house. I felt tickled with what I found. As we walked out of the store into the main hallway, I saw a man facing away from me. Mother saw him at the same time. As he turned around, my heart skipped a beat. He resembled Ajax so much it was almost unreal. Mother and I looked at each other with surprise on our faces.

With tears streaming down my face, I could hardly move. At the mall exit, there were benches and vendors with food. I walked toward the benches and sat down, trying to get myself together and stop crying. Mother got sodas for us and pretzels for the little ones. She sat down next to me, but didn't say a word. Sipping on my soda, I got the children situated with their pretzels. Not being able to hold back my tears, now I was crying hard.

Mother asked, "What is it? Why are you crying?" I was able to hold back the tears to talk. I told her of my dream about Ajax a few nights earlier. I had never told anyone about the other dreams but this one had me upset because he wanted me to come with him. I told her how he told me twice that he was always with me and that nothing would ever happen to me.

As I tried to explain the dream, we heard what sounded like a few gun shots outside. Then more shots rang out again, only this time there were many and people were screaming and running. I jumped up and grabbed Lilly and reached for the stroller. I told Mother to grab Craig's hand and run. I wanted to get away from the entrance doors just incase the gunman came running inside.

As we ran, I thought about my dream; that I was again acting quickly, as if forewarned. We continued to run down the long entrance way until we could turn the corner into a big department store. I went far into the back of the store near the fitting rooms so I could slip into one, if need be. I was shaking from fear, not knowing where the shots were coming from or if the gunman was coming into the mall. The halls were soon evacuated and quiet. There were announcements for everyone to stay where they were and not to come out into the main concourse. Craig was crying, so I quickly gave him a piece of gum, hoping he would get happy and stop. I was overcome with fear of what might be happening. Finding a fitting room door that was open, I told Trip and Craig to sit on the bench inside and be very quiet.

I sat down with them, holding Lilly and Kelly in my arms. I felt scared but tried to stay calm so the little ones wouldn't get upset. I managed to grab my diaper bag but left the stroller outside the fitting room, away from our immediate area, thinking we would be safer if nobody knew we were in there. I had slipped into the handicapped dressing room because there was a larger bench area in the corner. I recalled those doors lock automatically when closed, so I was surprised to find one that had been left open.

I told Mother to sit down on the bench. She glared at me with panic in her eyes and asked, "Did he say we would be alright?"

I said, "He told me he is always watching over me and that no harm will ever come to me."

Trip, being the nosy one, asked what I was talking about, but I told him to hush and be very still so that Craig and Lilly won't be afraid. Then suddenly we heard more screaming and Craig started to cry again. Pulling him closer to me, I whispered in his ear that if he cried, Lilly and Kelly would also cry, so he stopped and snuggled up closer to me. By that time, the baby was asleep in my arms. We could hear a lot of commotion but couldn't tell exactly what was going on. Suddenly, there was another shot and more screaming, then silence.

Within minutes, sirens blared, seeming to come from many directions. About an hour later, the police were in the main hall telling people that it was safe to go to their cars. I wanted to get out of there and go home but I was afraid to move with so many children in tow. When we decided to leave, we made our way out of the store and left the mall through the glass doors at the end of the concourse.

Walking to my car, I could see the police were standing near it. I asked an officer what had happened. He pointed to the cars and said the gunman was in custody; that the man had a shotgun and had been hiding between the cars, waiting for his wife and her boyfriend to come out of the mall. When his victims came outside, he shot them both. I felt weak-kneed. I could hardly hold myself up. I realized the gunman had been hiding between my car and the one beside it. I leaned on my car and threw up. By now, Mother had realized what happened.

She was saying "Oh my God, we could have all been killed."

The officer asked me if that was my car. I could hardly speak but managed to shake my head yes. He reassured me that they had shot the gunman in the mall and they had him in custody. Putting my little ones in the car, I quietly thanked Ajax. What if that dream had not come to me? What if we had left the mall as usual? We could have been in the line of fire or witnessed two people being gunned down.

The bodies were gone but there was still a lot of blood on the pavement. The sight of blood alone was enough to make me feel sick. On the way home, we didn't say much. Mother asked if Dane knew about my dreams. I said "Nobody does, except you." And I silently continued to thank Ajax.

That night, when I told Dane our story, he said I must have a guardian angel on my shoulder. If only I could have told him about the dreams but I didn't dare. I thought he might have known more than he shared with me about Ajax's last days at home. It almost seemed we had an unspoken agreement with neither of us discussing those weeks. Undoubtedly, he loved me and the children. Why stir the pot and make it spill over? Our marriage was good. I didn't want to disturb our tranquility over a past that couldn't be changed.

Of course, the shooting incident at the mall made the front page of the newspaper. The last shots that we heard while we were in the dressing room were the police shooting the gunman who was trying to escape through the back of the store we hid in. He turned to shoot an officer and he was shot first. We were at the other end of the store so we were safe, but didn't realize it. I relived the fear and panic that I felt when I saw the news that night on the TV.

How freakish, I thought, *we were in the wrong place at the wrong time but it turned out okay, thanks to my dream, and thanks to Ajax's promise.*

Our home was coming along wonderfully. I was excited for the weekend to come so that I could see what my kitchen was going to look like. It was every woman's dream to have a big kitchen where she can cook and bake. I was going to have exactly that.

Saturday morning I was up at the crack of dawn getting everything ready for the long workday at the new house. There were no refrigerator or stove present yet, so I needed to pack a cooler and carefully plan ahead what I would need for my little ones. They were so well behaved, I was able to accomplish a lot while I was there. I couldn't believe it. Craig and Lilly played in the house and Trip was busy with the neighbor boys playing behind our house in the woods. It was wonderful. I knew we would be happy living there. Young girls Craig and Lilly's age lived next door, so our neighbor took my children to play at her house sometimes. She was kind. I liked her and her girls were adorable.

Installing kitchen cabinets proved more difficult than we thought, but around four-thirty, Dane's parents arrived with dinner and his father helped after we ate. After his parents left, Dane and I stood in the kitchen admiring it all. He reached for me and pulled me close, hugging me. His arms felt so good around me. Given he was tall and muscular, I felt quite protected in his arms, almost like a little girl, again. I suppose that feeling was intensified because I didn't experience it when I was little.

He hugged me to his chest and said, "See? I told you not to worry. We won't be living in the streets."

We both laughed as we looked into each others eyes. He kissed me gently and whispered, "I love you."

It was already seven thirty. Kelly was getting fussy. It was close to her bed time. I had brought her pajamas. I figured we would be there until late. After she fell asleep in the car, I would be able to lay her into her crib and call it a night.

Sure enough, Kelly fell asleep on the way home, so that was one down and three to go. With all the little ones finally in bed, I crashed on the couch. Dane had poured us each a glass of wine. I felt hesitant to even drink it for fear I would fall asleep with the glass in my hand while taking a sip. I drank my wine and went to take a shower.

To my surprise, Dane was still up, watching television and having a second glass of wine. I snuggled next to him on the couch to enjoy the moment.

He said, "Wasn't that shooting incident something? The one that happened at the mall the other day. Thank goodness you left the concourse so fast. Who knows what could have happened if you hadn't? It seems like you are always one step ahead," he said.

All I could think to say was, "My instincts kicked in. I knew we needed to get out of there quickly."

Then he hugged me closer and said "I would die without you and the children. Thank goodness you thought fast and did the right thing. I love you Desiree, so much."

Again, I didn't want to talk about it, so I answered with, "Aw, I love you too. Please don't talk about it. It still upsets me to think about it."

After that, we watched television and then made our way upstairs to bed.

Before long, we were ready to move in. We were both so excited but, of course, Mother still acted cold, as if we had been the ones who decided to move out. She never addressed all that we spent renovating her house. We decided we would wait to put down flooring in the play room until after we moved in, when we had a little extra cash.

When Mother came to see the house, she noticed there was no flooring in that room. She suggested that she would like to buy it "for the kids," as she put it. Dane didn't want it. I told her it wasn't necessary but she went ahead and got it anyway and had it delivered. Dane felt really angry that she went ahead and did what she wanted without our permission. At that point, I was just happy to be moving and I left it alone.

I did chuckle to myself, though, when I thought about the thousands of dollars we put into her home, that she was moving back into, and now she bought a little piece of carpeting supposedly as an exchange. That lame gesture was her way of trying to justify it. In what kind of mind could that be a balanced equation?

When moving day came, I felt so happy. Between doing things at the new house and painting it, I still managed to do the packing. All was ready when Dane went to get the truck. He asked some of our friends to help. Dane's parents stayed at the new house so someone was there between truckloads. The night before, we took the beds apart and took the mirrors off the dressers. Moving everything went quickly.

I cried when I walked out of Mother's house. I had worked so hard to make it special. Then, after doing all that work, she made such a fool of me. It seemed like I was a total stranger to her and it was fine that she told me to leave, even knowing I was pregnant with my fourth child. She wasn't even content to wait until we were out. She started moving her things in and complaining that the carpeting didn't really go with her furniture. I couldn't believe she was complaining about the color of the new carpeting that she got for free. My tears soon turned to happiness, though, when I arrived at our new home and saw most of the furniture in place.

Everything looked so good. Our new kitchen set had come that morning. That completed the kitchen. We got an oversized wooden table with a bench on one side. That really looked great in the large dining area. Glass sliding doors were there at the end of that area. The table fit perfectly. I stood there for a minute and took it all in. Our home was beautiful and spacious. I couldn't help wondering how something that good resulted from something that was so bad. Now, nobody could throw us out or tell us what to do. This was our home. Now we were free of Mother's evil ways.

Dane's mother brought dinner for us all and put it in the refrigerator. I was so surprised when I saw it. She was a kind woman, who genuinely liked me, and I could feel that in what she did.

Everything seemed to go smoothly but then Dane and I tried to organize and insure it went well. With all the furniture and boxes moved in, I felt like I had come home; that this was now, indeed, our real home. The kitchen was already organized. Dishes, pots and pans and pantry contents were all transferred to the new house a few days before the move. I set the table for all of us to eat our first dinner in our new home without paper plates and without searching through boxes to find dishes and silverware.

What a treat I, thought, *to have such a pleasant first meal in our new home.*

I held on to hope that Mother would stop by but she didn't. I just had to put it out of my mind. I knew in my heart that she was a fundamentally miserable person and that ironically, because of her mean spirit, Dane and I were now living in our very own home and we felt as happy as we could be. Everyone was hungry and happy that our first meal was pure pleasure and so delicious. Our children got excited to be living in that neighborhood with many other children for playmates. They ate quickly and asked to go back outside to play. After we loaded the dishwasher and cleaned up the kitchen, Dane's parents helped us put things in order. I could see they felt proud for their son.

I knew our little ones would be tired from playing outside most of the day. I went upstairs to make sure I had all their sheets on the beds. As I made the little ones' beds, I had a very warm feeling come over me, as if someone had come up behind me and put their arms around me. I stood still, not knowing what to think, and then the feeling was gone. I attributed that to being tired, knowing I was way too young for a hot flash.

The spacious bedrooms shared a very large bathroom for the children. I peeked into the bathroom, with towels in place and art on the wall, and thought of all the baths that would happen in this huge room.

Entering our master bedroom, I paused in the doorway for a moment to admire how beautiful our furniture looked there.

I thought, *Lots of romping will happen in this room, too,* as I put the sheets on the bed.

Glancing into the master bathroom, I was pleased with what I saw there. That room was also furnished and I loved having our own, private bath. I had finished all three bathrooms a few days earlier. That day, I felt pleased I had taken the time. I wanted to be gone from Mothers house. I felt ill-at-ease there, so had I counted days until we could go. Standing in our bedroom, I thought about how ironic life can be; how some things are simply meant to happen. In the end, Dane and I came out better than even, house-wise, all things considered. We were able to repay his parents in thirty days. It seemed everything worked out for the best, despite Mother's meanness toward us.

After we were in our new house for about a week, Author called on the phone to ask if Dane and I would go out to dinner with him and his new girlfriend. I was surprised, given the last time I saw him I had threatened to call the police if he ever came to my house again. When I discussed him with Dane, his take was that perhaps Author went about trying to help Trip and me all wrong, and he realized that, so maybe I should find it in my heart to forgive him.

We both laughed as he said "Seventeen years with your mother would cause anyone to go nuts. Lets go, and just see what he has to say. He was good to you when you were a kid, if you recall."

"Wow. That's stretching your imagination. He was drunk and singing all the time," I said.

"Well, look at you. You're hot. The poor guy probably fantasized about you," he answered, and he laughed. "Come on, lets meet his new woman."

On that Saturday, when we had the date to meet Author and his new girlfriend for dinner, the sod for our lawn was delivered. When we were laying it down, it rained. Not only a little sprinkle; it rained hard, starting when we were only halfway through. When the sod was soaked, it became much heavier to lift. By the time we finished, not only was I beat, but also, we were so muddy that I took my clothes off in the garage and put them in the laundry room which was right off the garage. I talked Dane into postponing dinner that night. Then I called Author to tell him what happened. He understood. He said he would call us again to see when we could make it. I went to shower happy to stay home in my new house.

Yes, we were happy, more than ever before. Our little ones were in their glory, having other children around. We had chosen the right location. As more homes were built in our area, we realized even more that we had made the right choices. We had our friends come over to visit often. We enjoyed such a happy and cooperative marriage. We liked one couple in particular. We invited them often because the man worked with Dane on the same crazy schedule that Dane worked. Their work shifts changed frequently. Although there was a pattern, keeping track of it was hard. With Dane working weekends, it was hard to find couples who could visit during the week when we could entertain.

Greg and Leslie had two children. Their daughter was the same age as our Craig and Lilly. Their son was the same age as our Kelly. Our large playroom turned out to be a plus. The children loved it and all their toys had a place, so I loved it.

Greg and Leslie had heard about a clothing outlet in Pennsylvania. They asked us if we would like to go there on a day when the guys were off work. Of course, we said yes. We went there the following week. It took us about three hours but it was fun to be talking and joking along the way. When we arrived, we couldn't believe our eyes. It was even more spectacular than we had heard.

While walking around, I noticed they had men's dress pants for two dollars. Those dress pants regularly sold for twenty-five to twenty-nine dollars. I couldn't believe my eyes. I took Dane aside and told him about an idea that came to me. We decided to talk more when we got home and could talk more freely. The deals we had found excited me. Immediately, my mind was churning with ways to make money.

I had developed innovative ways to supplement our income before but what I was thinking about this time was a winning idea. Later that evening, when our little ones were in bed, Dane and I were sitting together. I told him what was on my mind. By then, my enthusiasm was showing. I laid out some numbers. With a hundred dollars we could buy fifty pairs of those two-dollar pants. If we sold those at the flea market for ten dollars a pair, we would gross five hundred dollars. If we then reinvested that in more pants, we could grow that profit even farther, and so on.

But I faced a dilemma: that was Greg and Leslie had found the opportunity and shared it with us. It would not seem fair if we started profiting from their find, unless we gave them a chance to participate. Dane agreed. He told me to discuss it with Leslie. He would discuss it with Greg at work, the next day.

I told Dane I had no idea how well we could do but I had a feeling we would do very well. I noted that Leslie and I could take pants to the flea market together when our men were working.

He reminded me of the time I made Barbie Doll clothes to sell for Christmas. He didn't think I would do that well but he didn't want to disappoint me by saying something negative.

Afterwards, he said, "You blew me away with the money you made. I couldn't believe it." He then followed with, "Knowing you, we'll make a fortune. I say, go for it."

He then leaned and kissed me with a lot of meaning. Before long, he was encouraging me to follow him upstairs so he could show me how much he loved me. I believed if you keep your man happy at home, he won't wander and I acted from this belief. I followed him upstairs to our beautiful bedroom. After I checked on all the little ones, I quickly showered. My thoughts were focused on the money we could make rather than what I was about to experience.

I didn't know if it was passion and love for me, or if Dane simply knew how to please women but whatever the reason, he showed consistent desire to please me and to assure that I'm satisfied. My girlfriends would complain about their husbands being selfish, not taking enough time with them, but I couldn't complain. Dane was truly impressive in bed. Also, he never failed to tell me how much he loved me.

This was one of those nights when he was really into making love and his kisses showed it. When I stepped out of the shower, he was lying on the bed in all his glory.

He said, "Come here and let me show you just how much I love you."

I laughed as I thought, *Men have no modesty at all. They just lie there and grin like a possum eating a sweet potato.*

I dropped my towel and climbed into bed. He pulled me close, so our bodies touched. He squeezed me, told me how happy he is with me and how lucky he feels to have me as his wife. He held my face with his hand as he whispered "I love you." My body trembled with desire.

He kissed my face. Then my neck. Then my breasts. Then my tummy. I throbbed with anticipation, knowing what would come next...

Lying in each others' arms in the afterglow, I wondered again why I couldn't let go and give my heart to him completely. I had this void inside that just didn't allow me to go there.

I gave Leslie a call the next morning and told her what I had planned with men's dress pants. Although I wasn't surprised that she liked my idea, I was surprised with her enthusiasm. She was talking so loud and fast that I had to slow her down.

They came over to our house that night and we had a pleasant discussion about how we could handle the project. I had already called the flea market to see what it would cost to rent a booth big enough to contain a makeshift fitting room. I even figured in gasoline cost to pick up our stock. I was good to go and ready to try our venture.

We decided that we would buy stock on the next day our men would be off work. I could think of nothing but this project until we made that run. With four of us buying, we figured we would each buy six pairs of slacks and then go back again later and get another six each. But to our surprise, it worked out even more smoothly because no limit was set on the amount you could buy. I was seeing dollar signs.

Dane and Greg made a small fitting room out of the lumber we had left over from the house. We were in business within two weeks. Even I was surprised by how well those pants sold. After the first weekend, we sold almost every pair. Our orders filled a whole eight by eleven sheet of paper. With cash we made from the first weekend, we bought around two hundred more pairs of pants. That paid for our booth at the flea market and the gas we burned going to the outlet.

The next weekend, first thing Saturday morning, there were so many people at our booth there was not enough room for them all. They were grabbing pants without even trying them on. By the end of the day, there were very few pants left and our pockets were stuffed with cash. We had another sheet of paper with more orders. My husband was singing my praises.

When we went back to Pennsylvania next, I suggested we buy some of the men's dressy polo shirts. Everyone agreed. We continued to sell those men's pants and shirts for about four months. Then, we had to find a little store to continue expanding. We were in that little store for about six months when we added other lines of clothing. We were then buying direct from sales reps and doing very well.

Nobody could believe it, but I did. I knew it was a winner. The weather was treacherous outside but even so, customers just kept on coming. We told them that we were expecting a shipment of men's suits; those should be in stock by Saturday morning. The roads were icy and our shipment was sitting on a dock in Cleveland, about an hour away. There was a problem. The trucking company had sent all drivers home due to the weather. So there were no trucks running.

There we were with the store full of people waiting for suits. I made coffee for the people who were standing outside and informed everyone that the suits would be available in about two hours. If they wanted to come back, they could count on the suits being there. But nobody wanted to leave. When Dane and Greg arrived, the suits were all sold in a matter of minutes. I was able to grab a suit for Dane and one for Greg, and that was it, they were all gone.

We soon outgrew that little store, as well. We had to move into a much larger space in a shopping center. Here I was once again, painting and decorating this monster of a store. Leslie and I got along exceptionally well in every aspect of the business and also as friends, but I definitely was the one with the business mind.

After painting all day, I came home with my little sidekick, Kelly, and crashed on the couch. Dane was working days that week so he was home right after I got there. I felt so tired that I decided to order pizza delivered for dinner. That suited the family just fine. After eating, I sat down to rest for a few minutes before it was my bath time. Dane offered to get the boys their baths and then ready for bed. I felt pleased because that gave me time to wash some laundry before bathing the girls.

That night, I was quite tired from all my work during the past week. The new space was huge. I worried about getting it all done in time for our grand opening. I showered quickly and flopped into bed. The minute my head hit the pillow, I was dreaming.

> *"Hi, Pretty Woman," I heard, and there he was, in front of me.*
>
> *I reached out to him and hugged him close. I could feel his soft kisses on my lips.*
>
> *Then he whispered in a quiet voice, "I'm so proud of you. Look what you have achieved. I love you," he said.*
>
> *Then he hugged me tighter and said, "You must listen very carefully to me, you must. Do not leave the store for any reason except at the end of the day. Don't leave for any reason, no matter what."*
>
> *He pulled back and looked me in the eyes and said, "I love you so much and though I want you to be here with me, you're not ready. So trust me and believe in me."*
>
> *He started to pull away.*
>
> *I pulled him back, saying, "Please don't leave me. I've never stopped loving you."*
>
> *But with our kiss the white cloud enveloped us and he was gone.*

Dane woke me up, then. He told me that I had been dreaming and that I said "Please don't leave me, I've never stopped loving you." I just laid there not able to speak.

"Who were you dreaming of?" he asked. I wanted to cry, seeing the look on his face, but all I could do is say, "I don't know, I don't remember."

He didn't buy it but that was all I could think to say.

I snuggled up to him and whispered "I love you, good night."

I was up early the next morning, getting Trip, Craig and Lilly ready for school, and trying to make sense of what I had dreamed the night before. As usual, my dreams made no sense until after everything they were about actually happened.

I was ready to leave for the store as soon as the bus picked up our little ones in front of the house. My little sidekick was ready to go, with her toys packed for the day. What a precious child Kelly was. I just couldn't get enough of her. The way she talked was the cutest thing I have ever heard. She pronounced her words so sweetly. It seemed as if she was attached to my hip.

I assured our store was large enough so that, after school, the children could have a room of their own. Leslie and I furnished it, including a refrigerator, so that she and I could take turns going back there with the children when they came in after school. It worked out well that our children were the same ages.

Having only one more day of painting made me happy. When that was done, the carpeting would be delivered.

Yay, I thought, *"soon we will be open."*

I finished the next day as planned. Then I wanted to paint the private bathroom in the back. Leslie was going to go to get her hair cut. She wanted me to go to lunch with her and her son, afterward. I thought it would be a good break for the little ones, so I agreed. Kelly climbed into their car behind Leslie. Her son was sitting in the seat behind the front passenger seat. I went to sit in the front but then I remembered my dream.

Changing my mind, I said to Leslie "Wait, I think I will stay here. Come on, Kelly, let's get out."

Kelly wanted to go so she started to fuss. I said "Okay, let's go." Then just as abruptly, I said "No, I want to stay here. You go get your hair cut and then call me. I'll meet you then."

Leslie looked at me as if I were nuts. Kelly started to cry. But I was afraid to leave. I unlocked the door and went back in. About ten minutes later, Leslie called. She screamed, and she was crying so much that I couldn't understand her. I told her to calm down.

"Come and get me," she screamed, "come quickly!" I knew something was very wrong by the way she was crying. I told her I would be right there. Then I grabbed Kelly and went to her.

When I arrived at her location, Leslie's car was off the road. She was standing nearby. A plumbing truck was also pulled off the road. The plumbing truck had slammed into her car's rear end. Some pipes flew off the truck's rack. One pierced the rear window of her car at an angle, passing through the car where Kelly would have been sitting, and out the front window, through space where I would have been sitting. Either, or both of us, could have been hit in the the head. The accident could have killed us both. It was a rather large, metal pipe, so there was even a possibility we could have been beheaded.

My knees felt weak.

Leslie kept crying and repeating, "Thank God you didn't go with me."

Once again, I silently thanked Ajax for warning me.

With the store's carpeting installed, we needed to build display racks for all our jeans. We wanted that section to have a rugged, outdoorsy look, so we decorated it with wooden racks. Standing back in disbelief, Leslie and I felt astounded by what our men accomplished with wood that was mostly scrap. When it was distressed with a mallet and stained, the finished look was perfect.

We purchased some round, display racks from a store that was going out of business. That saved us a lot. I was beside myself with excitement. We had accomplished this all, starting with a hundred dollars' worth of men's dress pants a little more than one year before.

When opening day was upon us, we were all quite excited. We looked at each other in awe, not being able to believe the throng of customers who came in that day. The store looked quite attractive and the area for the jeans was a focal point in the store that pleased us all.

I made arrangements with the school ahead of time to drop my little ones off at the bus stop by our store. That made things easier for me. It was one less thing to worry about each day. I only had to be concerned with my youngest, Kelly. I didn't quite know what to do with her. She did not do well going to a day care. In fact, each time I attempted to take her there, she threw up. Then the center would call me to come for her. I even tried staying there with her for a while but that didn't work, either.

She was such a good little girl, absolutely no trouble at all, but I thought she should have children to play with instead of just playing by herself in the back room or hanging around with me in the store. She was such a beautiful child that I was afraid someone might grab her behind my back. That placed some extra stress on me. During the days when Dane was either off work, or working a shift when she could be with him, there was no issue. On days when he worked, she worked along with Leslie and me.

Dane enjoyed working in the store on his days off. We arranged things so he could and I would stay home to catch up on my chores. There seemed to always be laundry to wash and dinners to prepare. I usually cooked a few meals at once so we had something ready if I was late coming home from the store.

Business was fantastic. Leslie and I went to the dry goods shows in New York and came back with wonderful deals to sell. The show was in the New York Hilton. It filled twenty six floors with different lines of clothing. All that was overwhelming at first but we soon became accustomed to it. Buying came naturally to me. I had a way with the vendors. I made very good deals on many different styles of clothing. We were now also carrying women's clothing. That made the buying trips even more fun for us.

Because we were an independent store and just starting, I got good deals on some items that made excellent money. One vendor gave us a line of sun dresses for a dollar and twenty-five cents. We sold them for twenty five to twenty nine dollars. We sold thirty of them in the first week that we received a shipment.

I also made friends with a young man who ran a women's boutique. Through him, I got some great woman's clothes. He would buy items by the dozens, sell me only a few at a time, and give me a discount that usually only came with larger volumes. I would drive to his store and pick out what I wanted. Then, we would go over the invoice to tally the cost and I would pay him. It worked out great for us, since we were just getting started with new styles in our store.

Life was wonderful then. I was so happy and proud not only of our business but of my life and my family. Dane and I still got along quite well. Even at times when we had deadlines to meet, or had tension from outside sources, we never got upset with each other. We were a team and we respected each other.

Greg and Leslie weren't that even-keeled. They seemed to be at each others throats all the time. Sometimes, that got to be tiresome. I didn't mind so much if they had differences but I didn't like when she would come in late and tired because they had been up all night trying to make up. That got on my nerves. I was playing nursemaid. She was so tired she would put her head down on the counter by the register and not be able to move. I didn't think that was good for customers to see.

My little one was a better salesperson than Leslie was. Kelly wandered around thinking she was helping. When someone walked in, she would go up to them and say "Mommy got new shirts. Come here and see them. They are pretty." The customers loved her. She was so cute, with those two curly, dark brown pony tails, and the way she talked, she really was a little doll.

I came into the store about an hour early one Saturday with Kelly so that I could put out shipments that came in late on Friday afternoon. I opened at ten a.m., as usual, and stocked the shelves. I was alone that morning, feeling uneasy for some reason.

I reminded Kelly, "If Mommy tells you to go sit down, I want you to listen, okay?" Of course, she was okay.

At about ten-twenty, two young men came into the store. I felt very uncomfortable, but again, I didn't know why. I told Kelly to go sit down. She sat under our counter where she could not be seen. I went to the phone and called the store next door. I did what we had arranged for times when either of us sensed danger: I ordered a fish sandwich for lunch and told them to get one for my husband also, who would arrive any minute.

So the men next door knew something was wrong. They came to my store's display window and looked in, after calling the police. One of those young men who were scaring me hung around near the entrance. The other took a bunch of clothes into the fitting room. Just as he came out of the fitting room, he took a running leap at me, knocking me into the counter, demanding the money from the register.

I told him, "Okay, just let me up and I will get it."

I was scared he would discover Kelly under the counter. I was afraid she might start crying so I tried to act as if nothing was wrong.

Just as I turned to get the money, the other young man started to yell "Let's get out of here," and both men left the store.

Within a minute, the police were in my store asking questions, when another distress call came from the drugstore at the end of the plaza. Those scary young men had left my store and gone into the drugstore to rob them. The police were so close that they caught them as they were leaving the drugstore. When the police left my store, I looked for Kelly. There she was, sound asleep with her blanket under the counter. She didn't know anything about what happened. It all worked out well, but it left me nervous about Kelly's safety in the store. The men next door came over and joked about how well the fish sandwich routine worked. We never thought we would need to use that for safety, but it did work.

After the incident in the store, I decided Kelly should not be there as often as she was. No matter what I had to do, I was going to make other arrangements. Mother remarried to an entirely different man and he basically wanted her to stay home. She offered to watch Kelly and Leslie's little boy Randy until I made other plans. It was a long drive but I was desperate. Our relationship basically involved me turning a blind eye to unkind things Mother did and trying to move past them.

Dane couldn't forgive her that easily. I had seen a caption in the weekend newspaper that showed a woman from the side, standing with her arms extended up and to the back of her as a breeze blew her hair.

The caption said, "When you choose to forgive those who have hurt you, you take away their power."

That made me think long and hard. I had such resentment in my heart because she cheated me out of a house and then acted as if we had wronged her by moving out of it. After I took that caption to heart, I knew her power to hurt me was taken away and she could never hurt me again. I don't fault Dane for feeling the way he did, but for me, this other path was easier.

The holidays were approaching much too fast to suit me. With the weather turning cold, I hated taking Kelly all the way to Mother's house but I had not found someone else to care for her. When I picked her up, I could see she wasn't happy. That bothered me, but right then, we had to live with it.

Dane sometimes picked up our little ones at Mother's house when he worked days. He was going past there anyway. On the way home one day, Kelly pointed out a local pool hall. She told me that Daddy had taken her and Randy, Leslie's boy, to that place the night before.

I was surprised. At first, I didn't believe her. Questioning her, I realized she was telling the truth. In fact, Dane did go there with the two little ones. Even worse, he had left Randy in the car sleeping while he took Kelly inside with him.

When I asked her what they did there, she just said "Daddy gave some man money and he gave Daddy a lunch bag."

Still not understanding her, I asked her again and she told me exactly the same thing, only the second time, she elaborated: the lunch bag was just like the one Trip and Craig take to school. I was stunned and confused because I thought Dane would never go into a rough pool hall, especially leaving Randy in the car. She then told me that Randy woke up when they were in there. He was crying when they came back to the car. Now I was really confused but I didn't say anything that night when Dane came home at midnight.

The following night, both Leslie and I went to pick up the little ones. This time, Randy pointed out the pool hall and said he cried because he was left in the car alone. I thought Leslie was going to hit the roof. To my disbelief, Kelly piped in, saying that it was okay because Daddy just got a lunch bag and they came right out. Leslie reacted exactly the same way I would have. This was astonishing. I couldn't imagine what he bought, although the lunch bag told me it was probably something he shouldn't have.

I let it go and I asked Leslie to allow me to get to the bottom of that, rather than blowing up, which would prevent me. She reluctantly agreed. When I got home, Dane's car was in the driveway since he didn't go to work until midnight. When I got out of my car, I tried his car door but it was locked. Now I knew something was wrong, for sure, because he didn't usually lock his car doors. My stomach felt sick. This didn't make sense but because he had never given me reason to wonder about anything, I tried to wait it out and see what would happen. The next day, Leslie wanted to know if I had talked to him and what he said. She was really hot and I couldn't blame her.

I convinced her to not worry, saying, "I'm sure it was nothing." Then she said something that cut me to the core, "You have no idea about him do you?"

"What are you saying?" I asked.

All she said was, "I guess ignorance is bliss."

There were quite a few customers in the store so I had to drop the subject but I really was upset. When we were ready to close up and leave, Leslie said, "I love you and I don't want to hurt you, but *wake up*. He's not what you think. I don't want him ever picking up Randy again."

What could I say except "Okay, I understand, but let's not be upset with each other because I really don't know what is going on and I can see you are not going to tell me."

Leslie and I got along quite well. On days when the weather was bad we just kept the two little ones with us in the store. Crazy as it seems, when the weather was bad we were packed with customers. If it were me, I would stay home with a fire in the fireplace and not go anywhere. On the other hand, we did quite well with business.

Thereafter, I paid more attention to Dane. I looked for some sign that would tell me what was going on but there was nothing. Soon, we were almost into the holidays. I didn't know how I would be able to handle working more hours and still take care of my family. Dane and I decided we would hire someone to take care of our little ones while they were home during the holidays. I found a pleasant young girl who the school highly recommended. My children just loved her. It was such a treat for me because she did the laundry and made our dinner. That wasn't part of our agreement but it was sincerely appreciated and welcomed. I paid her extra money for all the extra things she did. She was so excited. It worked out well. I decided to keep her, on a part-time basis, so that I could devote more time to the business. She was taking college courses so this worked out well for her, as well.

There would be no way to leave Kelly at home every day but I was able to leave her at least a few times a week. With the rest of the children home, Kelly was a lot more willing to stay home. Craig and Lilly were so patient with her. They included her in everything. Craig was the best brother any girl could ever ask for. He was fiercely protective and yet so patient with both of them. Trip, on the other hand, couldn't be bothered. He went about his own business. He was the kind of brother who picked on his siblings until someone was in tears.

We bought a huge Christmas tree and had a wonderful time decorating it with the children. By then, we had collected Christmas decorations that they looked forward to putting out, each year. We put the tree near the fireplace. Because the stone surface continued across the room, the tree looked beautiful with that stone background. When the tree was lit, the mica specks in the rock and the glitter in the popcorn ceiling sparkled everywhere in the room.

I made a fire in the fireplace and made hot chocolate for everyone. I was so happy; I just couldn't see anything out of the ordinary with Dane. He was just incredibly loving and attentive to me and the children.

"Dane and I are going Christmas shopping tonight," I told Leslie. "I love this time of year."

She agreed but didn't elaborate, so I thought perhaps she and Greg might be arguing again.

With the day finished at the store, we locked up and I went home. Dane was waiting for me and soon we left. We went to one store looking for a particular toy but they didn't have it. We peered through the store windows when we were ready to leave and we saw that snow was falling, hard. As we came out the door we began to run. Suddenly, Dane picked me up, turning me around in his arms. I was laughing as the snow was falling on my face. He put me down, and there in the parking lot, he took my face in his hands and kissed me with passion.

He said, "I love you more and more every day, promise me you will never leave me."

I was surprised, but being the comedian that I am, I smiled and said, "Who else would make love to me as well as you. Besides, you laugh at my jokes when no one else does."

He opened my car door and leaned in and kissed me again saying, "I would die if I didn't have you."

We got a lot of shopping done and we came home happy. There was a small fire smoldering in the fireplace when we got home. I poured some wine and put another log on the fire. We sat down to watch the fire and look at the tree. The children were already asleep and the house was peaceful. The only sound was the crackling of the fire.

"How peaceful everything is, tonight," I thought. "I am one lucky lady."

Sipping our wine and enjoying the evening was just what the doctor ordered. Unwinding as we chatted always seemed to bring us even closer. When we finished our glass of wine, I asked Dane if he would like another one. He told me he would like another glass and in vivid detail, he described exactly what he would like to do after he finished his wine.

Oh boy, I thought. *Am I ever in for a treat tonight. Wild horses couldn't keep me away from that kitchen to pour our wine.*

As we began to enjoy our wine and some cheese and crackers, he raised his glass to toast with me.

"To the most beautiful wife any man could possibly ask for, and she is mine."

We clinked our glasses together and took another sip of wine. I snuggled next to him on the couch as we enjoyed what was left of the evening.

The fire started to slowly die out. It was getting late. We decided to go upstairs to bed instead of putting another log on the fire. After I checked on all the little ones, I showered. Showering with anticipation, I hurried to finish. I toweled off and slipped into a nightgown, brushed my teeth and returned to the bedroom. Dane had lit a few candles and he laid there, sound asleep on the bed. I chuckled as I looked at him sleeping so peacefully. I blew out the candles and laid down next to him. Sleep came easily and the next morning arrived much too early.

Going into the store early was a pleasure because I didn't face the chaos of getting the children ready for school that morning. I accomplished a lot in that extra hour before I started work. Leslie came in on time that morning. She was surprised by how much I had done. We changed displays and racks frequently enough that each time someone walked into the store, it looked different.

The ceilings were high. I made use of that space with large pieces of cork board. I displayed complete outfits up there, so customers would see how things looked good together. Our two display windows were quite large and easy to decorate. I usually changed those each week. I'm blessed with good energy so I would put it to good use. Kelly loved to get into the window area and decorate it with me. She was a big help. She handed me things or get down off the ledge to fetch something I may have forgotten. What a sweetheart she was. Who would have thought a girl so young could be so wise and so helpful?

Leslie and I ordered many small gift items for the holidays. To our surprise, they were selling quickly. I placed a reorder within four days of their arrival. What surprised us most was the sexy men's underwear. We were reordering that, constantly. I loved watching the guys stand there and take the underwear out of the tube to see the colors. Raising their eyebrows with a satisfied smile, they usually took three pairs instead of only one. That clothing line came with a circular rack to hold the tubes in place, according to size. We placed that near the cash register. Most men looked at them and then couldn't resist. The funniest part was when they would ask me what I thought about a certain color they have chosen. Of course, I liked more than just one.

With less than two weeks until Christmas, our store stayed busy all day until closing. I was happy we had someone to stay with our children, because I didn't have a minute during the day to even eat lunch, much less to keep an eye on children. Leslie's mother-in-law was watching her children. That gave us peace of mind, knowing that they were well cared for. I came home tired but happy about what we accomplished. Not many young couples our age with four children had what we did and the happiness we shared.

We decided one year that we would take some cash out of the business and pay ourselves bonuses. Previously, we had put almost all our cash back into the store. This was going to be a wonderful Holiday Season for all of us.

I started to notice a difference in Dane's behavior though I couldn't quite put my finger on what I was seeing. He definitely was more quiet. He seemed a bit distant. Leslie and I were the ones who mostly took care of the store. So it wasn't as if more pressure was put on the men. Even Leslie and Greg had asked me if there was something "off" with him. They both noticed a subtle change in his behavior. There was a nuance in his skin tone, an almost pasty look.

I handled most everything that needed to be done. If something needed to be taken care of, I would hire someone and have it done without even blinking an eye. Dane was nice to look at but not much of a handyman. I made sure I cooked meals so Dane only had to heat them up for the little ones while I was gone to New York for the shows. The store was no burden for the men at all. It made so much money, more than we ever thought would be possible. Only now, during the holidays, our hours were extended. Otherwise, the store was closed by six p.m. every day.

I had seen this look on Dane before but I was not sure what was going on. I asked him if he felt alright and he looked at me like I was crazy so I just let it alone. I noticed that when Dane was home with the kids on his days off, Kelly was acting strangely toward him, almost stand-offish. She ran to me when I got home and didn't leave my side for a minute until I put her to bed.

"Maybe she's just missing me these past few weeks," I thought.

When Christmas was almost upon us, on the last Saturday, we decided the four of us would go out to dinner one evening after we closed. The shopping plaza extended our hours for the holidays so it would be a late dinner. We'd go straight from the store to the restaurant. I made arrangements with our baby sitter to stay, so we could enjoy the evening without worry about getting home. We ordered a bottle of champagne to toast our successful business venture. I noticed a distance between Dane and Greg that I had not seen before. I thought maybe everyone was just tired. Leslie and I would be leaving for New York in a few weeks. Although I loved the buying trips, this time I felt a little apprehensive. The men decided to take us dancing after dinner and though Leslie and I had tired feet, we went along with their idea since we were closed on Sundays.

It can be amazing how one gets their second wind. I so relish a chance to dance. No matter how tired I might be, I am game. We got home around one-thirty a.m., and Kelly was up waiting, half asleep on the couch. The babysitter said Kelly was so upset that she thought it best to let her sleep on the couch next to her. Kelly's behavior was beginning to puzzle me. I knew Dane would be eager to go to bed and make love, so I calmed Kelly down, put her in her bed, then got into the shower. Even though sleeping in was an option, I rarely took advantage of it because there was always so much for me to do on Sunday.

We were slammed the last few days before Christmas. We closed at four p.m. on Christmas Eve. Since the bank was going to be closed the next day I took the money bag home with me to deposit it Monday morning. I was so proud that day. We grossed over eight thousand dollars. I did not stop all day and neither did Leslie. We hardly had time to go to the bathroom. Coming home that night, I was on cloud nine with pride in what we had achieved.

Kelly came running to the door again as if she had seen a ghost only this time she was crying. Getting her calmed down was a little more difficult today, though I kept telling her Santa was coming tomorrow. This year, Christmas eve was going to be at Dane's sister's house, with all of Dane's family. They never invited Mother because she was always so sarcastic with everyone but there really was nothing I could do about it.

I gathered everything I was supposed to take along, then wrapped the nieces' and nephews' presents. We were all ready on time and left for the evening. I loved the holidays, and Dane's family. They make it even more wonderful. Getting home around eleven-thirty p.m. and trying to get all the children settled in bed, was quite a task. They were so excited. I think I was just as excited as they were. I had wrapped all the presents the Sunday before and left them at the store so no one would peek at them. Trip was especially mischievous about finding things. When everyone was asleep, Dane went to our store to get all the presents so we could put them under the tree. Once they were placed, we sat down on the floor, with me sitting up against him, in his arms.

I am so happy, I thought.

I said a little prayer thanking God for all my blessings.

We sat there for about a half an hour, then decided we'd better go to bed since there was no doubt we would have an early wake-up call. I couldn't wait to see the little ones' faces when they saw all their presents. I made sure Christmas was always peaceful and pleasant since I never wanted my children to go through what I had to endure on Christmas when I was little. Having to sit and watch my presents without opening them, because Mother and Author were fighting. That sort of thing was never going to happen to my children, no matter what.

When we lived in the big house, Mother would come over Christmas morning to watch the little ones open their presents. Now that we were in our own home, I had my own Christmas with my children and didn't invite her for the mornings. She could come later but this was my special time and I didn't feel I wanted to share it with someone who would turn on us. Though I had forgiven her, I would not forget.

As expected, at six a.m., everyone was up and excited to open presents. I didn't care because I was too excited about the wonderful day that was starting for us. The children were squealing with delight with each present they opened. They were all such beautiful children that I watched them with pride. Each year, I loved receiving the gifts that the children made for me either in school or on their own.

Everyone was so excited they could hardly eat breakfast. I looked around and realized how lucky I was. The day was so wonderful that I hated to see it end. With all the children in bed, the house was quiet but with a subtle feeling of happiness. I don't often think about my father but that night, I wondered what he would think if he was looking down at my home, seeing all the happiness that my whole family experienced.

That poor man, I thought, *he just didn't have a chance.*

That Christmas fell on Saturday so we had another day to relax before starting into our routines again. That morning, everyone was calmer and better able to eat breakfast.

I loved to cook, so creativity with food came naturally to me. I often tried something new. Since we had a beautiful fire going in the fireplace, I thought we would roast hot dogs and marshmallows instead of eating leftovers from Christmas. The children loved to do that. With the tree up and the atmosphere pretty and fun, I thought they would especially enjoy that. One would have thought it was a gourmet meal, given their enthusiasm.

When we built the house, we made the hearth wider than usual so I could decorate it easier. It served as a great place to set a tray of food or where we could sit. Everyone was very happy with the presents Santa brought them. So the day went well. Everyone played with their new toys. When it came time for dinner, I suggested that we roast hot dogs and everyone was thrilled.

That works for me, I thought.

I made a few things to go with the hot dogs and we were good to go. I always got a kick out of watching Craig roast his marshmallows. He had to brown them perfectly all the way around. What a wonderful little guy he was. He really looked out for his sisters, always protecting them and staying by their side. At first, Lilly couldn't get up the steps on the school bus. He would stand behind her, helping by giving her an extra boost. As far as Kelly was concerned, there was a special bond between them. That was obvious even at an early age.

Monday morning, Dane went to work the early shift, and the babysitter's dad dropped her off to watch the little ones. They were excited to show her all their new toys so I knew that would be a pleasant day for them.

I went to get the money that I had hidden behind the china cabinet so I could take it to the bank before I opened the store. At the bank, I handed the teller the zippered bank bag with the money and checks in it. When she counted the cash, she said it was short. The cash didn't add up to the amount I had written for the deposit. I thought she had to be wrong because both Leslie and I had each counted the money. Both of us counted it to avoid mistakes. I asked the teller to count it again. Once again it was exactly one thousand dollars short. I made the deposit and went to the store to discuss that with Leslie. I knew she was going to be surprised because we both counted it separately.

What happened when I arrived at the store was unexpected.

Leslie said, "We need to talk and we need to talk *today.*"

Surprised by her attitude, I didn't know what was going on. I knew that after Kelly told us about Dane taking her to the pool hall, both

Leslie and Greg weren't the same, somehow. We had about forty-five minutes before we opened the store.

So I said "Okay, what is it, is there something wrong?"

"Yes. Desiree, there is something wrong and you need to wake up about Dane before it's too late."

My head was spinning. I absolutely had not a clue what in the world she was talking about.

She said, "You need to open your eyes and see what is going on."

At that point, I begged her to just tell me what it was, and she did. My whole world, as I knew it, came to an end that morning. The words she spoke ripped my heart out. Everything started to make sense, all the incidents I had overlooked or made excuses for... everything. It was like a flashbulb going off inside my head.

At first, I shed some tears. Then I dried my eyes and asked her to help me so that all the hard work that we did wouldn't be lost. She hugged me and gave me her word that she would see me through this and that our friendship was strong and true.

She said "You have to understand that Greg works with Dane, so it is harder for him to keep his mouth shut."

"Please, please," I begged, "there are four children and there is our business to think of."

I then asked her why I didn't see it. Her only answer was that he knows how to hide his actions and cover them by telling you something you want to hear.

"We're scheduled to go to New York in two weeks, so I have to really think this through," I said. "But trust me, this will not happen again. I promise you, and I mean every word of what I am saying."

Leslie had no reason to disbelieve me. She was the one staying out late with various men in New York, not me. I had never said a word, even when she had a hard time with waking up in the morning, basically leaving the buying work to me for the first few hours until she could function. We opened the store and it was busy within a few minutes. We were lucky that most of the people wanted to exchange their items for a different size rather than returning them.

Not being able to concentrate at all, I was happy that things went well with customers.

At one point, I looked at Leslie and I couldn't help thinking, *Here I am, doing everything at home, in the store, and in New York, and I am the one who's being lied to and deceived by everyone.*

I acted like nothing was wrong when I got home, but before I opened the garage door, I got out of my car to see if Dane's car was locked. It was. I also noticed it was still warm.

Damn, I thought, *he's hiding something in his car and that's why he's locking it.*

Because there was nothing I could do, I got back into my car and pushed the button to lift the garage door. Going in through the garage like I always did, I didn't notice anything out of the ordinary, but then again, what was ordinary? Taking a deep breath, I walked into the kitchen as if nothing was wrong. Dane had just gotten home and the sitter was still there, which was a little unusual since he got off work about three hours before then, but I said nothing and acted as if I did not even think twice about it.

No one had been in our home since I came home from the store Christmas eve so there was nobody else who could have taken the money. The children were too young and Dane was the only one who knew where I hid it. The babysitter soon left and I quickly fixed dinner. I felt torn between keeping my mouth shut and just blurting everything out.

The next day, I discussed as much as I could with Leslie. Even though I didn't sleep the night before I was able to function well, and take care of the customers with her. That day around noon, we had a break in sales. Leslie ask me what I thought about the robbery we had in our previous store a few months before we moved into the big store. I found out the owner of the building thought he saw Dane leaving the store by himself around ten forty-five p.m. the night of the break in.

She told me that Greg already knew that Dane was fooling around with drugs and that is why they were so upset when he took the kids to the pool hall. I felt sick inside with fear. Pure panic was going through me.

I then asked her, "Why did you and Greg stay in the business?"

She then said Greg had a talk with Dane and Dane reassured him it was "only once in a while, just recreational," and that he "had no intention of ever getting hooked again." I looked at Leslie and realized that I had just received my answer, in that one word "again."

Leslie and I went to New York for our summer stock but my heart was not in it. She stayed out partying until around three-thirty that first night. The next morning, I found it hard to hold my tongue. When she was so tired, I had to start work myself until she joined me at noon. She's not a pretty woman, and her figure is very old fashioned-looking, so I know the men aren't buying her drinks just to enjoy her company.

Now the big picture hit me like a ten-pound hammer. I realized all three of my "partners" were riding on my shirttails because I was the one who did all of the buying and planning in the store. Leslie didn't even help decorate the display windows. I had to do that, too.

That night I had a talk with Leslie. I tried to explain that I had a lot of responsibility and that I needed her to help me, not stay out partying all night. She didn't receive my comment pleasantly. She told me that she and Greg weren't getting along well anymore and that she just needed to get her life together.

Oh Lord, I thought, this is not good. I reassured her that I was there for her no matter what. But that didn't sit well with her, either.

She snapped at me with, "What you're facing at home is in the way of you being there for me. Your hands are going to be full with surviving."

I could see she was tired and not at all in a good mood. This seemed to be her general demeanor lately, so I just left it alone.

I made arrangements ahead of time with the sitter for her to stay at the house while I was gone. That at least gave me peace of mind as far as the children were concerned. Our buying trips usually lasted about four days. I couldn't bear wondering what might be happening at home with the little ones. Dane and Greg were working second shift so they wouldn't be getting home until midnight. I figured it was best she stayed all night.

I spoke with her parents and they thought that was okay with them. She was nineteen and very responsible. I really liked her. She came from a black Baptist family and always read the children's bible to them. Talk about the best fried chicken well, this young lady could really cook and didn't mind doing it. I had no plans to keep her after the holidays but was happy that I had left it open because it gave me peace of mind on this trip.

Days turned into weeks and weeks turned into months with me noticing more and more Dane's strange behavior. I had tried to avoid the changes hoping they somehow would disappear. They didn't. He became more withdrawn and Kelly became more stand-offish with him. One day, I wasn't feeling all that well so I asked Leslie if she could close by herself. Of course, she said yes since she could see I wasn't feeling well.

When I got home I knew I needed to take the bull by the horns and do something drastic. As I walked quietly in the door Kelly was crying and Dane was acting strangely with his head on the floor and his feet up against the wall. Kelly was definitely upset and it really ticked me off. His eyes were very blank and I could see he was stoned on something. Immediately he asked, "Why are you home so early?"

My heart sank as I told Kelly to go into the play room with her brothers and sister, who were doing their homework.

She cried and said, "Daddy was mean to me. He told me to go away."

I hugged her and asked her again, "Let me talk to Daddy. You go into the playroom, okay?"

Agitation showed all over his face but I did not care. I asked him to come into the kitchen so I could start dinner while I talked to him. In all our years together, we never had harsh words with each other and I didn't want to start that but I needed to let him know I was aware of what was going on, and I needed an explanation. I quietly told him that I knew about the staged break in at the first store, and that he was the only person who could have taken the store money during Christmas time.

He started to say something but I cut him off, saying, "Dane, no one else knew I brought that money home. No one knew where it was hidden. No one else was in the house until I went to the bank on Monday morning."

He didn't respond. Then I went over to him and wrapped my arms around him and said, "I'm willing to do what ever it takes to save this marriage and our family."

I then told him that I loved him and would do anything it took to make it work.

He looked at me and said "I don't have a problem, you do. I don't need help, you do. So if you're done, I would like to watch the news."

I could hardly believe my ears. He didn't address anything. He ignored all the things I said. I turned around to remove the pan from the stove and when I turned back around again, he was gone.

A few weeks later, Dane got really sick with what seemed to be a bronchitis infection. I kept telling him to go to the doctor but he refused. After he slept in the girls' room for three days, while they slept in my room, I convinced him to go to the doctor before he gave it to all of us. He went, got some medication and told me it was a sinus infection that settled in his chest. He told me the doctor said it would clear up in a few days with the meds he gave him. I believed him and thought no more about it.

I started having the children come to the store on weeks when Dane worked afternoons so that I didn't need the sitter as much. They loved it. I always had some kind of surprise snack for them. Kelly was in her glory, being able to stay with me, although I still took her to Mother's every so often. I needed them around me since I was not handling Dane's behavior very well.

One night, while he was sitting on the couch, I got down on my knees in front of him and begged him to get help, saying that I would do anything it took to help him. He looked at me and took my hands in his.

He said "I love you so much. I never imagined loving someone so much, but honestly, you're the one with the problem, not me."

I was so shocked, I could hardly believe my ears. Although he did not raise his voice, and he said the words "I love you" with emotion, he was letting me know he had no intention to seek help. As far as he was concerned, it was me who needed help.

When I asked him how he felt about upsetting the baby with his actions, he thought a minute and then said, "She'll get over it. It's no big deal and I think you are over-reacting."

I was dumbfounded and he knew it.

Feeling defeated, as I got up off my knees, he reiterated, "I don't have a problem. You do."

Devastated and heartbroken with his attitude, I told him "You will have to leave until you get yourself together. There is no way I will allow our children to be upset over your actions."

Very calmly, all he said was, "Fine. I'll leave as soon as I eat."

Watching him eat made my heart ache. He ate very slowly and seemed to enjoy every bite, as if he knew this was the beginning of the end. He did not say anything to the children as he got up from the table and went upstairs to get some clothes. When he came back down, I watched as he went to the front door, opened it, and stepped through.

Hearing the door close, for the second time in my life I was left to think, *he is gone.*

Chapter Eight

So many emotions tore at my heart but there was no way I could allow my innocent children to be upset over someone who obviously set a priority on something other than his family.

Standing at the sink, I wondered, where is my life heading, what will happen next?

Of course, the two older children asked where Daddy went. It seemed the girls didn't pay attention to him leaving. Of course, never missing a thing, Trip asked why he took a duffle bag with him. By now my tears had started to flow. I didn't know how to answer. Try as I might, I could not stop the tears.

I simply said, "He's going away for a while but he'll be back."

In my mind, that is what I wanted to happen. I thought maybe saying it would make it be.

Craig came to me and hugged me so close as he told me, "Don't worry Mommy, I will take care of you."

I looked down at my son and somehow I knew if he possibly could, he would. The depth of his perception of what had just taken place surprised me.

"Craig, since the day you were born," I whispered, "you are the one who I can always count on. You always think of your family first. You are such a good boy and I love you so much."

He hugged me back and answered "I love you to Mommy. You'll see. I'm going to take care of all of us."

I was so nervous I was just about ready to jump out of my skin. I needed to calm myself somehow. I thought I would read the newspaper and maybe that would keep my mind off the situation at hand.

At one point, I put the paper down in my lap and that is when I noticed all four of my beautiful children were sitting on the floor near me. They all had something to keep themselves busy and they were all sitting very close to me. Even though my heart was aching, I looked at each one of them individually and realized how fortunate I really was. They were all so different and yet all so precious. Because of them, I would find whatever strength I needed to take care of us.

I picked up the paper again so that I could hide my tears but very soon, Kelly crawled into my lap and laid her head on my chest, almost as if she knew I needed her close to me. Kelly and Craig both always wanted to be close to me, to not venture very far. Their personalities are a lot alike. They are both very sensitive. Holding Kelly close, I caught the scent of baby shampoo in her soft hair. It made me realize just how young and innocent she was. I tried to think positive but right then, that was impossible.

The first night Dane left, going to bed was a serious challenge since all the children decided they wanted to sleep with me. My goal was to create calm and normalcy. I reassured all of them that Daddy would be back, that he just wanted to go away for a few days, and then he would return. They seemed to believe me, except for Trip who wanted to know why he left and how long he would be gone.

Not knowing what to say, I asked him to help me by not asking questions that his brother and sisters would hear and maybe not understand.

He smiled with a big boy look and said "Gotcha, Mom."

My big fear was that something would happen to Dane before he could get himself together and come back home. I was so naive to any kind of substances that I literally feared the unknown.

Greg and Leslie were present at the store when I arrived in the morning. This was a surprise since Leslie usually didn't get there until right before ten a.m., when we opened. I knew something was up but I didn't expect what I was about to hear. I always got the pot of coffee ready at night, before I left, so that all I had to do in the morning was press the "On" button, which is what I did that morning.

When the coffee was ready, we each poured ourselves a cup. Since we still had at least forty-five minutes before the store opened, we sat at the little table in the back. I could see that Leslie had been crying but I didn't say anything about it, I just wanted to hear what they were about to say. I was in for a surprise.

They decided that because of their marital state, they didn't want to continue with the store. If I had explained my thoughts, calling that "a shock" would have been to put it mildly. Greg said that after the two incidents with the store money, he just didn't feel he could trust Dane. He thought they should bow out graciously, right then. I could not believe what I was hearing. I knew they were having a lot of trouble in their marriage but to give all this up was crazy.

I just sat for a minute trying to take it all in.

Then Greg said "Give us a few thousand dollars and we will leave. You keep the inventory and anything else there is."

The money was not the issue. I knew I could easily give them money but I was left with no help, whatsoever. I wondered if they knew that Dane had left the night before, so I asked them. They did not know but Greg said he was not surprised.

"You are going to have your hands full Desiree, believe me, I feel sorry for you," is what he said next.

Leslie then said she would work another two weeks so that I can get someone else to take her place. I simply could not believe my ears. We all worked so hard to create this store and now they wanted to walk away for a measly few thousand dollars.

That's crazy, I thought.

Asking Leslie if she was going to stay that day was harder than I thought. I started to cry.

Greg left and it was just Leslie and me, as usual, until we opened. She tried to smooth things over but in the back of my mind I knew there was more to their decision. Immediately, I wondered what exactly Greg knew about Dane that he was not telling me.

As the weeks went by, I became more nervous and anxious, to the point I felt myself falling apart. With Leslie gone, I asked Mother if she would like to come and work with me for a while, until I could see exactly where I was, financially. She agreed, and I had her helping with changing displays and all those things that I now didn't have time to do. I couldn't count on her all the time even though she knew I needed to get my act together and get everything in order.

Leslie got a job right away, managing a boutique. She didn't stay the full two weeks like she said she would. I wasn't sleeping at night and during the day, I dragged like a horse that had already plowed a field all day.

Mother told Dane to come and stay in the little house that was now empty. To my surprise, he did that, saying he did not want to go to his parents' house and we couldn't afford to spend money on an apartment. When she told me what he said, the word "apartment" hit me like a truck since it sounded so permanent. It seemed to me that this time, she was trying to help us.

Mother was helping me in the store on the third Saturday after Dane left when the phone rang and I answered it. It was Dane's father. He started out sweet but soon became very demanding. He insisted that I tell him the truth about Dane. I wasn't sure what Dane had told them and not wanting to cause any trouble, I asked him what he meant.

He angrily said, "All I want is to know the truth and I know you will be honest with me." What he said next, I was not prepared for, "Is Dane dying or is it something else?"

I almost dropped the phone.

I burst into tears and told him, "I don't know what is going on, but I begged him to go and get help and he refused, telling me that I am the one who has a problem, not him."

His voice softened. He told me that he had seen Dane the day before and he looked terrible. Not knowing exactly what to say, I decided in that moment that the truth was the best. I explained to him what had happened and that I told Dane he needed to get help or he had to leave.

To my surprise, his father told me I was right, the kids don't need to see that. I talked to him for about fifteen minutes. He told me they would see what they could do to force him to seek help. I thanked him and said goodbye.

I was quivering all over which caused Mother to tell me to calm down before I got sick and became of no use to anyone, including myself. I looked at her and didn't say anything since there was really nothing to say. Getting more nervous by the day, I felt myself getting sicker and sicker until I couldn't stand the pain in my legs and arms. Every day, it seemed to get worse. I decided I had better take care of myself, since I knew there was nobody else I could count on. I went to the doctor to see what was causing the pain in my joints. The doctor examined me and asked me questions. After a few questions, he told me to come into his office so he could talk to me.

The doctor had become a friend because he came into the store frequently. He was always so kind and friendly and always bought things. In his office, he got a serious look on his face and said he would have to run some blood work on me but he suspected a lot of my problem was nerves. He sent me for blood work and said he would have me come back in after he received the results. They took the blood at his office and I went back to the store.

A few days later, I got a call from the doctor's office saying the results of the blood work were in and I should make an appointment to come in. By now, I could hardly stand the pain in my joints and I was in some serious misery. The doctor's office gave me an appointment early the next morning. I had to take Kelly with me since I didn't have anyone to watch her. Not minding at all that I took her, she just chattered away, telling the receptionist about our store. She is such a sweet little doll, everyone loved her. The doctor came into the examining room and informed me that I needed total rest and that my nerves had thrown me into a condition that will take a while to settle. He told me that this was the way my body was breaking down; that if I wasn't careful, I would end up in bed until my body healed. He gave me medication and told me to go home and try to rest.

I had no one to take care of the store regularly, only a few part time girls. I was in a serious dilemma, but figured I would calm down and somehow everything would be alright. That was wrong. When I woke up the next morning, I could hardly walk, I was in so much pain.

There was no way I could go into the store. I could barely even get the little ones ready for school. I was in near-agony and scared to death. I called Mother to see if she could go and open the store for me because my part time help were girls that were still in school. She said she would but it would have to be later since her husband was working a second shift and she thought she needed to stay home with him until he left.

Instead of just saying nicely that she should stay home, she had to follow up with, "I have a husband, you know, and I have responsibilities, but your store is not one of mine."

I felt so hurt by her attitude with me. Pure panic set in because I had no one to open up the store. There was no way I could even force myself to go since I could not even walk up our steps to the bedroom to get dressed. I laid down on the couch and asked Kelly to just give Mommy a few minutes to rest and then I would get her breakfast.

When I woke up, Kelly was playing with her toys in the family room where I was laying. I glanced at the clock and I froze because it was almost one in the afternoon. I had slept for over four and a half hours. I wanted to cry, thinking, as young as Kelly was, she never tried to wake me to get her something to eat.

I jumped up and told her I was so sorry. She giggled and told me she ate some raisin bread. I couldn't believe my ears, she had gone into the bread drawer and helped herself to the raisin bread.

"What a precious little girl," I thought.

The doctor was right about the situation getting worse before I started to get better. Dane wanted to come home to take care of me but I was hesitant. Not having a choice, I had to agree and just accept that was the way it had to be, hoping in my heart he would decide his family was more important than his problem. He stayed at the house for a few weeks. Although he was a big help, it was also a daily reminder that we were not important enough for him to stop whatever he was doing.

I was afraid to have him go to the store because of what had occurred in the past but he really wasn't interested in opening it up and he let me know it. I couldn't believe we had worked so hard and now the three of them were just walking away.

I notified the owner of the shopping plaza that I was ill and would open as soon as I was able. To my surprise, he was understanding and told me the most important thing was that I get better. As I struggled to get around, I could not believe that all Mother was interested in was Trip staying at her home. She did not say a word about the other three, just him. Reluctantly, I let him stay there so that the other three would have some peace. It seemed the older he grew, the more trouble he liked to cause. He was constantly picking on one or the other.

It took me six weeks to start seeing improvement in my ability to move around. It also took that long for the pain to ease up enough that I could reduce the medication. I was able to get back to a somewhat normal life, meaning to open the store and take care of my children.

Dane went back to Mother's little house. Soon he would move in with his parents. His father called me to say he insisted on Dane moving back home so he could watch him, since he now knew there was a problem. He told me not to blame myself, this was his problem, not mine, and I didn't do anything to cause it. His kind words stuck in my mind. I appreciated hearing that from him.

When one of my orders for leather jackets came in, as usual, I wrote a company check. The bank called me to say that my account balance would not cover it. Thinking this had to be impossible, I decided to go to the bank during lunch hour. I hoped Mother would come in so I could spend as much time as would be needed there. I gave her a call telling her what happened. She said she was coming in but not until around one-thirty p.m. That was fine. It enabled me to review my banking records. Leslie had always kept the checkbook. I figured I would only have to go over a few months. I was the only person writing checks so I knew there was no way a check could have bounced. I never bounced a check before so the bank covered it until I could come in and see what was going on.

The manager of the bank sat down with me to go over my business checking account. I originally thought there was just a slight error somewhere but what I soon learned was devastating. Never reviewing Leslie's work caused me quite a dilemma. I didn't know where to begin, except to go back to the very beginning and check everything. None of the monthly statements corresponded with the balances I showed in the check book.

I deposited enough money to cover the check that bounced. I told the bank manager I would try to make sense of this mess and get back with them. Upon receiving a copy of all the monthly statements, I thanked her and left.

I had been very active in local community affairs. I was scheduled to have dinner with a woman, Esther, who was on a public housing board that I also served on. During dinner, she asked me how things were going. She was a good friend, so I opened up and told her about my recent troubles. After dinner, we decided to go into the bar for a drink. She advised me to get an accountant to review the books to see exactly what happened and to also check the store inventory to make sure nothing was missing. I hadn't considered that some of the inventory could be short. My head was spinning with all that I now needed to do.

I went to the bar and ordered another glass of wine. An extremely handsome bartender took my order.

When he returned with my wine, he said, "This one is on me."

I smiled and responded "Thank you so much but I would rather pay for it."

He smiled broadly and said "It's already taken care of, just enjoy."

I went back to the table and told Esther what just happened.

She said, "Instead of wine, you should have asked him to audit your books to see what happened with your money. He works for a large accounting firm."

I chuckled and said, "With his infectious smile, he's dangerous."

I recalled how Ajax used to growl at me and that seemed the only way I could describe this man: with a big growl.

After a while, I went home. I didn't like keeping the babysitter working too late. I hated to burden her father with picking her up at a late hour. Nor could I leave my children home alone until I took her home, myself. They were kind people. I felt lucky to have found them. As we were leaving the bar, I glanced back but did not see that handsome accountant.

He must have left for the night or gone to the stockroom, I thought.

Walking out with Esther, we met two women who had set up a jewelry display in a hallway of the restaurant's lounge. We stopped to talk to them and to look at what they were selling. One woman was chatty while the other seemed reserved. The talkative one had grotesque buck teeth but her manner was pleasant enough. I felt drawn to the other gal so I spoke with her. There was something about the woman that touched my soul. It was a *déjà vu* feeling. Somehow, it seemed I had known her before.

While checking out the jewelry, I looked to my left and saw a long row of windows. I looked through them and saw two men playing tennis.

"Oh my Gosh," I said to Esther, "there's our bartender."

She came over and he looked up at us and waved, as he smiled at me. I walked back to the display table and continued to look at the jewelry. I asked the quiet woman if she had a business card. I saw on the card that they also staged house parties.

I said, "That might be fun and I know enough women who I could invite."

Esther laughed and said, "Your mind is usually working on ways to make money. I have to give you credit for coming up with some good ideas."

"I wouldn't get money for having a party but I might get some free jewelry, and besides," I thought, "those women are working hard to make a living. Why not help them?"

I went into my store as soon as my children boarded the school bus, hoping I would readily find the error in the checking account. Starting three months back, I expected it was only an oversight on Leslie's part. Nothing matched. Nothing was even remotely accurate. Then I went back a few more months; same thing, nothing was correct. Not knowing where to begin, I decided to get someone who knows what they are doing to find where the error begins. Deposits all matched but not a single balance was right.

I was confused because I had trusted Leslie to balance the books every month. That was something I hated to do. So when she offered, I was happy to turn it over. I never had a reason to not trust her. Even when the tally didn't balance, I still didn't think she would ever steal anything. I was sick to my stomach not knowing what to think or who to trust.

When it was time to open the store, I put the checkbook down. I figured I would have to start at the very beginning and go from there. I had plenty of money in the account to carry me over so I knew I had time to figure it all out. I was slammed with customers that day and made good money. I decided not to make a deposit that night. Instead, I took the money home until I could go to the bank the next day.

I went in early the next day to make sense of the mess I was in with the checking account. I didn't have any orders due in until the next week so I still had time to find the error. The check book itself was correct but the bank was showing something else. I was confused. Once again I was very busy and for the next few hours didn't have time to think how I should handle the mess.

I forgot the money at the house so I didn't deposit it. At the end of the day, I decided to not deposit those receipts, either. I was uncomfortable with what had happened and since Leslie and Greg were no longer a part of the store, it was me alone handling everything. Having no one to answer to except myself, I took the cash home again.

Lilly was such a big help. I could count on her to help me with everything. She was far wiser than her years. She always seemed to be right there when I needed something, whether it be to help dust the displays or to keep Kelly busy until I could do something for her. Without Lilly and Craig, I didn't know how I would manage. Trip was way too busy causing havoc to think about much else. Since the day Craig was born, Mother favored Trip and seemed compelled to pit my two boys against each other. I called her on this many times but she denied it each time. Sometimes I wished I could just pick up and move far, far away.

I managed to get everything organized and finished before bedtime. Happy for the peace and quiet that afforded me, I decided to lie down early. My body still aching, I tried to relax and soon I was sound asleep.

"Hello pretty woman. I'm so sorry I haven't come to you sooner but now I'm here," Ajax said.

We both reached out for each other. He kissed me, ever so sweetly.

"I love you," he said. "I haven't abandoned you. I've been with you every step of the way, my love. I love you so much."

I held on to him, wanting to never let go.

"Listen to me carefully" he said. "You must read every paper that is put before you. There will be many answers in them."

*He kissed me again and then kissed my eyelids as
tears rolled down my cheeks.*

*He said, "I still have your tear in my pocket. I will
carry it with me for all eternity. Don't cry, my love, I will
always protect you. I'm sending someone to help you, so
you will be fine."*

*Kissing my lips again, he said, "I must go now but
remember to stay near your car so that you are not hurt.
I love you Pretty Woman. I wish you could come with me
now. Until you can, I will always be with you, just as I
told you the night I left."*

*He kissed me one more time. Then the white cloud
enveloped us. I reached for him but he slipped away
from me.*

Waking up the next morning, I remembered this dream. Wondering
what he meant about "papers," I accepted that I would know what he
meant when the time came. Not wanting to get all upset and cause
myself more problems, I left the check book alone and figured I would
continue to hide the cash for a few more days. As always, I put the cart
before the horse. I was worrying ahead about taking care of the house
and children. I felt concerned about having enough money to take care
of everything. I thought long and hard about seeking advice from an
attorney, but put that thought on the back burner, also.

I had a doctor's appointment. I made sure Mother would show up at
the store so I could leave. She surprised me when she came in early. She
was in a good mood so she talked to me with a happy tone instead of
resentment. The doctor's office was the same old situation, hurry up and
wait. Once inside the examining room, I waited for another ten minutes
before the doctor came in. He examined my arm, hands and leg joints
thoroughly and then told me to get dressed and come into his office.

In the office, I waited again, endlessly, it seemed. When he came in
he was so pleasant I felt relaxed. Fear of what was to come left me. He
sat down and leaned back in his oversized leather desk chair and started
to ask me questions about my condition and my personal life. Then I
broke down and cried.

Being so understanding, he continued to talk. His manner enabled me to admit the truth about what was going on in my life. As I poured my heart out, I told him about Dane and the fear I had that his problem would never go away and I would be left all alone raising four children.

I said, "I have to ask the question, 'Who in the world would want me and four children to raise?'"

He stood and said he would be back in one minute. Drying my tears, I sat back in the chair and waited for him to return. He came back with a mirror in his hand.

He handed it to me, and said, "Look in this mirror, please."

I did, and then I looked at him, waiting for him to tell me what I was looking for.

"Do you see yourself?" he asked. I replied, "Yes, but why am I looking in the mirror?"

He then told me something surprising, "You are a very beautiful woman. Not only are you beautiful, but you are also smart and you can run a business all by your self, starting from nothing. Believe me, Desiree, there will be plenty of 'someone's' out there who would be proud to be your husband and raise those equally beautiful children. Now dry your tears. Believe me, you are going to be fine," he said.

Then he did something that surprised me. He said, "Wait one more time, I need to get something."

He was back in the room rather quickly. He brought a file folder in his had.

He looked at me very seriously and said, "I want you to listen to me now. You need to move on in your life; to make a new life for yourself and those beautiful children of yours. The situation you are in will not change soon, if it ever changes."

I didn't understand and I said as much. Opening the file folder, he leaned forward and said, "for what I am about to do, I could lose my license. But you are a decent woman and I am willing to take that chance."

He put the open file on his desk and said, "Excuse me for a few minutes Desiree. I need to take care of another patient. Then I will be back. It will only be about fifteen to twenty minutes. Sit here and wait for me please."

I said, "Okay," and he left, closing the door.

I sat there for a minute and then the memory of my last dream hit me like a bolt of lightening. Ajax had said, "Read all the papers that are left in front of you. There will be a lot of answers in them for you."

I leaned forward, turning the open file around, which enabled me to read it. Looking at my watch I thought, *Fifteen to twenty minutes will do.* What I read in that file cut me to the very core. Reading Dane's medical records gave me many answers to so many questions. His problem went back many years. I was astonished to think he was able to hide it from me.

Clinical notes from his last episode with pneumonia stated, "Patient refuses blood work. Eyes appear ashen on outer areas. Follow up visit required. Patient's history of drug abuse..."

It went on and on with his medical history, going way back into time before we were married. My heart ached as I tried to decipher all the words I was reading. They were heart-wrenching words about his problem and what it was causing.

Leaving the doctor's office that day, I realized more than ever that I had to do something: either get Dane to seek help or face the fact that he will never exorcise his demons. If the latter is the case, then I should make a life for myself and my children, without him. I deeply wanted him to admit he had a problem and get help but, in my heart of hearts, I knew he would not. He was adamant that it was me who had a problem.

Dane would call every night to talk to me. There were times when I could tell by the tone of his voice that he was not himself. I hated to even guess what his problem could be. I put that out of my mind and ignored it, but deep inside, I knew I couldn't continue like that forever.

He would stop by for only a few minutes at a time. This made me wonder why he wasn't staying longer to spend time with the children. I knew he had to miss them even if he didn't miss me, but each time it was just a short visit, in and out again. He offered no help. He never asked about how we were doing or if we needed anything. He remained completely self-involved.

I tried to keep things going the best I could. It was hard on me to work all day and then take care of a big house and do laundry at night. The health episode that I suffered left me weak and tired. My only day off was Sunday, when the store was closed. The weather became very cold with a lot of snow that year. Normally, I would love snow but in that year, the wind and cold cut to the bone. There was no way I could play with the children in the snow like I typically would. Business was slow due to the weather. Although I kept my head above water, the slow business played havoc on me.

After more than a week, I still had not gone to the bank to deposit the cash. I still hadn't figured out what happened with the checking account. I felt confident that Leslie didn't take any money so I just kept thinking it was an error. A major error. I was actually afraid to find out what happened. That old saying did apply, that "Ignorance is bliss."

Knowing I had to get to the bottom of it sooner or later, I thought I would ask Esther if she could recommend someone to help me. We planned to have dinner together again in a few days. I didn't want my business discussed all over town, so I thought it better to go to someone she knew who I could trust. Her husband prepared taxes every year. I figured she would know someone capable and reputable.

Coming home absolutely beat, I intended to make dinner and then relax and call it a night. That was not in the cards, though. I could see Dane's car was parked in our driveway as I approached the house. I felt sure something was wrong because he would not come by without calling first. The closer I got to the house, the more anxious I became, until finally, I pulled into the garage.

The children were with me in the car. They were not happy to see their father was there. Lilly spoke up first.

She asked, "Why does he come to the house? He doesn't talk to us and he scares Kelly. I wish he would just leave us alone, Mommy."

My heart ached as I told her to be nice. As I said the words, "He's your Daddy and he loves you," I felt sick inside, knowing his priority wasn't to love his children. Given how Mother trashed my father to me when I was little, I vowed that I would never do that to my own children, no matter what. My poor father never had a chance. No matter what he did, it was never good enough for Mother.

I felt sick to my stomach walking into the garage and then into the family room, not knowing what I would find, and rightfully so. Dane was lying on the floor but he got up when the door opened. The children scattered, each going their own way, except for Kelly, who clung to my leg. She wouldn't leave my side until I called Lilly to take her.

I sat down on the couch and told Dane we needed to talk, *really* talk, to decide how we could correct our situation. I told him I loved him and didn't want us to break up but I was not going to continue putting the family through this chaos.

That is when I realized how messed up he was. He looked at me and repeated that it was me who has a problem, not him. It was that look in his eyes that scared me, though. I didn't say anything more. I got up and went to the kitchen to start dinner. I was not happy with how he was coming along behind me. He could barely stand. I decided to call my girlfriend to see if she was busy. I acted as if she had asked me to come over but I was just talking for him to hear it.

With Trip at Mother's house for the night, I could put the three younger ones in the car and leave. I called to Craig and Lilly to get ready, saying that we were going to Sophie's house soon for dinner. They were ready in a flash, with Kelly in tow. I apologized to Dane. I told him that I had promised Sophie I would come over and have dinner with her. He believed my ruse and started to put on his jacket. He was so far gone that he could hardly stand still long enough to put his arms in the sleeves of his jacket.

I told the children to go get in the car, that I would be there right away. As they left, I looked at Dane and told him he was to never come to the house all messed up again; that if he did I would call the police. I opened the front door for him to leave. He looked at me as if he wanted to destroy me. I had never seen him look so mean and hateful. As he approached the door he said, "You'll be sorry for this." Then he left.

The wind was blowing and there was so much snow on the ground that driving was not a good idea. However, I wanted him to leave. I didn't know what else to do. We left the driveway at about the same time. I noticed he did not turn his headlights on. As I realized we would be soon on a main road, I pulled over to get out of my car and tell him his lights were off. As I closed my car door and walked toward the back of my car, I slipped and fell on the ice. My legs were still extremely sore. For a moment, I tried to move but couldn't. As I fell, I heard him accelerating, starting to pull around my car.

A loud voice in my head said, "Stay close to your car," just as Ajax had told me in my dream. I rolled over, against my car's back tire, just as Dane shot out from behind, almost running over me.

I laid there for a second and I could hear my children screaming, "Mommy! Mommy!"

Suddenly, Craig was helping me to get up. I was shaking all over from the fear of what could have been. I felt his car brush against my body as it passed. That was how close he came to running over me. What a terrifying feeling that was, to be up against my car's tire with not even an inch left to move away any farther.

With Craig's help, I got up and back into my car. While gathering my composure, I decided I would not try to reconcile with Dane any longer, under any circumstances. In his state of mind he could have killed me. What would happen to my children if I were gone? I drove down the road, not even thinking about the dream, just thanking God that I was safe.

When we arrived at Sophie's house, she made me a cup of tea and some dinner for my children and for her own. She and I had been friends for a while and I trusted her. I loved our conversations. Not only was she a wise woman, she was also a gifted psychic. When I found she was able to see the future it blew my mind. She had never told me of her ability. I asked her why. She laughed, saying she thought I might be uncomfortable around her if I knew. I had told her my story about that horrible psychic at the carnival and how what she revealed had haunted me for years.

With Sophie, there was no discomfort. In fact, I asked her what she saw happening; if the children and I would be safe. She didn't scare me like the fortune teller at the amusement park. Nor did she make me think my future would be gloomy. However, what she revealed saddened me to tears. Previously, I had thought Dane and I would grow old together and have a house full of grandchildren but that was not what she saw. She told me that he was a very troubled man; that I should be very careful with the children around him. She said no real harm would come to the children but there would be some scary incidents.

I asked her if I would ever again allow myself to feel the love I had felt for Ajax. I had never talked about him with anyone else. For some unknown reason, I felt at ease telling Sophie our story. That night, I told her everything about us, starting with dating in school, then wanting to get married, then to my dreaming of his death. She listened with tears streaming down her face.

Then she said, "He is always around you, protecting you, and he will always be right by your side until the day you die."

She then went on to describe him in full detail, as if he were standing right there. I told her about the dreams when he says things that don't make sense until I'm in a situation and react as he instructed. She and I talked for hours that night. We became best friends.

As I was leaving, Sophie said to me, "You'll find out Dane took money out of your business, not your partner. Her husband knew what Dane was doing. Your partners didn't want any part of it."

I hadn't mentioned any of that to her, so it surprised me that she could talk about it.

She followed up with "You'll be just fine. A very handsome young man will go over your books. He'll let you know exactly what occurred… and, oh, is he ever going to like you a lot." Then she laughed.

I had to wonder if she was the person Ajax sent to help me. She had helped me greatly with her kind words and understanding. I was left with a feeling of great relief after talking to someone who understood about Ajax. I went home knowing that no matter what might happen, I would have the strength to endure. Drifting off to sleep, I had a peaceful feeling for the first time in months.

I became afraid of Dane for the first time. I was not going to take any chances that he might come into the house again with out me knowing. I changed the locks on the doors and programmed a new code into the overhead garage door's remote control. The only other doors in the house were the glass sliders in the eating area. I blocked them with a board in the track.

Esther called me at the store to remind me of a housing authority meeting that I had to attend the following night. She also wanted to know if I would like to go out to dinner afterwards, her treat. The meeting was to be short, so we would get home early, she said. I was happy to get out but I reassured her that I could pay for my own meal. She was so much fun that I really enjoyed doing things with her.

When the half-hour meeting was finished, she and I went to the same restaurant where we had gone the week before. This time, a waiter served a glass of wine at my table, saying it came compliments of the lounge bartender. I looked at Esther and knew it was that handsome young man who had given me wine the last time I ate there. I asked the waiter to please thank him cordially for me.

Esther laughed and we continued our conversation. After dinner, Esther again suggested I ask that bartender to go over my books to discover what happened with the money. Then that I told her about the night when Dane almost ran over me with his car. I also told her how I visited Sophie and all the things Sophie told me. Esther was all ears.

She said, "See? I told you to ask him."

I laughed. Esther's husband was going to pick her up late. She asked me if I would wait with her until he got there. I said "yes" because she would never leave me sitting there alone. We moved from the restaurant into the lounge area. She ordered drinks for us. This time, the handsome bartender served them, introducing himself.

He sure is nice to look at, I thought, as I leaned back to get a better view. Then Esther pulled a fast one.

She said, "Aren't you the man who works for that accounting firm in Cleveland?"

He looked at her with surprise and replied, "Why yes, I am. How did you know, are you a client?"

She then told him about her husband doing accounting on the side and that her husband recognized him one evening when they were at dinner. I sat there frozen, thinking she was going to put me on the spot right then and there by saying something about my books, but she didn't.

Instead, he introduced himself as Pete and handed us each a card. He said that if we ever have a need, or know someone who needs an accountant, just give him a call.

As he handed me his card, he smiled broadly again as he said "I understand you own the clothing store in the Oberlin Avenue Shopping Plaza. If ever you need someone, please let me know."

I smiled and took the opportunity, saying "As a matter of fact, I do have a little problem that needs solving. Can I reach you at this number?"

By then, he was grinning like the Cheshire Cat. He told me that he was off the next day, and that if I would like, he would stop by then, but any day he would be at that number. I chuckled silently over his enthusiasm and admitted to myself how good it made me feel. He then asked if I would like him to call me in the morning after I checked my schedule. I agreed, and gave him the store number. I said that I was usually there by nine a.m. but we didn't open until ten, so if he would call by nine fifteen I would know by then what was happening. He smiled his winning smile once again and left us.

After he went back to the bar, out of ears' reach, I looked at Esther and said "Smooth move woman, smooth move."

She laughed and said, "See how easy that was? Now you have someone to look at you books."

I laughed and wasn't sure if I should say thank you or wish she hadn't done that. Thank goodness her husband came on time because I really needed to get home and do a few things before I called it quits for the day. Kelly wouldn't go to sleep until I got home so the baby sitter just let her sit up with her until then. My little keeper, I thought. This little one is glued to my hip and to think I was absolutely dumbfounded when I discovered I was pregnant with her. With two other children a little over a year apart, and Trip being a one-man demolition squad, I wasn't certain I was ready for another child, but she absolutely became my little buddy and I wouldn't trade her for the world. She is every mother's delight as a daughter.

At exactly nine-fifteen the next morning, the phone rang at the store. I chuckled when I looked at my watch and saw the time.

At the other end, I heard this happy go lucky voice: "Good Mornin'. Am I late?"

I laughed so hard I almost choked on my coffee. I asked him if he was always so happy in the morning. Somehow, his happiness rubbed off on me. For those few minutes while we talked, all my problems seemed to take a back burner. He asked me what I needed to get help with. I explained what happened when I wrote that check for leather coats; I was taken aback because there were no funds in the account. I tried to be brief and yet convey the problem, without going into my personal life.

He told me what I needed to provide him, some invoices and old statements. He asked if it would be alright if he came by in a few hours.

His professionalism surprised me, pleasantly. I agreed to have everything ready. I forgot to ask him if he would be taking the work to his office or if he would work in my office. It didn't matter, as long as I knew what had happened, in the end. I was unsure which would be a better outcome: if Leslie took the money, or Dane. Either way, I was soon to find out. It took quite a while to gather all the paperwork he needed. I felt happy that I had a few more minutes to gather more paperwork before customers started coming in. I opened the store at ten, as I usual.

When he arrived around noon, I had almost everything he needed. I needed a few more minutes. The noon lull enabled me to finish. When Pete walked in, I was impressed by his looks. He looked even better in the daylight than he did at the lounge. He was wearing a red polo sweater which really made his jet black, curly hair stand out. When he smiled, which he seemed to readily do, his teeth were perfect, giving him a smile to die for. Kelly, my little sidekick, chatted with him about the new shirts we received the previous day. He laughed, and kept quite a conversation going with her, asking her to show him where they were so he could look at them. Like a little mini-me sales clerk, she said "Follow me and I will show you." He laughed again, and followed her over to the display table.

Then, to his amazement, she asked, "What size do you wear?"

He looked over at me and laughed as he said "She really knows what she's doing, doesn't she?"

I was so proud of her. *She's such a beautiful little girl and so smart,* I thought, *what would I do without her?*

Getting to the business of his visit, Pete asked me if there was an office where he could work, to see if he could find the problem quickly. Otherwise, he would have to take the paperwork with him. I showed him where my office was and also invited him to sit behind the counter at a little desk.

Choosing to sit at the counter, he told me what he needed. Then he started reviewing everything from the very beginning when we opened the store. I waited on customers and watched him from the corner of my eye. He was intensely engaged and definitely going over everything with a fine-toothed comb. Watching him made me even more apprehensive because now I knew the truth was going to come out and I was afraid of what I would learn.

About an hour and a half into his sorting through everything, I asked him if I could get him something to drink. We both laughed at the reversed roles we were playing. I reminded him that there was no wine there, but I did have coffee or sodas. He asked for a cup of coffee which I happily made for him. Bringing coffee to him reminded me of getting coffee for Ajax. Still intensely going over everything, he stopped to take the coffee cup from my hand and he took a sip. I sat down near him. I asked if he had found anything that would give me an idea as to what happened to all that money. I didn't want him to think I balanced the checking account, so I explained to him that my partner did the books and I took care of buying and ordering.

He smiled that great big warm smile and said, "I'll find out what has happened. It may take me a while but I'll get to the bottom of it. He asked me if I knew where the missing checks are and I didn't know what he was talking about since I thought everything was there, neatly filed. Leslie would put the invoices into a folder until the checks for the shipments cleared. Then she would attach the check to the invoice and then put it in the company file. He showed me some of the checks were missing. In some cases, only the packing slip was in the file, not the invoice.

I realized that this would become a long process. I asked if there was anything I could do while also helping customers or at home in the evening. He told me it was better if he did it all himself so he could see if there was an overall pattern. He reassured me once again that he would figure it out and get to the bottom of what was going on. He took a break while he drank his coffee and asked a few questions about the store and about buying for the store.

He thought that sounded so neat; to go to New York and buy a bunch of clothes. I laughed and told him it isn't quite as simple as it sounds; that it's quite a challenge to remember all the different styles and, out of twenty-seven floors of clothing, on which floor you saw something. I explained that I had to take notes at first, so I could keep things straight, because all those floors of vendors with different clothes were mind-boggling.

Some funny stories about the first buying trip brought us both to laughter. From then on, there was a comfort level between us. I felt relaxed around him. I no longer felt ashamed that I didn't realize what was going on behind my back. He told me stories about some of the accounting firm's big businesses that had been ripped off, just as I had been, and they were in business for many years.

I had to excuse myself to assist customers but I returned quickly to continue our conversation.

What a happy personality he has and he isn't bad to look at, I thought to myself.

The afternoon went quickly. We had quite a few big sales. He asked if he could take everything with him to his office and work on it there, the next day. Of course, I agreed. I gave him phone numbers where he could reach me if he had questions, and he left.

I decided to go to Sophie's house. I made dinner earlier so we could visit for an hour or so and get home in time for baths and bedtime snacks. I brought some cookies for all the kids.

Her husband worked second shift at the local Ford plant, so she welcomed company in the evening. I really enjoyed talking with her. Her compassion and understanding were extraordinary. She had a way of helping me feel at ease, as if all was going to be okay, so there was no need to worry.

Soon she and I were sitting in the kitchen having a cup of tea. She took my tea bag and looked at it. She told me about things that were going to happen. I sat quietly, taking it all in, not really knowing what to say.

"You will divorce your husband," she said, "and the sooner the better. Just be careful with your children because he's not stable. He might act out. Something tragic will happen to him in his early fifties. He will be alive but his mind will be gone. He will spend the rest of his days that way."

I asked her what she meant, but she said she only knows that he has been unstable for a very long time and he will not be good to the children. That didn't surprise me because of the way he would upset Kelly and not even feel badly about it.

I asked her if I would be able to take care of myself and the children with the income from the store. She said I would close the store but I should not worry because someone would love me and accept the children as if they were his own.

I picked up that tea bag and looked at it but I didn't see a thing. This made her laugh. "It's just a tool," she said. "It helps me to see things, that's all."

Looking at the tea bag one more time made absolutely no difference. I still saw only a wet tea bag. At home that evening, I went over her words. Even though they were hard to digest, there were also words of encouragement and happiness. It would take a special kind of man to take on a woman with four children. But I hoped Sophie would be right; that eventually, someone that special would enter my life, which comprised working all day at the store, then taking care of children at night.

Sundays were still the same; I tried to get everything finished in one day. Most of the time, I was successful when the young woman who watched my children on Saturdays would help me with laundry and vacuum cleaning. She liked the extra money I gave her for helping me and I really appreciated that help, so it was a win-win situation.

The following week, my mind was consumed with Pete getting to the bottom of the missing money puzzle. I could hardly wait for his call telling me when he would bring back my files and have the answers I so desperately wanted. I was quite busy with the sale I was running. I felt so proud of the cash I was bringing in. Shipments arrived almost daily, preparing the store for the spring season.

Soon, I would go back to New York for another show. That thought made me weary because I was so uncertain about everything. Also, it would soon be time to negotiate the new lease. I felt nervous about a potential rent increase. The first two years of the lease were very reasonable but I had no idea what to expect after that. With my life in such a turmoil, I was afraid to put my name on anything binding, in case everything went to Hell.

Pete called to ask when we could get together in the evening at a location where we could talk without interruption.

"Oh. That sounds serious. Let me think about it for a few minutes," I said. "Could you call me back in about fifteen minutes?" Being afraid of what I would soon hear, I thought I would ask the babysitter if she could watch my children while I met with him. Then I wouldn't have to take them with me. It would only take about an hour, so I thought the best place would be the store, after closing. There, nobody would bother us and it would be quiet. In my office we wouldn't be interrupted.

My stomach was in knots until I reached the babysitter. She said she would be happy to watch my children. When Pete called back, I explained what I thought would be the best place to meet and asked him what evening after work would be best for him. We set a day and time. We spoke a few more words and then hung up.

When the day came to meet with this accountant, my stomach was a mess. Store hours almost over. I waited anxiously for him to arrive. I closed the doors that day not knowing what the next day would bring. I sat quietly for a few minutes to calm myself. I tried to relax and willingly allow what ever was meant to be. Sitting in my office, I heard a knock on the glass door. Quickly getting up, I said a little prayer that I would have strength to face whatever he had found.

Going to the door seemed like walking the length of a football field. When I got there, I saw this wonderful, smiling Italian stallion. I unlocked the door. He entered like a breath of fresh air. His presence was so stately.

I said, "Let's go into in my office where we can meet without being bothered," as I led the way into the back area. He had my paperwork in the box I had given him. The checkbook was tucked under his arm. Laughing as we walked through the store, I asked if all his clients gave him files in a box like that.

He chucked and replied, "I wish they would provide a box. Usually, it's just a torn grocery bag."

We laughed and went into my office. It was already getting dark outside. I had turned my office lights on. Sitting down, I said that I felt sick to my stomach because I was so scared about finding out where and when the money disappeared. He reassured me that he had discovered how it disappeared and that he would go through it all with me if I had time. That remark scared me even more. It made me aware that money had been taken over a period of time. It was not only a one-time thing.

Half way through the mess, my stomach started to growl. I realized I had not eaten. After laughing at how my stomach was talking to me, I asked Pete if he had eaten yet. He said no, so I asked him if he would like me to order a pizza.

"Sounds wonderful," he answered. While ordering the pizza, I felt my hands trembling. I shook my head in disbelief about what I had learned by then. I began crying, because I had worked so hard for so long, only to be robbed. I was the one with four children to care for; the one with a big house to keep up; and the one who had to do all the ordering because Leslie was too busy enjoying herself while in New York. Now I was the one left in this big store and finding money had been embezzled so perniciously. At that moment, everything seemed to cave in on me. My tears flowed freely.

Pete reached over and touched my arm. He said "Please don't cry. I got to the bottom of it. I can show you where and when every penny was taken. Please don't cry. I hate to see a woman cry."

I dried my cheeks with a tissue and told him how thankful I was, and how much I appreciated his help.

When there was a loud knock at the door, I knew our pizza had arrived. Going to the door seemed like a long trek again because my legs felt so weak due to what I had just learned. I paid for the pizza and brought it into the break room. Pete came from my office and sat down. I was getting soft drinks out of the fridge when I boldly asked if he would rather enjoy a glass of wine. He agreed, so wine it was.

I opened a bottle and poured for us. This was my first opportunity to relax and chat with him. I found him charming and intelligent in addition to his astoundingly handsome looks. As we talked, soon he had me laughing again.

What a personality, I thought. *Jeez, this man has it all.*

While we finished our pizza and drank another glass of wine, I felt more relaxed and better able to handle whatever he might reveal.

Pete asked if I remembered him from another time when we met previously.

He laughed, then said, "I certainly remember you."

I was stumped. I asked him where he knew me from.

He said, "Think about it . . . do I look familiar at all?"

Then he resumed our conversation about my books. What had taken place with my accounting was quite simple, in essence, but given how simple it was, Leslie should have caught it. She took the path of least resistance. She overlooked what the figures were saying. She cheated, forcing the balance. I felt all along that Dane was a thief, but in my heart, I had hoped it was just a mistake that had been overlooked. By manipulating each month to balance, she gave him another opportunity to steal the following month. This had gone on for several months.

Then it dawned on me: this was why Leslie left the store. She knew money was missing and that it was Dane who was taking it. Couple that with whatever Greg knew about Dane, and together, they probably felt it was better to run away than to face a confrontation. Since Greg worked with Dane in their day jobs, there could be serious complications.

After finishing with the money issues, I asked Pete if he would like another glass of wine. He gladly accepted. We sat in the back room and talked for at least another hour and a half. I returned to his previous question about whether I recalled knowing him before. I asked when and how we had met.

He chuckled and said, "You may not remember me. I was much younger then but don't I look familiar, even now? I delivered the newspaper to your apartment, the one off Kingsway. I recall that black silk robe you wore. I used to fantasize about you in that robe, and now, here I am doing your accounting."

I remembered him then but certainly not as vividly as he recalled me.

"What a small world," I thought.

He said. "I couldn't believe my eyes when you walked into the Derby. I kept waiting for you to recognize me then, but it has been quite a few years..."

We laughed and laughed as he shared more memories. When he realized how late it was getting, he decided to go. I asked him how much I owed him for his accounting help.

He said, "How could I take money from you? You have one partner stealing and another covering it. Please, let it be my pleasure." Saying that he could not take payment, he then asked me if I would let him take me to dinner in lieu of payment. I reminded him that I was still married and even then, he would not take money. He chalked it up to a good learning experience and flatly refused.

As we left the store, he said, "If you change your mind about dinner, give me a call. Or simply order white wine, instead of red, the next time you're in the lounge. Until then, I'll just keep on fantasizing about you in your black robe."

We laughed again, and then he walked me to my car.

At my car, he once again said "No strings. Just dinner and conversation."

I smiled, and told him I would think about it. My ego had been inflated but I hoped, beyond all rationality, that things would somehow work out for the children's sake as well as mine. I still valued my marriage.

As the weeks passed, without any money coming from Dane, the only way to get some child support was to force his hand in some way. I filed for a legal separation to get some help with our children. If this was an example of what the future would be, I simply did not know this person I had married. With the first hearing scheduled, I felt not only anxious but also heartbroken. I knew this was, in fact, the beginning of the end.

When I went to the doctor for a final check up, he asked me how things were going at home. I began to cry as I told him that I had to file for a legal separation to get some money for the children. The doctor leaned forward in his chair. His face became serious as he told me I had to make a life for myself and my children.

He said, "As a doctor, I've seen cases like your husband's far too many times. Believe me, given that you and those four beautiful children don't stop him, he will never stop until it's too late."

I sat up straight in my chair. I made a critical choice: to become strong. The last time I saw this doctor, he allowed me to read Dane's medical file by leaving it open on his desk when he left the room. In this next visit, he was warning me that Dane wouldn't change.

Finally, I got it. I had to play cards with the hand I had been dealt. I left the doctor's office that day a changed woman with a conscious mission. That was to raise my children the best I could, without hope of redress, without reservation, and with no regret.

I worked hard in the store. I only took what little money I needed for basics until the child support would start. I put my house up for sale. I made up my mind that, no matter what, I had to take care of my children. They calmed down after Dane departed, especially Kelly. I took her to the store more often because I could not afford a sitter. The three older ones came to the store after school by bus just as they had in the beginning. We were happy then and we were getting by.

Weeks later, as I looked up from the cash register one day, I saw Pete walking in the door. I felt surprised but greeted him calmly. He walked straight up to me and put his hand on my arm. He asked if I would like to go out to dinner with him. I laughed and said, "Persistent, aren't you?"

He laughed, too, and then said, "It's not about me, so much. You are so beautiful and I simply enjoyed your company. So I would love to take you to dinner. Remember? I said 'No strings,' just dinner." I was smiling from ear to ear and once again my ego got a tremendous boost from him.

As I was about to accept, Kelly came running out of the back room and went straight to Pete and stopped. She stood there smiling.

He stooped down and said "Hi there, Little Sales Clerk. Did you get any new shirts in, lately?"

I waited to hear what she would say. Although I was not blown away, what she said surprised me: "We did get some new shirts in, but you didn't buy any last time."

She spoke in her sweet little grownup manner. He laughed, and said, "Well… lets see if we can find something I can't live without this time."

Having filed for a separation months prior, I was willing to accept his dinner offer. He told me to dress up because he was going to take me out on the town after dinner. I did dress up, and with a charge of anticipation for what the evening would be. I enjoyed every minute of our evening. I hoped he would call again. He was still incredibly good looking, of course, and with a crazy personality, too. He had me laughing all night long.

We went dancing after dinner. Although he didn't dance nearly as well as Dane, it was enjoyable. It had been many years since I went out with anyone but Dane. In the back of my mind, I faced the facts: I really didn't know Dane; and now, his children and soon-to-be ex-wife were not his priorities.

When our evening ended, I didn't want to let it be over. When we came back home, I invited him inside to wait until the babysitter's father came to pick her up. When he first came to get me, I was ready to go. So he only entered as far as the foyer and didn't see much of our house. This time, when he walked into the family room, he made a whistling sound in astonishment and said, "This is your house? It's so beautiful!"

I thanked him and offered a drink. He asked if he could have a cup of coffee. With the babysitter gone, we talked for hours. I didn't need to get up early to open the store. So I kept on enjoying our evening. He told me he would love to get together again. I agreed, and he departed.

The following week, Esther and I went out to eat again after our meeting. This time, I had a lot to share. I ordered a glass of wine, and this time, I ordered white. I watched Pete laugh about my drink selection, over at the bar. He brought our drinks to the table personally, and once again, he said that our drinks were on the house. When I told Esther about my dinner date with him, she was all ears.

After Pete and I had gone out a few more times, there was an unexpected, extreme freeze in our town. The water mains had broken. We experienced terrible flooding in my neighborhood. Huge chunks of ice were scattered everywhere. The road became impassable. Before the phones went dead, I called Mother and told her I could not get out, that everyone was stranded.

As I was talking, the electricity went off. My phone also went down. With plenty of firewood in the garage, I knew I could keep the family room warm for the kids, at least. I put sheets up to block the doorway to the garage, to confine some heat in that family room. I had recently added a booster unit to the fireplace to improve heating efficiency. I built a large fire and turned on that unit, which blew hot air out from pipes laid under the fire. At first, the room was too cool but it soon felt unbearably warm.

About four hours later, we heard pounding at my front door. I opened it and there stood Mother with her husband. They had taken their car as far as they could drive, then walked the rest of the distance to rescue us. We were going to her house for the duration of the emergency.

As we started out, I saw that my legs still were still too painful to walk in the deep snow. The wind was blowing hard. It was snowing so much that one could hardly see. I told Mother to take the kids and I would stay back but her husband, Michael, wouldn't hear of that. He found one of our neighbors trying to get out with their van. Michael asked that man if we could try to get out with him. He agreed. They had a new baby. They handed the infant to me in the van. Then the remaining four adults somehow pushed it far enough that we were able to get beyond the ice mounds. The neighbor had to rock his van back and forth many times before we had it going down to the road. When we reached the main road, we were able to get to Michael's car and continue onward to Mother's house. I had been scared and the pain in my legs still hurt so badly that I didn't know what to do. At Mother's house, we felt safe and warm.

The news reports showed photos of the main water pipe broken. It was gushing water. They were sending in the National Guard by helicopters that night, to get some of the people out. By the next afternoon, the road crew had scraped some of the ice away so we could get into our homes. I was afraid there would be a lot of break-ins because the entire development had evacuated.

When the electricity came back on, I wanted to go home to check on the house and get my car. I had talked to Pete a few minutes before the power went out. He said if he could do anything to help me, I should call him. So I called him to come and take me to my house. He was more than willing to try to come and get me. The snow had started to fall again and the roads were icy but he said he would try.

Once we got to my house, Pete had to park on the street. Piles of ice at least six feet tall blocked my driveway. The street crew had cleared the road but they pushed the ice into our driveways. The mounds of snow and ice almost blocked our front doors.

At least the electricity was back on, so I could warm up the house for our return. It wasn't very cold in the house because the heat automatically came back on when the power was restored. I built a fire in the fireplace to warm up the house faster. Then I made a pot of hot tea. It was getting dark outside and the phones were still down. The television news reported that phone lines should be working within a few hours.

Pete and I sat down on the floor in front of the fireplace and enjoyed the snapping and crackling fire. I felt very comfortable and at ease with him. He was someone who makes you think all is well, no matter what. At around nine that evening, the phone came back on.

I called Mother to see how the children were doing. Craig and Lilly were in bed but Kelly was waiting for her mommy. To get the car out, I would have to shovel the driveway. Knowing how sore I was, Mother told me to wait until morning before trying to get on the road. I had told her that Pete had to park on the street because of the driveway blockage. That day was when she first met him. She considered him very good looking and pleasant. She thought he had gone home at that point so she didn't hassle me about waiting until morning.

Back in the family room, I sat on the floor in front of the fire, grateful I had a few hours to myself to do nothing but relax and chat. That feeling had eluded me for years, so I welcomed it. By then, the fire was blazing, producing copious heat. I asked Pete if he had eaten because I had nothing since breakfast. I was starving. He got some lunch at noon but he hadn't eaten since. So I went into the kitchen to see what I could throw together quickly. I came back with two plates of leftover roast and mashed potatoes. I was so hungry that I hardly knew what I was eating but he, on the other hand, was enjoying every bite.

At around ten p.m., not knowing if he was going to try to drive home, I asked him if he planned to fight the elements or stay put for the night. I brought us wine and we talked for hours. We were warm enough that we could sit on the sofa instead of right in front of the fireplace on the floor. That was a sweet feeling, sitting there with him but I was not accustom to it.

It's so strange how our lives change, I thought. *One month, I'm happily married. The next, I'm separated and feeling devastated by the thought of my husband stealing a large sum of money from me. One month, I cry because I have to file separation papers to survive with my children. Then, the next month, I sit with a glass of wine in front of a fire with an Italian stallion. Go figure...*

Dane eventually came into my store looking quite "out of it." He accused me of causing him heartache. Not willing, for even a second, to be blamed for his chaos, I tore into him for the first time during our entire marriage. I let it all out, having discovered the actual evidence of when and how he had stolen money. I delivered an ultimatum: he had one week to check into a clinic or I would sue for divorce. Then I ordered him out of the store. He laughed at me. As he walked out of the store, he turned to look at me and he shouted, "File."

The divorce process took well over a year. During all the trials, tribulations and heartaches, Pete saw me through. Sometimes, he came to the store to sit with me and help with whatever needed to be done. I thought long and hard about continuing to see him. Every time I pulled back, he would come closer, telling me how much he cared for me. In every situation, he was there for me, whole-heartedly present. He and Kelly formed a bond. To watch the two of them together was heartwarming. She was so little and he was so loaded with daddy instinct that they got along from the very beginning.

Lilly and Craig did not miss Dane in the least. They also enjoyed having Pete around. Trip, being a little older, really didn't show his feelings, either way. During the year while the divorce was in process, Dane hardly visited our children. When he did, it was a disaster. Lilly and Kelly became more distant from their father with each visit. Abusing me verbally became one of Dane's priorities. That did not sit well with Trip or Craig. In fact, it caused many unpleasant situations with angry words between Dane and his sons. Dane had adopted Trip many years previously. He had treated Trip like his own child, before. Somehow, he stopped showing Trip the same affection he gave the others. Trip reacted loudly toward accusations his father would make.

Soon, I became close friends with Marie, the woman I had met as she was selling jewelry outside a restaurant. I found such comfort in her friendship. Her sons were the same ages as my boys. It was good for us to get together. Her sons liked my daughters. They brought a smile to my face each time I saw her boys rushing to the door to greet my girls. Sometimes, I would go to the lounge to have coffee or wine with Marie when she finished selling jewelry for the night.

Marie recharged me. She gave me confidence that everything would work out in the end. Having new friends was good for me. Sometimes Sophie would join us. We all had a pleasant time but I didn't realize that Marie and her son, Kyle, would play such important roles in my life story many years later.

As always, Mother didn't like my new friends, but I had stopped taking that personally when I finally realized it wasn't really about me or my friends, anyway. She simply didn't like anyone at all. Not even herself, deep down, in the foundations of her heart.

After all the unpleasantness happened, hanging onto the store became difficult, to say the least. Leslie departure put me in a difficult situation but I was not willing to give up easily. There was one more dry goods show that I wanted to attend, in Las Vegas. Thinking I might be able to pick up some good deals, I decided to go. I mentioned it to Pete one night and he suggested he could drive me there. I had to laugh, realizing just how far that drive would be. I thought it better to fly out there. He insisted, though, trying to convince me how relaxing and fun the adventure would be.

I gave in. We planned the trip. I hired some additional help at the store and asked Mother to let my children stay with her. I felt astonished when she said she would keep them. After all, she really was not the grandma type. She typically let only Trip stay overnight. But she thought it was a good idea for me to get away from all the stress Dane had caused. She told me to go enjoy a few days away from it all. By then, my divorce from Dane had been final for a few months.

What a beautiful trip that turned out to be. Every time we crossed a state line, Pete pulled the car over and gave me a long kiss. He made the drive pure fun, not to mention all the love he displayed. I couldn't believe how affectionate he was with me.

When we arrived in Las Vegas, I attended the show to see what good deals I could find, like overruns or promotional items that new designers sometimes brought. I took my time. I decided to go through the entire show before making a buying decision. This show disappointed me, both in scope and available deals. Even so, I went through it all meticulously, thoughtful at each step. This was the first day and given that it would run for several days, I had time to make decisions about what to order.

All along, I was also thinking through what would be the best way to handle the business reality I was facing.

That evening, I told Pete I was thinking I should try to sell the business instead of trying to keep it going. Was he ever surprised. I told him that there are some new lines that might sell quickly if I try them. But that I thought maybe I should just sell out, pocket the cash, and take my children somewhere else to live, where they would have a chance for a normal life.

This caught him off guard but he said he would support any decision I make. Knowing he wanted to go back to school to study law, I realized he would not be able to keep helping me as he had been doing. Then I really would be in an iffy situation. I loved the whole concept of owning a business but I had to face realities. I was a single mother of four younger children. Selling my home would only bring a little profit at that point.

Things looked difficult from every angle. Many nights, I had to take work home to keep up, even though I had a very good system of keeping track of invoices and money. Even though Pete did help me, it was still time consuming, given I had to care for four children and their every need. As I pondered it all, I realized one person, working alone, could not possibly cover everything, and get it all done right.

Pete leaned toward me and dried my tears with his napkin.

He told me "I love you with all my heart. I will always be there for you. Take your time and think it through before you make decisions."

He leaned back and continued, "Come on, dry your tears, we're in Las Vegas. Let's have some good times."

Though I smiled, it was for his benefit because no matter what fun we might have, my dilemma would remain until I could think my way through it.

Dinner was fabulous. After dessert, it was fun walking through the casinos but what came later really knocked me off my feet.

I felt tired from the emotions of the day and all the walking the show required. When Pete suggested we call it a night, I was glad to oblige. I put on a nightgown I had purchased especially for this night. It made me feel pretty and sexy. Somehow, that gave me confidence to relax and just be myself.

When I entered the bedroom, Pete said "I'm with the most beautiful woman in Vegas, and I know it."

"Wow," I said, "what a compliment. But really, it isn't necessary because I'm all yours."

He got up from the chair and came over to me and kissed me with such passion that it took me by surprise. He lifted me up in his arms and carried me over to the bed. He laid me down as he bent over and kissed me again and again. Then, laying next to me, he touched me with a feverish passion that he had never revealed before.

His kisses engulfed me as he whispered "I love you Desiree. You are mine and I don't ever want anyone else to touch you. Marry me. Marry me right here, while we are in Vegas. Desiree? Will you marry me?"

I looked up at him and whispered the words "I love you too." Kissing me again, he leaned his head back and he asked again, "Desiree, will you marry me and go with me to California to study law?"

This time, I said, "Yes."

Chapter Nine

We were married two days later in one of the prettiest little chapels on the Las Vegas strip. Being caught unprepared, I needed to shop for a dress and shoes, but to my surprise, it all went very smoothly. That is, until it was time to pick out my flowers.

The wedding chapel had many bouquets to choose from. Pete pointed to the only one with yellow roses. "Oh, I like this one. They match your golden blond hair. Plus, they are like sunshine and you're my sunshine" he said.

I froze, not knowing what to say. I had not told Pete about Ajax and the yellow roses, and now was not the time.

So I looked at all of them again, chose another, and sweetly said, "I really prefer this one." Of course, he went along with the one I chose.

The clerk told us that the flowers would be ready when we arrived the following evening. I walked out of the chapel numb. I smiled, not letting on that I was shaking inside. I wondered if Pete's attraction to those yellow roses and his repeating of the same words that Ajax used to say to me, was a sign from Ajax that Pete is the one who Ajax was sending to take care of me. Sometimes, I thought it was Sophie with her unbelievable ability to see into the future but now I wondered. Sophie kept telling me I was going to have a big surprise on this trip. When I asked questions, she said she didn't want to ruin it, but to be prepared for a wonderful surprise.

Sophie was the first person I called after we were married. I couldn't wait to tell her. She giggled and said, "I told you there would be a big surprise."

Her daughter took the phone and said congratulations and that her mother had told her I would come back married. Pete's parents were wonderful on the phone. Even though Pete was ten years younger than I was, his parents were happy for him. Especially his father, who I really got along with well.

Mother, on the other hand, was not happy and she took it out on Kelly the rest of the time I was gone. When I got home, Craig and Lilly told me they did not like how Mother treated Kelly; that she was even mean to her. I gathered the details and decided that instead of confrontation, I would simply not have them stay there again. That was the last time my children stayed overnight at their grandma's house. Not that she ever asked to have them. That just wasn't her thing. Her husband Michael was good to me but he wasn't a children person either.

I sold my home way too fast. I found it difficult to walk away from it. There wasn't much equity in it; we each only got about eleven thousand. I had to agree to the sale, according to the court, so I decided to accept what I got, and be satisfied. We found a place to rent but it wouldn't be ready for two months so we stayed in Mothers little house until we could move.

Mother let Trip sleep at her house because the little house was so small and I only had one set of bunk beds. Two bedrooms for four children can feel crowded, even temporarily. The memories in this little house overwhelmed me but I accepted that for a short time. Within those two months, I figured I could sell the rest of my inventory from the store. Those goods were in Mother's basement, so being nearby was convenient.

Our new landlord needed an additional two months to finish the house we wanted to rent. That didn't sit well with us but we decided to accept the wait. We both really liked the new house.

Sometimes, when I would lie beside this beautiful man at night, I could only think of the night when Ajax kissed me goodbye. Those memories haunted me on many occasions. Knowing it was just that, a memory, I tried to find something positive about the present moment and to dwell on the positive. But it was hard to think of pleasantries and even harder to hide how I felt.

I thought I was not in my best form because of our living conditions. I simply didn't feel well. But I soon learned otherwise. Waking up nauseated each morning left little doubt about what was going on inside me. I told Pete right away that I thought I was pregnant. He felt ecstatic. He wanted a baby very much and although I always wanted six children, that was not a good time to be pregnant.

The morning sickness went on for weeks. Eventually, I went to the doctor. Sure enough, there was a little one inside me. I felt blessed, although scared at the same time. Four children were a handful in our financial condition. A new baby worsened that. I received so little child support. Asking Dane to buy anything for our children was completely out of the question.

If I set our difficult finances aside, I really was happy about another baby. After a few weeks of morning sickness, I started to feel good again. Pregnancy always agreed with me. I felt very healthy during the times I carried babies. But somehow, I felt different with this one, though I couldn't put my finger on what was different. One afternoon while the children were in school, I laid down and closed my eyes. I was so tired that I felt myself drifting off to sleep quickly and right into a dream.

"Hi, Pretty Woman," Ajax said, as he kissed my lips again, "I love you so much!"

I responded to his kiss but before I could speak he said, "I've come to warn you that you must not wait, you must go to the hospital right away. You will not carry this baby to term and your safety is at risk. If you listen to me, you will be fine. It is not meant to be that you should have this child or any others in the future.

I do love you so, and I miss you so much. Be at peace, you will soon move out of this house and go to a faraway place, where you and your children will find a new life."

I was not able to speak a word before the white cloud came. I reached out to him but he was already gone.

Waking, I cried when I thought of his warning. If I could have recalled him ever being wrong in the past, I might have been able to doubt the dream. But he had been right, consistently. His words haunted me. I tried to put that dream out of my mind, thinking it might be the first time his prediction could be wrong.

I was so weepy, anyway, that I found it hard to stop crying, but I managed to dry up before the children came home from school. I had prepared a wonderful dinner. I tried to live in the moment, forgetting everything else.

One evening, we had some friends over for a meal, which proved to be quite a challenge in that tiny house. The children were playing in the bedroom when suddenly we heard a loud thud and then a scream. I ran into the bedroom. I saw blood splattered on the wall and Kelly holding her forehead. Given the amount of blood on the wall, I knew it was serious. I ran for a towel to stop the bleeding.

It was a serious gash on Kelly's head. I called Pete to come.

With one look at her, he said "I'll get the car keys. She needs to be stitched."

I called Mother to come for Craig and Lilly and we left right away. At the hospital, the doctor took the towel away from her forehead. When I saw the gaping gash between her eyes, I passed out on the floor. As I came to, Kelly was leaning over the hospital bed, asking, "Mommy, why are you on the floor?"

Pete helped me up as the doctor called in a plastic surgeon to do the stitching so there would be minimal scarring.

Back home, our friends returned for a glass of wine. As we talked, they mentioned that the apartments where they lived had a large room where we could take some clothes from Mother's basement to sell them. I liked the idea and discussed it with them. It seemed there were wrought iron gates closing off the room so the clothes would be secure there. Thinking this would be a good way to sell off some of the inventory, we agreed upon a weekend when we could do it.

We decided to take only the sweaters as an easy way to begin. I didn't want to take it all because I wasn't sure if the goods would even sell there. It took me a short time to carefully pack all the sweaters so they would not get wrinkled. I felt excited to get something sold. I thought Mother would be happy to reclaim some space in her basement.

On a Friday night, we laid out all the sweaters on tables. Then we stayed until the iron gate was locked. The next morning, very early, we got a call from our friends saying that someone had taken the entire iron gate off the wall during the night. They stole all the sweaters. I felt so upset but I took the news in stride, especially since there was nothing I could do about it anyway.

Every day, I had to change that bandage on the bridge of Kelly's nose. At first, it was difficult for me but soon it became routine. The doctor told us how lucky she was, that if the cut been a sixteenth of an inch longer, she would have been in serious trouble, requiring plastic surgery. I treated the cut every day with vitamin E. Before we knew it, her scar was almost invisible.

One Sunday afternoon, we were watching a football game on television when my stomach began cramping. At first, I didn't think much of it, but within a few minutes, I knew something was very wrong. Within an hour, I was in serious pain. I started to hemorrhage. My recent dream was the first thing I thought about at the first sight of blood. Of course, I had Pete take me to the hospital immediately. By the time I arrived, it appeared to me that everything was shimmering, as if the whole world was vibrating.

They admitted me right away and started to give me blood. A doctor came in to examine me. He told me that I had lost the baby and that I needed immediate surgery.

I cried because I felt so sorry for Pete, who was looking forward to this baby. I silently thanked Ajax as I cried, knowing his dream was probably true, so there would be no more children for me. At that moment, I knew I would be okay, but the immediacy of my loss was tearing me apart. The look on Pete's face and the tears in his eyes reflected his own heartache.

I told him, "I'm so sorry. We'll try again," all the while thinking about my dream.

The day arrived when the house we were to rent became available to us.

"Thank God," I thought, "I really need to move away from all these gut-wrenching memories."

The slightest thing brought bad memories flooding back to me. I seemed to have no control over the sadness they brought.

The move went smoothly. We felt so happy to be in our own home. Mother never bothered us but the way she favored Trip made the rest of the children feel left out. She seemed obsessed with him staying overnight at her house. Michael, her husband, was not happy about that.

Having moved right across the street from the elementary school, I automatically thought the children would be safe and happy. Little did I know it would prove to be a nightmare. After living there a month or so, I was standing in the kitchen one day when, through the front window, I saw a man pull up in a car, jump out, and try to take Kelly. I screamed and she ran, foiling his attempt to grab her. I grabbed the phone and dialed nine-one-one. Through my terror, I managed to describe the car and what had just occurred. In the meantime, Pete snatched the car keys and chased the man, trapping his car at a convenience store parking lot, as he attempted to take a three year old girl who was left in a car while her father went into the store. Soon after all that, I discovered the worst place to live is close to an elementary school because that is where pedophiles lurk.

With that misadventure behind us, we moved on to a more normal existence. I worked on weekends with my best friend Marie at a local catering company. The job paid well. Plus, we could take home leftover food and deserts. Both of our families looked forward to the new weekend food supply. We also loved how that helped us, financially.

One night, Marie and I worked late at a party where an abundance of food was surplus. The boss gave us a choice of going home early or staying to help clean up. My children were with their father for a weekend trip so, I figured, why not stay and help? We wanted to take some of the overstock home.

We were dividing up the surplus food when my phone rang. Looking stunned, and wondering who in the world would be calling at eleven p.m., I grabbed my phone. It was Dane, and he was very angry with the girls because they wouldn't sleep in the same bed with him.

I tried to explain that Lilly had matured now and she wanted her own bed. That did not affect his anger. He started blaming me for them not wanting to spend time with him. Although I knew this was not a time for finger pointing, I simply told him to calm down and everything would be fine.

Then I heard Kelly whimpering, so I asked Dane if I could talk to Lilly. That was when all Hell broke loose. He started to talk with a whole different tone of voice. He sounded like he was losing it.

He told me, "I have all four of the kids lined up against the wall and I am going to shoot them. They are going to die."

I panicked and started to plead with him, saying "Allow me to talk to one of them. Any one of them." But he refused. I figured the only way to handle him when he acted like that was to side with him. That is what I did. I knew begging him to let me talk to the children would not appeal.

So I said, "Dane, you know what a snippy little thing Lilly is. She thinks she's older than she is. Why take it out on the rest of them just because she won't sleep with you. Have her go in the boys' room and sleep." And I continued speaking this way.

I could hear that he was calming down after a few minutes, so I told him that I had just gotten home from a job so I needed to go to the bathroom. I asked if he could call me back in a few minutes. He agreed, and we hung up.

I called the police and quickly told them what was happening. I begged them to get to his house quickly. They told me they would send someone right away. Then they told me to meet them there. I lived about thirty minutes away, so I called Mother and Michael and told them to go quickly.

Marie went with Pete and me. We made it there in record time. I had told the police how far away I lived and what route I would be taking so I would not be stopped for speeding. Mother and Michael were on the scene when I arrived. There were three police cars and a paddy wagon and officers armed with shotguns. There were no flashing lights. The cruisers were parked down the street. Police officers blocked cars from the street.

I got out of my car and ran to the police in front of Dane's house. They told me that they had run a check on his name and that he had been known to sell drugs. That information I really did not care about. I only wanted my children out of that house.

The officer had me stand by a brick pillar near the entrance to the porch. Dane's father answered the door. He had no clue about what was going on. He had been asleep in a bedroom. He did not know any of this was going on. He yelled up to Dane in a very stern voice and Dane appeared at the top of the stairs. The officer told Dane to release the children and to come downstairs immediately and step aside.

As he was coming down the stairs, the officer motioned for me to come forward and get the children.

When Dane saw me, he started to yell loudly, "She can't come in here. Keep her out."

Another officer went upstairs to retrieved the children. They all came running down the stairs except for Kelly. The officer was carrying her. She was so scared that she was trembling. The three older children ran out the door. The officer handed Kelly to me, and I handed her to Marie who then guided all the children to our car. Kelly was trembling so much that even her little head was shaking.

In my car, the children opened up and told us what had happened. They said Dane threatened them with having the police take them away so that I would not know where they were. When Trip looked out the window, he saw police. He panicked, thinking his father had, in fact, called the police and they had come to take them away. Feeling like a female protagonist in a grade-B movie, I vowed that night that I was going to move far away so this sort of thing could never happen again.

During the Christmas gathering at Dane's sister's house, my children had to sit at a separate table. They were treated like outcasts. Dane's parents hardly spoke to them. After that Christmas, the three older ones refused to ever go anywhere with him again. Dane re-married and his new wife's jealousy toward my children began immediately.

Her actions concerning my children were unacceptable. I had never met her but I knew of her by reputation. When Kelly was a little over two years old, she told me about a woman who came to our house while I was far away, shopping for the store. She meant while I was in New York on a buying trip.

She said that the lady smoked cigarettes and "Daddy was mad at her 'cause she rang the doorbell."

I wasn't in a position to discuss that with Dane. Half the time, we were conflicting with his working hours. Keeping it in the back of my mind, I stored it for future reference. Kelly was upset when she was telling me the story. She said her Daddy made her go upstairs and stay in her room. I thought that was strange because we had a huge playroom where she could have played with her toys.

Never loosing sight how much I wanted to move far away, my mind was in a constant whirl, wondering how I could get permission from the court to leave the state. We were in our rented house for over a year when the landlord decided they wanted to move into the house we had rented. Then we had to find another place to live.

We found a brand new home in another school district that was great for the kids. We loved this new house and living there but even after that change, I still wanted to move much farther away. Dane didn't bother with the children often but when he did, it was very upsetting for them.

This year, at Christmas time, I really had to fight with the children to get them to go to Dane's family gathering. When they returned, I was angry with myself for having done that. Once again, they had to sit by themselves while everyone else had fun.

I couldn't believe Dane's parents did that to my children, but they did. They hated his new wife and made that very obvious both in their actions and in words to others. They couldn't see what Dane was thinking when he hooked up with her. She was quite chunky and her personality wasn't the most pleasant, but she was his choice. My only concern was how well she treated my children.

When the children got home that night, they told me about the ski boots that Dane's step children got for Christmas along with many other gifts. He gave his own children each a sweater. The girls got a Barbie doll picnic table that his wife's father made for them. They were heartbroken and they spoke up, saying they were never going to go there again.

About three weeks after Christmas, one of my girlfriends of many years asked me if I would like to go to Florida with her. She was going to meet with an elderly man who wanted to open a boutique on Clearwater beach. He wanted her to manage it. Since I already had experience in owning and operating a clothing store, she asked me if I would be interested in meeting him and possibly working with her. Jumping at the chance, we left a few days later for the long drive to Florida.

The trip was filled with anticipation and tinged by my desire to make a good impression. I realized this job could generate an opportunity to present a strong argument to a judge as persuasion for me to leave the state with my children. So I travelled eagerly.

Meeting with this business owner proved beneficial. It was a go from the very moment I met with him. The man was very wealthy, in his eighties, and he still had lots of business savvy and energy to spare. He respected my experience. He told me the sooner I could move, the better. At the beach area, he showed us where he planned to rent space for the boutique. He told us in detail what he wanted to do.

I was on cloud nine. I felt eager to get home to start the process of departure. Being still weak from that miscarriage only a few weeks earlier, the long drive home seemed endless. That pregnancy had been fraternal twins. Losing them played havoc with my hormones. I was exhausted. I felt like a limp rag when we arrived home.

My marriage was not faring well. Pete couldn't fathom my condition. I kept having miscarriages and might not be able to bear a child of his. He wanted a child intently but I had to consider my health and safety as my first priority. Also, I knew in my heart there was no one to raise the children I had already borne if something ever happened to me. I would have rolled over in my grave if Mother were to take my children. Also, after the bizarre threat incident with Dane I could never trust him again.

I tried to stop his visitations, but to no avail. It boiled down to my word against his. Considering all the things that happened to my children during his visits, I shuddered about our legal system. How could they allow children to go through all that they had to bear without intervening? How could they allow a man to visit children and destroy them both physically and emotionally? How many front teeth needed to be chipped, how many kidneys bruised from being thrown up against a wall? How many young girls had to tell stories about being taken into a bathroom while their father openly urinated? These nightmares haunted me daily. All I could do was find a way to legally leave the state with my children and as quickly as possible.

A solid business opportunity in another state would equip me to petition the court to let me take my children away from Dane to make a new life. My plan about leaving included maintaining secrecy. I hired an attorney to represent me and set a court date for a hearing. I used the money from the sale of my home to hire a moving company to carry my furnishings.

Being afraid that a judge might not allow me to leave with my children, I asked the moving company, "If I don't get permission to leave the state will you take my furniture to another state, secretly?"

Of course, they had to ask which state I was moving to.

I simply replied, "By the time the truck gets to Route Ten, I will be out of court, at my mothers house. The dispatcher can call me there at one p. m. on Monday."

The question they asked was, "If not Florida, which State do you want the furniture taken to?"

I replied. "Houston, Texas. That's why I want them to call when they get to Route Ten."

The man laughed and said "You got it all figured out, don't you lady?"

I did have it figured out. I would not stay there to witness my children being destroyed. I would not stay on behalf of someone who claimed to love them but who used them as a pawn. A man who wouldn't face the fact that he had a problem.

Absolutely not, I thought to myself. *This mother is getting out of here and making a new life for herself and her children. With or without Pete, my children come first. They're the most important factor in my life.*

On the weekend before we left, a heavy snowstorm dumped fifteen inches of snow on us. Taking the opportunity to enjoy it, we built two large snow figures. One, we made into a man. We spray-painted a blue bathing suit on him. The other, we made into a woman with a red bikini. We made a large beach ball that sat next to the male snow person and sprayed it yellow, blue and red. We had such a good time building these that we even spray painted the woman with yellow hair and the male with black hair. They each stood about ten feet tall.

Just as we finished the sculptures, the local news crew came by. They took photos of our creations for the evening news. There appeared on the news that evening.

The following weekend was Mother's Day. I spent the day at Mother's house. That was quite stressful because I had just told her that we were leaving the following day. Her first reaction was anger. She told me that if it were her, she would simply tell the kids to get used to the situation, that this was the way it was going to be.

Then she said, "You will be gone six months and then be begging me to send you money to come back."

After all the years that had passed, she still didn't know me. I would clean toilets before I begged her for money to come back where my children were tormented. No way. I truly would scrub toilets with my toothbrush before I would put my children through any more pain than they had already endured.

Being lined up against a wall and threatened to be shot, by their father? That is simply not something any child should ever experience. No matter what, I would never again allow myself to receive such a gut-wrenching phone call as that one had been. When I gathered all four of them and told them what I had decided, they were visibly relieved by knowing that soon it would all be over, that they would not have to go through such abuse any more.

They didn't even care where we were going as long as we left the area. When they heard the word "Florida," they were thrilled. At first, the only one who wasn't excited about moving was Trip, although he soon became as thrilled as the others. Packing our clothes felt exciting because I knew that, one way or another, we were leaving. The only people who I would miss were Marie and her boys. They had become part of our lives, especially her youngest son, Kyle. I felt fond of him. I took him everywhere with my own children, whenever possible. He was like one of my own children because he was with us so much as they all grew up.

The Court date went well. The judge granted me permission to go to Florida. He gave Dane the typical visitation rights: two weeks during summer and a visit at Christmas. I agreed to anything the judge said so I could leave the state without kidnapping my children. Dane would have to pay to fly the children to Ohio for a summer visit. Therefore, the judge granted me only twelve dollars per week, per child, for child support, to offset Dane's cost for airline tickets.

Nothing mattered to me as I stood there before the judge. I finally felt free for the first time in five years. Knowing I'm a survivor who's not afraid of working, I knew we would be alright. Pete decided to go with the children and me to Florida and to work things out between the two of us.

Trip wrecked my car two weeks before we were scheduled to leave. We left town that day in a borrowed car.

As I pulled out of the driveway, I thought, *Wow, here I am leaving this state forever with four children and a dog and cat; in a borrowed car; with a marriage on the rocks; and with six thousand dollars to my name.*

My love for my children erased all fear that I might normally have felt. Survival mode kicked in. When we approached the main highway, I started to sing, "On the Road Again," just the way Willey Nelson sings it and with just as much enthusiasm. We were on our way to a new life in a new state. There would be no tears for any of us, only happiness ahead.

Chapter Ten

*I*n Florida, in the middle of May, we settled into an entirely new and different life. Our furniture took a lot longer to arrive than we expected but our new neighbors took us under their wings. They kindly provided us with all essentials to make our initial few weeks tolerable.

After I settled the children into school for the few weeks that remained, I began meeting with my new employer. This wonderful man not only gave me the opportunity I needed to leave Ohio but he also gave me an exciting chance to do something I loved. Mr. Beech and I got along well. We seemed to agree on everything. We chose a wonderful store space right on the beach, with a view of the water. I was in Heaven. I could hardly wait to go to the shows and select clothes for this awesome venture.

About six weeks into our planning, designing, and ordering, I was driving back after taking everyone to school one morning, when an overwhelming, terrible feeling came over me. I felt like I wanted to cry yet I had no apparent reason to feel that way. Suddenly, the scent of the cologne that Mr. Beech wore filled the car. I knew something had happened so I prayed he was alright. I hurried home and tried to call him but he did not answer. After calling all morning, I tried to think positive, but my fear was hard to shake off.

The next morning, I received a call that Mr. Beech had died from a heart attack the morning before. My world crumbled as I realized this wonderful man had come into my life so I would have the reason I needed to move so we could start a new life. It wasn't a coincidence. It was meant to be.

I looked for a job and found one within two days. The job was managing a different type of boutique that carried high end clothing. God was on my side. With a new job, in a new state, I was ready to conquer whatever came my way. The boutique flourished and the owner was so happy with what I was doing that she soon let me take over the entire shop. I love it and the customers loved me.

Pete didn't really want to work. He took his time trying to find something. He was handsome, so nice to look at, but looks soon get old when you are trying to do it all. The marriage took a turn for the worst when he returned to wanting another child. He questioned everything I did, as if I had any extra time to do much of anything.

When he found a job, I so hoped it would keep him busy enough to realize I was working hard to keep us afloat. He landed a good-paying job but getting him to go to work was like another job for me. Each morning became a struggle and I started to resent it.

After losing my last pregnancy, I decided that was the end of that; there would be no more attempts at bearing children. That did not set well with Pete. He soon started to act out. At times, he treated me hatefully.

I worked hard at the little boutique and really did well for the owner, tripling her sales within a few months. I also modeled on the side for a very expensive jewelry store. I was paid well for that. I received a large bonus during the holiday season for selling an eighty thousand dollar necklace. Smiling at the customer, I could not have helped but wish the necklace had been mine. Life was good except for Pete who felt life was not worth much without a child of his own.

One night, while I was showering, Pete placed a box cutter knife on the night stand so that I would see it there. When I asked why it was there, he said that if I thought for one minute he was going to let me go he would show me that no one would want me when he was finished with me.

I could not believe my ears. I tried to act as if it didn't bother me; that it was no big thing. I lived like that for over a year, with a fear inside me that, in his jealous mind, he might think I was looking at other men.

When I had enough money stashed that I could make it on my own, I left with my children in tow, filed for a divorce, and had him served at the house in the morning, before he left for work.

So sad, I thought. *I was so crazy about him that I would have never even looked at another man.*

All those rich men who came into the jewelry store meant nothing to me. I was happy in my marriage but something dark inside him surfaced and his jealously took over his mind.

The divorce was over within a matter of weeks. I moved into another home with my children. At the courthouse, Pete showed up for the final hearing. As we stood outside the courtroom, he approached me very humbly and began crying as he slid down the wall.

He said, "What have I done to us? Can you ever forgive me?"

I forgave him. However, as I walked from the court house, I never looked back. I only looked forward. I lived in fear for over a year, not knowing if he might butcher my face in some jealous rage. Finally, I was free of that terrible fear.

As two years passed, I kept my head above water and survived, taking care of us all. With Trip at boot camp in California, we settled back into a routine. There was a void in the house though, because Trip's presence almost always meant turmoil. He loved to aggravate everyone, especially his brother Craig. Kelly had been his target for some time but he eased up on her during the last few years before he departed. With Craig, there was a terrible rivalry. It spanned years, going back to when Mother would pit Trip and Craig against each other. I had words with her about that habit but she continued anyway. I was so happy when I moved to Florida. Then life became about the four of them building something new together, as brothers and sisters.

I made a decision to earning some steady money rather than working for a friend's husband in a multi-level company. I thought about going to school to become a nail technician. I had heard they made good money. It would be easier than constantly trying to recruit everyone I met to do the multi-level thing. The nail course lasted only a few months. I could do it at night while working during the day. I worked for one of my friend's husband a lot but my schedule was flexible. Signing up for the course, I found I enjoyed the school and the work was a piece of cake. So I felt satisfied.

One day, my friend and her husband came over and brought along a man who needed some typing and secretarial work done. They introduced me to Titus. Although I had more than my share of work, I agreed to help him. He took to me.

He told my friends, "They sure have beautiful secretaries in Florida."

Although that was a pleasant compliment, my only concern was to make enough money to take care of the three children I still had at home.

Working for Titus proved more beneficial than expected. He paid well. He wasn't demanding, at all. One night, I needed someone to receive a manicure from me at the beauty school. I asked Titus if he would like to be my guinea pig. He laughed and said he would.

What a crazy time we had that evening at the school. He was so much fun we had the whole class laughing. After class, he asked me if we could get something to eat together because he had not eaten since breakfast. We went to a lovely restaurant and continued to have a wonderful time. I noticed, by the way he was looking at me, that he had more in mind. But I needed to stay focused and finish this nail training so that I could take a board test and start working. The owners of the house where I was renting decided they would move back into the house as soon as my lease was up. Again, I was looking for somewhere to move. It would be a few months before my lease was over but I always planned ahead.

I discussed this with Titus at dinner that night. He told me he held a lease option on a house near where I was living. He said that he wouldn't be moving to Florida for at least a year to eighteen months. He suggested that I move to that house because he had to pay rent every month when it was sitting empty. Not wanting to be obligated to him, I graciously declined and thanked him.

From that evening onward, Titus would ask me if I needed someone to work on for my course. I told him that he had caused such a riot the night he came, that the teacher didn't want me to bring him back. He laughed and kept in touch, almost daily. I did a lot of work for him and he paid me well.

When he began to come to Florida regularly, he took me out to nice restaurants. He wanted to spend more time with me each trip. On every visit, he would remind me that his leased house was still sitting empty. He never even stayed in it when he came to Florida. He stayed in a hotel. I consistently refused. Then, one evening he took me by the house, as if to tease me. I was surprised by how spacious and beautiful it was. When we went inside I saw he hadn't lied, it was empty. As we left, he locked the door again told me, he really didn't mind if I lived there. He promised there would be no strings attached.

I showed my children the house. That seemed to be a mistake because it really was so beautiful and spacious. One of Kelly's girlfriends lived about three doors away. I decided to take him up on his offer, with a provision that he would not ask us to move without ample notice. Then I wouldn't be on the street with three children. He laughed, and gave me his word that nothing like that would ever happen.

My children and I packed everything. They were delighted that we would stay within their same school district. As we made this move, I thought about how the children had grown to become such beautiful individuals. They were a great help to me in every aspect of living, from helping around the house to being my very salvation. I didn't know what I would have done without them.

It had been at least twelve years since Dane had seen them. He still sent his lousy twelve-bucks-a-week child support, which came directly out of his paycheck, but he had not even phoned them one time in all those years. He never even sent them a birthday or Christmas card.

How sad, I thought, *they are truly such good looking children with such wonderful personalities. I'm sure by now he would not even recognize them if he passed them on the street.*

Titus started coming to Florida more often. Each time, he stayed in a hotel, never once asking to stay at the house. More and more, I enjoyed his company and looked forward to seeing him. He started taking me to business meetings. I soon became his right hand, knowing what needed to be done next. After a meeting that had been out of town, I needed to take paperwork to an attorney the next morning.

Getting up early, I set out to run all the errands on my list. I figured I would go to the farthest place first. I set out for Clearwater, to an attorneys office. Not many blocks from the destination, as I came to a yellow light, an ambulance was approaching the intersection very fast from my right, with flashing lights and siren screaming.

Not wanting to interfere with the ambulance, I stopped abruptly, instead of running the yellow light. The car behind me did not stop. It hit my can from behind, going at least sixty miles per hour. The impact shoved my car through the intersection, causing the ambulance to nearly hit me. The force of the collision knocked the wind out of me. Unconscious, I did not even know I had passed through the intersection.

The driver stopped the ambulance and came to my car to make sure I was alright. I was stunned. When I came around, I reassured the ambulance driver that I was alright; that he should get the patient in the ambulance to the hospital. I tried to get out of my car but I felt unstable. I had to sit for a few minutes until I felt better. I pulled my car over to the side of the road and got information from the driver who hit me. He admitted he didn't even see that I was stopping when he hit me. When all that was done, I felt more sure of myself. Then I continued to the attorneys office. I didn't think I could go to the other places that were on my list. The attorney advised me to go to a hospital emergency room.

I called Titus after I got home. That proved to be an eye-opener. He told me he would catch the next flight and be in Florida within a few hours. I kept telling him I was okay but he insisted that he was coming down. He flew in, got into the car that he always left at the airport, and arrived at my home within a three and a half hours.

At that point, our relationship took a turn. He completely took over. He took my children school, out shopping, and made sure they had everything they needed. He assured I had the best doctors.

The headrest had struck the back of my head so hard that it caused trauma to my eyes. I had to put drops in my eyes every night for the following year. Once the drops were applied, I couldn't do much of anything because the drops dilated my eyes. It took a full twelve hours until I was able to see properly, again. Putting them in early enabled me to drive Kelly to school the next morning.

Treatment two or three times a week for my back also continued for months. Being messed up from the accident was bad enough but what really bothered me most was that I had just started working for a nail salon. There were days when I made a few hundred dollars a day. After a few months, the doctors gave me some bad news, that I would not be able to continue doing that type of work. I was devastated but Titus kept telling me not to worry about anything, that he would take care of it all. I have no reason to doubt him.

Night after night, I put those drops into my eyes. When the year had passed, my eyes had healed but I still had pain in my back. I suffered like a dog with constant pain and continued to need therapy. All this time, Titus never faltered in taking care of me and my children. Never once did he complain or say a word about me not being able to work. I knew he felt responsible because I was delivering paperwork for him, but he went above and beyond his duty to me.

I don't know what I would have done without his never-ending help. When I became able to travel, I started to travel with him again on short day trips for meeting all over the state. I tried to go back to doing nails again but I found the pain in my neck and shoulders unbearable. He was so understanding, never once suggesting I get a different type of job. In fact, quite the opposite, he told me he preferred I work for him rather than anything else.

Titus came across some brand new townhouses on Lake Tarpon. He took me to see them. The one we viewed was beautifully furnished. It also had such attractive landscaping outside that I was taken with it. He only wanted my approval and the next thing I knew, we moved into the townhouse. It was even nicer than the house we had lived in before it. I was happy to make the move to somewhere new with other neighbors. The neighbors where I had lived before were snooty. They thought they were better than others. He gave up his option to buy the previous house and we moved. After telling my friend Laura about the townhouses, she and her husband looked at them. They also decided to move there. I was so happy when she told me. She moved to a location about four units away from us. We couldn't have been happier.

Our friendship was very close. Titus traveled a lot so I was thrilled to have her living so close. Laura's husband had become friends with Titus. They were trying to put some deals together for importing coffee beans. With the men off doing their thing, Laura and I saw each other every day. We spent a lot of time together. Every evening she would venture down the sidewalk with her after-work cocktail. One could hear her swirling ice in the glass as she approached our door with her little dog, Pepper. We spent many hours at the pool on weekends or sitting in one of our kitchens, talking. Our friendship was very loyal. Being an only child, I treasured her friendship. She seemed more like a sister, one to whom I could tell all my secrets.

Titus asked me to marry him about twenty times; each time he came to Florida. And each time, I would find an excuse. I felt afraid to marry again. I thought it was better to continue living like we were. I was happy with it but he wanted more. I thought he drank way too much. I didn't want to put myself in that situation. After another year passed, I agreed that if he did not drink for a year, I would marry him.

The year passed and he did not drink, so I agreed. We told a few of our friends about it and they all decided to attend our ceremony. It wasn't anything elaborate but we all had a wonderful time. Titus had owned a jewelry store in Texas, but he sold it a few months before he permanently moved to Florida.

When he first put my wedding ring on my finger, I nearly fainted. It was beautiful to see and the huge center diamond was every woman's dream. Our friends caught the expression on my face with the camera as I looked down at my hand. I never imagined he would give me such a huge, three and a half-karat diamond. Titus had told Lilly and me to shop for what I would like, so he would have an idea, but what I found in stores was nothing compared to the ring he gave me. After the wedding, Titus insisted that I not work at all. He wanted me to help him with what he needed and to take care of the children and the house.

Works for me, I thought.

Lilly was in her senior year at high school and Kelly was in the ninth grade. Thinking things would start to calm down was just an illusion though, because they didn't. Craig was working and living in Tampa after a short trip to Ohio. During that trip, he tried to establish a relationship with his father. Needless to say, it did not work. Given that he never had a relationship with Dane previously, it wasn't devastating to him. I'm sure he hurt inside but he really didn't want to talk about it. After that, he permanently wrote his father off.

I was happy when he was back. I had been absolutely miserable when he left because I missed him so much. Words cannot describe the void I felt in my heart. He's such a decent young man and he loves his sisters so much that he would do anything for them.

Our new life with our family together made for a wonderful Christmas that year. The girls were quite popular in school, which made for a constant houseful of high school kids. No sooner did I take a batch of cookies out of the oven than they were consumed, in a matter of two minutes. I was happy and proud to see how my children flourished after our scary move from Ohio to Florida. Hating to take the tree down, I reluctantly put it away, wishing the season had lasted a little longer.

After the school year, Lilly went off to Europe to model so it was just Kelly and me. At first, I worried about Lilly, because she was so headstrong, and defiant toward authority. She danced to the beat of her own drum.

The rest of the children were gone and Titus was out of town often. Kelly and I had a chance to enjoy each other doing whatever we wanted. With Laura living so close, when I did or said something that annoyed Kelly, she would go to Laura's house to vent. Laura loved it and although Kelly and Craig were always were her favorites, she really developed an even stronger love for Kelly.

When the war started in the Middle East, Trip was sent overseas. To say I was a mess put it lightly. Fear destroyed me as it took over my every thought. My tough love act, insisting that Trip join the military, could have costed my son his life. I prayed harder than I prayed in my whole previous life.

I turned to the only source of true love that I knew. I started praying to Ajax, begging him to guide my son. My saving grace was the phone calls I received from Trip. Our local phone company allowed soldiers to call home for next to nothing. That was a big help financially. I would treasure each minute of our conversation. I lived for those calls, not wanting to hang up for fear it might be the last time I heard "I love you, Mom," from my firstborn.

Soon, I realized Titus was showing signs of jealousy. When Trip would call he got huffy and would leave the room. I had sensed it before, when Craig bought me a beautiful emerald ring for Christmas.

Titus tried to find some fault with it instead of being happy for me. His jealousy was only with the boys, not with my daughters. Craig bought me an outstanding gift for every occasion. Titus tried to take away the specialness of it. Being I was as headstrong as my daughter Lilly, I ignored Titus's attempts to take away my thunder.

With Titus out of town, after hanging up with Trip one time, I laid in bed, consumed with fear that something would happen to him. I dozed off to sleep. Hours later, I could feel the warmth of Ajax kissing me and the sense of his presence.

> As he appeared he said, "Hi, Pretty Woman, please don't cry. I am with your son every step he takes. Nothing will happen to him, I promise. I am watching over him."
>
> I continued to tremble, and I told him, "I am so scared that because of me insisting on the military, he might not come home."
>
> He reached out to hold me in his arms and he told me, "You have my word. He will come home safe and sound and will live a long life."
>
> I looked up and our lips met. He kissed me ever so lovingly with tender affection.
>
> I could feel his lips and the warmth of his arms around me, and as the white cloud started to engulf him he whispered, "Please know your son is safe and my love for you will never end."
>
> Then he was gone.

When I woke up, my face was, as always, wet with tears. But my heart was no longer filled with such terrible fear for my son. Instead, it was filled with the warmth of Ajax's undying love. I longed for him.

I couldn't let go of my fear that if I loved a living man again, my love for Ajax would leave me. When I felt myself starting to feel love for another in my heart, I froze. When that competing love died down, the controlled feeling would return. Even knowing it was unfair to the men in my life, my need to control my emotions remained more powerful than my ability to let go of my fear of loss and just let love bloom as it would, naturally. I could still close my eyes and hear the door closing as Ajax left for the last time. I would get a sick feeling in the pit of my stomach each time.

Life remained calm as long as I didn't ask too many questions. Titus seemed very secretive about certain things. I noticed when I would go to the store or to the pool, he seemed get phone calls. Then, he would pack and go away again. There was something going on there but I couldn't figure out just what it was. He had more reasons to leave suddenly than anyone else I knew. Before we married, he told me he formerly worked with the government but that had ended. So I didn't know what to think.

If I asked too many questions, sometimes he would get defensive but other times he would say this crazy little thing: "You get the kittens and I'll take care of the mama cat."

When he said that, I knew to not ask again.

Laura and I loved times when both our men were gone. Then, we could just kick back and talk, which was something we did well. Her husband was a man like Pete, who wanted sex continually. So she was happy if her man was doing something with Titus. Then, she didn't have to play "the good wife" role. Titus was not like that by any stretch of imagination. One could never say he didn't enjoy or want sex but he wasn't the kind who wouldn't leave you alone. I never felt it was a chore making love with Titus, but then again, he was gone a lot, so I would get a break, compared to her.

While having coffee one morning, Titus got a very serious look on his face. He asked me to listen very carefully. He told me he had to go out of town for a few days. There would be some time when he would be completely out of contact. Not understanding, I asked him, "Where are you going and how long will you be gone?" He only said "Please, don't ask me questions. This is something I have to do. I will call you the minute I can."

That was not good enough for me and he knew it. But he said, "I'll explain later but for now, please understand. I'll be okay and I will call you the minute I can."

All I said was "whatever" and I went to the pier. The pier was very soothing to me compared to the pool, where usually someone wanted to talk. As I sat quietly, I heard my name. I turned and I saw Titus standing outside our townhouse. He waved goodbye to me. I didn't wave back. I simply turned around to watch the water. Then I knew he had lied about not working for the government anymore.

Four days later, I got a call from Titus, acting like nothing had happened. He told me he would be home the next night, late. He had a car he used to go back and forth to the airport. I had no idea where he was coming in from because I didn't pick him up. At that point, I really didn't care but I probably should have cared.

When he arrived home, I was happy Kelly was spending the night at her girlfriend's house because I wanted answers and I was about to force them. One look at Titus when he walked in the door told me he had been to Hell and back during the few days he was away. He looked as white as chalk and I could see he had not slept.

He walked over to where I was sitting.

He bent over and kissed me as he said, "It's so good to be home."

I didn't know what to say so I said nothing. He asked if there was something he could eat since he had not eaten all day. I got up to check the refrigerator for something I could put together quickly.

When he finished eating, he put his plate in the sink and said, "I have a favor to ask of you."

Remaining quiet, I said "What is it?"

He asked me to go get my tweezers. He said he needed me to do something for him. Going up the stairs to our bedroom, I wondered why he needed tweezers. When I came back down, I was shocked by what I saw. Titus had taken his shirt off. His chest was raw looking and full of glass fragments. There were also some in his scalp and in the tops of his feet. His green eyes looked at me sadly. He begged me to pick the glass bits out and to allow him to explain later. I started taking the fragments out, one by one. I used peroxide to treat all the little wounds after each piece was removed. I worked on his chest for over an hour and a half. Then I took care of his head. Then the tops of his feet.

When I was finished, he kissed me and told me how much he loved me and how he appreciates me giving him time to explain. He promised he would tell me the truth somehow. The next morning, his chest was raw with little holes and the tops of his feet looked terribly sore. I still didn't say anything, knowing he would tell me something once he got a cup of coffee in him and woke up.

He told me again that morning he would find a way to tell me; that he needed to collect himself; that he had been through a lot during the last few days. I was clueless and at the point of not caring. I did not like the way he left so frequently and this event was over the top, as far as I was concerned, but I gave him the time he needed. I knew he was not cheating on me. He was in love with me and considered me the love of his life.

Two days later, the morning paper was sitting on the table, opened. As I poured myself a cup of coffee I felt something was wrong. Titus was sitting out on our patio with his coffee so I went out to sit with him. He looked at me and told me how lucky he is to have me and that there is something in the newspaper he would like me to read.

He said "give me a minute and then I will go inside with you." I agreed, and started to drink my coffee. Just as I finished, he stood up and went in and I followed.

His tennis shoes were sitting on the floor in the front entrance and he went to get them and place them by his chair. I poured more coffee knowing I was going to need it. He picked up the newspaper and handed it to me. It was folded open to a small article on the second page that read, "Agent killed installing surveillance cameras in Honduras…"

The article was brief but told the story. That agent was killed in the bus by Honduran guerrillas armed with machine guns, as our agents tried to flee the area. Other men suffered massive amounts of shattered glass fragments. As I read on, I became sick to my stomach as I realized Titus was one of the "other agents" involved.

I went over to him and hugged him. Titus broke down and started to cry as he told me, "The shoestring on my tennis shoe broke. I bent down to tie it so my shoe wouldn't come off as we ran. We had changed our clothes from night garb. As I tied my shoestring, it broke. That guy who died ran past me as I tied my shoe. He took my seat in the bus." He paused as he choked up again. Then went on to say, "That could have been me who was killed." He picked up his shoe and showed me the knotted shoe string.

I stayed silent, trying to digest it all. I didn't ask Titus many of the wrong kinds of questions after that day. In this case, I figured ignorance may not be bliss but at least it's less stressful than knowing too much detail.

Trip had been overseas one year when he came home to California's Camp Pendleton. I was beside myself with excitement and relief. I could hardly wait to hug and kiss him. I made arrangements to fly out to the base and then to take a trip to Las Vegas for a few days. Mother and Michael were going to the base with me. Then we would meet Titus in Las Vegas.

On the long plane ride to California, my thoughts drifted from one thing to another. I felt disappointed that Titus was not going with me. I felt hurt that anything could be more important than my son coming home but happy that I would be present when he arrived. My thoughts drifted to my last dream of Ajax; to how he reassured me that Trip would be safe; and that he was watching over Trip every step of the way. I marveled at how these dreams came and how his kiss felt so real.

Even to that day, it still amazed me. My tears were real enough. I could feel them on my face after he was gone. But his kisses, how could they have felt so vividly authentic? There was no doubt in my mind that he was there for us, watching over me and my children. He had warned me so many times of things I could not possibly know about, otherwise.

Laying my head back, I whispered to him, "I love you, too."

Meeting my Mom and Michael at the airport worked out well. The timing was perfect. The next day was the big day. I felt so excited. This was the first time I had been away from Trip for such a long period and being the Mom I am, that was difficult for me.

At the base, we registered for the "Welcome Home" ceremony. We met with other wives and mothers who had made arrangements so we would know where to go, and what time to be there. I was surprised that they told us to be on the pier at four-thirty a.m. But, then again, I would have stood there all night, had I been permitted. We ate breakfast at the Burger King on-base. From there, we went into the barracks to help distribute fliers. I felt so proud and happy to help. I simply stood there at times, and took in the moment, reeling with happiness. I smiled so constantly that my cheeks hurt.

The morning couldn't have come soon enough, as far as I was concerned. I was out of bed and ready to go, in a flash. During one of our conversations, I had promised Trip that I would have a bottle of Champagne on ice in the car and ready for celebration. Since I try to keep my promises, I did that. Going down to the ice machine, I giggled over the thought of Trip opening that bottle. I also brought along some champagne glasses. With the ice bucket filled, I got the champagne from my suitcase and started it chilling.

When we arrived at the pier, many people had started gathering. Far out on the water, I could see large vessels moored. Knowing one of those ships carried my son was bone-chilling. Suddenly, we saw an amphibious tank go into the water from the ship. The American flag on it was whipping in the wind. Chills ran up and down my spine. I cried tears of relief and joy that the dangerous journey was over for my son.

Standing there on the pier, I was mesmerized by the sight of many amphibious tanks that, one by one, began the last leg of their journey home. I looked up at the sky and quietly thanked Ajax. I felt a huge burden was lifted from my shoulders. I thanked him over and over again.

A tap on my back brought me back to reality. As I turned to my left to see who had touched me, a woman stood beside me. She smiled. She handed me a yellow rose.

She simply said, "Here, this is for you."

Tears flooded my eyes as I looked down at the perfect yellow rose in my hand. I turned to my right where Mother was standing with a stunned look on her face. Then I turned back to see where the woman had gone. She was nowhere in sight. Turning back to Mother, I was speechless. No one else on that pier had a rose, only me.

One by one, the men assembled. They stood in formation as all of us waited with anticipation. A man in uniform came around to all of us as we waited. He chatted with us. He held a microphone in his hand. As he approached a small boy about four years old, he asked the boy what he wanted to say to his daddy.

He placed the microphone near the little boy's mouth as the tyke shouted, "Daddy! I can't wait no more. Please come here."

The crowd all said, "Aww…" in unison.

We all had tears in our eyes. Then the uniformed man came over to me. He asked who I was waiting for.

I replied, as I pointed to my son, "I'm waiting for Trip." Then I shouted, "I have champagne in the car on ice."

Everyone laughed and the officer yelled into his microphone, "Trip! The Champagne is chilled. Dismissed!"

All the men fell out of formation and ran to their loved ones. Still holding the rose, I hugged Trip fiercely.

When we stopped hugging, he looked at my hand and asked me. "Where did you get that rose?"

I only smiled and said "It's for you."

I handed it to him. Popping the cork on the champagne put a big smile on Trip's face. As we toasted to his safe homecoming, without saying a word, I slightly lifted my glass to toast Ajax.

Having served almost eight years in the military, Trip got his discharge. He was heading home, unscathed. Mother tried to bribe him to move back to Ohio, even going as far as to offering him the big house, the very house she cheated me out of, so many years earlier. He refused, and came to Florida where we all lived.

I guess she will never quit being *that woman*. Many years previously, she even put in a swimming pool, trying to bribe Trip to live with her instead of me. The rest of my children laugh at her absurd favoritism. But in my heart, I knew it was her compulsive jealousy that tormented her and made her lash out. Like an insane devil, that jealous rage tried to reproduce itself through her behavior, so it could also torment everyone around her, as well. As the years passed, none of my children developed a loving relationship with her. She did that to herself. Nobody else drove that wedge that split her away from us like a chunk of fuel for the flames of her self-hatred.

After living in our townhouse all those years, Titus decided he wanted to build a house for us. He told me to look around at some models to get ideas for what I would want. He didn't have to ask me twice. I only looked for a while to gain a good idea of what I would like. Staying within the amount we had set aside was my main goal. No matter what, I was determined to do that. There was a fear in me that would raise the question, "If something ever happened to him, what would I do?" Even many years after the rear-end collision, I still suffered. My back hurt, constantly, and I hated the idea of servicing a house payment. Titus had a tendency to think "Texan," always big, but I was more down-to-earth, wanting to stay within our means.

I found three houses that had certain features I liked. We intended to combine what I liked, to incorporate these aspects into our house plan. The thought of breaking ground was exciting. I could hardly wait to get started. I was even more eager to move in.

I didn't think life with Titus would ever be easy. It was constantly tumultuous when he was home. But I did know he loved me. He tried to provide me with everything any woman could want.

He told me, "You are the only good and pure thing in my life."

The third time he said that to me, I still did not know what to say.

Only that time, he followed up with, "Sometimes, I feel like I'm competing with a dead man. I simply don't know how to compete with a ghost."

My heart was beating so fast that I thought it would jump right through my skin. I managed to stay calm.

I respond with, "What a silly thing to say."

Then I got up from where we were sitting and went into the kitchen to start dinner. But his pronouncement weighed heavily on my mind. I found it difficult to sleep that night. The next morning, he left early, so I didn't have to deal with what he said or why he said it.

After several months, our home was almost finished.

"In a couple weeks, we will move in. How exciting!" I thought. It had been a long time since I moved into my own home. No wonder I could hardly wait. Though Kelly was excited about the house, she didn't like changing schools.

In the fullness of time, one after another, my children got married. First Lilly had a son. Then Kelly had a son. Kelly's little boy absolutely stole Titus's heart. Titus couldn't seem to spend enough time with him, from building a cabin to play in, to teaching him how to use tools. After that, Kelly had another son, and then a little girl. The entire family fussed over this last little one. Being the first granddaughter, she attracted special attention.

Trip married a Philippine woman who he met while serving in the Philippines. After five years of marriage, they still didn't have any children and their marriage ended. My handsome, easy-going son, Craig, found a partner that we all dearly loved and he was happy. Craig and I shared a special bond because we we were in business for years and we worked together every day.

Even after many years, life with Titus did not get easier. I had everything any woman could want, materially, but feeling secure wasn't part of the package. I called him "The Hurricane" because when he came home, he acted loud-mouthed and controlling but then he would be gone again before I knew it. This was a given and a continuous condition of life. He disappeared often without me knowing where he was, but most of the time he could be reached by mobile phone.

We had many businesses and he traveled continually. That probably kept our marriage intact because there was no way a sane woman could have lived with him on a daily basis. Absolutely no way. I cared for Titus dearly, but I carried a hollow, empty feeling inside me, as if my heart were missing. Sometimes, when I heard the garage door going up, I knew it is Titus coming home. I would get a heavy feeling in my chest, almost like I wanted to run out the back door and never be found. I lived for my children and grandchildren and pretended the married side of my life wasn't there.

When our little princess of a granddaughter was one year old, on a Saturday afternoon, we were going to have a birthday party for her. She had brought so much joy to our family with all her fussy little dresses and sandals. Her little toenails were polished pink from the time she was four months old. As far as Titus was concerned, he worshipped the ground she walked on, but then, he had always adored Kelly.

It was obvious Titus didn't feel good that day, but he insisted on staying for the baby's whole birthday party. Although he spent most of the day laying back on the sofa with his legs up, he didn't want to leave. It was clear he wasn't enjoying himself, as he usually does. At one point,

I looked at him and felt dismayed by just how pale he was, like all the life had been washed out of him.

Thinking back, I realized just how much this man had done for me and my family, from taking care of me, to buying school clothes and cars for my children, to even building a home for Mother. He did all this without complaining. Even when he was building Mother's home, he only required that she leave it to me so I would have security if he was gone.

All that seemed so long ago.

Chapter Eleven

Ever since I first knew Titus, he was an emotional mess during the Christmas Holidays. From the time the Christmas tree went up until it was taken down, he was unbearable to live with. I relived the way Author ruined all my Christmases with his drunken behavior. Many times, I told Titus to go to a hotel until Christmas was over but he never left. Instead, he got caught up in trying to forget whatever drove him into such unhappiness. Every year, I prayed that it would get better, but every year it was exactly the same. It seemed I was not meant to be happy during the holidays.

One year, he was the best he had ever been, but I could still see demons lurked beneath the surface, taunting him until the Christmas tree came down.

My birthday came and went without Titus even getting me a card. He was in so much pain that I'm sure dinner was the last thing on his mind. This was the first time in twenty years that he didn't take me out to dinner and present me with a beautiful gift before the desert arrived. Focus on selling our ore mine was his first priority. He seemed desperate, as if there was no tomorrow.

As his condition continued to worsen, the doctors still couldn't figure out his problem. His VA doctors decided to run blood tests and sonograms. He was such a healthy, well built man that nothing serious ever entered my mind. When the initial tests were complete, to my relief, it was only gall bladder stones. With surgery scheduled within a few days, we prepared for him to be out of commission for a few days to a week.

When he had sold the ore mine, he made arrangements for the buyers to rent temporary equipment to mine the ore deposits. The initial paperwork had been signed and the initial down payment received.

Titus decided to take care of our bills so that he could rest in the hospital knowing nothing was due. Just before the Holidays, he had put in new kitchen cabinets and a granite countertop, along with wood flooring. We still had those bills due. Then, with just one day before surgery, he paid everything off. We still had a pretty good cushion so we both felt at ease.

He was as pale as could be and feeling excruciating pain but the doctors were scheduled to remove the stones the next day. According to the doctors, he would get total relief. He laid down in the spare bedroom early that night, so I went into our bedroom to watch television. I fell sound asleep within a matter of minutes.

> *"Hi Pretty Woman. Come here and let me hug you,"* Ajax said.
>
> *I eagerly slid into his arms and lifted my face to accept his kisses.*
>
> *"I miss you so much,"* he said, *"but I want you to know I will help you get through what's coming next and you are going to be fine. I will guide you, I promise. You will be able to handle everything with my help.*
>
> *"Oh Desiree, I love you so much! I wish I could take the pain away but I can't. I can only guide you."*
>
> *I was still in his arms. We hugged, and he kissed me before the white cloud appeared. Then he was gone, once again.*

That dream left me with a feeling of total panic. Through the years, I learned to interpret the dreams. They came at a time when I would need to be aware of what was coming. I knew a dream about Ajax meant something serious and this was the beginning of the end for Titus. Going to the VA hospital on Ajax's birthday was difficult for me. Not being able to change the situation was the reality. Knowing I would be guided was the consolation.

I was waiting for Titus's final test results, all the while thinking about my dream from the night before. I couldn't allow fear to take over. I stood strong and prayed for more strength. From the tests, we learned that Titus indeed had gallstones and also, a spot on his liver, which would have to be biopsied after his gallstone removal. The next day he would go into surgery. My horrible nightmare was about to begin.

Surgery went well that morning. Titus enjoyed instant relief from the pain. Then we waited for biopsy results. After they brought Titus back to his room, he was groggy for hours and very sore. I thought he would be going home in the morning so I allowed myself to relax and cross-stitch a baby blanket. We were unaware of what the next day would bring. He woke up and felt hungry. He joked about the pain from the biopsy. Like me, he relaxed, thinking it would be alright the next day.

I arrived at the hospital very early in the morning, thinking Titus would be coming home. The doctors arrived around ten a.m. to discuss the results.

Their spokesman pronounced, "You have liver cancer. We advise you to get your house in order."

I heard those first two sentences. The rest was a total blank.

The doctor told Titus he would try to let him go home for a day or so but he couldn't guarantee even that. Titus broke down when the doctors left. He repeated, over and over again, "I am so sorry." The last time, he looked at me with tears streaming down his cheeks and he sobbed, "I'm so sorry to do this to you."

I tried to be strong but that was impossible when I looked at my husband and saw the total helplessness in his face. Once he told me how sorry he was, he got up and moved to the head of the bed, sat down, and then pulled his legs up, laying his head back. It seemed like he was accepting his destiny.

That was the last time I spoke with Titus. Immediately after the doctors left the room, the nurse came in with an injection that caused him to drift off to sleep. I stayed for hours, getting home after ten p.m. He slept peacefully. I couldn't help feeling thankful that he was unaware of his surroundings, not able to think about dying.

I was present at the hospital by at least eight a.m. every morning. I thought I would at least get to talk to him one more time but it wasn't meant to be. The nurses would tell me about how he ate his breakfast and how he talked about me with such love but I didn't witness it, nor was I able to speak with him. I felt so frustrated.

I tried going to the hospital at all hours, to no avail. The nurses continued to tell me about what Titus did in the morning. One even told me what a crazy personality he had and how, after he showered, he told her how much he loved to dance with me. I looked at him lying in the bed with his mouth hanging open, unaware of my presence. I wondered how he had showered and how could he have said all those things, when he wasn't even moving. If it wasn't for a man in the bed next to him, I would have never believed the nurses but that man told me the same things.

Not really wanting to leave his side, at least I went to the hospital daily after he was diagnosed, hoping to tell him that I loved him. At night when I came home, I went into my walk-in closet to change clothes. One evening, I got home from the hospital after ten p.m., exhausted. I noticed fiberglass on the carpet. Total panic struck me because I knew someone had been inside my home while I was gone. They went into the crawl space above the closet, scattering fiberglass. I felt so helpless. I sat down on the floor and burst into tears.

I promptly called Mother. I asked her if she and Michael could come to stay with me until the ordeal was over. They said they would, and that they would travel as soon as they could get a flight. I couldn't believe whoever went into the crawl space was so thoughtless that they would leave evidence that they had been there, knowing it would scare me. Strange as it seemed, I did not think it was someone who wanted to rob me. Instinctively, I knew it had something to do with Titus' secret life.

He would, at times, tell me "Just don't ask, Darlin'."

I didn't know what was up there in the crawl space. That was left to my imagination.

The next day, I called my girlfriend Marie and told her what was going on. I explained to her how the doctors were treating me like Princess Diana. They were asking me if I had eaten and even bringing me coffee. I told her how they sat with me, and held my hand and talked to me to comfort me. This simply did not make sense given a veteran who was in the Army for less than two years.

I told her how he had revealed that he was involved with a government agency before we were married, but that he quit. Now I wondered exactly what agency he worked with and if he ever did actually quit. Why would someone go into my crawl space above the closet? And what could they be looking for?

So many times, Titus would disappear. He would not show up where he said he was going or when I would call, it would sound as if a relay system was transferring the call. There was no sense in trying to discuss that with him because the attempt would only cause heated words.

Marie told me she knew someone who might be able to tell her something and that she would get back to me. I couldn't believe my ears but I thanked her repeatedly. As we said goodbye, she told me to give her a few days and then call her back. Hopefully, by then she might know something.

While Titus was still able to talk, he had called the social worker at the hospital without my knowledge. He requested that no visitors be allowed except for me and my children, or at least that was what I was told. They respected his so-called wishes and a note was inserted into his file.

A few days later, Titus's children from a previous marriage called. I tried to put the phone to his ear so they could say they loved him and say goodbye to him but he became agitated after speaking to his oldest son. He knocked the phone away from his ear. Two of his three daughters begged me to allow them to come to the hospital but even though I said I would try to get them in, they never showed up. Instead of driving straight through to the hospital, they decided to spend the night in one of the casinos along the way, and by morning, they had decided not to come ahead.

I never again heard from any of his children. During the twenty years I was married to Titus, he did not have a relationship with his own children. It was like his three daughters did not exist. His grandson lived with us for a short while and then he was gone, never to be heard from again.

I arrived at the hospital earlier than usual one day. I found three doctors all standing in his room along with four interns. As I entered the room, one doctor came to me and asked if he could speak to me outside the room. Outside, he told me that there was no hope; that I needed to decide whether or not I wanted to take him off life-support. Only fluids were nourishing his body, prolonging the inevitable. They told me he had a strong body and it might take anywhere from one to three or four weeks before he passed. Standing there numb, I thought that my only choice had to be whatever was best for him. I started to cry. The doctor reassured me that he would not suffer; they would still give him pain medication but no fluids would continue to prolong his inevitable death.

I looked back into the room and saw someone who had been a very strong, outgoing man, who now was weak and passively awaiting resolution of a terminal illness. My mind returned to a conversation when Titus said he was competing with a dead man; he did not know how to fight for my love. He told me he loved me dearly but my heart belonged to a man who no longer existed. I cried even harder, knowing that through all our married years, he had it right. After Ajax, I couldn't let go and allow myself to truly love again.

Now he was about to leave this world forever and there was nothing I could do but pray for him. I prayed that whatever he did for our government for all those years was not something he was paying for so dearly now, with his life. Our government had used him to achieve what it needed, then it left me alone to pull those tubes.

I gave my consent. Within a matter of minutes, the tubes were removed. Titus appeared to be napping then, as he so often did in the afternoons. All the doctors and nurses left the room. Then I sat there alone with the man who had been my rock for so many years. My mind flooded with vivid memories like when I had breast cancer and he slept on the hospital floor next to my bed because he wouldn't leave me alone.

I had taken Titus's phone home about six days after he was admitted into the hospital, fearing it could be stolen or somehow lost. He was out of it, so he would not be able to make or receive calls. There was no need to leave the phone with him. He was moved to a private room. He was never left alone. A nurse was present twenty-four hours a day. On the third morning after we took away life support, the night nurse asked me for his phone.

Not knowing what was going on, I stammered. I asked, "Why?"

"Oh, he asked for it last night," she said.

I looked at him. He was lying still, with his mouth open. I knew quite well he had not asked for his phone. Nor could he have asked for anything, at that point. I told her I took the phone home many days previously. Then she left the room.

Just another strange thing, I thought.

Not being able to wait another day, I called my friend Marie that evening. I received the shock of my life. Hearing those words from my friend's mouth was like being thrown into a cold, rushing river. I was speechless as I listened to her talk. She was so kind and gentle, choosing her words so the information would be thorough yet brief. I asked her if her source was reliable. She reassured me that she knew him well and for quite some time. I seemed to float home, not remembering the drive at all. Anxious to get to the house to tell Mother, I literally jumped out of the car as soon as I pulled into the garage.

On one hand, I felt proud of him and on the other, I felt our life had been a lie. I couldn't help wondering if some part of our life had been truth or if perhaps it all had been lies. Whatever was true, I knew one thing without a shadow of doubt: that he protected me to the very end. He never told me anything significant. Even if I would get on his case about his travels he never faltered, or revealed clues to what was going on. It came quickly to mind that the hospital had kept him drugged. We never had the ability to talk.

They did that purposely and I resented it. He never told those nurses that he loved me or that he loved to dance with me, as they had said. It was all lies to pacify me. Now I wondered about everything, including the cancer. There was no chemotherapy, no radiation, no surgery, nothing at all to prolong his life. They were done with him. They only needed me to cover their final act by pulling the plug.

I wanted to contact Titus's business partners. I needed to somehow access Titus's phone to get their numbers. Such an innocent act proved to be so hurtful. No words can aptly describe what came next.

I called the mobile phone company. They readily unlocked his phone so I had access. Being in my office with my son sitting across the room proved beneficial because what was about to happen became devastating. I had contacted two of his partners when I realized he had a message in his voicemail. Thinking it was nothing important,

I continued to contact all the people who Titus had business dealings with. One by one, they were caught unaware and asked if there was anything they could do for me.

After contacting the most important people, I thought I better listen to the voicemail messages in case there was something I needed to do for the final closing of the ore mine. One by one I listened.

Eventually, I heard a woman's voice say, "Honey Bear, where are you? I'm scared to death something has happened to you. If anyone gets this message, please call Mary at this number."

At that point, I felt my heart sink to the floor.

I played the entire message for my son who got a disgusted look on his face. "What next?" he said. "That man makes me sick."

I couldn't believe my ears. Titus consistently told me I was the one pure thing in his life. The thought of another woman just seemed surreal. Could this be true? Could he have seen someone else on the side?

Calling the number was hard. When I heard the woman answer, I was at a total loss for words. Stammering, I asked if Mary was there. From that point onward, the call was a nightmare. At first, the woman acted nasty toward me, thinking I was some horrible woman who refused to give Titus a divorce. She gradually realized she had been led down the garden path. Then the whole conversation changed. She asked me if there was anything she could do to help me. I couldn't think of anything but I thanked her.

As I was about to hang up, she blurted, "What about his storage?"

I didn't know anything about a storage space but soon I learned I didn't really know anything at all about his secret life. As the days passed, Titus slipped deeper and deeper into a coma. Every day, I wondered about our life together; about why he lived a lie of such Byzantine proportions to keep me contented and yet have ability to do what he did for the government.

Marie said there was a lot more to tell me but I couldn't dwell on details right away. Getting through the mainstream of it all was my first priority. I wondered what else would be revealed but the rest had to wait.

Titus was moved to hospice where he passed quietly with Trip sitting at his side. I laid down on the couch next to his bed and fell asleep. My son woke me up to tell me it was over. Titus was gone. He had been admitted to the hospital on February second. He died on February eighteenth, a total of sixteen days from start to finish.

After he passed, the doctors requested my permission for an autopsy. I agreed. He was taken from Hospice back into the VA hospital. That was not something the VA typically does. I was told once a patient leaves a VA hospital they are no longer responsible in any sense. While asking to do the autopsy, the doctors informed me that it would be at the hospital's expense. Also, that they would take the body to the cemetery after it was completed.

With all the arrangements made, I found that everything was taken care of. I didn't have to pay for any of it. Again, I thought that was strange for a soldier who was only in the military for a short time, then got a general discharge before his enlistment commitment was satisfied.

During and after Titus's death, the doctors were very kind to me, trying to help me understand but without telling me much. Prior to his death, after finding out there might have been another woman, I asked the doctors if they could test for STD's, just in case I needed to be aware of any potential problems I might face. They weren't allowed to do that without his signature but they did it anyway for my peace of mind.

Standing at the grave site, my mind went back to many things we shared. I thought about things I questioned and I realized I would never know what really happened. He was always on the go with endless energy. Somehow, I could not imagine him now at peace, with his purpose in life completed.

When his twenty-one gun salute began, I thought of Ajax and how I had heard those guns before at a distance. Now, half a lifetime later, I heard them fire yet again.

Chapter Twelve

I had no time to grieve for Titus. There were so many things I needed to attend to that I did not know where to turn first. One by one, I took care of the things that seemed most important, trying to assure that each detail was dealt with properly.

Heartache after heartache fell upon me as, one by one, I managed each issue. Learning Titus led a double life was not easy for me. I began to question everything about him and us. Who was this man to whom I had been married to for so long? What strange fact would I uncover next?

Going through his storage proved quite painful. The woman who left the message on his phone tried very hard to "help" me. All along, I kept wondering why. My friend Laura went with me to Texas which proved to be a blessing. I was to meet this anonymous woman at a local restaurant. While we waited for her, Laura looked out the window and said "Oh my God, brace yourself. She's here." Not knowing what she meant, I froze. I was facing away from her as she approached us.

As the woman entered the restaurant Laura said, "Okay, be prepared."

I stood up and turned around. With one look at me, the woman gasped, and said, "You aren't what Titus described." She then told me the whole fabrication he had created for her. When finished, she took me to the storage that Titus rented and left me alone with all that I was to find.

I saw furniture that I thought had been sold months before and clothing that I never knew existed. That hurt like someone driving a nail into my heart. But the real pain came as I started to go through box after box of receipts. The boxes were stacked, row upon row, totaling approximately thirty boxes in all. They were stuffed with meal receipts and airline tickets to places I had no idea he visited, all there in front of me. Finding a box of sophisticated phone devices made so many things more clear to me. I recalled all the times I had called him at a hotel when, once I was connected to the room, I heard relay sounds. Now that hit me like a bolt of lightening. He was not at that hotel. My calls were relayed to his actual location.

There in that storage space, I decided to move the furniture around to see if anything else was there. I looked down at the floor and found a beautiful string of pearls lying there. During our twenty years of marriage, the only thing I ever asked for was a string of pearls, which I never got. I picked them up and kissed them, thinking he placed them there for me to find.

Everything was falling into place as I discovered more and more details in that twelve by ten foot storage locker filled with unbelievable covert operations equipment. In one corner hung a black suit, white shirt and black tie. This struck me because during the twenty years when we were married, Titus would never wear black clothing of any kind. He would not even wear black socks much less a black suit. It hung there neatly and had a slight scent of his cologne on it. One by one, I went through everything and then just threw it all away in the dumpster, including the string of pearls.

The strange woman made arrangements for her son to take the furniture to a youth ranch. She told me to take what I wanted and her son would come later with a truck and clear it out.

"Why?" I kept asking myself.

Why would a woman help the wife of a man who had supposedly lied so terribly to her? She said he had promised her so much, even telling her they would marry, once his divorce was over. Yet we were not divorcing and neither of us had ever even hinted about any divorce.

It was all so confusing and heartbreaking. This woman was quite frumpy, with thinning gray hair and dirty fingernails. There I was, with long, blond hair and definitely well maintained, with polished nails to go along with my expensive jewelry. One could not even begin to stretch the imagination enough to compare us. I knew instinctively that there was more to whoever this woman was.

The next morning, I had an appointment with the attorney who had sold the tile roof plant that we owned in Texas. Once again, more upset and more confusion.

So much confusion that even the attorney said, "This was the most unusual closing I have ever experienced."

All I could say to him was, "If you think this was confusing you should have been to the storage locker."

Was the tile roof plant a front he used to gain information on people? I suppose that will never be known.

Once that whole trip was completed, I faced going to Europe to retrieve contents of his lock boxes. Again, this proved to be a perplexing nightmare. In London, I soon learned how unwelcome I was at his bank. Although I had all the proper court papers, the bank was none too eager to hand over the cash that was in his safety deposit box. While they appeared to be friendly on the surface, some underlying force was in play.

Laura and I were first taken down a flight of stairs, and then we had to wait for a man to unlock a door. Once we were inside the next tiny cubicle, we had to wait for a buzzer to allow us through another door. Now we are standing in a very narrow hallway, once again waiting for a buzzer to allow us into an office area. In that office, a man asked us to wait for him to go back upstairs to get an assistant to join him. When he let the door close, that created such a vacuum that both of us sat toward the front edges of our chairs. We waited for forty minutes before they came back. In the meantime, we wondered what was next in store.

When they entered the room, only one man spoke. He was not very pleasant in demanding to know what was in the box.

I tried to be pleasant enough as I told him, "I'm not sure about all that is in there but I know there is a large sum of money. Because my husband has died, I am here to retrieve it."

One would have thought I was a drug dealer given what happened next.

The two men stood up and one of them very forcefully said, "Come with us."

I looked at Laura and wondered how many more locked doors we would have to go through. In the room with the safety deposit boxes, I had a sick feeling inside. My fear caused me to feel weak in the knees. Opening the door, they stood aside. At that point, I tossed my brief case into the door jam so that the door could not be closed.

The men did not like that but I quickly said, "I am not comfortable with all this nonsense. Please allow that door to remain open."

Then they took out the safety deposit box and forced me to count the money in front of them. I felt it was none of their business what was in the box, since it now belonged to me. But they forcefully demanded that I count the money in front of them. After I was finished counting the last thousand dollars, they informed me that I could not take the money. They asserted that they would keep it for me until I got legal representation.

I was having no part of that but I figured it was more important to get out of there in one piece, so I smiled and asked for envelopes and tape, then I put the money in the envelopes and taped each one shut, initialing over the tape.

The next bank was a lot easier since they had opened up the box before I got there and they informed me that the box was empty.

Imagine that, I thought.

There was nothing I could do about this in a foreign country but I questioned their authority to open the box without me present. There were also three checking accounts in Europe but most were drained with very little remaining. At the end of the day, I just admitted total defeat, not knowing what to think about how Titus and I had lived.

Laura and I decided to go out to dinner. We ventured out into the falling snow that was creating a blanket. Outside, she and I looked at each other and joined arms. We sang the Lavern and Shirley television show theme song as we skipped along the sidewalk. Everyone stopped and stared at us but we didn't care.

We went to the US embassy after my initial visit to the first bank. That visit proved to be the only time anyone would admit to me that Titus was listed as a CIA agent. Although Langley headquarters made two calls to me, nobody would directly admit Titus had been associated with the government. Laughing to myself, I realized they must assume I am stupid enough to think they are asking me questions for no reason. The last call was quite unnerving. Finally, I told them not to call me again.

When we returned to the States the next nightmare began. I found out why that "helpful woman" had been so nice to me. That was scary. She and her son were members of a theft ring. She was hoping to access the storage to see what was, supposedly, Titus's "art collection." I wondered at the time why she tried to hang around the storage locker but I didn't open up it right away. Instead, I did some shopping first. I waited to open the unit until after I returned with some boxes.

When I learned the truth about this woman, all I could think was: *Imagine that. A cowboy pretending to be an art collector.*

More and more reality hit me in the face revealing how deeply Titus was involved with the powers that he served. After about a week had passed, one evening I received a phone call from that strange, "helpful woman." She spoke sweetly, asking me how I was doing and wondering if Titus's art collection was in the storage locker.

I silently giggled to myself and thought, *I'll make you squirm and sweat.*

I replied, "Art collection?—Titus wouldn't know the difference between a reproduction on paper and an oil on canvas."

She sounded nervous then when she said, "Well, maybe he was going to surprise you with the paintings."

I played along and baited her with, "Really? Did you see them?"

The phone went silent. Then suddenly, she cleared her throat and said "Well, no. But he said it was in his bedroom."

I laughed, and with a scorned woman's voice, I replied "Believe me, he was no art collector."

Then I thanked her for calling and wished her well.

Afterwards, weeks stretched into months. I learned much more about the man who I had shared my life with. I'm still astonished by how he kept his hidden life such a deep, dark a secret from me. I should have realized there was something bigger than "us" going on but I suppose I didn't actually care that much. Asking led to nothing good. I soon learned to accept and ignore what didn't seem right.

Cleaning up the aftermath proved next to impossible. I found myself pacing the floor, befuddled, most nights. Sleep eluded me as my mind constantly reviewed everything I learned or any specifics I was trying to clear up and finalize.

Living with Titus was difficult. He was not an easygoing kind of guy. On the other hand, he absolutely worshiped the ground I walked on. He tried to show me that, in so many ways. I respected him ever more, after watching him die with such personal dignity. Even when he could no longer speak, he still tried to say "Thank you," each and every time the nurses came in with his pain medication.

I almost wish I had not learned about his secret life. At times, it becomes more than I can handle. Knowing about it only makes me resent our government even more. Losing so many men and women in war seems, to me, completely senseless and tragic. It was bad enough being told that my husband was sent to meet with three rogue operatives to turn them back to America's interests. Then to find out they injected him with a cancer serum… That was not something I wanted to know or needed to know. They were trying to paint him as a hero but what they accomplished was to show me how our government uses people to destruction. Then, when agents are no longer needed, they dispose of them like embarrassing garbage that could create a liability.

They forced me to make the decision to take my husband off life support. Now, I wonder, where was this self-important government that had used him up? When it came time to make that gut-wrenching decision, the government didn't say, "Let us help because he did so much for us." Instead, they kept him drugged so he couldn't speak to me. Then, when the time came, they had me make the decision to end his life.

I remember very clearly when Titus came home from our tile plant, severely bruised all over his body. He told me that he had fallen down the metal steps outside our office. His face was bruised. So were his knuckles. At the time, I joked with him, asking if he was sure that he wasn't in a fight. He couldn't even eat because his stomach was so painful. It was hurting because, he said, he fell on some icy steps. That pain was actually due to mayhem: three rogue agents versus a lone, sixty-six year old man.

I often had late-night conversations with Kyle, my friend Marie's son, who had spent so much time in my home as a boy that I felt like he was one of my own children. After one of our chats, I put two and two together. What I figured out made me shudder and it gave me goose bumps. From a previous slip of Kyle's tongue, I guessed the identity of the information source who had told him about Titus.

I felt afraid to say too much on the phone.

So I began verifying my discovery by asking Kyle, "That man who your mother contacted for information about Titus when he was sick: is he sort of family to you?"

Kyle went silent.

Then he said, "That took you long enough. It has only been a year now. I didn't think you would ever figure it out. Yes, he is family to me ... sort of."

I trembled when the source was verified.

What a small world, but in a very big way, I thought.

I never mentioned the informant's name, or that he was actually Titus's government agency partner, as well as his business partner and also a friend of the family. Titus had told me his partner died many years earlier. I felt stunned to find out this informant was not only someone close to me but also still very much alive. I referred to him as "the Family Source" thereafter, never mentioning his name or that Titus had told me he had died.

Chapter Thirteen

For almost a full year, I tried to settle Titus's estate but I was still nowhere near closing it. Between trying to continue with my own business and trying to close all the doors related to the estate, I was left exhausted and angry. More and more, I realized just who Titus really was. I found it hard to accept that our whole life of twenty years together was based on lies on top of more lies. I had to wonder if any of it was true or if his love for me was also a lie.

The sum of money that I wanted to rely on seemed to be going out the door to lawyers as fast as was coming in, if not faster. No matter what I did, I couldn't stop that.

My days were filled with what seemed like fighting against the whole world. Strange people kept coming out of the woodwork like undiscovered species, claiming this or that. I couldn't seem to find peace anywhere.

I went to my office to take care of what was most important but somehow, I would end up dealing with estate issues. I felt guilty that my business was sliding. Although I was able to readily switch from developing products with the chemists to handling the rented equipment for our ore mine, somehow I had lost any choice in what took precedence in my time management. I thanked God for my son Craig, who had been such a rock for me. Without him being there every day for me I would have crumbled.

The new kitchen cabinets and granite counter top that Craig and Titus installed for me, just before Titus died, were so beautiful. It almost seemed like Titus knew he only had a few months to live. They installed the counter top on Christmas Eve and then he died in February. I look at it now and wonder if the horrible story I was told has any merit to it. Did he really know his time was limited?

There were so many stories and so many facts to back them up that, when I reviewed them mentally, I could not imagine what Titus's life must have been like during those last few months. Titus would continually tell me, through the years, that I was the only pure and decent person in his life. After the information that trickled back to me, I wondered just how true his statement was.

A close friend of mine arranged an introduction with someone who had worked for Interpol for many years, in many countries. I met with him in his office. I was taken with all the job-related souvenirs he had on display. He requested that I bring information and pictures along with me. He said he would try to help me locate things.

Two weeks later, he called, asking me to meet him in the parking lot of a local store where he needed to shop.

He confirmed a few larger items and then advised me, "Just leave it all alone and move on with your life."

He also told me that our government will never allow me to claim these items since Titus used them in his work; and that if I valued my life, I would just leave everything alone.

With that information, I realized that my husband gave his entire life to serving our country and in the end, after they had used him abjectly, they threw him to the wolves. Titus would have wanted me to just leave it alone, too. I'm sure my personal safety would have been his priority.

The company that bought our ore mine reneged on the purchase payments after they found out Titus had died. Then they stopped making yearly payments for related land leases. Because I no longer owned the mine, I could not make the lease payments to Bureau of Land Management. So the leases reverted to the state of New Mexico. Then they were granted to another company. Once again, I was left to wonder how this all came about.

Also, the contractor in Kansas who bought our roofing tile plant decided, since Titus had died, he would file bankruptcy. Then he stole the processing machinery and equipment from the building before it could be secured. Going after him was senseless because bankruptcy laws protected him.

Our one last deal was completed, a multimillion dollar contract with an insurance company to purchase our valuable German bearer bonds. The FBI went to the bank vault where the new owners were keeping them and seized them, claiming they were stolen. Not knowing whether they could be part of Titus's cover, I decided to let it alone, to lick my wounds and move on.

I kept Titus's phone on the charger in case one of the business partners needed to contact me. Titus's phone kept showing a message in Spanish along with an SOS message. I tried to reach out to one of the offices for the CIA but met with total rudeness and questions, none of which pertained to the SOS on the phone. More importantly, they wanted to know what I knew and why his phone was still in use. Within an hour of this call, his phone went dead even though it was fully charged.

I wanted to see if Titus had known he was ill. So I went to the Veterans Administration center to retrieve his medical records. Only three days after he died, when the woman tried to access his records, the whole computer screen went black. She tried again, but the same thing occurred. I left there completely confused. The paperwork that I requested along with his military records came back heavily redacted. That was the end of me trying to fit the puzzle pieces together. I was done.

My doctor discovered I had a small lump in one of my breasts. I needed a biopsy. Wondering what would come next, I was left incredulous. I felt depressed. While on the operating table, I chose to have local anesthesia instead of sedation during the biopsy. The doctor told me that my body was breaking down from all the stress of the estate settlement. He warned me that I had to turn over all the problems to the attorneys before they destroyed me.

As I laid on the operating table, I started to cry, not for myself but for Titus. The doctor wiped my tears with gauze as he tried to comfort me. I needed to talk because so much was bottled up inside me. In that moment, I felt trust in someone for the first time in over a year. That encouraged me to unburden myself.

"Doctor," I whispered, "do you believe in our government?"

He looked at me strangely and asked, "Why?"

I asked him if he knew what a rogue agent is.

He answered, "Yes. But why do you ask?"

I began to recount the whole saga of Titus: "I heard many stories about my husband. Slowly, events confirmed my growing suspicions, especially when US Embassy staff in London confirmed that Titus was listed as a US government agent. A slip of the tongue by a man who grew up spending a lot of time in my home, led me to guess the identity of a key informant.

"My husband lied to me to protect me because he knew that his government agency partner was a family relative of my best woman friend. Just before we were married, Titus revealed he had worked as a government agent. Titus also said, about himself, that because his partner died from a heart attack, he thought he was getting too old to represent our government effectively. So in effect, Titus told me he was no longer a government agent."

The doctor smiled and said, "Well, I see he loved you very much; enough to protect you by lying. I'm certain you were never meant to know who his partner was, or that he and your husband were still working for the government."

I continued telling the doctor, "There's another part of Titus' story that I can't let go. It's how my husband was sent to persuade three rogue agents that they were making a mistake and to somehow talk some sense into them."

The doctor kept listening as we waited for the biopsy results to come back from the lab.

I continued, saying, "I was told a fight broke out and the three rouge agents beat my husband quite badly. Also, one of them injected Titus with a cancer serum."

The doctor looked at me strangely. He gently asked me if I believed that.

"Yes," I replied, "because my husband came home from a trip severely bruised from head to toe. When I questioned him about all those bruises, he shrugged it off, saying he fell down a flight of stairs at our tile plant."

Trying to comfort me, the doctor said, "Well maybe he did fall…"

Somehow, I knew the doctor didn't really think that but he wanted to convince me that he did. I then told the doctor the whole story about

Titus's death and how he had only been in the military for ten months when he was discharged; yet the government did everything for him afterwards for free. He stayed in private rooms and then went to hospice. After he passed, the VA requested me to allow them to do an autopsy and all of this was done at no cost to me.

My doctor intently asked me what the autopsy had revealed. I took a deep breath and told him the pathologist who did the autopsy reported back to me before sending the report. He said that my husband had "rhabdoid cancer" and that it had manifested in his liver. I asked him what that meant.

He said that rhabdoid is the most aggressive form of cancer. He told his students who were witnessing an autopsy, that in their entire careers as doctors, they probably would never see it again.

Just as if someone knew my story was over, the doors opened from the lab into the operating room and the results were ready. The doctor sat down next to me on the operating table. He took a deep breath, then gave me bad news. Making the decision to receive a double mastectomy was terribly difficult. I felt like my whole world was coming to an end.

Looking at my beautiful granddaughter later that day made me realize Titus's estate was the least important thing in my life. My beautiful family was what truly mattered. I gave twenty years of my life to a man who I really did not know, a "mystery man." My son Craig suggested that I inscribe that on his tombstone. Finally, that part of my life was over.

My surgery was a success. My four children were wonderful sources of strength. One by one, each step of reconstruction surgery was successful until I felt whole again. Never venturing far, I went to work at my office and straight home again at night. My home became my safe haven where I felt no one could ever hurt me again. One by one, the lawyers won all the lawsuits and one by one, all that had apparently belonged to Titus seemed to be taken away from me, one way or another.

After I had been alone for several years, my friend Laura kept after me to start going out, to start making a new life for myself. We spent hours talking about it. She always encouraged me not to be afraid but I was. I was very afraid.

Chapter Fourteen

On a Saturday that began the same way as all previous Saturdays had started for the last four years, I woke up early and made a pot of coffee to go with my morning paper.

Then having finished both the paper and the coffee, I decided to call Laura for a chat. Her husband Phil was golfing, as usual on a Saturday morning. That gave us time for some girl talk.

Our conversation ended as usual with Laura telling me it's time for me to start meeting people and enjoying myself. I listened as I always do and ended the conversation as it always ends, with me voicing my concerns and fears.

After hanging up, I went into my home office and checked email as usual. Upon not seeing anything important, I decided to start cleaning my house. I loved my home and felt lucky to have it paid for. That day I was full of energy so I really got into cleaning. Room by room, I cleaned the entire house. I even scrubbed my hardwood floors.

Periodically, I checked emails and went back to cleaning. As I moved the furniture in the family room, I realized that during the week since I had cleaned no dirt or dust to clean had even appeared. I sat down on the floor behind the sofa and started to think about my life and where I was that day as compared to five years previously. I realized that time was slipping away as I sat alone night after night with my two little Boston Terriers. *Maybe Laura is right*, I thought, *maybe I should go out and meet people. But where?*

I finished scrubbing behind the sofa and went into my office to clean that final room. Sitting down at the computer, I checked my email again and saw a dating website. I thought, *What the heck, I'll just look.* And so began my next chapter in life, "Nightmare!"

I filled out the form for the dating site and within a matter of minutes I started getting emails. *This is fun,* I thought. At my age, to start dating again did seem adventurous and exciting, even thought I was scared to death. I never thought so many people were looking for a companion. Soon I was inundated with emails. One by one, I sorted through them and soon I was chatting regularly with the select few I thought might be safe and fun to go out with. Very quickly, I had a date almost every night and I chuckled to myself about all the free meals I would have.

After dating like this for about a month, one man stood out from the crowd. I thought he might be someone I would want to see more often. Being afraid to allow anyone to come to my home, I would meet a guy at a restaurant, far enough from my house that I could make sure no one followed me home. This man seemed sweet and not pushy at all. He was willing to meet me anywhere I chose. We continued meeting for a few months. Slowly, I stopped seeing other men and just kept meeting this Victor. He seemed a gentle soul. He had a powerful position in a large corporation. Many people worked under him and was a competent businessman. I liked the way he could carry on a conversation about any topic and he always seemed eager to please me.

After about three months, I thought it was safe to allow him to come to my home to pick me up instead of going somewhere to meet him. I felt nervous but Laura kept telling me to stop being so scared. I figured I was old enough to handle any situation. We went to a movie, then out to dinner, and all went well. So my fears were put aside and our relationship began.

We dated for around six months before I met the daughter who lived with him. She was in college. Like any typical college girl, she was always busy and she didn't care much about meeting her dad's friends.

She seems nice enough, I thought, at our first meeting.

She didn't look like her father and she seemed quite shy. There seemed to be something wrong; nothing I could put my finger on but something was lurking.

As our relationship grew, Victor started spending more and more time with me and started staying over on weekends. I was happy and no longer felt so alone. I noticed Victors daughter would call him a lot but I never stayed around when the phone calls came in. Instead, I gave him privacy.

Sometimes, on the weekends, we would meet her for lunch. Each time, I would get a feeling that something was not quite right with this young woman. She didn't seem like a typical college girl. She didn't seem to have any friends. I never said anything about my feelings but they were strong and they concerned me. She never did or said anything to me that was out of line or nasty. It was just a gut feeling.

Victor and I got along well, though, and I pushed my feelings about his daughter aside. He had another daughter who was married and lived out of state. I did notice that she did not call very often but again, I chose to ignore all these things.

Our first Christmas together was wonderful. My children welcomed Victor with open arms or at least that's what I thought. They thought his daughter was strange but they didn't say anything to me about her at first.

We flew to Victor's home town so I could meet his mother and family. That visit went extremely well. His mother and I formed a bond. My heart ached for the woman because I soon learned she had a rough life and was now confined to the house. During this visit, Victor's mother told me she had never seen her son look at a woman the way he looked at me and that it made her happy to know he met someone who loved him in return.

We spent three wonderful days sightseeing. Victor showed me where he went to high school and college. On the second day, Victor went to a donut shop to get donuts for breakfast. While he was gone, his mother said to me, "Desiree, don't let Victor's daughter come between you two."

Of course I asked her, "What do you mean?"

She got nervous and made me promise not to say anything, which of course, I promised. She didn't say much but what she did say caught me off guard and I couldn't help reacting.

"Please," she again said, "Victor won't speak to me if he knows I said something about Betsy, but please, don't let her come between you two like she did in Victor's last marriage."

I told her not to worry, but I was worried, especially since I had sensed something was "off" about his daughter to begin with. The rest of the trip went well and our bond continued to grow. We flew up to Georgia to meet Victor's other daughter and her husband, soon after their baby was born.

Again, I was warned by that daughter to be careful about Betsy. She told me that Victor thinks she can do no wrong but Betsy is "unstable." She told me that she doesn't want Betsy around her baby but she tries not to cause trouble. I wanted to ask her some questions but we were alone for only a few minutes and I did not get another chance that day.

The most valuable new acquaintance I made while visiting Victor's family turned out to be Diana, Victor's sister, soon to be sister-in-law of mine, who thought my appearance there was important enough to make the trek from her home to their mother's house to meet me. We hit it off right away.

Both of us immediately felt that we had a special bond. Though we didn't discuss that until later, we wanted to stay in touch, so we exchanged email addresses. Thereafter, we kept up a correspondence, electronically. That proved to help me later when she became my touchstone as things grew difficult for me.

After living together full time for about a year, Victor and I decided we would get married. We planned a beautiful wedding on the beach at one of the nearby resorts. It was breathtaking, with all my children and grandchildren playing parts in it. Victor's daughter Betsy was also in the wedding but his other daughter could not attend. Being a detail person, I left nothing unplanned and the entire few days were beautiful.

When we arrived at the Bahaman Islands for our honeymoon, I became sick and stayed in bed for the first twenty-four hours. After I recovered, I was hit in the face with something I did not know how to handle. On the first night when I was recovered enough to leave our room, we had dinner and went back to the hotel.

Victor said to me, "I'm going to sit outside on the balcony and read." Being happy on our honeymoon, I replied, "Okay, I'll get my book out and come out to read, also." Then I followed with, "I bought some snacks at the shop downstairs. I'll bring them out."

Like a hammer, he hit me unexpectedly with a nasty tone of voice: "I'd like to be alone and read by myself, *if you don't mind*." Caught off guard, I was surprised. I felt hurt. I could hardly hold back the tears after hearing the sharp edge in his voice. From that very moment onward, I simply did not know this man.

He was no longer the Victor I had grown so fond of. He was someone else who was quite abusive. I tried to ignore that evening and move past it but his continued abusive behavior could not be ignored. I feared that a nightmare was beginning.

The rest of the honeymoon was pleasant enough, but the sick feeling in my stomach continued past the time to fly home.

We lived in my home and Victor's daughter lived in Victor's house. About three weeks after returning from the honeymoon, we received the bill from the resort where we were married. I opened the bill and what I saw astounded me. Across our entire guest list consisting of twelve rooms of people, not one person charged anything to their room except Victor's daughter. She charged seven hundred and ninety dollars during three days. She emptied all the liquor from the bar in that room, not once, but several times. She even ordered steaks and a leg of lamb right before the wedding, instead of eating at the wedding. She watched a lot of X-rated movies. I was rather upset when I saw the bill but figured I had better stay calm and just show it to Victor and let him handle it. His mother's and oldest daughter's words, about not letting Betsy come between us, played in my head as I sat thinking how to handle this situation.

What came next, I could have never imagined. After dinner, I told Victor we received the bill from the resort. I handed it to him to read. With some attitude, he looked at me and said, "And what's with the extra charges?" I very sweetly showed him they were from his daughter's room. He flew into a rage. It was not about his daughter charging so much in three days. His anger was because I was supposedly making it an issue.

Before I could say anything more, he informed me that if his daughter wanted to charge two thousand dollars on the room, it was none of my business. I couldn't believe my ears but I tried to remain calm as I reminded him that none of the other guests, even those who had little children, charged anything to their room. His rage only grew worse and he came at me as if he was going to hit me. I turned and walked away but he didn't want to let it go. He started screaming about how he was fed up with people picking on his daughter. Then he left the room.

I sat still for a minute, realizing I had not even raised my voice nor did I pick on his daughter. His mother's words came back loud and clear yet again, as did the oldest daughter's.

Victor did not come home that night. Nor did he ever come back to live in my home. I did not see him for about five weeks. Instead, he sent me emails, saying I needed help and that I was scarred from being married to Titus. I thought perhaps I had been scarred from all that I had discovered about Titus. I decided to seek some advice from counseling.

Talk about an eye-opener; I sure experienced one during the first few sessions with the psychologist. She listened to me intently, as if she was analyzing every word I spoke. I felt comfortable with her from the very start. I knew she was not judging me, she was only trying to understand and help.

I didn't go into the situation about Titus until I felt a total comfort level with her. After all, how do you tell someone that kind of a story without them thinking you are nuts? I only touched on it and spoke of his death. From the very beginning, the therapist told me Victor suffers from abandonment issues and that he self-medicates. Those words, "self-medicates," screamed loud and clear to me. I did not realize it at that time, but those words spoke more truth than I could ever imagine.

I continued to see this wonderful woman. I learned a lot about myself and why I feel and react the way I do. She continued to insist that Victor self-medicates and that she feared for my life. I somehow could not see that level of danger but kept it in the back of my mind.

Victor and I would talk and meet for dinner or a walk on the beach but he was not planning on coming back to my house. Instead, he wanted me to move to his home. His daughter had moved out and was living on campus. I thought if there was a way to save the marriage, I should try. Of course, I found every excuse available to justify my moving there, but the psychologist didn't buy a single one.

I moved right after the holidays. For a few months, things were beautiful. The campus wasn't far from our home. At first, we were able to live a normal life. Then, suddenly Betsy decided to call three or four times a day instead of stopping by every few days. Every night, she would call right after dinner and their conversations would last sometimes for hours.

We did not have a moment to ourselves without the phone ringing with some crisis and his daughter crying on the phone. I didn't say anything but inside I thanked God over and over that this was not one of my daughters. This young woman could barely function. Months of this put a terrible strain on our relationship. I didn't know how to handle it.

Victor was sleeping in another bedroom because he claimed he had trouble sleeping and didn't want to keep me awake. But I soon learned the truth. In the still of the night, I heard a slight noise and when my one dog sat up to listen, I knew that I did hear something. I got out of bed and quietly walked toward my husband's bedroom door. I could hear him talking very softly to his daughter. I could see by the clock it was after three a.m. This went on for weeks before the truth came out. His daughter had been sending large amounts of money to an exchange student from another country who had been using her to move money. If I thought I was experiencing a bad dream after coming home from the honeymoon, what I was about to experience was a full-blown nightmare.

I went back to bed quietly and tried to sleep but I tossed and turned for hours. I heard Victor get up and leave for his office. I laid quietly, waiting for his car to pull out of the garage. I couldn't believe what I had discovered the night before but I realized there was nothing I could do to help. I was exhausted and fell sound asleep.

"Hi Pretty Woman. Come to me, let me hold you," Ajax said.

I reached out and ran to be held by the one love who I knew would never betray me.

"Ajax," I whispered, "please help me.

"Hush now, just let me hold you."

Then he lifted my face and kissed my lips as he softly told me, "Listen carefully to me. Do not allow yourself to be drawn into this man's life in any way. Bide your time and keep your eyes and ears open to the truth."

"I don't understand."

He kissed me again. "It will all come to you. Just listen."

As I started to speak, the white cloud came and he touched my face. "I love you, remember that I will guide you."

And then he was gone.

I woke up wet with perspiration and went to the shower trying to digest that dream.

Thinking I wanted to go back to my own home, but knowing I had rented it out, I had six months before the lease would end. During the next two months, my life became unbearable. No matter what I did or said, it was never right or good enough, so I just withdrew quietly and reminded myself to do as advised: not allow myself to be drawn into this man's life in any way. I would bide my time and keep my eyes and ears open to the truth.

Things started to go missing. I knew that while I was out on errands, Victor's daughter was coming into the house. I tried to bring it to Victor's attention but he would not listen to me. Strangely, an item would be missing and then, a few weeks later, it would be put in another place for me to find, like on my desk or on my printer with a sheet of paper over it.

The psychologist told me that this was the way his daughter was telling me I was in Victor's home, not mine. I started to never leave the house when Victor was gone but instead to leave on days when he was home. Then one night, the phone rang and Victor stepped outside to take the call. Knowing it would be a very long call, I just picked up my cross-stitching and started sewing the towel I was making for Diana. As I picked it up, I thought back to the first time I met her and how lucky I felt that I was to have such a sweet woman as my sister in law.

Another night, gone on the damn phone, I thought.

But little did I know what I was about to hear this night.

As soon the conversation started, he said, "Betsy, what do you mean you want to give up everything here and move away?"

Then, his voice got louder as he said, "Betsy, *just how much money* did you give him?"

After that, he whispered and I continued to sew, wondering what would come next.

An hour later, Victor came inside and said, "That was Betsy. She is much better tonight. She wanted to talk about her next semester and what courses she should take."

I could hardly believe my ears when he said that. Of course, he did not realize I heard everything that was said. I wrote every day to my sister-in-law, Diana, in email but for some reason, I was cautious about what I wrote, as if I knew I had to be careful. She would warn me when we talked on the phone to be careful how I handled Betsy because of Victor's radical protectiveness.

It really seemed to be a sick relationship. There were plenty of chairs or sofas to sit on in our home. Yet they would sit right next to each other, side by side on the couch, to talk. Victor treated her almost like she would break, as if she was a fragile piece of china, not a young woman in college.

Trouble was never-ending with Betsy. I had come to know my time in this marriage would be short-lived. The straw that broke the camel's back was when a woman called Victor about Betsy, who was having a sexual relationship with this caller's fourteen-year-old son. The caller screamed into the phone so loud that I could hear her as if it were me on the phone with her.

By the time Victor finished twisting the situation all around, he had convinced that woman he would turn her in for allowing her son to run the streets and nobody would believe his daughter had done anything wrong. I couldn't believe my ears. I thanked God silently that I had asked the realtor that day to inform my renters they would have to move when their lease was up. They had four months yet to go but I thought I would keep my mouth shut and wait it out. Quietly, I sat watching television the rest of the evening. I pretended that call never happened.

The next morning, instead of emailing Diana, I called her because something I found in the garage drove such fear in me that I was afraid to mention it in writing. It made me sick to my stomach. I felt like I was going to throw up.

How can I last another four months, I wondered.

When Diana answered, I was trembling. I could hardly talk but I managed to ask her if she was located where no one could hear our conversation.

"Yes Sweetie," she replied, "what has Betsy done, now?"

I told her my boxes had been moved in the garage, so I was straightening them up and I noticed a small box there in my stack. Thinking the box was mine, and I opened it.

"There was only one piece of paper in it and it was folded. The paper was hand-written not typed," I said. "Diana, it was written and signed by Betsy. It spoke of horrible things she could do and what she would feel like when she did them. I went on to read her the list of things Betsy wrote.

"Desiree," she said "that doesn't surprise me. I tried to tell you this young woman needs help."

She tried to calm me down but all I could think about was getting back to my own home, where I didn't have to go through all this craziness.

We talked for a long time that morning before she said "Desiree you don't deserve all this. Get out. It won't get any better. She has been like this since she was a little girl. She was babied and babied. I wonder who Victor will blame now, when that note is written in Betsy's handwriting."

Time seemed to drag. I told no one anything about what I was going except Laura and Diana. My children knew nothing. I felt that would be safer. I would talk to Laura daily but I always chose to talk to her on my mobile phone. I felt afraid to talk on the land line phone. Victor took a total dislike for Laura because she had voiced a general opinion one evening. He thought she was directing that opinion toward his daughter, so that did it, he hated her, ever after.

I noticed Victor was locking his car even when it was in the garage. At times, when I was sewing, he would accuse me of saying something when I hadn't said a word. While we were separated, he came to my house to get some clothes. When he bent down to the drawer his nose started bleeding profusely. He told me he had problems with nosebleeds since he was young. Right then, I had no reason to doubt it, but later, he was getting them frequently.

I overlooked everything, until one night after dinner, the phone rang and I made a disgusted face to him and said "Again? Can't we have one night without these phone calls?"

When he hung up, I was already washing dishes. He came at me and body-slammed me so hard that my head hit the kitchen cabinet. I felt totally shocked.

I didn't say anything until he started to scream, "My daughter can call anytime she wants! You don't have any say in what she does!"

He then slammed into me again, really hard, and once again, my head hit the cabinet. Again, not saying anything, I walked away from him and I called the police.

As I dialed, I said "My mother didn't raise me to be a punching bag."

He ordered me to hang up or I would never make another phone call again. I hung up but I knew that once a nine-one-one call was made, the police would be calling me back. They did, and although I overtly acted like it was okay by then, they asked me if they should come out to the house. I replied, "Yes."

The police came over and made Victor leave for the night. After he left the house, the police asked me if they could talk to me for a minute. That night, I learned a lot about his daughter and the home I was now living in. I learned things I'm certain Victor never wanted me to know. The police wanted to know if I had Betsy' new phone number, and although I knew she had changed it again, I didn't bother to get it from Victor. She changed her phone number constantly. They advised me to leave this situation and I reassured them that I planned to leave as soon as my home became available.

Victor came home very humble the next day. Somehow, I simply didn't buy it. I had come to mistrust everything he said. Although I kept my mouth shut, I heeded my last dream strictly. I did exactly what Ajax had told me. I made a special effort to remember everything that happened from that point onward. I listened intently to everything making sure to not miss any detail.

Two months before my home would be available again, things went missing from the house while I went to get my hair cut. I tried to tell Victor about it. However, he did not want to hear it. I asked if we could talk. He said he was tired and had a busy day tomorrow. I let that go but it bothered me all night. I couldn't sleep.

In the morning, I got up early. I was already making coffee when Victor stepped out of the shower. He got dressed and was on his way to leave when he came back over to me and hugged me. He hugged me firmly.

He leaned back and said, "I love you so much, I really do." I didn't say anything. He kissed me, then he turned and out the door he went.

Strange, I thought, *he never does that, and he never goes into the office this early on Friday.*

I drank my coffee, wondering what the weekend would bring. That evening, six p.m. came and went, and Victor did not come home from the office like he normally would. The doorbell rang, so I went to answer the door. The man there asked if I was Desiree. Before I could even answer he handed me a letter and said, "You've been served," and he left. Back inside, I opened the envelope and saw it was divorce papers. I had planned on leaving in two months, anyway, but this caught me off guard.

The first person I called was Victor's mother to tell her what had happened. On the second visit to her home after we were married, she had told me that Betsy was evil and she does evil things. She wanted me to be careful of her. When I told her about being served, she started crying and told me how much she loved me and she knew this would happen.

She cried hard as she said, "The Devil is in that young woman. I am afraid of her. I always act like I am concerned about her studies but deep inside, I know she is the Devil."

I didn't expect all that but told her that I loved her too and I would keep in touch with her. At that moment, I was not strong enough to listen about anything concerning Betsy. In my heart, I knew she had caused all the problems that led to this beginning of the end.

The next person I called was my realtor. I confirmed that I needed my home as soon as the lease was up. While on the phone with my realtor, I heard a clicking in the phone line and figured it was Victor, which it was. He told me that he went to a lawyer on the morning after I had called the police about him a few months prior; and that he decided the night before to go ahead with the divorce. So he had planned this for months.

Thank God, I thought, *that I have my home to go to.*

Victor had convinced me, about three months prior, to give up my business, claiming it was putting us in a different tax bracket. He said that I needed to retire and enjoy life. He had planned all this even before he told me to close my business and become a stay-at-home wife. It was coming to me, all of it. This was all pre-planned.

The following Monday morning, I got a phone call from the FBI wanting to come to the house to talk to me. I kept asking why they wanted to talk to me but I received no answers, only a demand to meet. I refused to allow them to come to the house, claiming I had just received divorce papers so this was no longer my home.

After a few minutes, they called me back and told me to come down to their headquarters the following morning. I was so scared. I could not fathom what they could possible want from me.

At this point, I became paranoid about everything, including my computer, and especially the phones. Needless to say, I did not sleep well that night. I got up early and tried to calm myself but found that impossible. I was afraid to get in the shower for fear Victor might come home and I would not hear him come in. So I opted for a bath that morning. I was a paranoid mess.

Finding FBI headquarters was a challenge. As I drove to the area where I thought it was, I remembered taking Titus near there on two previous occasions. Once I got out of my car the real drama began. I walked up to the door and someone buzzed me in. Inside, two men passed an inspection wand all around me to detect any weapon. I then went through two more doors. There, I met the gentleman who had contacted me. He led me through a beautiful foyer, where there were real roses placed on the floor beside the names of fallen agents.

At this point, I had to give my purse to someone behind glass. Then, the agent and I went through another door when they activated the electronic latch. We went through another door which opened into the office where we would meet. Immediately, a younger man came into that room with a writing pad and pen. He introduced himself to me as he told me he would be assisting the agent that day. I was terrified. I did not understand why they wanted to meet with me.

Without delay, I asked them, "Why do you want to talk to me?"

They smiled at me and one replied "We will get to that in a minute."

They questioned me for over an hour. They asked all sorts of questions about Victor and his daughter. I had no idea what they were talking about most of the time. When I realized what they were asking me, I started to cry so hard I could barely contain myself. They did not give up, they just kept asking question after question. Although I thought I was of no use to them since I had no idea what they were talking about, they reassured me I was doing fine. I again started to cry and told them that I had been a widow for many years before getting married. I said "I never even so much as went out for a cup of coffee with another man. I just did my business and kept to myself."

Then one of the agents asked me, "What was your deceased husband's name?" He placed his hand with pen on the paper waiting for me to say the name. As I repeated my husband's name, the man put down the pen, leaned forward, looked at me and asked, "You mean Titus was your husband?"

I was so worked up I couldn't even talk for a bit. When able to speak again, I asked him if he knew my husband.

He said, "If it's the same Titus...," I cut him off by repeating Titus's full name, including his middle name.

He then replied "Yes, Desiree, I did know him."

That was a turning point where everything changed. The remainder of the meeting went quite differently. The two men continued to ask me questions but with a completely new tone of voice and a changed attitude. They now acted protectively. They advised me to get a restraining order against both Victor and his daughter.

They walked me out to my car. Before I drove away, they told me they would be contacting me again and they would see to it that I received the restraining order. I apologized for not being of more help but they convinced me that it was not so much what I knew, but more what I did not know, that helped them most.

Then the younger man told me, "Be proud of your deceased husband. He was quite a man." I thanked him, as tears once again streamed down my face.

Within one week, I started getting phone calls on the house phone from men wanting to speak with Victor. One call came from a Chicago company wanting to know if Victor wanted his reorder. At first, they would not tell me what the reorder was for. They said they would call back but after making up a story, I convinced them that he said he wants to re-order but he wants to increase the quantity.

They asked "Which product does he want more of?"

This, I found out later, was his supply of enhancement pills. I found that he and his daughter had a business with a foreign country, through California. That came as quite a surprise. I sensed something was going on due to some of the phone calls I overheard Betsy making but Victor being involved astonished me.

Bit by bit, the whole story came out. Now, recalling days when Victor would insist that I leave the house and go to a store that was quite some distance away, I began to pull it all together. He got me away from the house so that he could receive his couriered packages from California.

What a scum, I thought.

One of my friends suggested she could send away a bit of Victor's hair that I could recover from his hair brush, for testing, to determine what he was using. Still not believing my therapist about him self-medicating, I thought this was certainly a sure way of knowing my friend was wrong. Well, I was the one who was wrong. The drug assay came back positive.

So many things made sense, then.

Wow, I thought, *how could I be so blind.*

My computer had been acting up for a few months, so I took it to be checked and found out someone had installed some advanced spyware on it. I felt violated. I thanked God that I had been careful what I wrote to Victor's sister, Diana.

When my renters moved out of my house, I moved back to my safe haven. There was extensive damage to my home. With the help of my granddaughter, Angela, I was able to get it all back into order and feel at home again, at last. Through all those horribly stressful months, my constant companion had been Angela, my daughter Kelly's child. She was there helping me, not only to clean and paint, but emotionally, she was my light of day, my sunshine, and my ray of hope to get through all this drama and heal from it.

Angela was only eight years old but when moving day came, she directed the movers like an adult, taking charge. They found her so delightful that they were singing for her. They laughed about how she knew what furniture should be brought in next. I felt, at last, the Victor nightmare was over. Finally, I was safe.

Titus's former associates told me that I need not worry, I was being protected; that no harm would come to me; but I felt uneasy while I had remained in Victor's home. Now, at last, that whole ordeal was behind me.

On the first night in my own home, I felt such relief that I was able to relax. Going to bed that night seemed surreal, somehow, and I soon fell asleep.

> *I felt someone kissing me and suddenly, Ajax was there.*
>
> *"Hello, Pretty Woman. Let me hold you," he said. Then he let out one of his Roy Orbison growls.*
>
> *I slid readily into his arms and hung on. I welcomed his kiss and begged him to stay with me, telling him I'm safe.*
>
> *"You are safe from bodily harm," he said, "but you must get rid of the lawyer who is handling your case. He's not true to you. He is going to betray you.*
>
> *"I will guide you to another lawyer. You will then be in good hands. He will become your friend. I must go but do this now. Hire this new lawyer right away. You will win big. Oh, I love you so much, you will see, you will find true happiness."*
>
> *I touched his face and said, "I love you."*
>
> *While he kissed my lips, the white cloud came, and then he was gone.*

Feeling Angela's hand on my shoulder, I was startled.

"Who were you talking to, Nana?" she asked. "You said 'I love you.'"

Smiling at her, I said, "I was telling *you* that I love you."

I snuggled with her and soon she fell off to sleep. My mind was whirling with wonder about what Ajax had meant. How would I even begin to get another lawyer this late in the divorce? Then, knowing I better listen to him, when I woke the next morning I started to think about the dream and how I could go about this task at hand. I never felt comfortable with the attorney I had. I knew in my heart something was not right, and I better listen.

Getting a new lawyer was not easy. My divorce was in the final stages. It was difficult to suddenly jump into this case. The lawyer I found was a kindly man. He quickly grasped what was going on. I felt comfortable with him. I knew in my heart that he would do his best for me.

I called Kyle that evening. I told him about the new lawyer and that I felt he would do an excellent job for me. Kyle told me how happy he was for me.

Then he said, "I've been meaning to ask you, how did your visit with the FBI go?"

I could not believe my ears. I wondered how he knew about that and why he had waited so long to ask me. He told me he needed to be sure I was on a secure line before he said anything. We discussed briefly what they asked me and how they knew who Titus was. He chuckled and told me not to worry about anything.

He said, "You will come out of this very well, Desiree. All is taken care of."

Then he said to tell my new attorney to ask for a high amount of temporary alimony. I was dumbstruck, especially when he told me the alimony amount I would receive. I told him Victor had offered me four hundred dollars a month for three months as he cut me off. Kyle said he would love to be in the courtroom when the judge tells Victor how much he will pay.

I made an appointment with my new attorney the next morning. When I was sitting across from him in his office, the real challenge began. I explained the situation with the FBI from start to finish, including that they knew my deceased husband was a federal agent.

My new attorney looked at me strangely but not as strangely as when I told him that he needed to make a graph showing the court how Victor could afford this large alimony. I let him know that I had been told all along that I would get help with the divorce but before it actually happened, I did not know quite what to believe. At the pre-trial, a few days later, the judge reminded my attorney to make sure he submitted graphs to support his case. The look of bewilderment on my attorney's face was priceless.

The divorce took much longer than it should have because Victor fought about everything. I tried to warn him in the beginning that he would not win; that, in the end, it would cost him more to fight but his narcissistic personality took over. He assumed he was above the law and, to drive up the legal fees, his attorney encouraged him to fight. I'm sure he spent a pretty penny, only to lose heavily. He even thought he could fight the judge's decision by elevating the case to the Court of Appeals, but that only cost him another sizable chunk of money. Once again, he lost out when the initial decision was enforced.

In the beginning of the divorce, I asked for only enough money to get me on my feet until I found a job and could support myself. I thought that was fair since I had given up my business because of Victor's constant badgering. He refused to give me a dime, voluntarily. The judge did not take that lightly. The day the divorce was final, both Victor and his attorney were quite taken aback by the decision the judge handed down.

Sitting in the courtroom, looking at Victor, I thought, *What a waste of intelligence. He has a high-echelon position yet he is only a loser with a severely disturbed daughter.*

In the beginning, I felt drawn into his arms by what appeared to be honesty and gentleness. He had put on a stellar performance. He hid everything well, at first, but one by one, each bit of damning evidence came out. Even after his ex-wife's daughter called me and told me to run, I chose not to believe it. Remembering that call is what caused me to listen to my friend and test Victor's hair.

Winning did not take the pain out of knowing I had been fooled into believing this man truly loved me. How could I have ever known? Even my therapist told me he was a master of disguise. During one of my last meetings with that psychologist, she told me, "Desiree, if you had dated this man for five years before you married him, you would still not have known what he truly is like. He sweeps everything under the rug and hopes nobody can see it."

Those few years of pain and personal deprecation took a toll on me. I vowed to put my shield up even higher and to never trust or care for any man thereafter.

Chapter Fifteen

rying to calm myself down, I reopened the website that Omar sent me about Alexandria, Egypt. Once again, that beautiful yellow rose filled the screen and Ray Charles again sang "Georgia On My Mind." This time, I felt numb.

I listened and looked as the beautiful pictures of Egypt started to appear. One by one, I looked at each picture as it rolled by, wondering what it would be like to come to America at age seventeen, unable to communicate well, to start a new life so far from home and family. I could only imagine what he was feeling: his sense of wonder; the excitement of getting on a plane for the long journey to the USA; and his anticipation of starting six years of college.

After watching the entire film again, twice over, I decided to call him to discuss it. I could hear the pleasure in his voice as I described each scene I had viewed.

"It so beautiful in Alexandria. It's not like what people here think," he said.

"I want to go there with you. I want to see where you were born. Please, take me!" I replied with animated enthusiasm. But though I begged him to take me there with him, he evaded me, without any direct answer, and he laughed. Once I realized there was no use, I went on to tell him about the meetings I had scheduled for us the following week. I was staying home during the current week to get meetings scheduled out for the next few weeks. So far, I was doing quite well. I cherished every moment together with him. Each time we parted company, I felt an emptiness, but the familiarity of my home took over and once again, I settled into my separate life.

One of Celine Dion's songs includes the words, "I don't want to be an island anymore."

Whenever I heard those words, they hit home with me because I enjoyed having a relationship with my own, special someone, so much. But recalling the terrible mistakes I had made, abject fear would set in. I dropped back to the reality: that staying single and alone kept me safe. Fear limits a person's choices and I feared being hurt, yet again.

So many nights I sat here thinking, *So glad I didn't sell my house like Victor kept trying to get me to do.*

I was naive enough to believe him when he urged me to close my business and stay home instead, but somehow, I simply could not even imagine selling my home.

Where would I be today, I wondered. *What would have happened to me if I had done that?*

Most of all, what I wondered about was why did he feel compelled to destroy me? I was fortunate that the judge saw through him and saw to it that he will have to pay all my legal fees, and eighteen months of alimony. But that can't come close to restoring my losses, especially the income my business brought me.

I chucked to myself, thinking, *I wonder if he now wishes he had simply helped me like I asked. A few months of help would have been cheaper than what he has paid out for the divorce.*

He dropped at least a hundred and twenty thousand dollars, with legal fees, Court of Appeals costs, eighteen months of alimony, and other fees, all combined.

Sitting at my desk I thought, *I have so much to be thankful for when it comes to my Omar, that sweet and kind hunk of man.*

When he met me that first night at the dance hall, all I had been wanting to do was bury my head in the sand like an ostrich. I felt ashamed that I had actually believed Victor loved me when he only wanted to use me. Being so angry with myself, I found it difficult to forgive. With no appetite, I lost weight. I grew thinner and thinner. Even though the judge sympathized with me in court, I still felt defeated and used.

Then, along came Omar. He gave me reason to go on, a reason to get up in the morning, and most of all, a reason to feel accepted, that I was worthy, even though I had made such a wretched error by trusting the wrong kind of person. Throughout the previous few months, I knew, without doubt, that I had a true friend. To him, the most important people in one's life are one's true friends. A member of that elite group is more important than a lover or a spouse, because a true friend you can trust with everything and they never let you down.

We tell our rare, true friends the truth because there's no need to lie or cover up anything. We reveal even our weaknesses safely. Their acceptance is complete, unconditional and without contingencies. True friends accept us for who we are. They will never find fault or betray us. That unconditional acceptance came to me from Omar. No matter what he had to put up with, I knew that he believed in me.

Neither of us carries the typical expectations about us being "mates" for each other. We simply appreciate our deep, mutual friendship and respect it. We talk for hours. We confide in each other, revealing our most closely-kept secrets. I feel an undeniable trust with Omar. I find myself telling him things I have never told anyone; not even my closest girlfriends. I opened up and told him all that I had discovered about Titus. He listened intently and as I continued to talk, I felt tremendously relieved to let it all out and allow someone safe, a true friend, into my world.

I had never been able to forgive Titus until after discussing it with Omar and listening to his take on where Titus was coming from. With genuine understanding of Titus, I found I can let it all go, forgive him and move onward with my life, unrestricted by festering disdain for someone who I had truly hated. Omar cast a light of understanding on that whole experience in basic, simple words. Then, for the first time in the eight years since Titus's death, I could finally reach a state of inner peace about that entire chapter of my life and feel the forgiveness I needed to achieve to heal myself.

There was no way that Titus could have ever let me into his alternate reality. He truly did love me and so much that he protected me from his professional liabilities by telling me nothing about that side of his life.

Omar reassured me that Titus must have loved me deeply to keep his actual work life hidden from me, even to the very end, as he laid dying.

Gradually, I realized that the learning I gained through Omar's character and his wisdom were my golden treasures. His perspectives catalyzed a turning point in my thinking. At last, from then onward, I could feel forgiveness for Titus in my heart. His shared, compassionate insights freed me from the prison of my own self-hatred concerning my life with Titus. Such a simple man, Omar was; with the simplicity of the great prophets. His wisdom showed me how to forgive and move onward, living a richer life than otherwise.

During our long conversations, he would tell me more and more about what he experienced, through the years; like how he never faltered in loving his only child; and how he wanted to always be included as part of her life. Listening to him talk about her validated that impression of deep sadness I had picked up when I looked into his eyes, early on. I felt his ache in my own heart when I listened to him speak of all he had endured.

Yet he expressed genuine compassion for everyone around him, continually, in every aspect of living. He never became bitter or cold; he bore up despite becoming scarred and fearful. One usually thinks women are abused in a typical relationship. We hardly ever think the victim could be the man. One thing is certain: not all abuse leaves visible bruises; the sorrows delivered upon Omar took their toll emotionally.

I was so lost in thought about all these things that I startled when my phone rang.

Answering, I heard Omar ask, "How are you?"

Hearing his voice brought a smile to my face, I said, "I'm good. And you?"

"I'm good, hey, will you help me tomorrow? I have to go to my rental to clean it up but I have meeting at my office that I can not miss. I pay you good, if you help me. I can not do it all, myself."

I enjoy working with Omar. He does pays well when I work for him. Of course, I agreed.

"Can you come early in the morning before it get so hot we can not work?"

I agreed and heard the usual, "Okay, got to go."

Then he hung up, abruptly.

I laughed, and thought, *Some things never change.*

The next morning, I got up early. I headed to the office to see what work he had for me. I had helped him clean up his rental before, so I wore the appropriate clothes, but I was not prepared for what I found that day. The house itself was not too bad but the renters had neglected the yard completely. I didn't think we would ever get it back into shape.

It was a hot and muggy day. Neither of us knew quite where to begin. The yard was huge, with large trees and leaves everywhere. The leaves were layered so thickly that it was hard to rake them up. I made small piles. I hoped it wouldn't take as long as I thought it might. Omar went up on the roof and blew the leaves off. That made everything else look even more dismal. After about three hours, he looked at his phone and saw it was time to get back to his office for his meeting.

With his usual "I got to go," he left me to continue.

I looked around and felt overwhelmed with what still needed to be done but I continued to dig in. As the morning passed, afternoon heat became unbearable. I felt sick to my stomach. Determined to put a big dent in the work ahead of us, I kept on going. Suddenly, I got dizzy and weak. I leaned against the house and wondered why I was there in the first place. This was hard work. Sweat trickled off me.

My divorce had left me in a financial bind because I no longer ran my business. I knew in my heart that Omar continually found things for me to do, so that I could make extra income, but all this yard work was beyond the call of duty. It seemed to get hotter by the minute. I was sweating profusely.

I wondered why in the world was I in this predicament. One stupid mistake, and then, there I was. One thought led to another as I leaned against the house. I wondered how my life might have unfolded if Ajax's parents had simply left us alone and let nature take its course. I couldn't help wondering if I should even be there, right then.

I looked up to the sky and asked Ajax, "Should I be here? Does Omar really care?"

Suddenly, my mobile phone made a loud, blasting noise. It sounded like it was about to explode. I yanked it out of my pocket and looked at it. The loud noise faded into a video. I saw a man singing in Arabic. He and a woman were walking in sand. I didn't know what he was singing but I could hear and see from how he looked at her and sang to her, walking behind, that it was a love song. I could not believe my eyes. I looked up, and there stood Omar. He had been standing behind me for a bit.

He asked me what I was doing. He saw tears running down my cheeks.

"Listen to this," I said. "What is he singing?"

"How did you get that?" he asked. "That is an Arabic radio station. He is singing, in Arabic."

I stared at him in surprise and disbelief.

"But what is he singing?" I asked.

He then told me it was a love song. This man loves the woman, but she does not realize that. She cannot hear the call of his love.

"But how did you get that on your phone?" he asked again.

"It suddenly appeared there, on its own," I said.

How could I have ever told him that I had asked a dead man if I should be working there and this frustrated love scene was his answer?

That day, we bagged fifty-two large trash bags of leaves and twigs. We ended the day as filthy as two children who had been playing in dirt.

When we finished lining up all those bags at the curb, Omar said, "Let's go get beer."

"Sounds good to me," I replied. Back at his office, I tried to wash off some dirt. All that did was smear dirt into another area. Looking at all the dirt on my body and clothes, I laughed.

"Are you sure you want to be seen with me?" I said.

He looked at me, laughed, and with his intriguing accent, he teased me. "Sit away from me, at other end of bar. Then I will not feel ashamed to be seen with you."

We laughed together, both realizing we are way too old to do all that work in one day. I never enjoyed a cold beer before as much as I did that evening. The next morning, we loaded all those bags onto Omar's truck and took them to his office for the garbage truck to collect.

My life had settled quite a bit since my divorce from Victor. Although in the beginning, I had beaten myself up for acting so stupidly, I had learned to rethink that situation and see it all differently. I viewed the whole picture with new eyes, remembering what my therapist had told me about Victor being a master at disguise. She also revealed that his personality would lead to him pushing everything threatening under the rug, thinking nobody sees it.

He certainly had fooled me about his daughter. I felt happy that chapter of my life was complete. I made some strategic decisions; to not allow myself to dwell on of all that misery; to only feel happy to have escaped that situation in one piece; and to savor all that life had to offer me in the present.

I stepped from the shower to answer the phone and said, "Hello."

I heard my favorite "Hallo. . . You help me so much this week. Come, lets go to Shepard's and dance."

I didn't need to be invited twice. I jumped at the chance to dance outside, on the beach, at Shepard's.

"Ooo! My favorite place," I said.

"Come then… lets go," he said. Before he could say another thing, I agreed to meet him in an hour.

"I make you dinner, then we go dance," he said.

Dancing that night was a celebration under a beautiful sunset. When we looked out, over the water, it sparkled with glitter as waves gently rolled in. The weather was perfect. I felt happy to be alive. This was one of my favorite places. That night, we are both in a mood to dance and enjoy all there is to be happy about.

This Middle Eastern man loved to dance, probably as much as I loved to look at him. Even after all our months together, I still found him quite appealingly handsome. I still loved to make him laugh. I can dance all night long and never get tired until my head hits the pillow.

"Oh, Omar, listen to the song that's playing. I love that song," I said.

Come on, lets dance then," he replied.

Always ready to dance, I stood up. He took my hand and led me to the dance floor. Enjoying the music, I realized again how truly happy I had become. I leaned back in his arms to look into his face. A fine, misty rain was falling. I could feel it dance on my face. When I looked at the

Tiki lights, I saw the rain was making rainbow halos around them. I looked back to Omar smiling so beautifully at me.

"If I were to die this very moment," I said, "I would die happy and in peace."

Omar responded with gestures, not words. He kissed me lightly and pressed me harder into his bosom.

The next few months brought significant events. Omar's mother came from Egypt. Given that she was declining, he asked me to stay with her during the day while he worked. I did that willingly but soon I realized just how difficult it could be, at times. The language barrier wasn't a problem, as I thought it would be, but the dementia created difficulties.

I stayed with them for seven weeks, taking care of her every day until he came home from work. It was like relating to a child in an adult's body but, even so, I would not take back those weeks for anything.

Quite a few years earlier, we received news of Dane coming down with Alzheimer's. By the time I cared for Omar's mother, Dane was in a nursing home.

I couldn't help recalling how I told him, "Some day, your Karma will return to you for not taking care of your children."

He laughed at me then but I doubted that he laughed when his doctor gave him his diagnosis.

I grew to love Omar's mother for the innocence that she expressed. She just couldn't get over my blond hair. One morning, while we were out on the balcony eating breakfast, she looked at her son quite seriously.

She said, in Arabic, "Look at that poor woman. The sun took all the color out of her hair."

Omar was laughing so hard that he could barely interpret what she had said. She had once been a beautiful, well-groomed woman. She became childlike during the advance of the dementia. I didn't mind taking care of her. In my heart, I knew that without her, this wonderful man would not be in my life. When time came for her to return home, I realized she would never again be able to make the trip back to the United States. I felt sad that I would never see her again.

Omar sees the world from a special perspective because he is a structural engineer. He assumes nothing is, in essence, as it appears. I noticed that he looks deeply into everything and everyone. He readily analyzes things from the inside out. He has an enchanting ability to see through people's facades easily.

Our months together stretched into two years. Once again, my birthday came around. He was not telling me all that was happening in his life but I could see and feel that something serious was amiss. Engineering work were slow in coming. I sensed it was more than that but he was not talking about it. We made plans for him to take me out to dinner and dancing but, at dinner, I could see that troubled look in his sad eyes. I learned over time that he tells me when something is wrong but in his own time. I decided to leave his issue alone and only enjoy the evening.

Once again, he made my birthday special even though he was falling apart inside. That night, back at his condo, as we laid side by side, he held me close and firmly, as if seeking some peace and security. I laid in his arms, listening to him peacefully breathing while he slept. I moved and he reflexively tightened his grip. His cologne smelled delicious on his face. Once again, I took comfort in the safe familiarity of it.

Four a.m. came quickly, as this adorable man said, "Wake up. Look what I have for you."

His cute voice made me laugh. He was telling me that he had a wonderful present for me. As morning shined through the windows, I heard the ocean rolling onto the beach, far below. Not wanting to give up the warmth of his body against mine, I decided to lay quietly until he awakened. Feelings flooded through me as I recounted our history, from first meeting Omar at a dance, until that present moment. We had become deeply bonded friends who depended upon each other for many things, both simple and profound; from him providing me major moral support, to me simply helping choose his clothes.

Strangely, though I may return to my home for a few days, when I get back to him, it feels as if I never left. Omar counted on me for everything yet like me, he was also afraid to give his heart completely. When he felt himself getting too close, he would back off, but the distancing never seemed to last more than a day or two. We were two adults, so afraid of pain, yet both so full of love in our hearts.

On the way home, I relived our whole weekend from start to finish, including his little-boy smile when he had that morning present to give me. To say the least, I'm cautious. I try to protect my feelings, yet, like a hummingbird in a tropical blossom, I dive into love.

If only I could shake my fear, I thought, *and lose myself in this relationship with complete abandon.*

Night fell as I crawled into my solitary bed. I thought how lucky I was, first of all, to be alive; then, how blessed I was to have family and people around me who loved me and cared about me.

I want to go back into business, I thought, *because helping people always makes me feel so happy and complete.*

But starting business again seemed like such an impossible notion at that point. Sleep came quickly and then it was morning.

My little Boston Terriers' inner clocks never fail them. No matter what time they go to bed, they awaken, as if to an alarm, at seven a.m. Letting them out on this day was like any other morning except I had a lot on my mind and with no explanation. Life went as usual and the day ended just as uneventfully as did the next few days.

Then I heard my phone ringing one morning as I stepped out of the shower.

I answered it and heard Omar's familiar voice, saying, "Hallo, how are you today?"

I laughed as I thought, *Oh, what a perfect time to give him a steamy visual.*

So, I said, "Well, I'm good. I was just in the shower. I shaved my legs and washed my hair. Now I'm standing here naked, talking to you."

"Why you do that to me?" he said. "You make me horny and then I have to work all day thinking about you."

I laughed and joked back, "What will you be thinking?"

"Never mind. The reason I am calling this morning is to ask you if you want to come to my place tonight. I make dinner and we go for walk on beach."

Of course I wanted to go. I quickly told him, "Sure."

"All righty, now. I got to go. Come early."

Then the phone went quiet. I giggled as I thought, "I got him good, this time. He will enjoy that visual all day long."

I didn't have much to do, that day, so I counted the hours until it was time to leave. When I arrived, he was waiting for me with a big grin.

"Let's have beer first. Then we go for walk," he said.

I went to the kitchen to open our beer. Coming back to the balcony, I handed him his glass. I began to look at this beautiful man in a new light. On the night I met him, I had been taken aback by his looks and accent.

Now, I realized, *He is so much more than that to me.*

Taking a sip of beer, I looked out at the water. My thoughts drifted back to something I had once read:

> A man may dance like there's no tomorrow. He may even be more handsome than a Greek sculpture or wealthier than the grandest monarch. But the one thing a true partner must bring, above all else, is deep and abiding power to love and in expressing his love, an integrity that rules his life. Above beauty, beyond riches, besides worldly power, and along with all else that attracts you, what you seek in a partner is depth of character.

I had realized Omar brought that wonderful essence to me. Not only was his character as deep as a desert well in his homeland, he was freshly-showered and his cologne smelled delicious. My post-shower visual must have worked a spell. We finished our beer and out the door we went.

On the beach, we left our sandals at the locked gate. The evening deepened as the sun descended majestically into a breathtaking blaze. We had walked on this beach many times before but for some reason, tonight seemed different. It felt even more beautiful. We spoke in intimate whispers, walking along the shore. Seagulls wheeled and squawked in the darkening sky. Absorbing all of it, I felt the joy of simply being alive in the company of such a prince.

Balmy air puffed softly in our faces as we walked along the water's edge. I placed my hand under his arm and felt like a queen walking with the most handsome and loving king in history.

I looked at him as I had so many times, but this time, an ancient fear shot through my heart like a bullet; fear of risking too much; fear of caring and then being hurt; fear of falling, even if it were into love.

I looked up at the sky's glowing hues and thought of Ajax, how he has always been there, never forgetting his promise to guide and protect me.

Studying Omar's face, I thought, *If I ever needed guidance, it would be now. Let it come before I let go again and allow myself to feel a love that I can not take back, in the deepest part of my heart.*

In those few moments, I wondered if I could ever love anyone as I had loved Ajax. Was I even capable? So many years had passed.

I closed my eyes for a second, waiting. I could see Ajax's face as I silently asked him for a sign that I should let go and seize this chance to be Omar's truest friend, to allow myself to finally feel the love that is its own reason for being; the love that fills the heart so completely that it leaves no space for fear.

I opened my eyes and all I could see before me was miles of empty beach, white sand lapped by the sea, a perfect canvas becoming a masterpiece, tinted by waning light. A larger wave crashed and as it splashed our legs, we both looked down. There in the water by my foot we discovered the most beautiful yellow rose. I began to tremble as I bent down to pick it up. As I picked up the rose, I started to cry from joy.

Omar looked at the rose in my hand and asked, "What is this? Where did this rose come from? Why are you crying?"

He searched my eyes as tears welled up and rolled down my cheeks. I gazed across the water.

Yes, I thought. Only, *Yes!*

No trace of my fear to love remained. In that moment, I knew it had left my heart forever. A thrill ran through my body. Omar searched my eyes as tears rolled down my cheeks. I could not speak. I sniffed the rose, knowing my prayer was answered. Omar reached out to hold me.

Standing there, clutched in Omar's arms, I thanked Ajax for his answer that ended my quest. I could hear his voice as if he were standing there beside me:

> *"I gave you my word that I would guide you and never leave you, and that I would love you into eternity. Take Omar now and love him as he loves you. Never let go. You know there is room in your heart for us both."*

At last, I was free to love again, with complete abandon.

As the final sliver of sun disappeared below the horizon, all I could think of was Ajax. Throughout the years, he had truly loved me. He never broke his promises. Still, he sent me beautiful yellow roses.

Printed in the United States
By Bookmasters